A-Z BEDFORDSHIRE

CONTENTS

C000262153

REFERENCE

Motorway	**M1**		Car Park (selected)	**P**
Primary Route	**A6**		Church or Chapel	†
A Road	A603		Cycleway (selected)	
B Road	B660		Fire Station	■
Dual Carriageway			Hospital	**H**
One-way Street			House Numbers (A & B Roads only)	134 40
Traffic flow on A Roads is also indicated by a heavy line on the driver's left			Information Centre	**i**
Road Under Construction			National Grid Reference	505
Opening dates are correct at the time of publication			Park & Ride	Elstow **P+**
Proposed Road			Police Station	▲
Restricted Access			Post Office	★
Pedestrianized Road			Safety Camera with Speed Limit	**30**
Track / Footpath			Fixed cameras and long term road works cameras Symbols do not indicate camera direction	
Residential Walkway			Toilet:	
			without facilities for the Disabled	▽
Railway	Station Heritage Station Level Crossing Tunnel		with facilities for the Disabled	▽
			Viewpoint	☀
Built-up Area	HOCKLIFFE ROAD		Educational Establishment	▭
			Hospital or Healthcare Building	▭
Local Authority Boundary			Industrial Building	▭
Posttown Boundary			Leisure or Recreational Facility	▭
			Place of Interest	▭
Postcode Boundary (within Posttown)			Public Building	▭
Map Continuation	22 Large Scale Centres 158 Road Map Pages 161		Shopping Centre or Market	▭
Airport	✈		Other Selected Buildings	▭

SCALE

Map Pages 4-157	Map Pages 158-159
1:16,896 3¾ inches (9.52 cm) to 1 mile 5.9cm to 1km	1:8,448 7½ inches (19.05 cm) to 1 mile 11.8cm to 1km
0 ¼ ½ Mile	0 ⅛ ¼ Mile
0 250 500 Metres	0 100 200 300 400 Metres

Copyright of Geographers' A-Z Map Company Limited

Fairfield Road, Borough Green, Sevenoaks, Kent TN15 8PP
Telephone: 01732 781000 (Enquiries & Trade Sales)
01732 783422 (Retail Sales)
www.az.co.uk
Copyright © Geographers' A-Z Map Co. Ltd.
Edition 1   2012

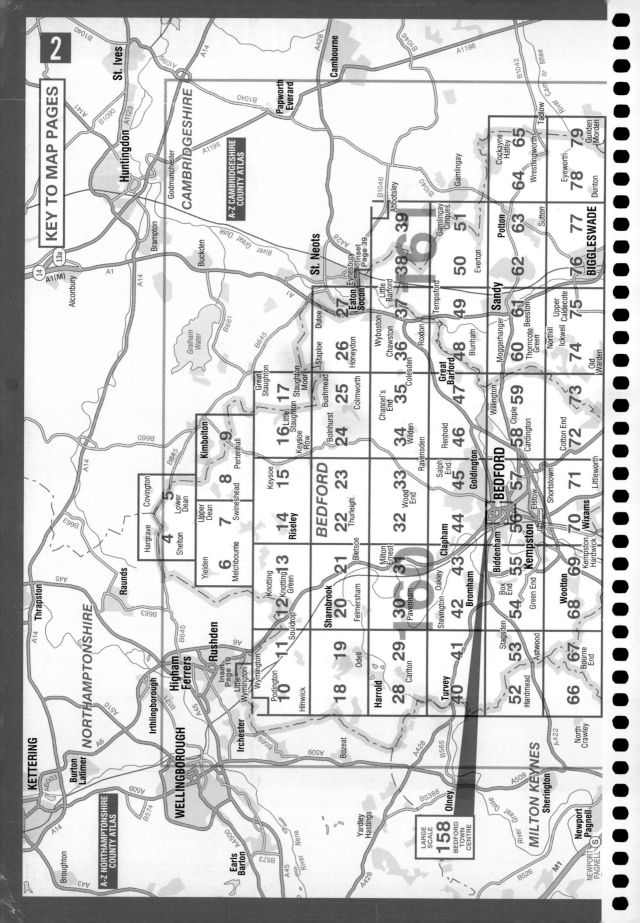

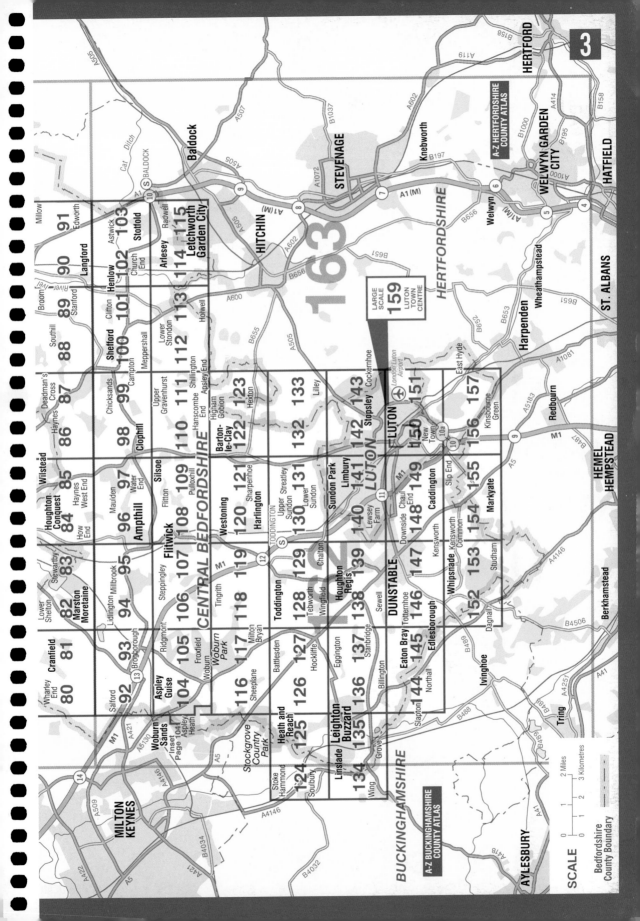

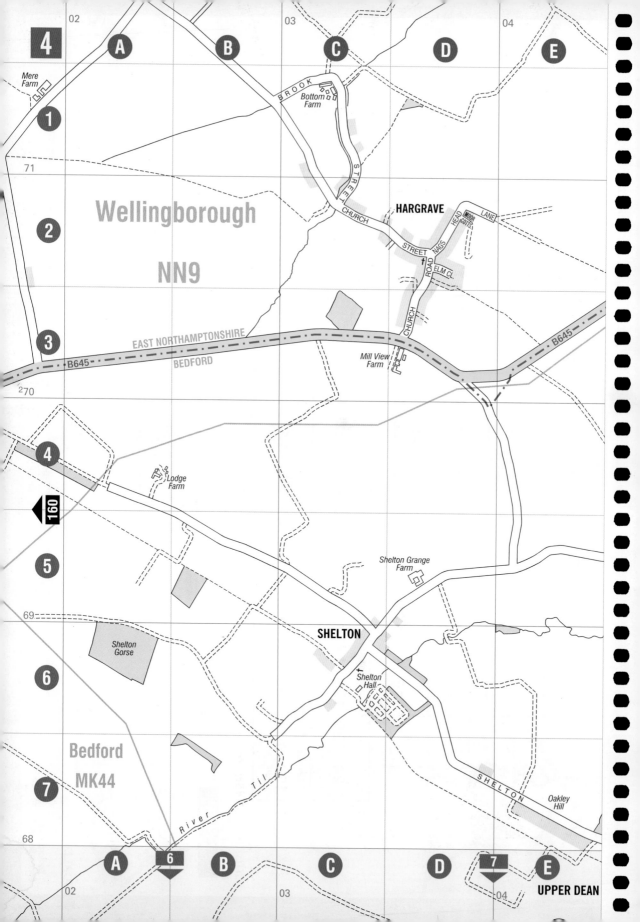

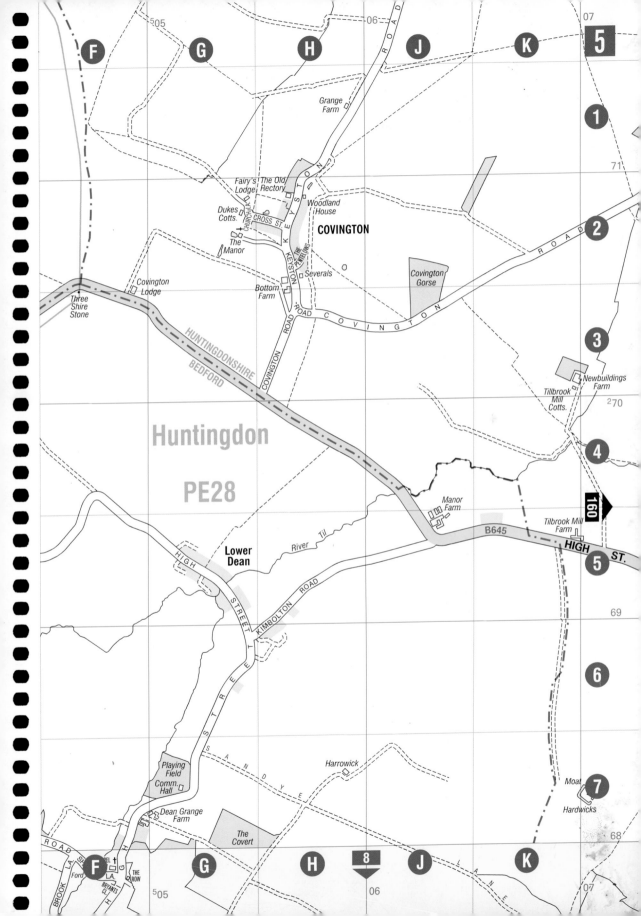

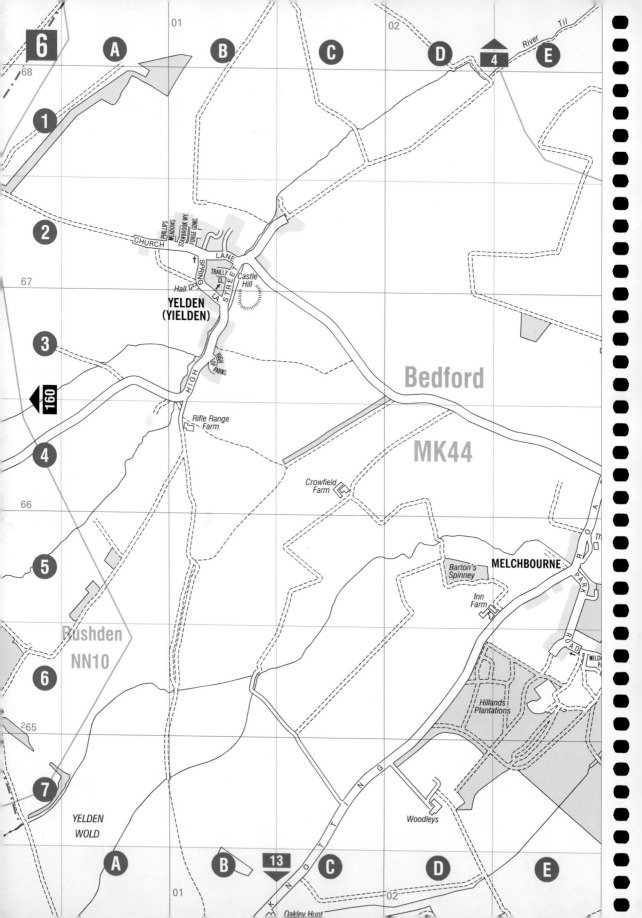

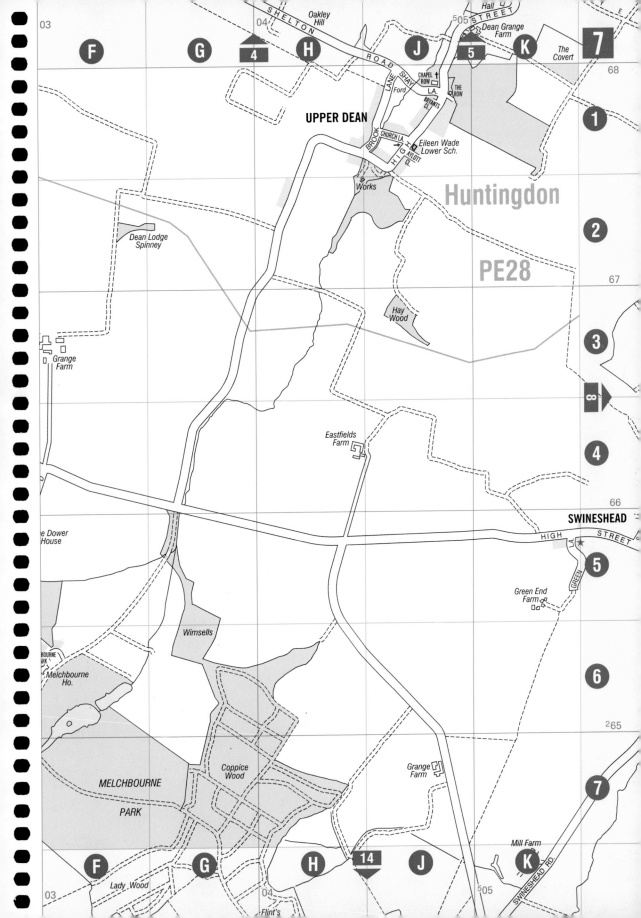

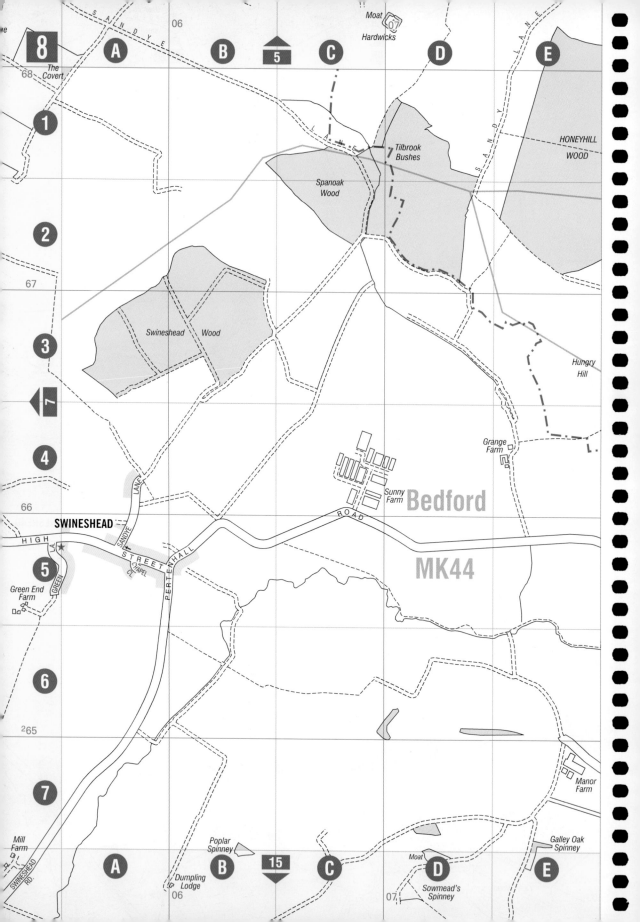

8

68

A   B   **5**   C   D   E

06

S A N D Y E

Moat
Hardwicks
07

The Covert

1

Tilbrook
Bushes

HONEYHILL
WOOD

Spanoak
Wood

2

SANDY LANE

67

Swineshead Wood

3

Hungry
Hill

7

4

Grange
Farm

66

Sunny
Farm

Bedford

SWINESHEAD

HIGH

STREET

ROAD

MK44

LA.

SANDYE

LANE

CHAPEL
CL.

PERTENHALL

5

GREEN

Green End
Farm

265

6

Manor
Farm

7

Mill
Farm

SWINESHEAD RD.

A   B   **15**   C   D   E

Poplar
Spinney

Dumpling
Lodge
06

Moat

Sowmead's
Spinney
07

Galley Oak
Spinney

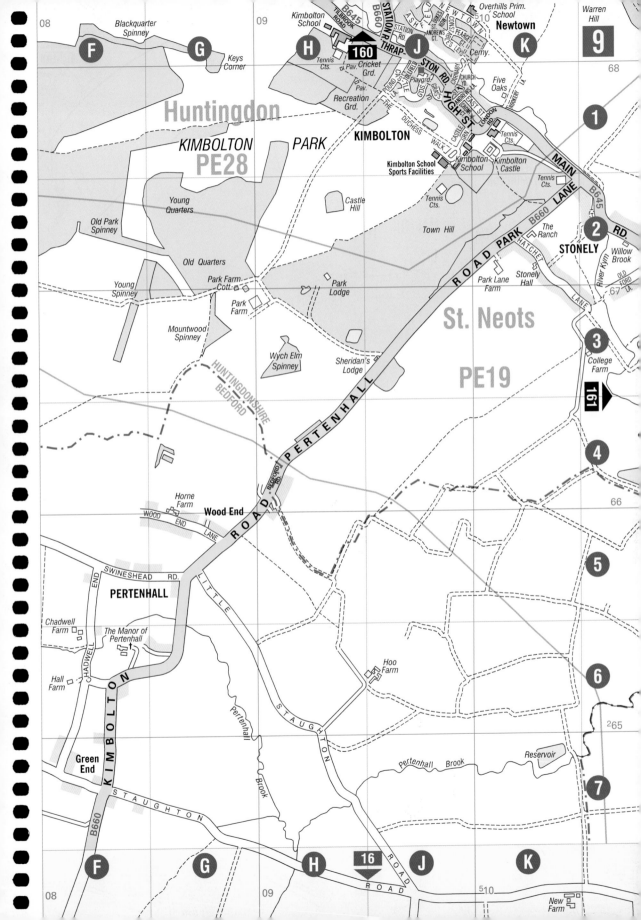

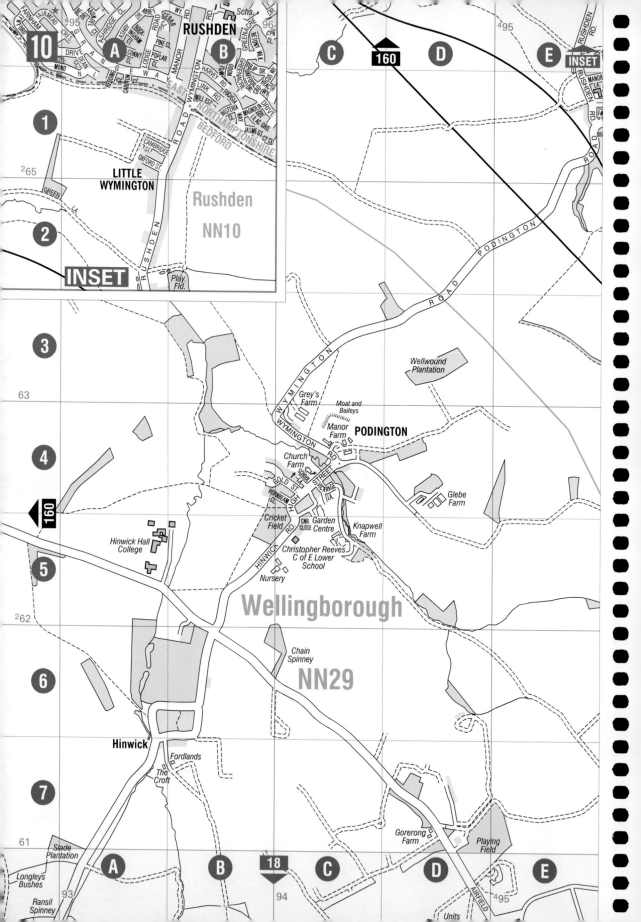

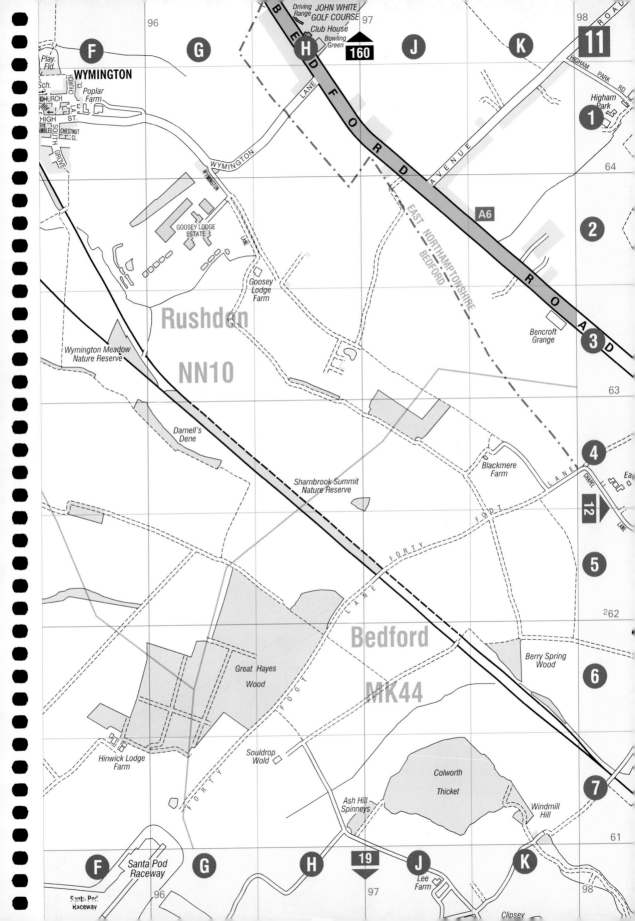

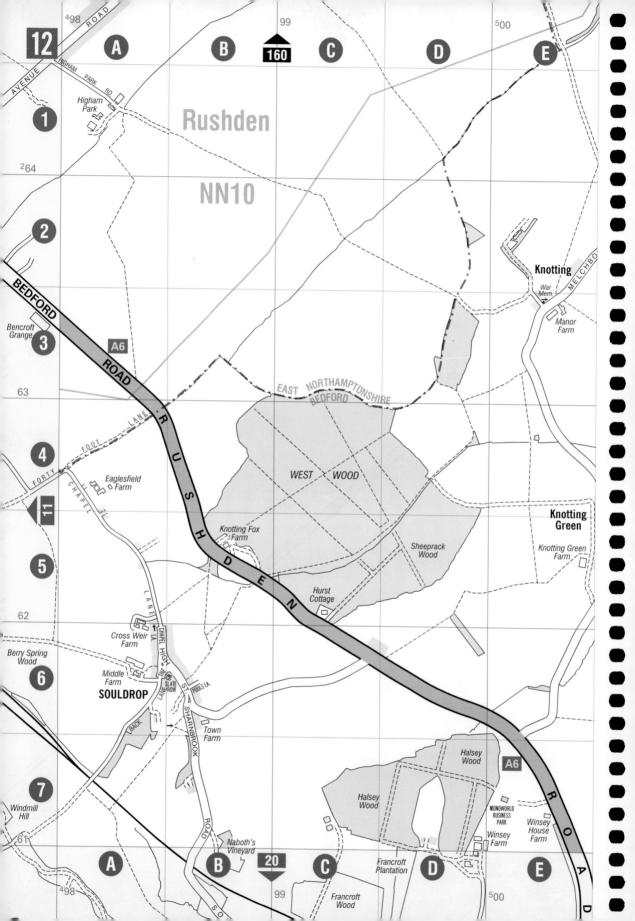

12

A   B   ▲ 160   C   D   E

498   ROAD   99   500

AVENUE HIGHAM PARK RD.

1 Higham Park

Rushden

264

NN10

2

BEDFORD

Knotting

War Mem.

MELCHBO

3 Bencroft Grange A6

ROAD

63

EAST NORTHAMPTONSHIRE
BEDFORD

Manor Farm

4 FOOT LANE

FORTY

CHAPEL

Eaglesfield Farm

WEST WOOD

Knotting Green

11

5

Knotting Fox Farm

Sheeprack Wood

Knotting Green Farm

62

Hurst Cottage

Cross Weir Farm

Berry Spring Wood

6 Middle Farm **SOULDROP**

LANE CHAPEL HIGH THE SLATE ROW POOL'S LA.

ST

SHARNBROOK

L BACK

Town Farm

Halsey Wood

A6

7 Windmill Hill

Halsey Wood

MONOWORLD BUSINESS PARK

ROAD

Winsey House Farm

61

Naboth's Vineyard

Winsey Farm

A   B   ▼ 20   C   D   E

498   99   500

Francroft Plantation

Francroft Wood

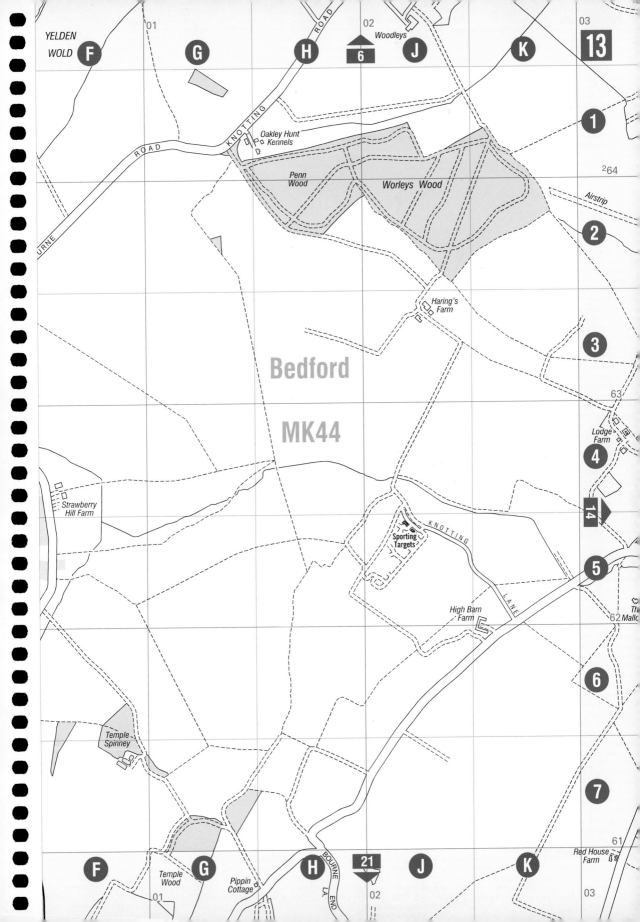

YELDEN WOLD **F**

G

ROAD

KNOTTING ROAD

H

01

02 Woodleys

6

J

K

03

13

1

264

Oakley Hunt Kennels

Penn Wood

Worleys Wood

Airstrip

2

BOURNE

Haring's Farm

3

Bedford

63

Lodge Farm

MK44

4

Strawberry Hill Farm

Sporting Targets

KNOTTING

14

LANE

5

High Barn Farm

62 The Mall

6

Temple Spinney

7

61

Red House Farm

F

G

Temple Wood

Pippin Cottage

H

BOURNE LA END

21

J

K

01

02

03

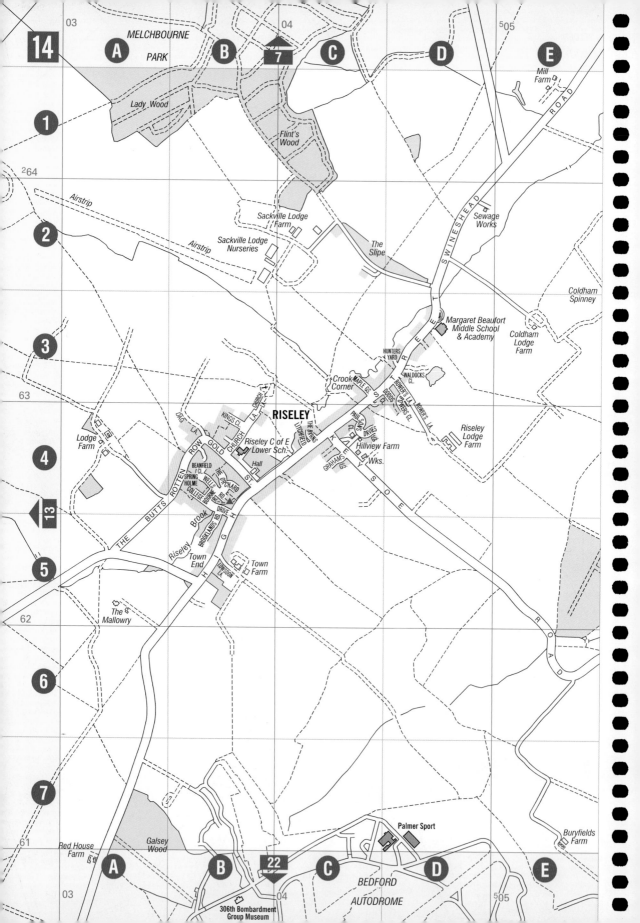

MELCHBOURNE
PARK

A **B** **7** **C** **D** **E**

Mill
Farm

1

Lady Wood

Flint's
Wood

R
O
A
D

²64

2

Airstrip

Airstrip

Sackville Lodge
Farm

Sackville Lodge
Nurseries

The
Slipe

Sewage
Works

S
W
I
N
E
S
H
E
A
D

Coldham
Spinney

3

Crook
Corner

HUNTERS
YARD

Margaret Beaufort
Middle School
& Academy

WALDOCKS
CL.

Coldham
Lodge
Farm

63

MAPLE GS.
THE AKINS

BOWERS LA.

DODDS

BOWERS CL.

BOWERS LA.

RISELEY

4

Lodge
Farm

OLD LA.
GOLD LA.
ROW
THE BUTTS
ROTTEN

KINGS CL.
CHURCH LA.
THE LOUBUSK

Riseley C of E
Lower Sch.

BEANFIELD
CL.
SPRING
HOLME
WELLS RD.
COLLEGE
BOURNE
DRIVE

Hall

LITCHFIELD
ST.
THE ORCHARD

PAUL'S
CL.
KEELING GS.
GRAHAM'S GS.
DAVIES GS.

Hillview Farm

Wks.

SOE

Riseley
Lodge
Farm

13

BROOK

Riseley

BROADLANDS RD.

THOMSON CL.

Town
End

Town
Farm

G
H

5

THE

H

62

The
Mallowry

R
O
A
D

6

7

Red House
Farm

Galsey
Wood

Palmer Sport

Buryfields
Farm

A **B** **22** **C** **D** **E**

BEDFORD
AUTODROME

03

04

⁵05

306th Bombardment
Group Museum

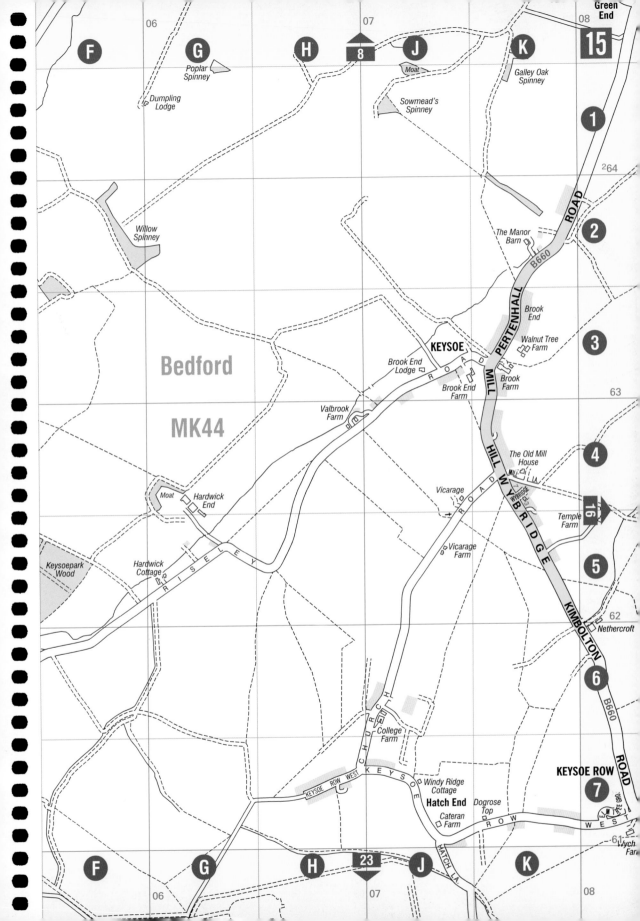

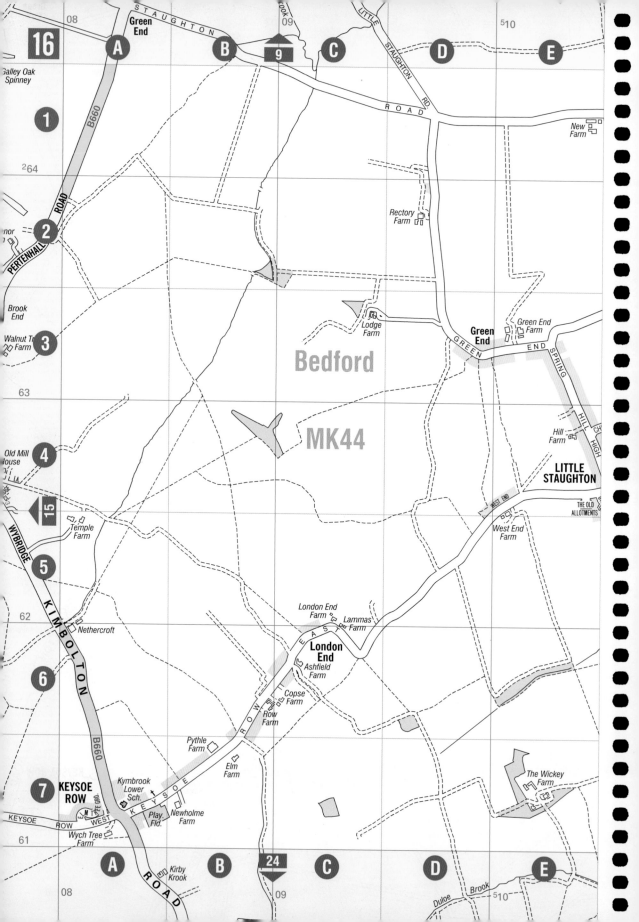

16

08 09 510

A **B** **C** **D** **E**

Green End

Galley Oak Spinney

1

²64

Manor

2

PERTENHALL ROAD

Brook End

Walnut Tr Farm

3

63

Old Mill House

4

◄ **15**

WYBRIDGE

Temple Farm

5

62

Nethercroft

6

B660 KIMBOLTON

7 **KEYSOE ROW**

Kymbrook Lower Sch.

Wych Tree Farm

KEYSOE ROW WEST

Play. Fld.

Newholme Farm

Pythle Farm

Elm Farm

KEYSOE ROW

Row Farm

Copse Farm

Ashfield Farm

London End

London End Farm

Lammas Farm

EAST

STAUGHTON

LITTLE STAUGHTON RD

ROAD

New Farm

Rectory Farm

Bedford

MK44

Lodge Farm

GREEN END

Green End

Green End Farm

Hill Farm

SPRING

HILL HIGH

CH

LITTLE STAUGHTON

WEST END

THE OLD ALLOTMENTS

West End Farm

The Wickey Farm

A **B** **24** **C** **D** **E**

Kirby Krook

ROAD

KEYSOE ROW

08 09 510

Duloe Brook

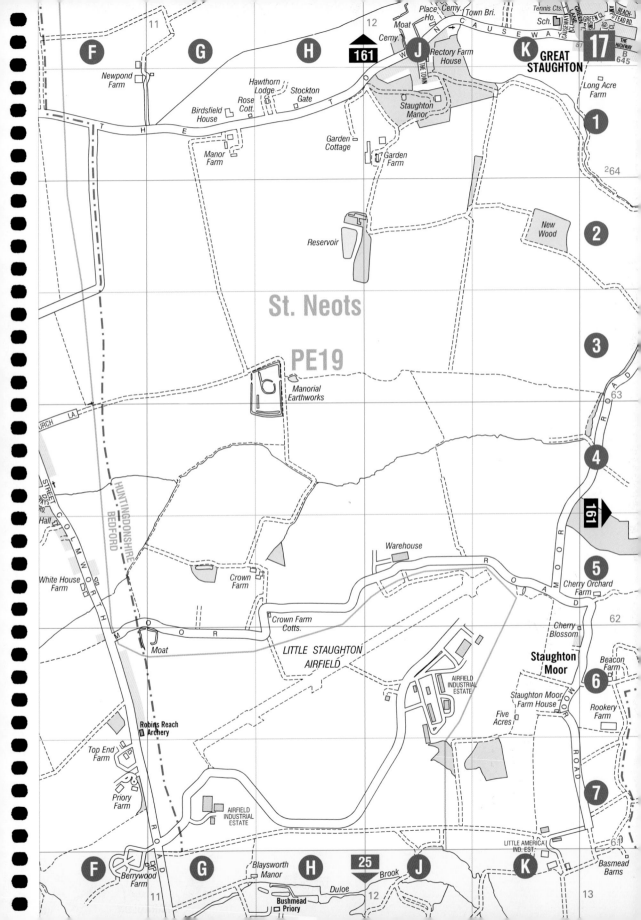

Newpond Farm

Hawthorn Lodge

Rose Cott.

Stockton Gate

Birdsfield House

Manor Farm

Place Ho.

Cemy.

Town Bri.

Moat

Cemy.

Tennis Cts.

Sch.

GREEN

161

J

Rectory Farm House

K

GREAT STAUGHTON

Long Acre Farm

Staughton Manor

1

Garden Cottage

Garden Farm

264

New Wood

2

Reservoir

St. Neots

PE19

3

63

Manorial Earthworks

4

161

CHURCH LA.

STREET

Hall

HUNTINGDONSHIRE
BEDFORD

White House Farm

Crown Farm

Warehouse

5

Cherry Orchard Farm

62

Cherry Blossom

Moat

Crown Farm Cotts.

LITTLE STAUGHTON AIRFIELD

Staughton Moor

Beacon Farm

6

AIRFIELD INDUSTRIAL ESTATE

Staughton Moor Farm House

Rookery Farm

Robins Reach Archery

Five Acres

Top End Farm

Priory Farm

AIRFIELD INDUSTRIAL ESTATE

7

LITTLE AMERICA IND. EST.

61

Berrywood Farm

Blaysworth Manor

25

Brook

Duloe

Basmead Barns

Bushmead Priory

11   12   13

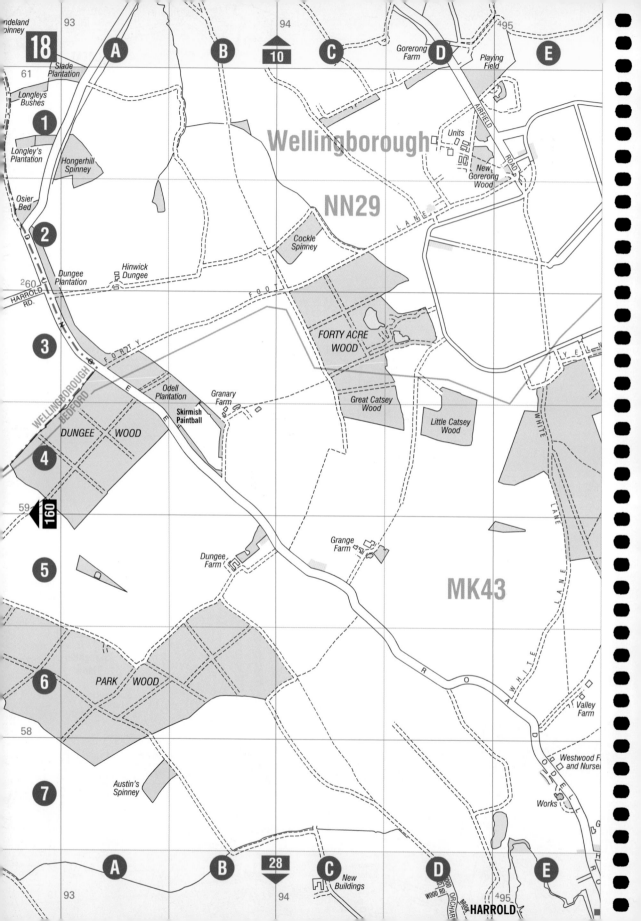

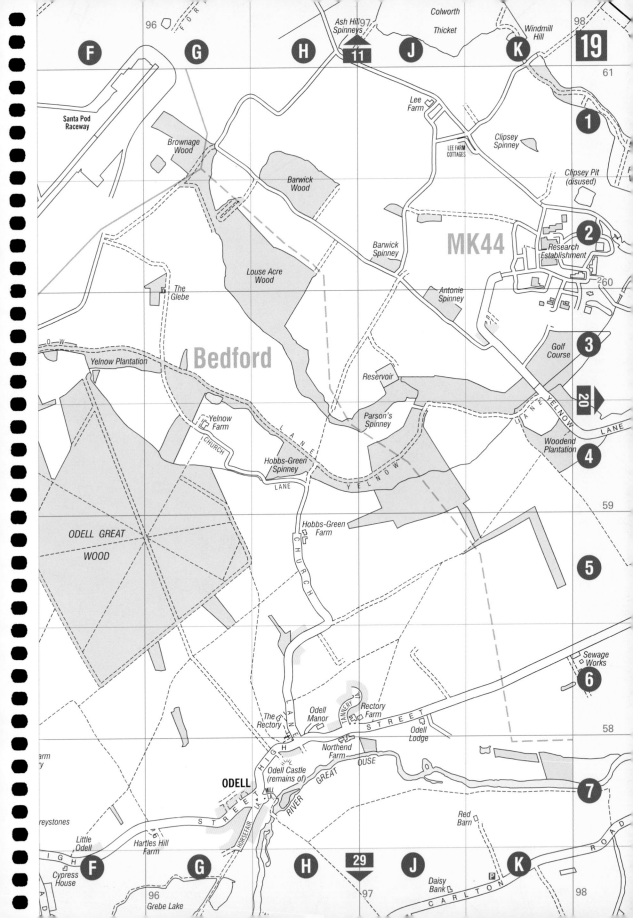

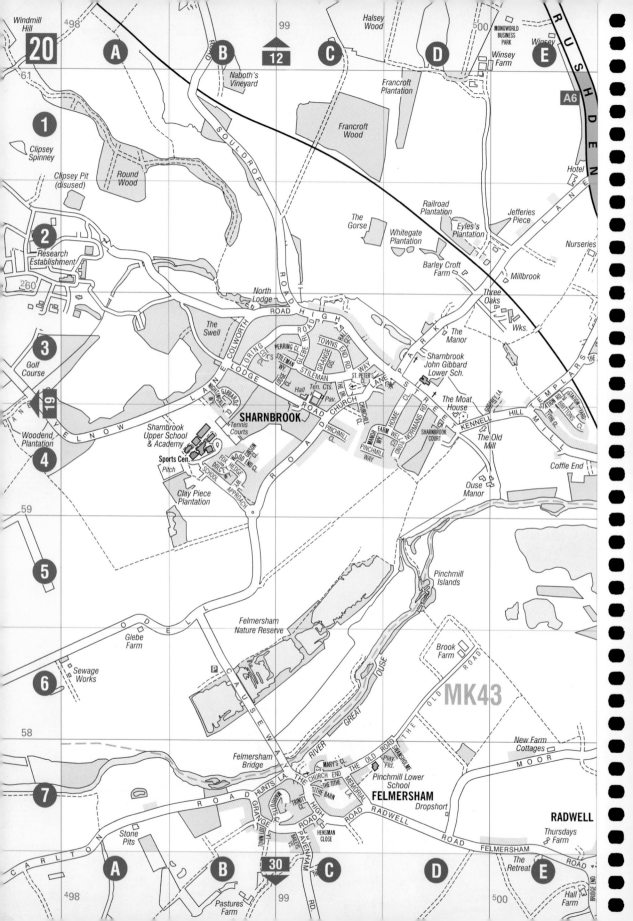

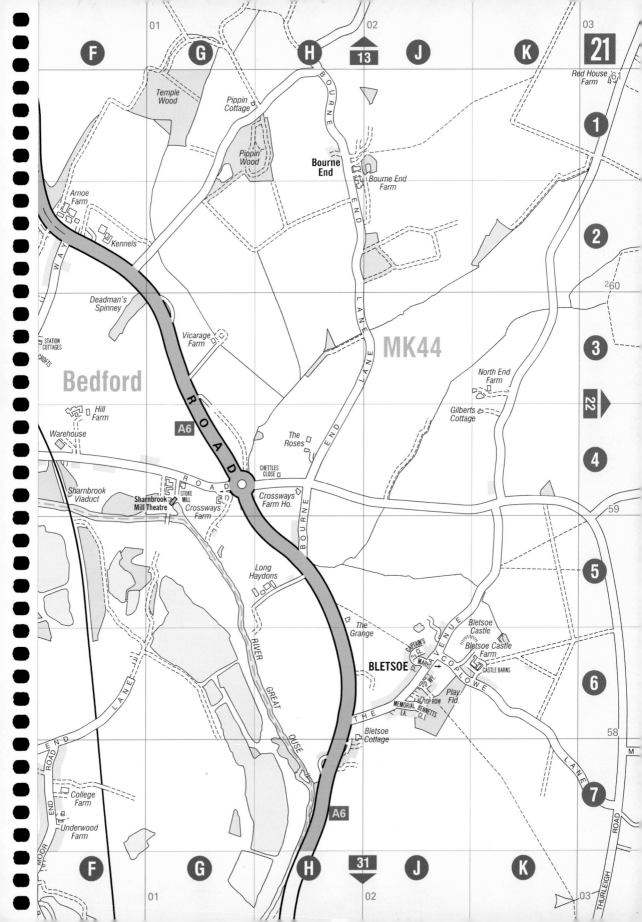

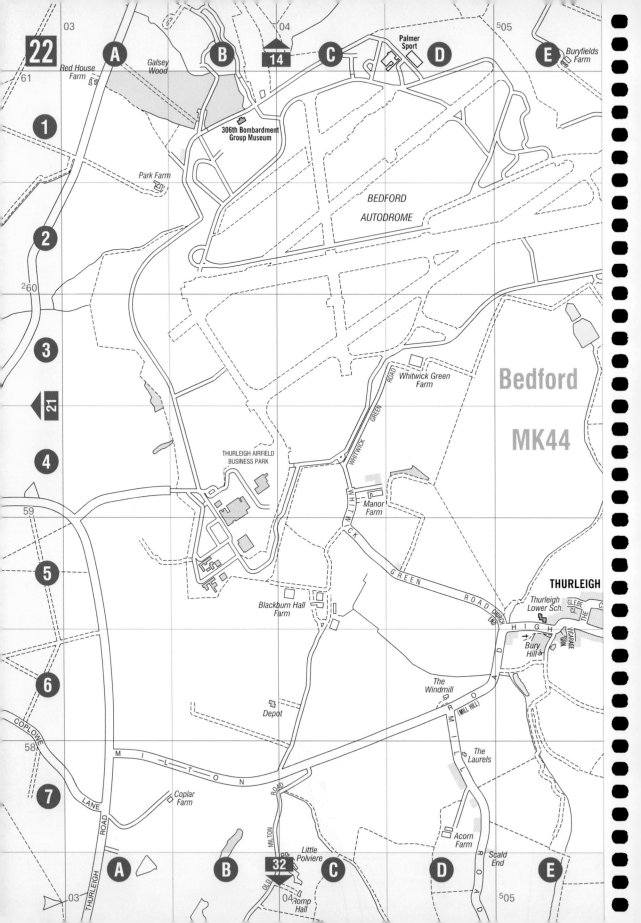

22

03 · 04 · 505

Red House Farm
61

Galsey Wood

A · **B** · **14** · **C** · Palmer Sport · **D** · **E** · Buryfields Farm

306th Bombardment Group Museum

1

Park Farm

2

260

BEDFORD AUTODROME

3

◀ **21**

Whitwick Green Farm

Bedford

THURLEIGH AIRFIELD BUSINESS PARK

4

WHITWICK GREEN ROAD

MK44

59

Manor Farm

5

THURLEIGH

Thurleigh Lower Sch.

Blackburn Hall Farm

GLEBE CL · THE · C

6

Bury Hill

HIGH

VICARAGE GRN

The Windmill

Depot

MILL HILL

COPLOWE

58

MILTON ROAD

The Laurels

7

Coplar Farm

LANE

MILTON ROAD

MILL ROAD

Acorn Farm

A

THURLEIGH ROAD

B · **32** · Little Polviere · **C** · **D** · Scald End · **E**

OLD

03 · 04 · Romp Hall · 505

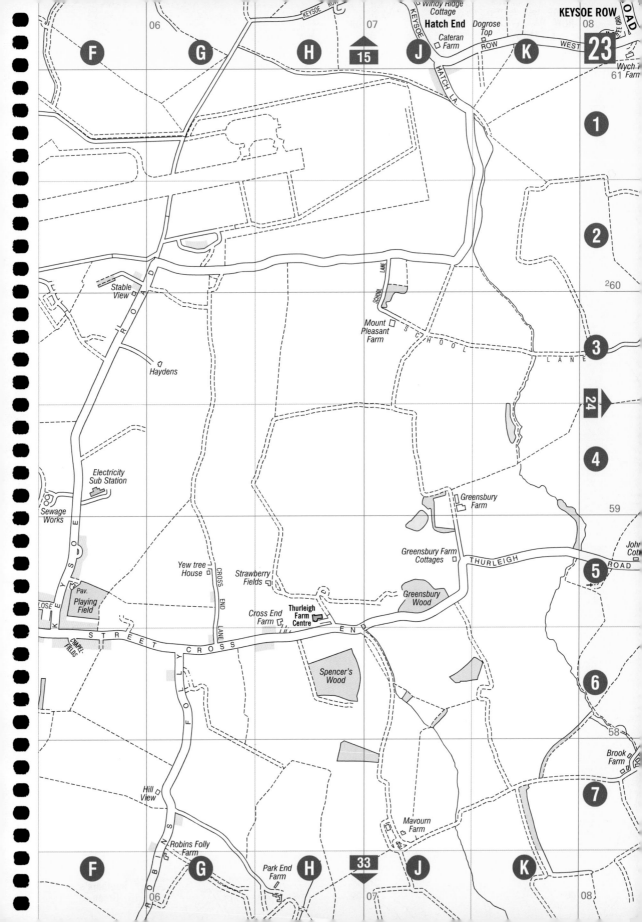

F G H 15 J K

Windy Ridge Cottage
Hatch End
Dogrose Top
Cateran Farm
KEYSOE ROW
WEST
Wych Farm
61

1

2

260

Stable View
SCHOOL LANE

ROAD

Mount Pleasant Farm

3

Haydens

SCHOOL LANE

24

4

Greensbury Farm

59

Electricity Sub Station

Greensbury Farm Cottages
THURLEIGH
John Cot
ROAD

Sewage Works

Yew tree House
Strawberry Fields

5

KEYSOE

CROSS END LANE

Greensbury Wood

Pav. Playing Field

Cross End Farm
Thurleigh Farm Centre

CLOSE

STREET CROSS END

CHPL. FIELDS

Greensbury Wood

6

Spencer's Wood

58

Brook Farm

HOLLY

Hill View

7

Robins Folly Farm

Mavourn Farm

ROBINS

F G Park End Farm H 33 J K

06 07 08

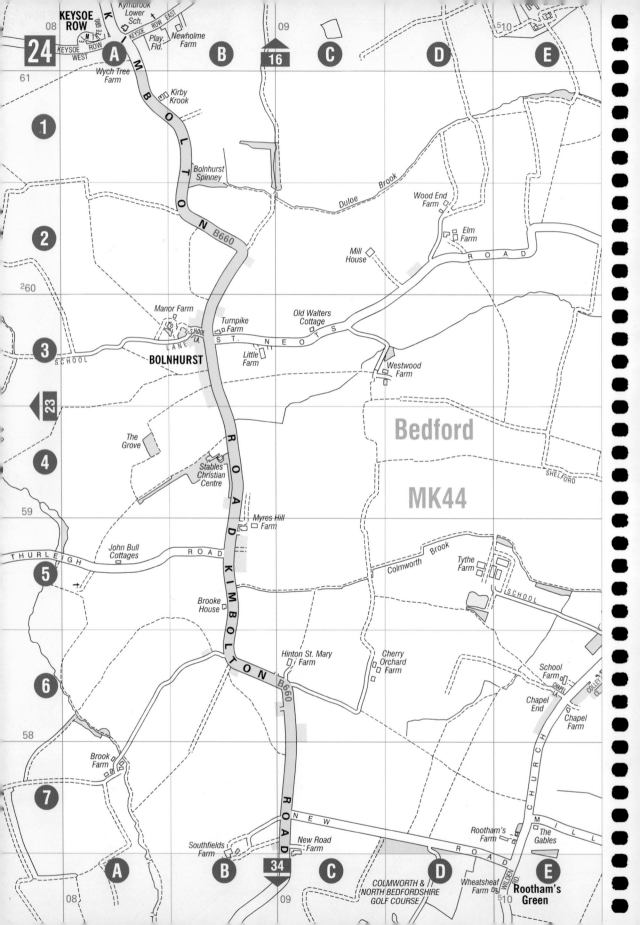

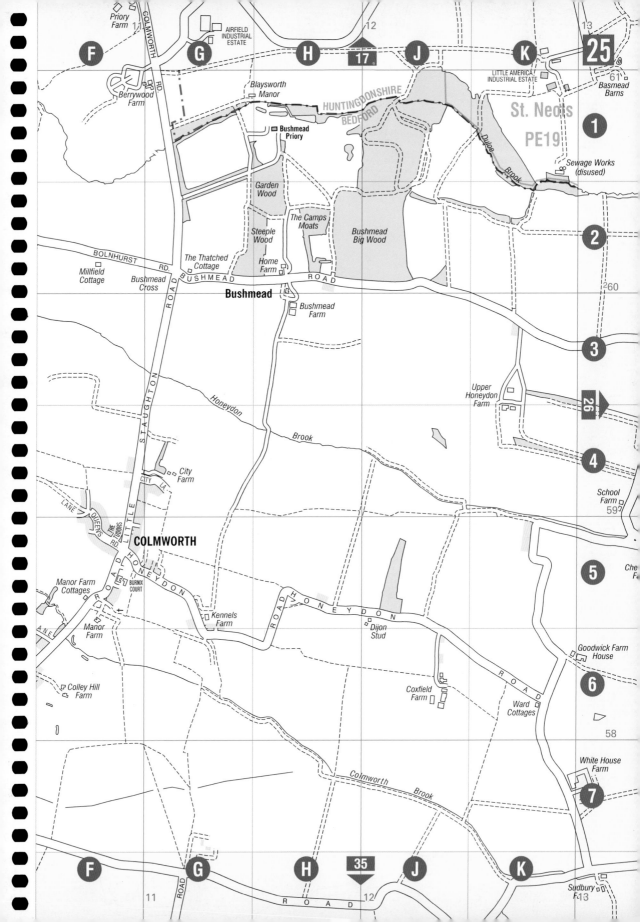

F G H 17 J K

1

Priory Farm

COLMWORTH RD.

AIRFIELD INDUSTRIAL ESTATE

12 13

61

LITTLE AMERICA INDUSTRIAL ESTATE

Basmead Barns

Berrywood Farm

Blaysworth Manor

HUNTINGDONSHIRE
BEDFORD

St. Neots

PE19

Bushmead Priory

Dulce Brook

Sewage Works (disused)

2

Garden Wood

The Camps Moats

Bushmead Big Wood

260

Steeple Wood

Millfield Cottage

BOLNHURST RD.

The Thatched Cottage

Home Farm

Bushmead Cross

BUSHMEAD ROAD

Bushmead

Bushmead Farm

3

STAUGHTON ROAD

Honeydon Brook

Upper Honeydon Farm

26

4

City Farm

School Farm

59

QUEENS RD. LANE

LITTLE HONEYDON

CITY LA.

THE TUDORS

COLMWORTH

5

Cher Fa

ROAD

BURNIX COURT

Manor Farm Cottages

Kennels Farm

HONEYDON ROAD

Dijon Stud

Goodwick Farm House

Manor Farm

6

LANE

Colley Hill Farm

Coxfield Farm

Ward Cottages

ROAD

58

White House Farm

Colmworth Brook

7

F G H 35 J K

11 12 13

ROAD

ROAD

Sudbury Fa

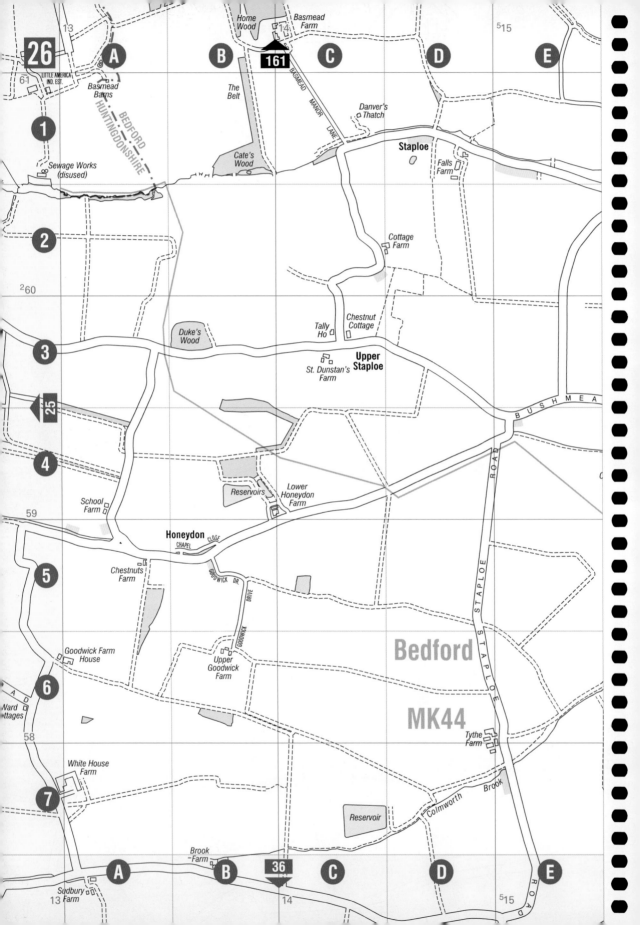

26

LITTLE AMERICA IND. EST.

6 1

Basmead Barns

Home Wood

Basmead Farm

BEDFORD
HUNTINGDONSHIRE

The Belt

Danver's Thatch

Cate's Wood

Staploe

Falls Farm

1

Sewage Works (disused)

2

2 60

Cottage Farm

Duke's Wood

Tally Ho

Chestnut Cottage

3

St. Dunstan's Farm

Upper Staploe

25

BUSHMEA

4

Reservoirs

Lower Honeydon Farm

School Farm

59

Honeydon

CHAPEL CLOSE

ROAD

5

Chestnuts Farm

GOODWICK DR.

GOODWICK DRIVE

Goodwick Farm House

Upper Goodwick Farm

Bedford

STAPLOE

6

Ward ottages

58

MK44

Tythe Farm

7

White House Farm

Reservoir

Colmworth

Brook

Brook Farm

Sudbury Farm
13

14

ROAD

5 15

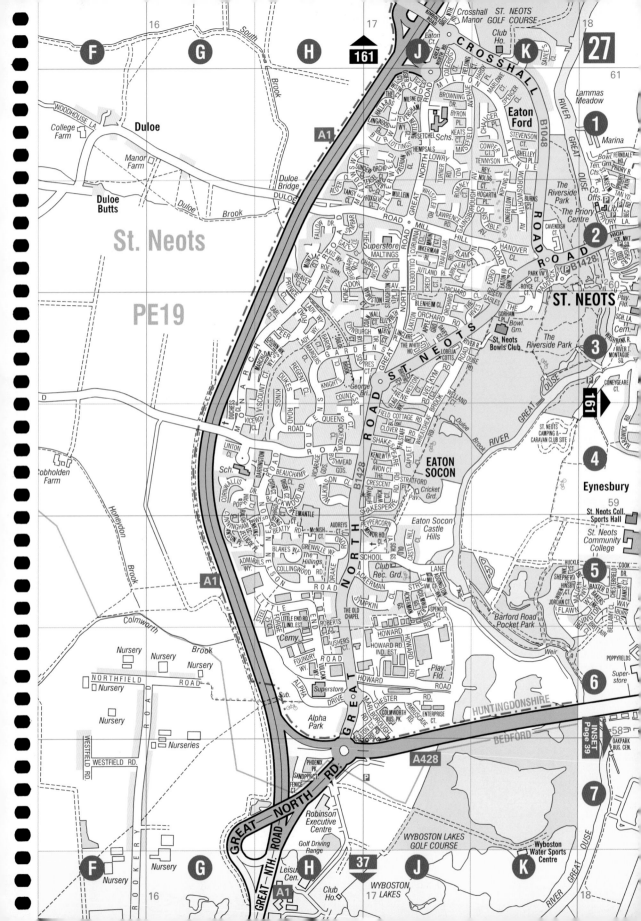

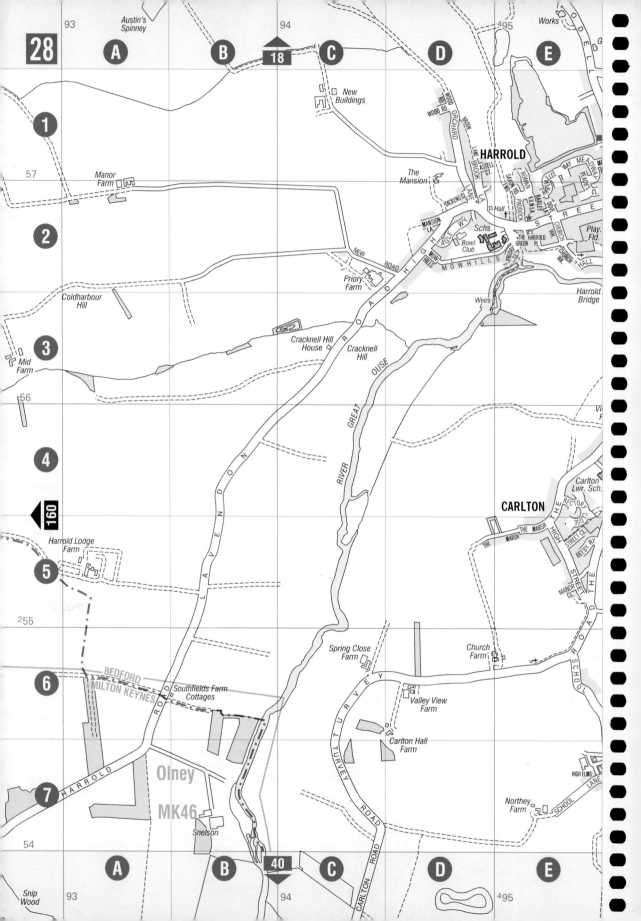

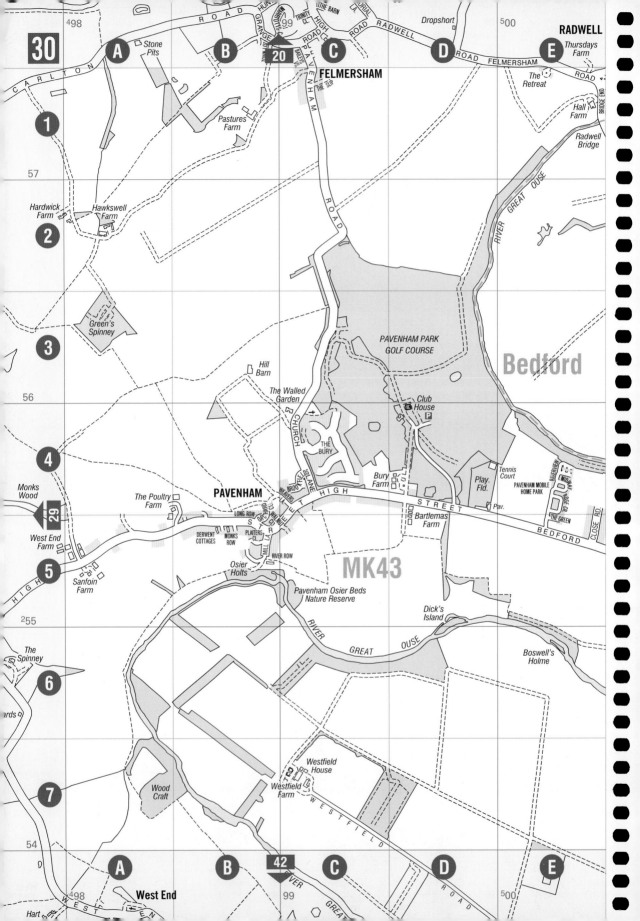

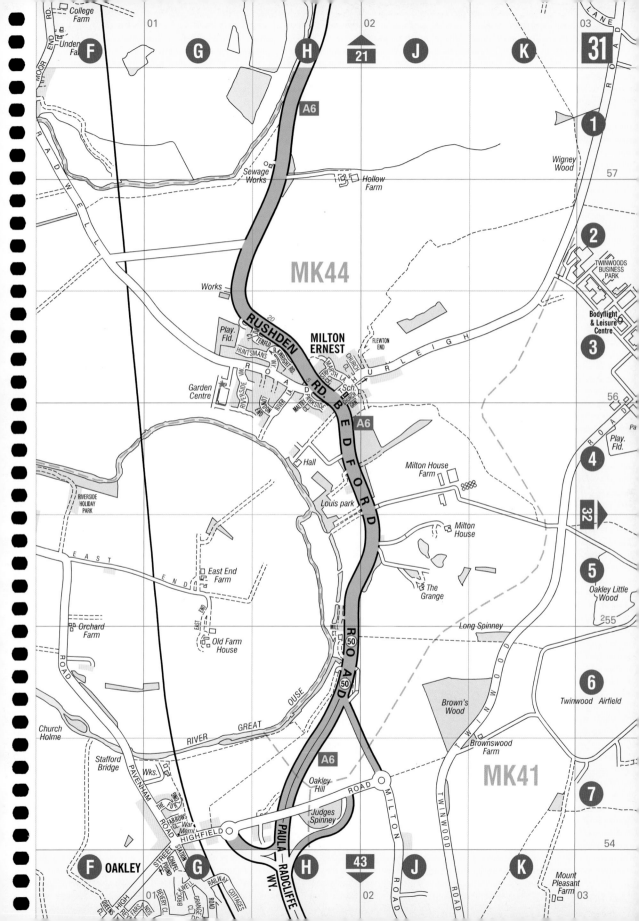

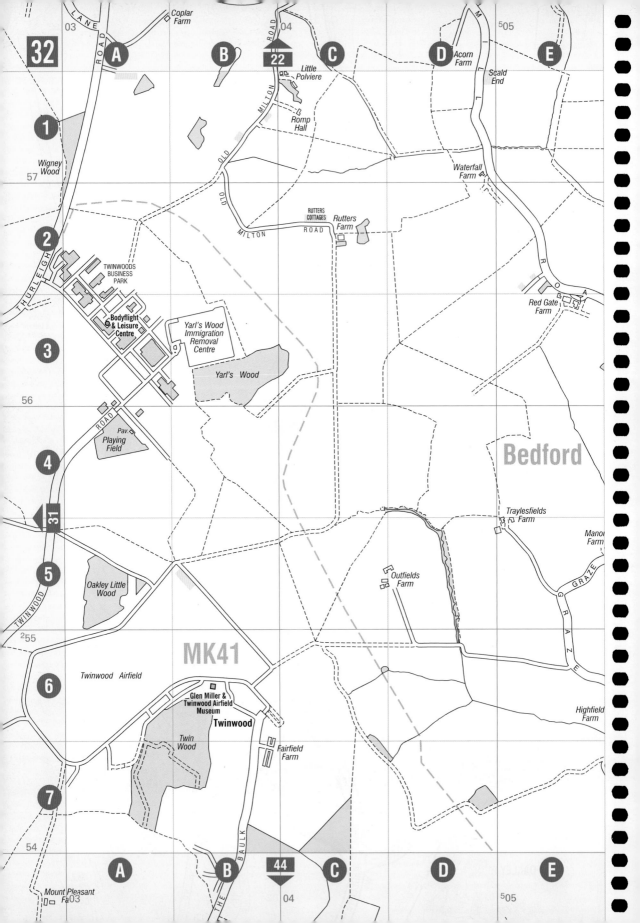

32

A **B** **C** **D** **E**

03 04 505

LANE

Coplar Farm

ROAD

22

Little Polviere

MILTON

Romp Hall

Acorn Farm

Scald End

1

Wigney Wood

57

OLD

Waterfall Farm

2

RUTTERS COTTAGES

Rutters Farm

ROAD

OLD MILTON

ROAD

THURLEIGH

TWINWOODS BUSINESS PARK

Red Gate Farm

3

Bodyflight & Leisure Centre

Yarl's Wood Immigration Removal Centre

Yarl's Wood

Bedford

56

ROAD

Pav.

Playing Field

4

31

Traylesfields Farm

Manor Farm

5

Oakley Little Wood

TWINWOOD

Outfields Farm

255

MK41

GRAZE

6

Twinwood Airfield

Glen Miller & Twinwood Airfield Museum

Twinwood

Highfield Farm

Twin Wood

Fairfield Farm

7

THE BAULK

54

A **B** **C** **D** **E**

Mount Pleasant Fa 03

44

04 505

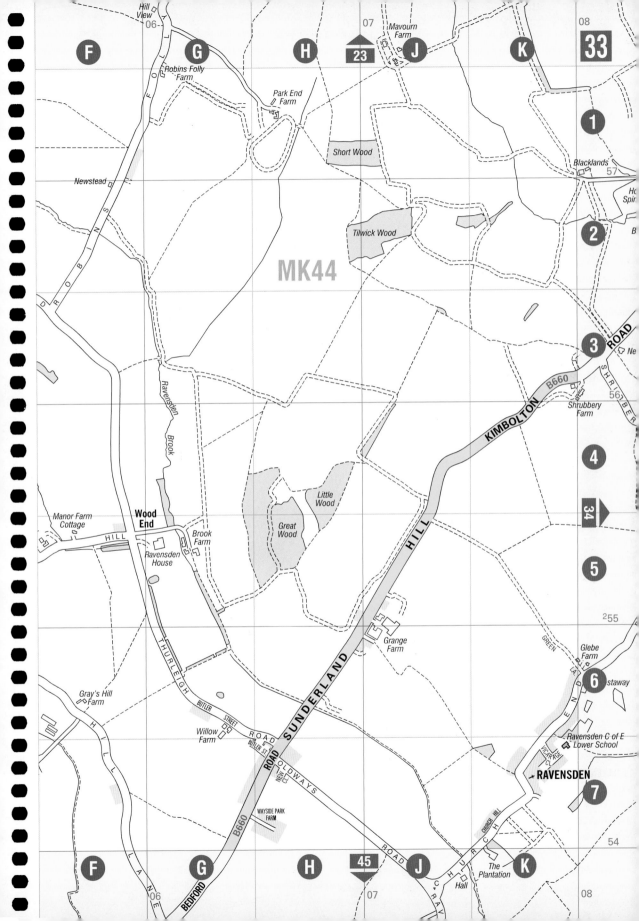

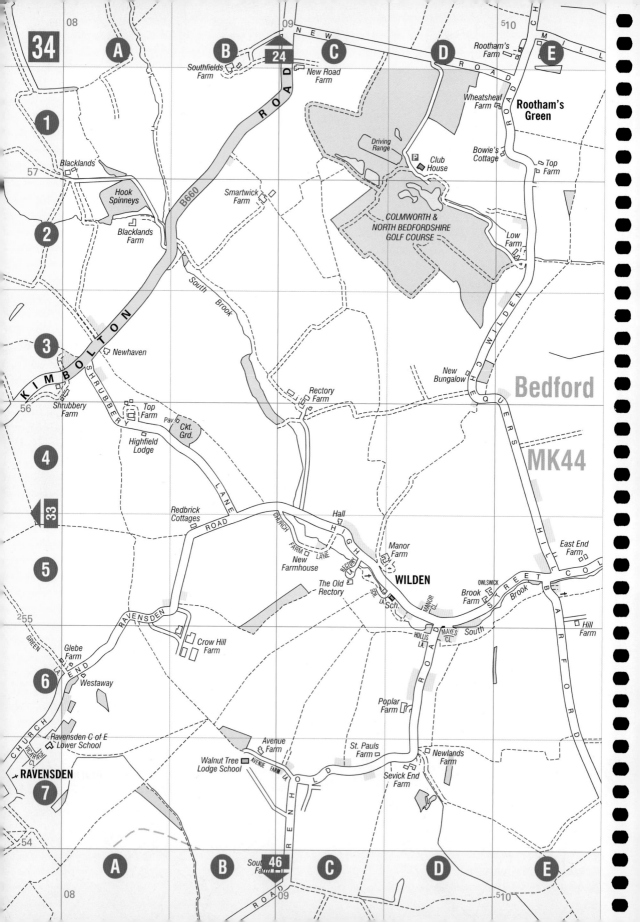

34

A B **24** C D **Rootham's Farm** E

Southfields Farm New Road Farm Wheatsheaf Farm **Rootham's Green**

1

Blacklands Driving Range Club House Bowie's Cottage Top Farm

57

Hook Spinneys Smartwick Farm **COLMWORTH & NORTH BEDFORDSHIRE GOLF COURSE**

2 Blacklands Farm

B660 South Brook Low Farm

3 Newhaven New Bungalow **Bedford**

KIMBOLTON SHRUBBERY 56 Shrubbery Farm Top Farm Pav. Ckt. Grd. Rectory Farm

4 Highfield Lodge **MK44**

33 Redbrick Cottages ROAD LANE CHURCH LANE Hall HIGH Manor Farm East End Farm

5 New Farmhouse FARM LANE RECTORY LA. **WILDEN** OWLSWICK Brook Farm South Brook Hill Farm

255 The Old Rectory SCH. LA. Sch. MANOR CL. MAYES CL.

RAVENSDEN Glebe Farm Crow Hill Farm HOLLIS LA. ROAD STREET BARFORD COL

6 Westaway Poplar Farm

CHURCH GREEN END Ravensden C of E Lower School VICARAGE CL.

RAVENSDEN Avenue Farm St. Pauls Farm Newlands Farm

7 Walnut Tree Lodge School AVENUE FARM LA. Sevick End Farm

54 GREENH OLD ROAD

A B **46** South Farm C ROAD D E
08 09 510

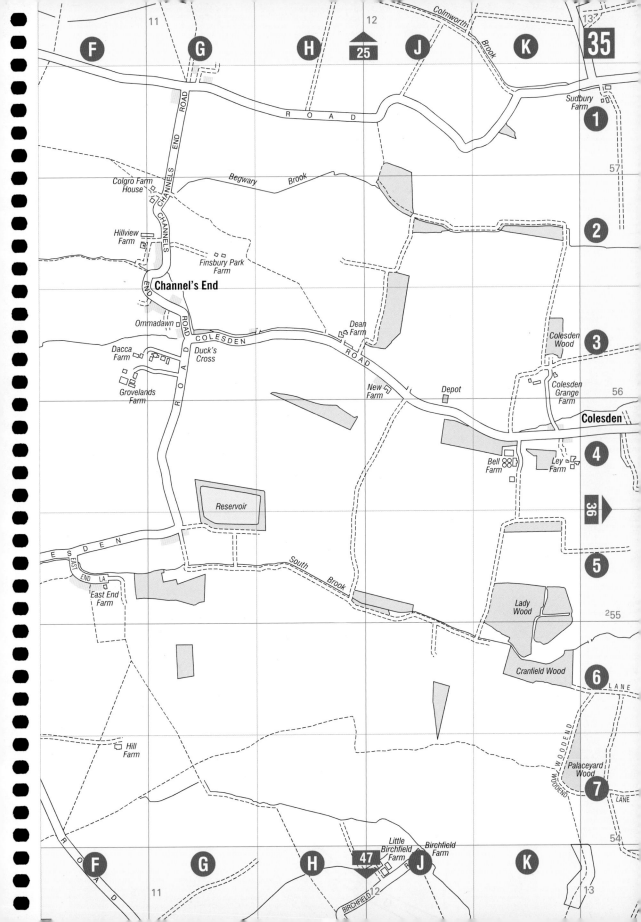

F G H ⌂ 25 J K

Colmworth Brook

Sudbury Farm
1

R O A D

57

Colgro Farm House
Begwary Brook
2

CHANNELS END ROAD

Hillview Farm

Finsbury Park Farm

Channel's End

Ommadawn
Dean Farm
Colesden Wood
3

COLESDEN ROAD

Dacca Farm
Duck's Cross

New Farm
Depot
Colesden Grange Farm
56

Grovelands Farm

Colesden

Bell Farm
Ley Farm
4

Reservoir

36
5

E S D E N

EAST END LA.
East End Farm

South Brook

Lady Wood
255

Cranfield Wood
6
LANE

Hill Farm

WOODEND

Palaceyard Wood
7
LANE

54

R O A D

F G H 47 J K

Little Birchfield Farm
Birchfield Farm

BIRCHFIELD 12
13

11 12

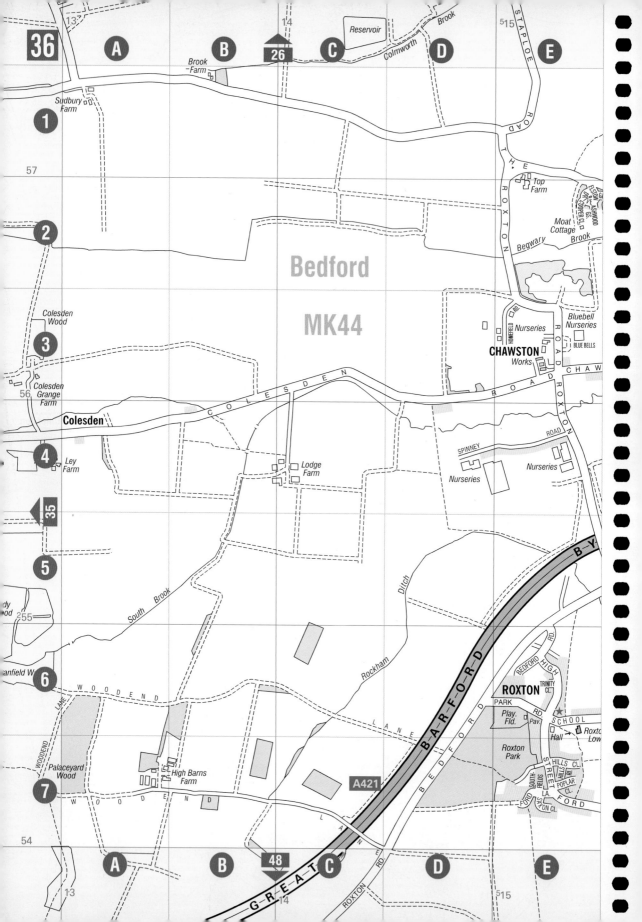

36

A · B · 26 · C · Colmworth · D · E

Reservoir
Brook
STAPLOE ROAD
515

13₃ · 14

57

1 Sudbury Farm
Brook-Farm

2
Bedford

Top Farm
ASHWOOD
DRY COPSE CL.

Moat Cottage
Begwary Brook
Bluebell Nurseries

MK44

3 Colesden Wood
Nurseries
CHAWSTON
Works
BLUE BELLS
Blue Bells

56
Colesden Grange Farm
COLESDEN ROAD
ROAD
ROXTON ROAD
CHAW

Colesden

4 Ley Farm
Lodge Farm
SPINNEY
Nurseries
ROAD
Nurseries

35

5
Ditch
B-Y

255
South Brook
Rockham
BY-PASS

RD
HIGH
BEDFORD
TRINITY CL.

6 WOODEND LANE
LANE
ROXTON
PARK
Play. Fld.
Pav.
SCHOOL
Roxton Low
Hall

Roxton Park
HILLS CL.
HILLS
POPLAR CL.

7 Palaceyard Wood
High Barns Farm
WOODEND
A421
BEDFORD
SOUTH STREET
FORD
STON CL.

54

A · B · 48 · C · ROXTON RD · D · E

GREAT
13 · 14
515

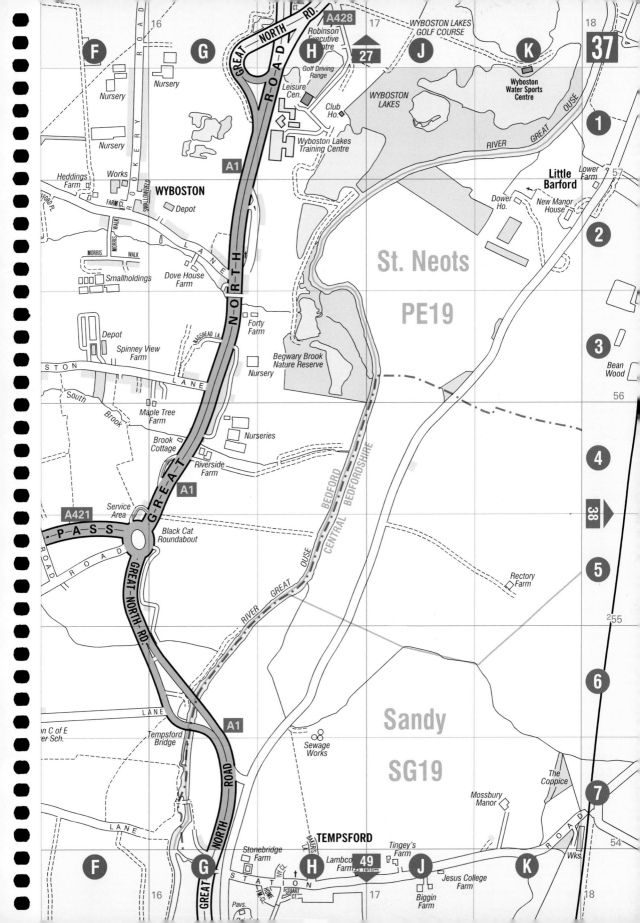

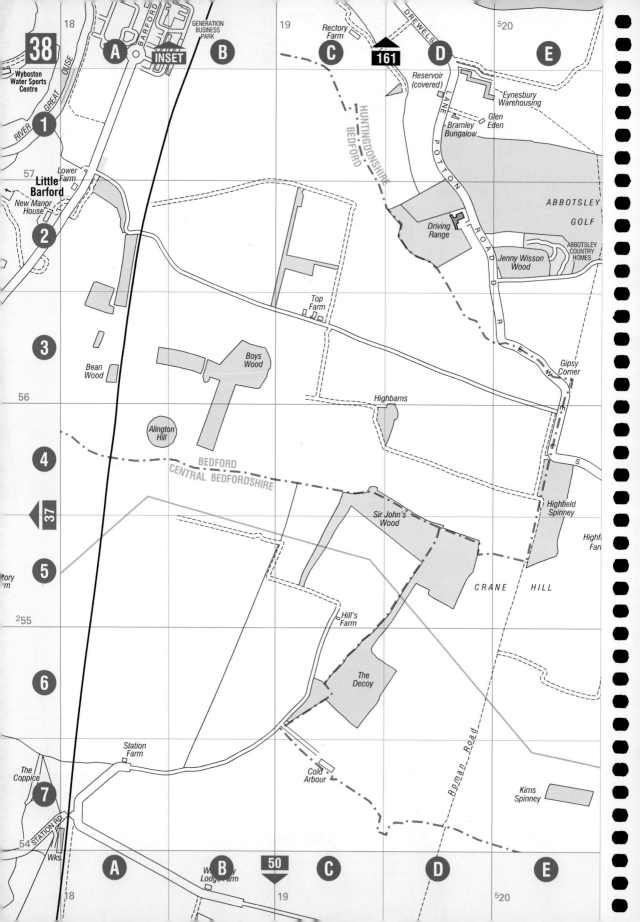

38

A INSET **B** **C** 161 **D** **E**

Wyboston Water Sports Centre

GREAT OUSE RIVER

BARFORD

GENERATION BUSINESS PARK

Rectory Farm

DREWELS

Reservoir (covered)

Eynesbury Warehousing

Glen Eden

Bramley Bungalow

HUNTINGDONSHIRE BEDFORD

POTTON ROAD

LANE

57 Lower Farm

Little Barford

New Manor House

Top Farm

Driving Range

Jenny Wisson Wood

ABBOTSLEY GOLF

ABBOTSLEY COUNTRY HOMES

Bean Wood

Boys Wood

Highbarns

Gipsy Corner

56

Alington Hill

BEDFORD CENTRAL BEDFORDSHIRE

Highfield Spinney

37

Sir John's Wood

Highf... Far...

tory m

Hill's Farm

CRANE HILL

255

The Decoy

Station Farm

Roman Road

Kims Spinney

The Coppice

Cold Arbour

54 STATION RD.

Wks.

A **B** 50 **C** **D** **E**

...by Lodge Farm

18 19 520

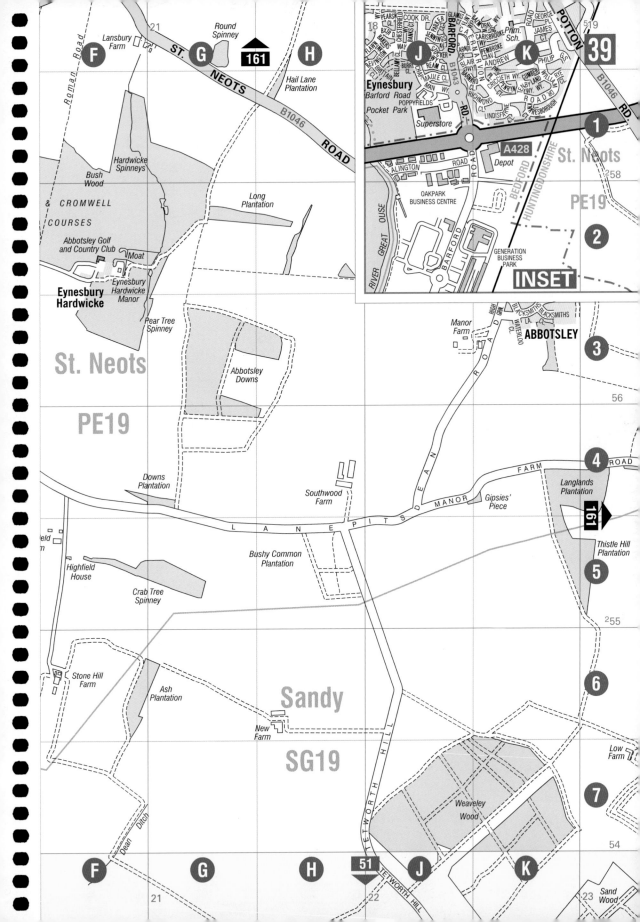

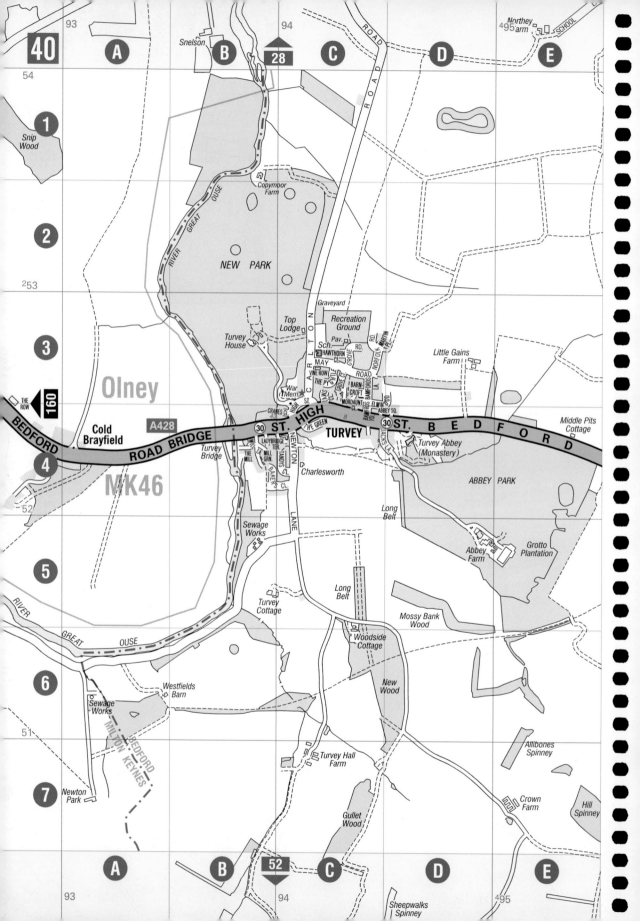

40

54

1 Snip Wood

RIVER GREAT OUSE

Copymoor Farm

NEW PARK

2

253

Graveyard

Top Lodge

Recreation Ground

Turvey House

Pav.

Sch.

HAWTHORN

Little Gains Farm

3 Olney

CARLTON

GROVE RD.

NORFOLK

MARTIN

MAY

VINE ROW

THE PYGHTLE

ROAD

LING

BARN CROFT

BAMFORDS

ELM

ABBEY SQ.

War Mem.

MORDAUNT CL.

THE ROW ◄ 160

BEDFORD

A428

ROAD BRIDGE

30 ST. HIGH

Cold Brayfield

Turvey Bridge

LADYBRIDGE TER.

THE MILL

MILL GRN.

NEWTON

PYE GREEN

TURVEY 30 ST. BEDFORD

Middle Pits Cottage

Turvey Abbey (Monastery)

Charlesworth

JACKS LA.

4

52

MK46

BAKER'S CL.

TANDYS

Sewage Works

LANE

ABBEY PARK

Long Belt

Abbey Farm

Grotto Plantation

5

Turvey Cottage

Long Belt

Mossy Bank Wood

6

Westfields Barn

RIVER GREAT OUSE

Woodside Cottage

New Wood

Allibones Spinney

Sewage Works

MILTON KEYNES

BEDFORD

Turvey Hall Farm

51

Crown Farm

Hill Spinney

7 Newton Park

Gullet Wood

94

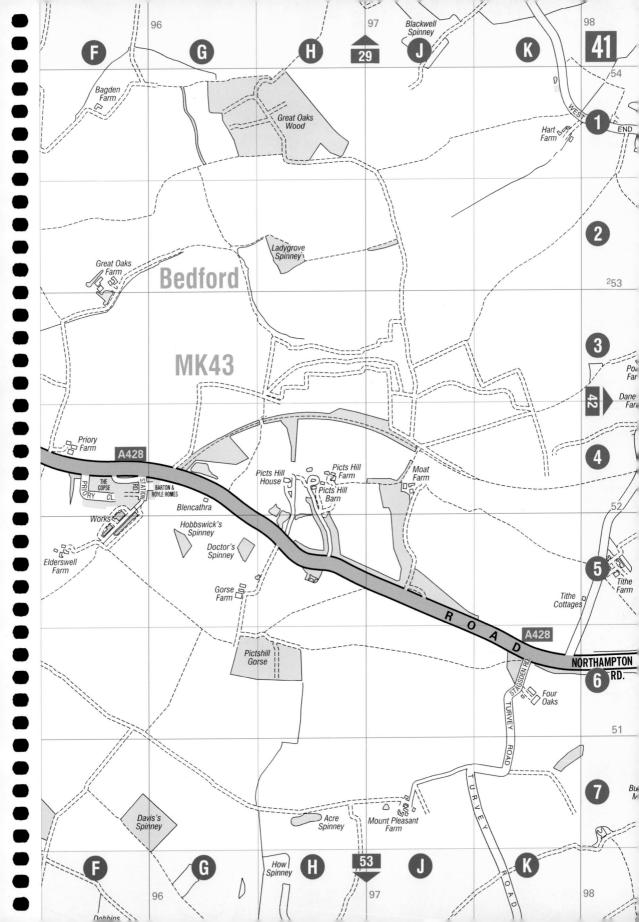

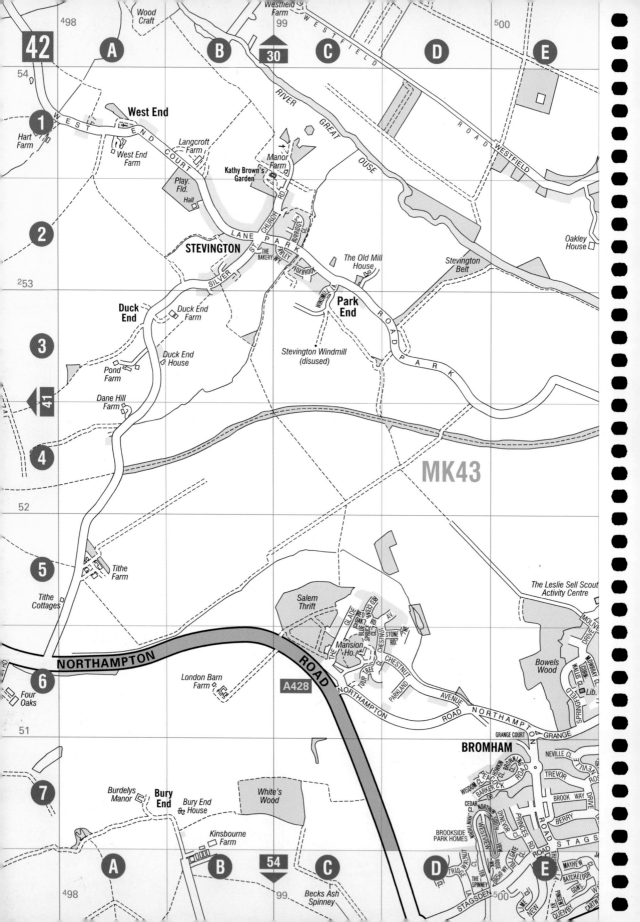

42

A   B   C   D   E

Wood Craft

Westfield Farm

WESTFIELD

99

▲30

500

54

WEST END COURT

West End

Hart Farm

Langcroft Farm

West End Farm

Play. Fld.

Hall

Kathy Brown's Garden

Manor Farm

RIVER GREAT OUSE

ROAD WESTFIELD

1

STEVINGTON

CHURCH RD

PARK WY

RILEY

BURRIDGE

Oakley House

2

253

SILVER ST

LANE

THE BAKERY

FOXBROOK

The Old Mill House

Stevington Belt

Duck End

Duck End Farm

WINDMILL

Park End

ROAD PARK

3

Pond Farm

Duck End House

Stevington Windmill (disused)

◄ **41**

Dane Hill Farm

4

52

MK43

Tithe Farm

5

Tithe Cottages

The Leslie Sell Scout Activity Centre

Salem Thrift

THE GLADE

RED OAK CL

BLUE SPRUCE CL

WALNUT CL

STONE RD

PINE AV

CHESTNUT

Bowels Wood

MOLIVERS DR

WOMBAT CL

WALLISFIELD

SPRINGFIELD

Lib.

NORTHAMPTON

ROAD

A428

Mansion Ho.

PULP TREE

PARKLAND

CHESTNUT RD

AVENUE

NORTHAMPTON ROAD

GRANGE

6

Four Oaks

London Barn Farm

51

GRANGE COURT

BROMHAM

NEVILLE CL

TREVOR

BROOK WAY

BERRY

NEVILLE CL

DRIVE

7

Burdelys Manor

Bury End

Bury End House

White's Wood

WISDOM CL

BARKER CL

PEACOCK

BROWN RD

ROAD

CEDAR CL

NORTH DYMOCK CL

PRINCES RD

WESTVIEW

ROAD

STAGS

BROOKSIDE PARK HOMES

Kinsbourne Farm

54

▼

Becks Ash Spinney

A   B   C   D   E

498

99

500

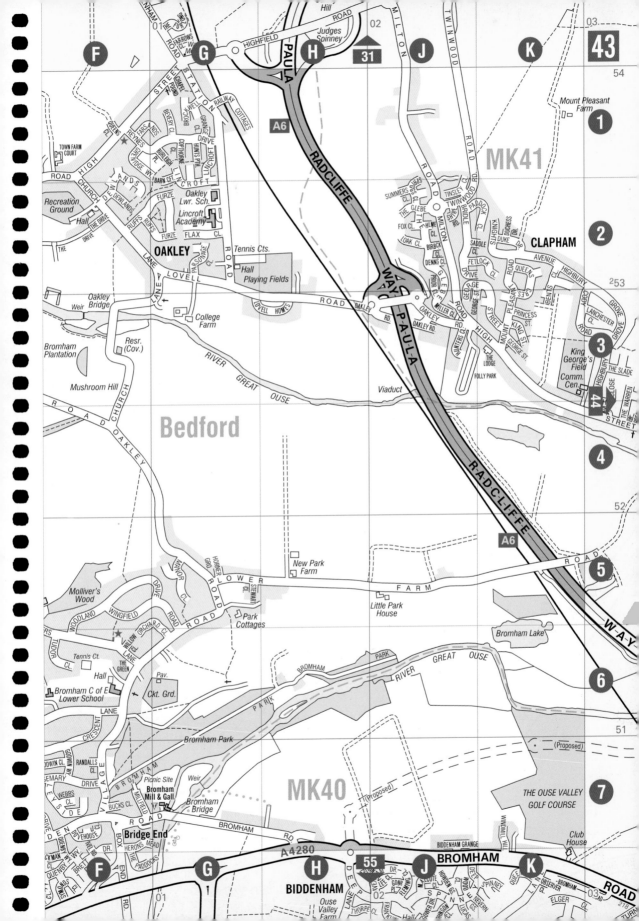

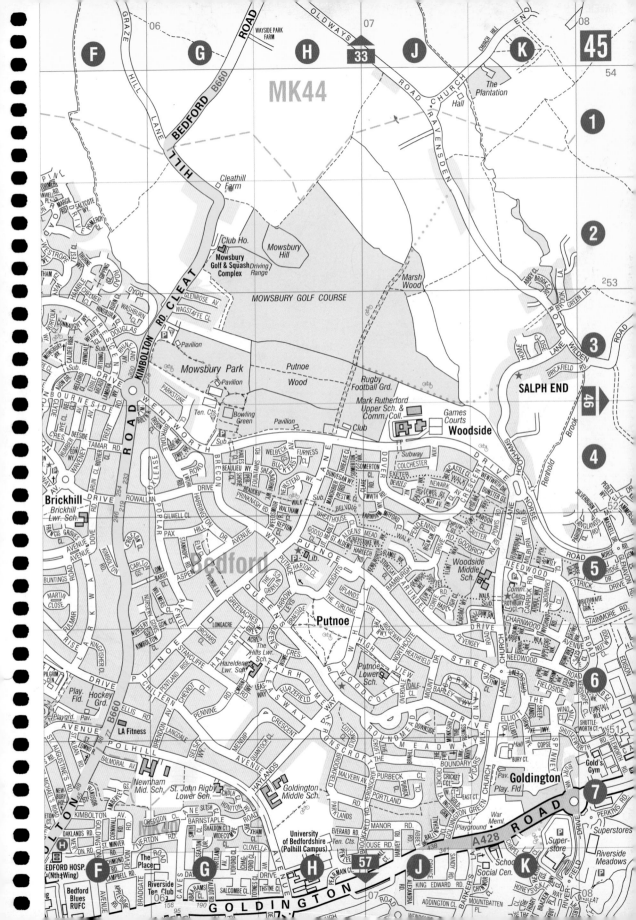

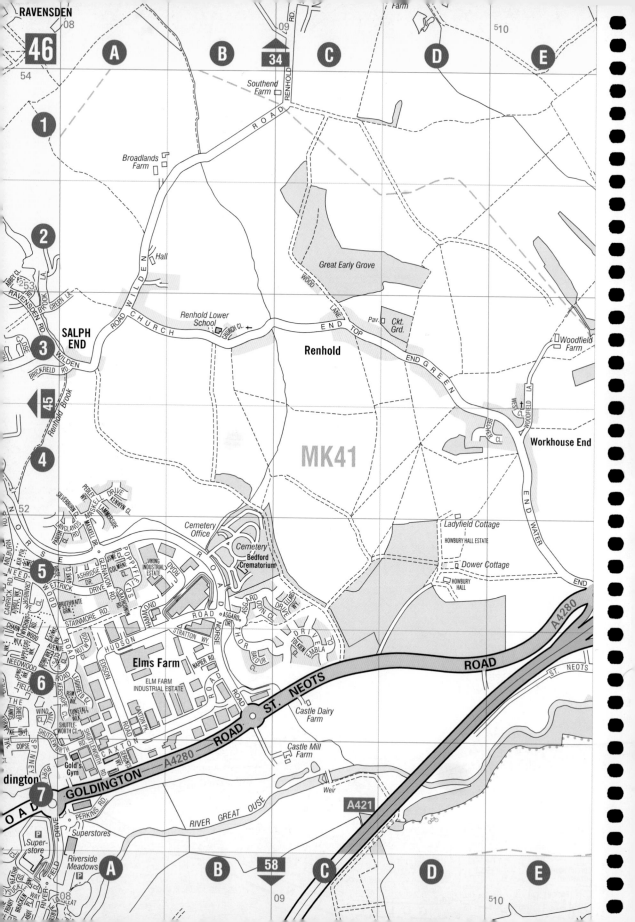

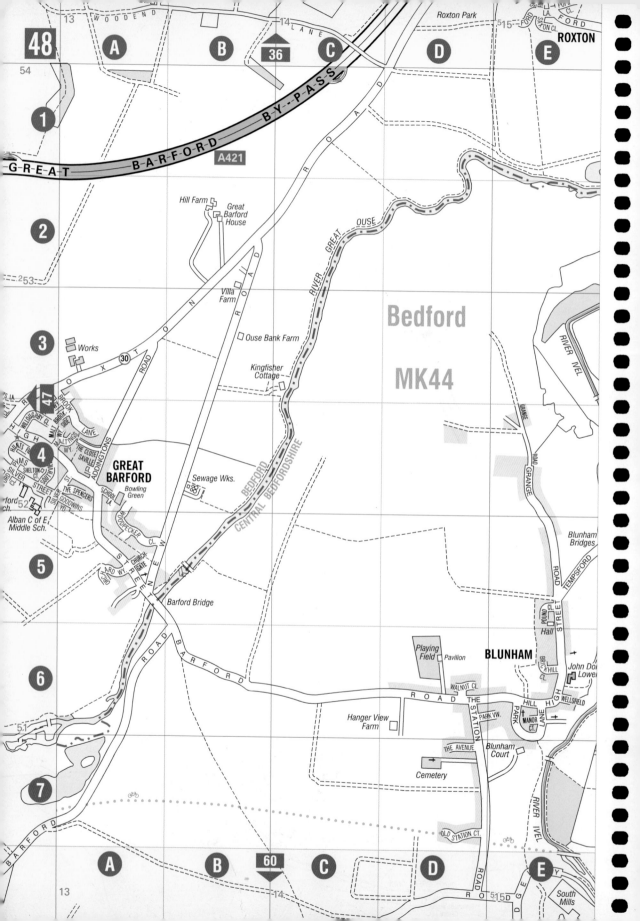

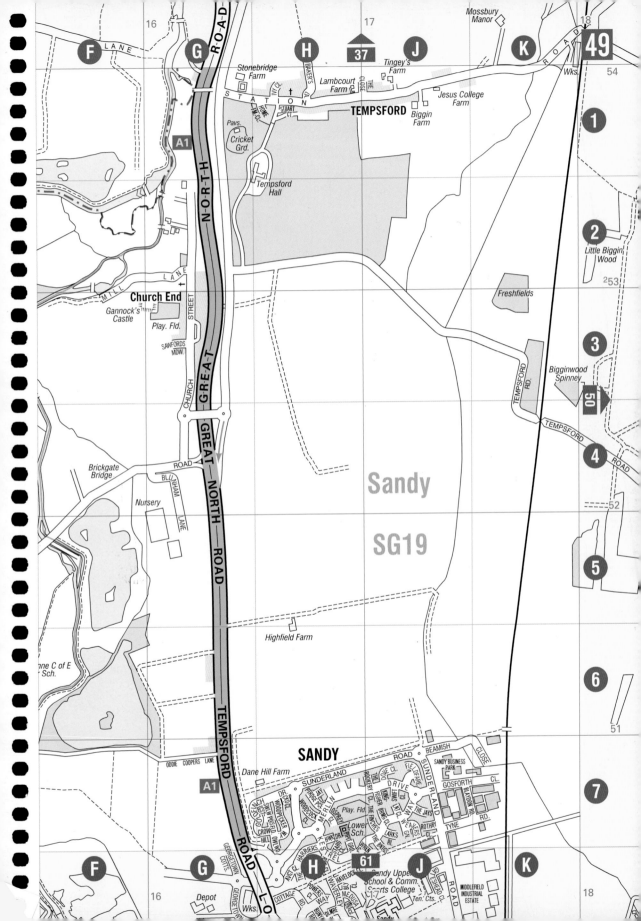

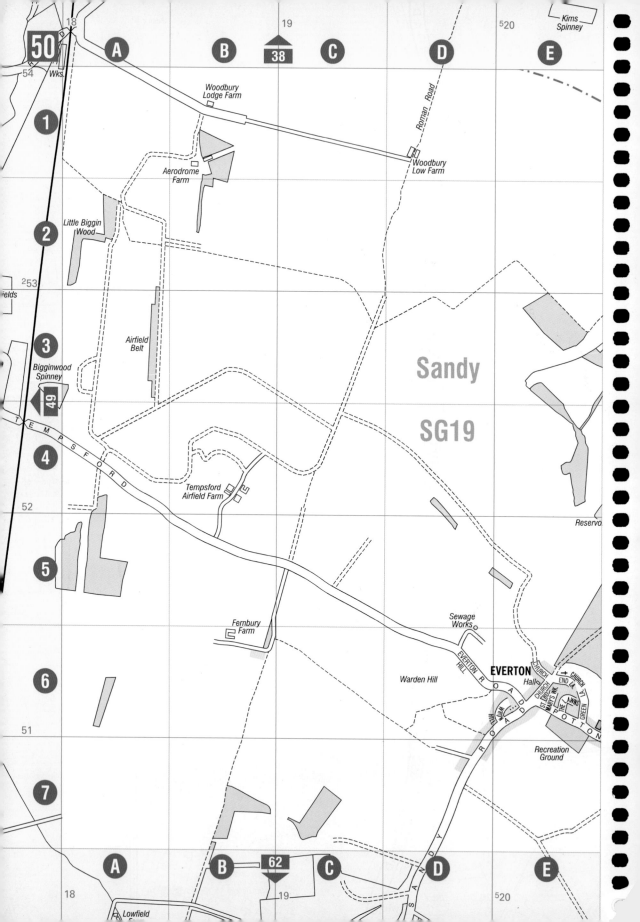

50

D Wks.
54

A   18

19   **38**   **C**   520   Kims Spinney

B   **D**   **E**

1

Woodbury Lodge Farm

Roman Road

Woodbury Low Farm

Aerodrome Farm

2

Little Biggin Wood

253 ²fields

3

Bigginwood Spinney

49

Airfield Belt

T E M P S F O R D

Sandy

SG19

4

Tempsford Airfield Farm

52

Reservo

5

Fernbury Farm

Sewage Works

6

Warden Hill

EVERTON HILL   **EVERTON**

Hall

CHURCH END LA

CHURCH

ST BROCK ST MARY'S INC.

GREEN

51

A.WNS

THE

P O T T O N

ROAD

ROAD FARM

7

Recreation Ground

SANDY

A   18   **B**   19   **62**   **C**   **D**   520   **E**

Lowfield

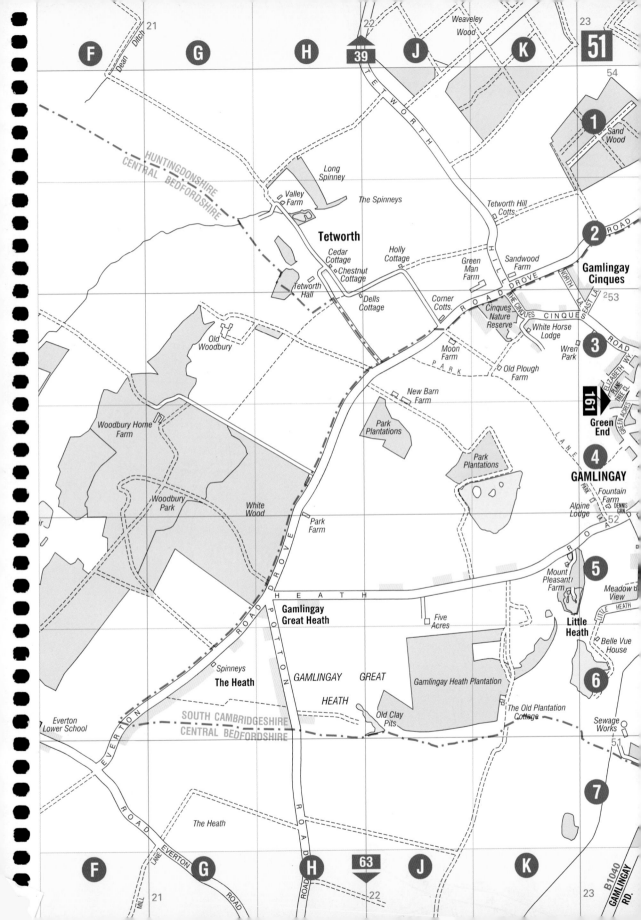

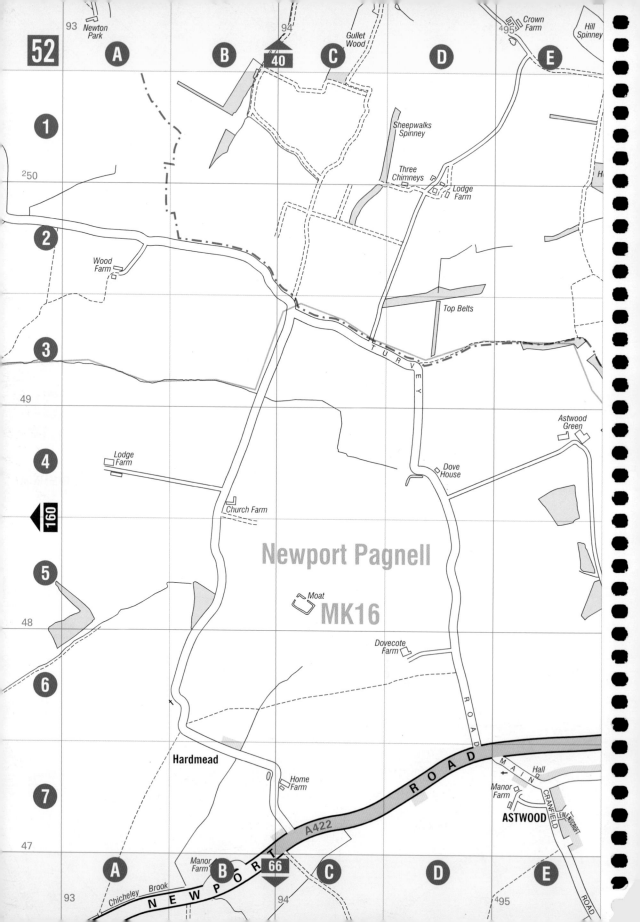

52

A   B   **40**   C   D   E

93   Newton Park

94

Gullet Wood

Crown Farm

495

Hill Spinney

1

250

Sheepwalks Spinney

Three Chimneys

Lodge Farm

2

Wood Farm

Top Belts

T U R V E Y

3

49

4

Lodge Farm

Church Farm

Astwood Green

Dove House

160

5

48

Newport Pagnell

Moat

MK16

6

Dovecote Farm

7

Hardmead

Home Farm

Hall

Manor Farm

ASTWOOD

R O A D

C R A N F I E L D

L E W E N S C R O F T

M A I N

47

A   Manor Farm   B   **66**   C   D   E

93   Chicheley Brook   N E W P O R T   94   A422   R O A D   495   ROAD

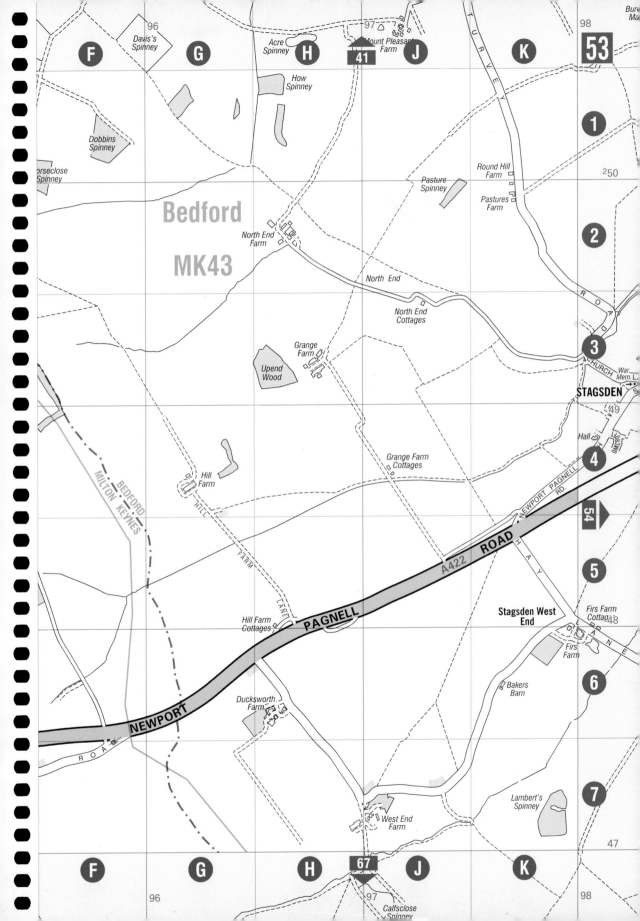

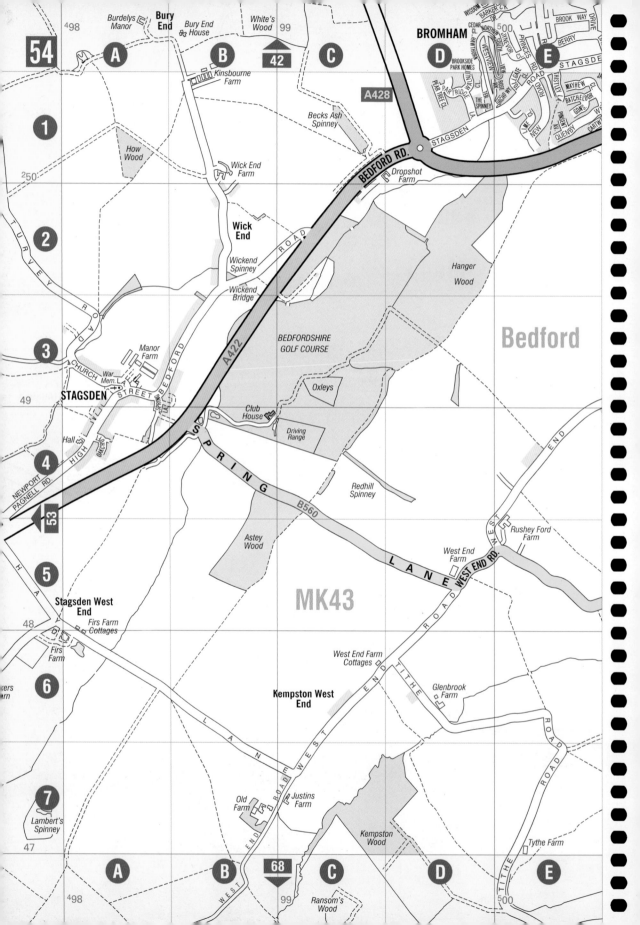

54

498   Burdelys Manor   **Bury End**   Bury End House   White's Wood   99

A   B   **42**   C   **BROMHAM**   D   E

Kinsbourne Farm

A428

Becks Ash Spinney

BROOKSIDE PARK HOMES

1

How Wood

Wick End Farm

Dropshot Farm

BEDFORD RD.

STAGSDEN

250

Wick End

2

Wickend Spinney

ROAD

Hanger Wood

Bedford

Wickend Bridge

A422

3

Manor Farm

BEDFORDSHIRE GOLF COURSE

49   **STAGSDEN**

War Mem.

Oxleys

BEDFORD STREET

Hall Cl   HIGH

Club House

Driving Range

Redhill Spinney

END

4

SWANS

NEWPORT PAGNELL RD.

SPRING

53

LANE   B560

Astey Wood

WEST END FARM

West End Farm

WEST

Rushey Ford Farm

5

Stagsden West End

Firs Farm Cottages

ROAD   WEST END RD.

TITHE

48

Firs Farm

West End Farm Cottages

Glenbrook Farm

ROAD

6

LANE

MK43

Kempston West End

WEST END

7

Old Farm

Justins Farm

Kempston Wood

Tythe Farm

Lambert's Spinney

47

A   B   **68**   C   D   E

498   99   Ransom's Wood   500   WEST   TITHE

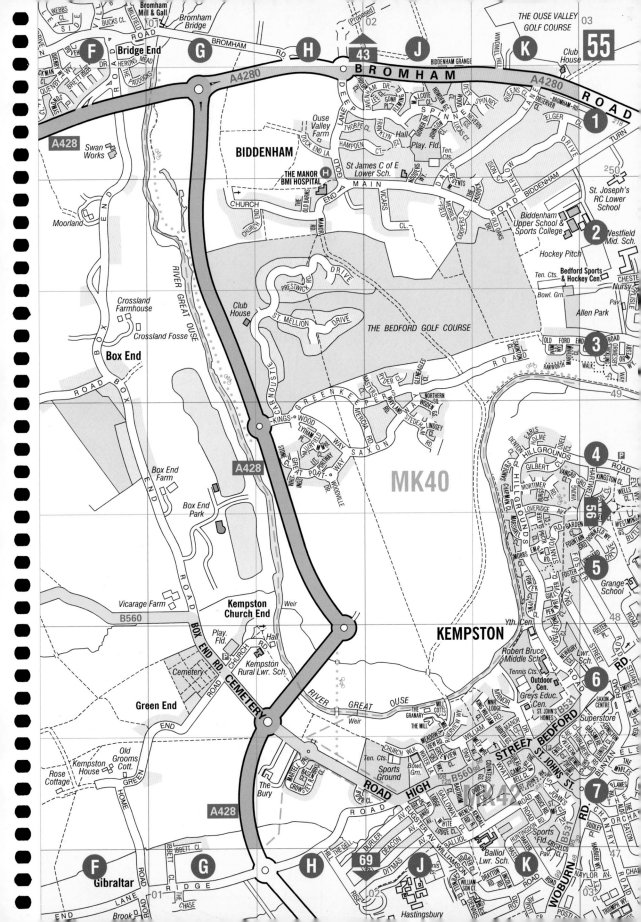

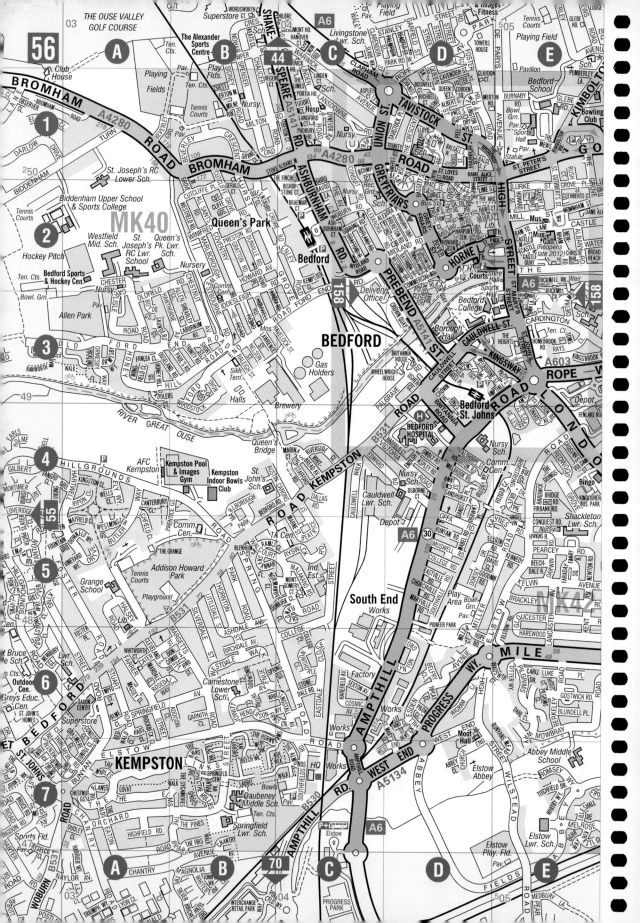

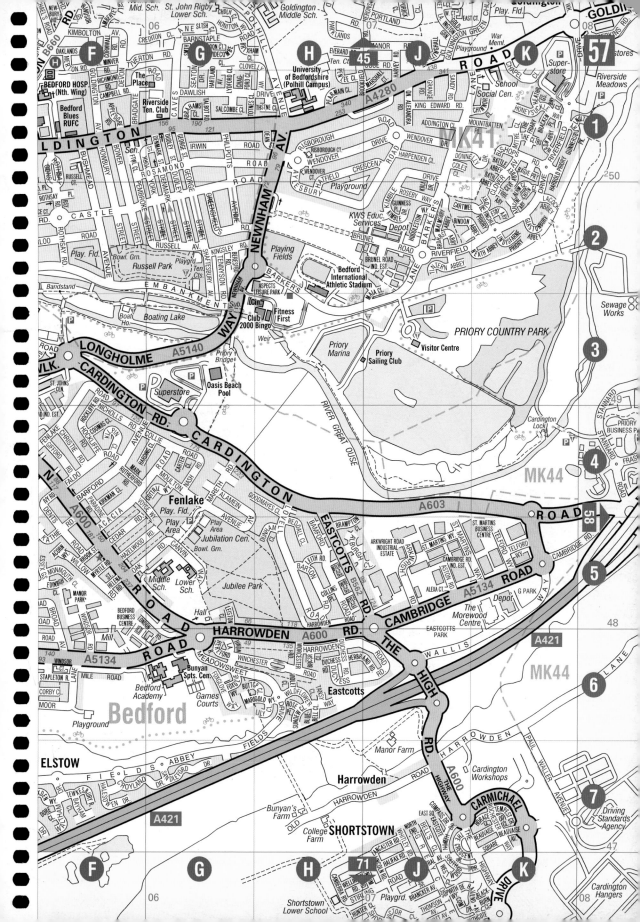

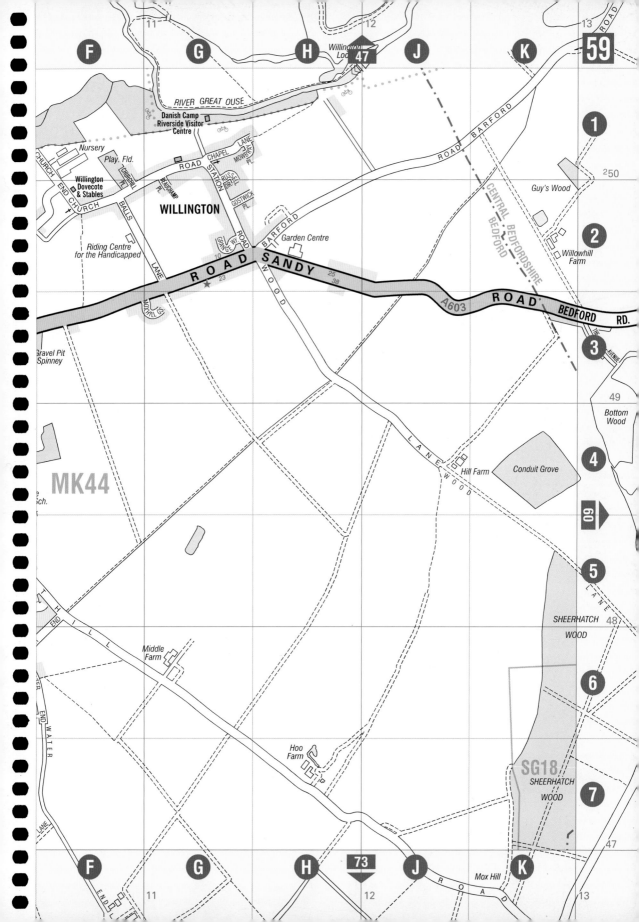

F **G** **H** **J** **K**

47

1

2

3

4

60

5

6

7

RIVER GREAT OUSE

Danish Camp
Riverside Visitor
Centre

Willington Lock

Nursery

Play. Fld.

ROAD

CHAPEL LANE

STATION

MOWSBY PL.

RUSCHEL DR.

GOSTWICK PL.

Willington
Dovecote
& Stables

BEAUCHAMP PL.

CHURCHILL PL.

CHURCH END

CHURCH

BALLS LANE

WILLINGTON

BARFORD

GARRAGE WY

GRANGE WY

ROAD

Garden Centre

Riding Centre
for the Handicapped

MILL LANE

R O A D   S A N D Y

23

19

10

25

38

WOOD

A603

R O A D   B E D F O R D   RD.

BARFORD ROAD

Guy's Wood

250

CENTRAL BEDFORDSHIRE

BEDFORD

Willowhill
Farm

THE AVENUE

49

Bottom
Wood

Gravel Pit
Spinney

MK44

Sch.

Hill Farm

WOOD LANE

Conduit Grove

**SHEERHATCH
WOOD**

48

LANE

Middle
Farm

THILL END

WATER END

WATER END

Hoo
Farm

SG18

**SHEERHATCH
WOOD**

47

Mox Hill

ROAD

F **G** **H** **J** **K**

73

11

12

13

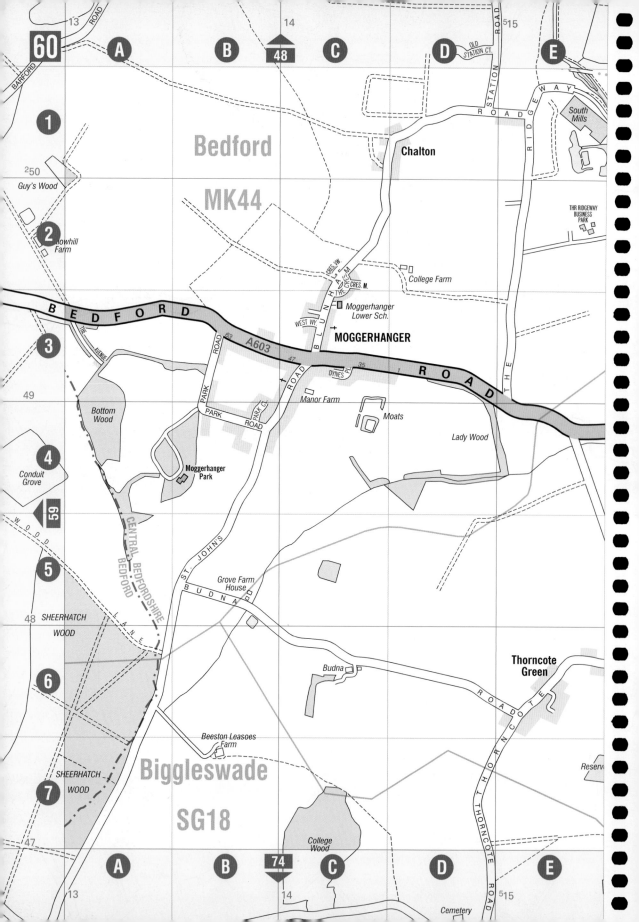

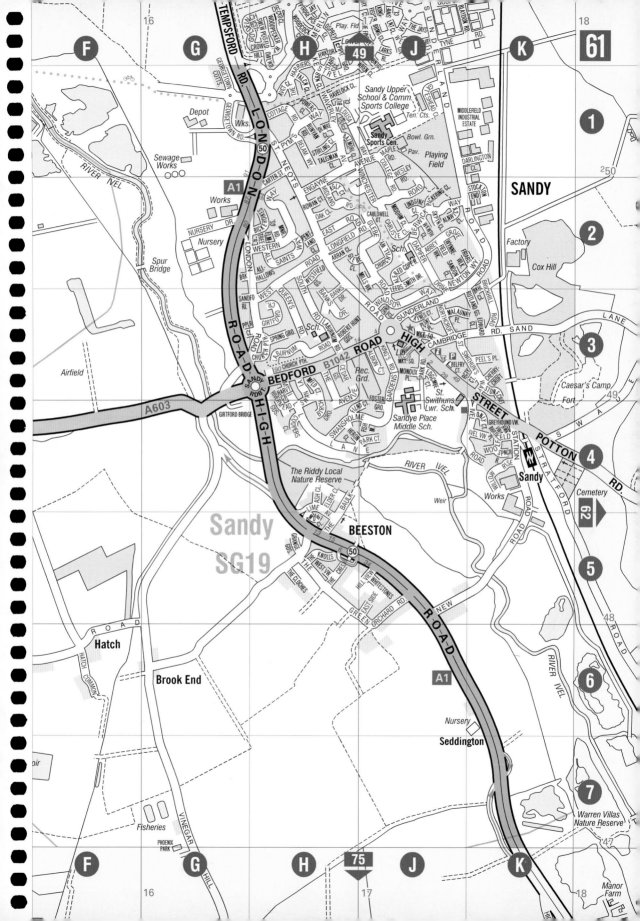

62

A B **50** C D E

1

Lowfield Farm

The Rookery

Hazells Hall Fm.

Hazells Hall

²50

Park Plantation

Sandy

2

ctory

Cox Hill

Lord's Wood

SG19

Oak Farm

R I D I N G

R O A D

S A N D Y

Sandy Heath

3

SAND

LANE

EVERTON

Quarry Hills

Caesar's Camp
Fort

49

S W A D E N

L O N G

4

STATION

Sandy

Swading Hill

Reservoir (Covered)

B1042

P O T T O N

R O A D

RSPB Visitor Centre

Redstone Hill

Cemetery

61

S T R A T F O R D

5

48

The Lodge Nature Reserve (RSPB)

Sandy Warren

Bunker's Hill

The Lodge

6

R O A D

RIVER IVEL

7

Warren Villas Nature Reserve

Biggl_eswade

SG18

47

A1

A B Sewage Works **76** C D E

18

Manor Farm

19

Biggleswade Common

Furzenhall Farm

F U

520

Resr.

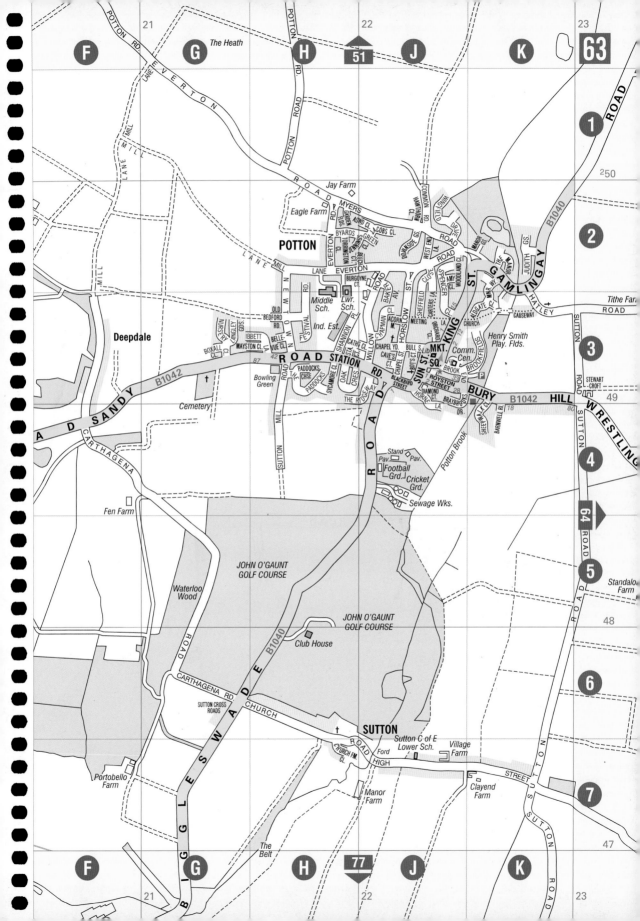

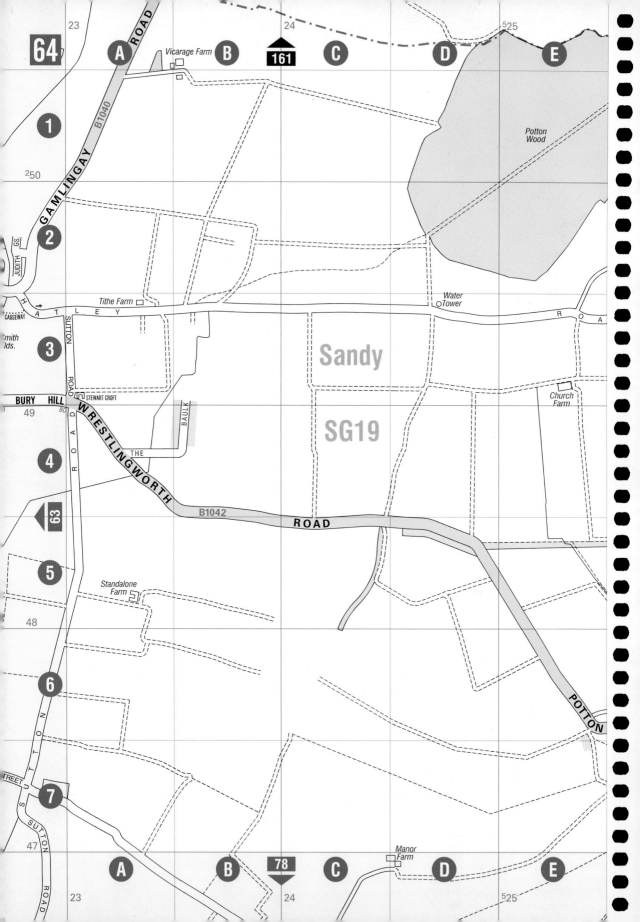

64

23   24   525

A ROAD B   ▲ 161   C   D   E

Vicarage Farm

1

250

GAMLINGAY B1040

JUDITH GS.

2

HATLEY CAUSEWAY   Tithe Farm   Water Tower   R   O   A

smith lds.

3

SUTTON ROAD

Sandy

BURY HILL   STEWART CROFT

49   80   THE BAULK

SG19

Church Farm

WRESTLINGWORTH

THE

4

◄ 63

B1042   ROAD

5

Standalone Farm

48

SUTTON

6

POTTON

STREET   SUTTON

7

47

23   A   B   ▼ 78   C   Manor Farm   D   E   525

24   525

Potton Wood

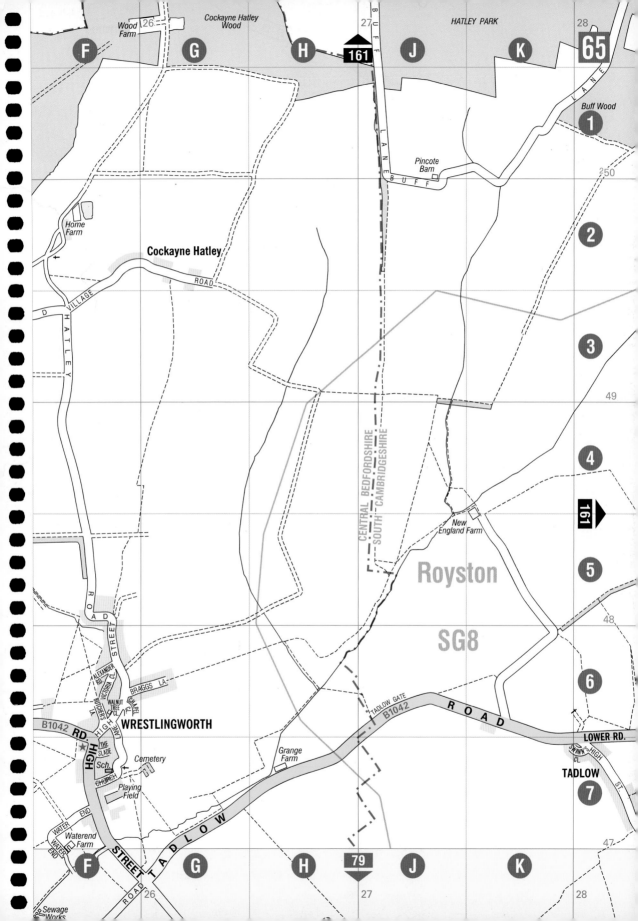

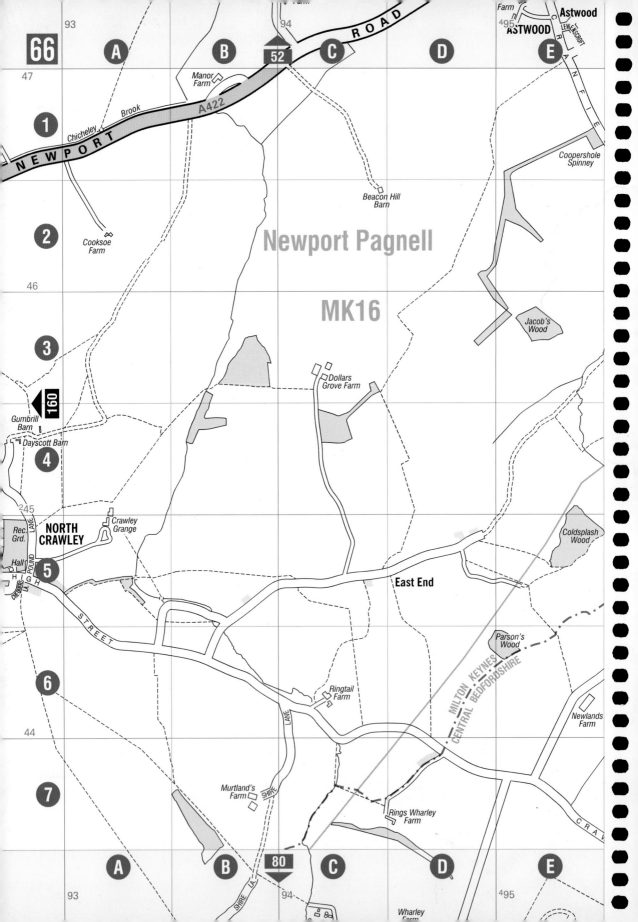

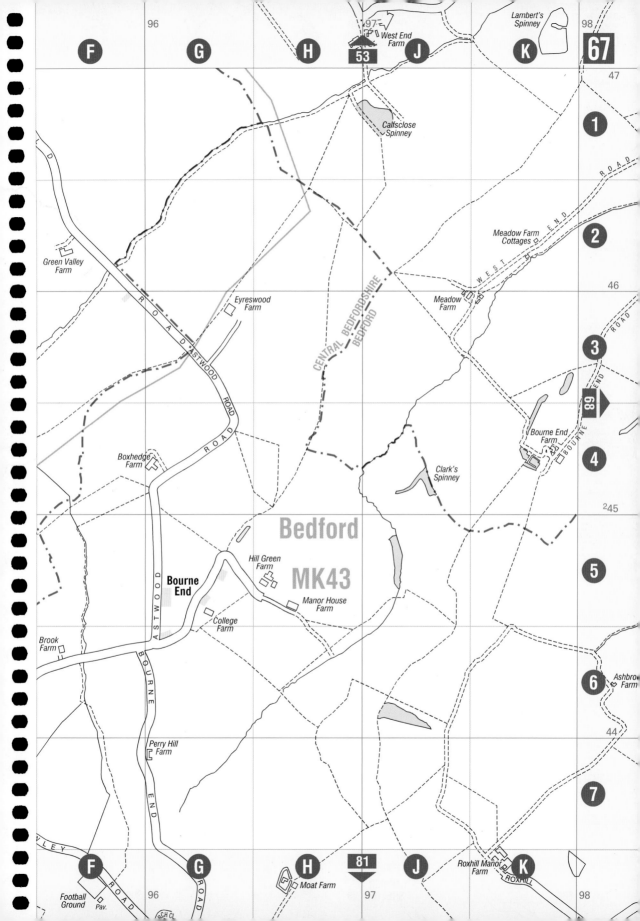

West End Farm

Lambert's Spinney

47

Calfsclose Spinney

1

Meadow Farm Cottages

2

46

Green Valley Farm

WEST END

ROAD

CENTRAL BEDFORDSHIRE

BEDFORD

Eyreswood Farm

ASTWOOD ROAD

ROAD

Meadow Farm

3

END

89

Bourne End Farm

4

BOURNE

Boxhedge Farm

Clark's Spinney

²45

Bedford

5

Bourne End

Hill Green Farm

MK43

ASTWOOD

Manor House Farm

College Farm

Brook Farm

BOURNE

6

Ashbro...

44

Perry Hill Farm

END

7

VLEY

ROAD

Football Ground

Pav.

CH CL.

Moat Farm

97

Roxhill Manor Farm

ROXHILL

98

96

96

98

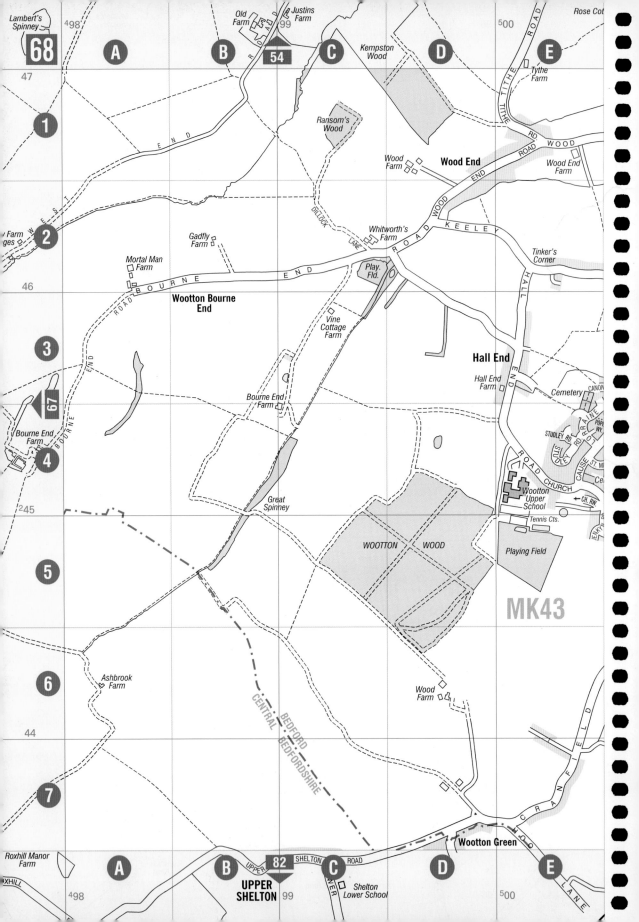

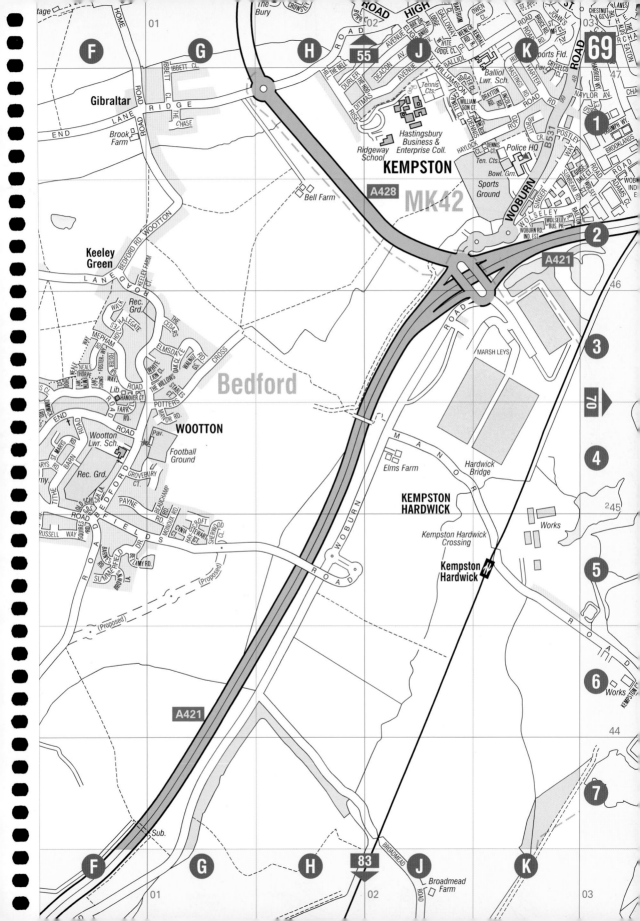

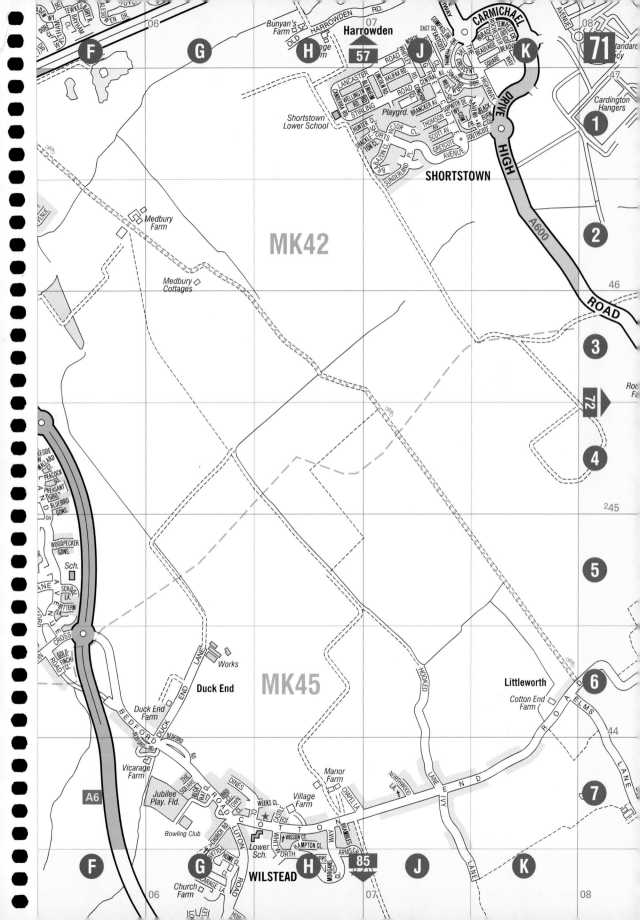

F **G** **H** **57** **J** **K**

Harrowden

Bunyan's Farm

OLD HARROWDEN RD.

CARMICHAEL AVENUE

Cardington Hangers

1

Shortstown Lower School

LANCASTER RD.
WELLINGTON RD.
STIRLING
BLENHEIM RD.
HALIFAX RD.
LINCOLN RD.
WHITLEY RD.
CANBERRA RD.
HUNTER CL.
VICTOR CL.
BAZON CL.

Playgrd.
BRANCKER AV.
CENTRAL AV.
COMPTON AV.
SOPWITH DE HAVILAND DR.
THOMSON AV.
SCOTT AV.
GREYCOTE
SOUTHCOTE
BLACK BURN COT.

SHORTSTOWN

SHORTSTOWN

HIGH DRIVE
A600
ROAD
47
46

2

3

72

4

245

Medbury Farm

Medbury Cottages

MK42

5

LAKESIDE
MALLARD CT.
PEACOCK
PHEASANT GRD.
BLUEBIRD GDNS.
WOODPECKER GDNS.
Sch.
SCHOOL LA.
BITTERN

GOLD FINCH CTC.
CROSS

BEDFORD RD.
Duck End Farm

DUCK END LANE
Works

Duck End

MK45

Littleworth
Cotton End Farm

ELMS LANE
ROAD
HOOKED LANE
44

6

Vicarage Farm

A6

Jubilee Play. Fld.

Bowling Club

THE SQUARE
BEDFORD RD.
DINES
WEEKS CL.
CASTLE
HAMPTON CL.
WISSON CT.
MORGANS CL.
BRAMBLES
CHAPEL LA.

Manor Farm

Village Farm

NORTHWOOD LA.
LANE END
IVY LANE

7

Lower Sch.

CHURCH RD.
LUTON RD.
HOME CL.
VICARAGE LA.
COTTON
WILHM

Church Farm

WILSTEAD

F **G** **H** **85** **J** **K**

06 07 08

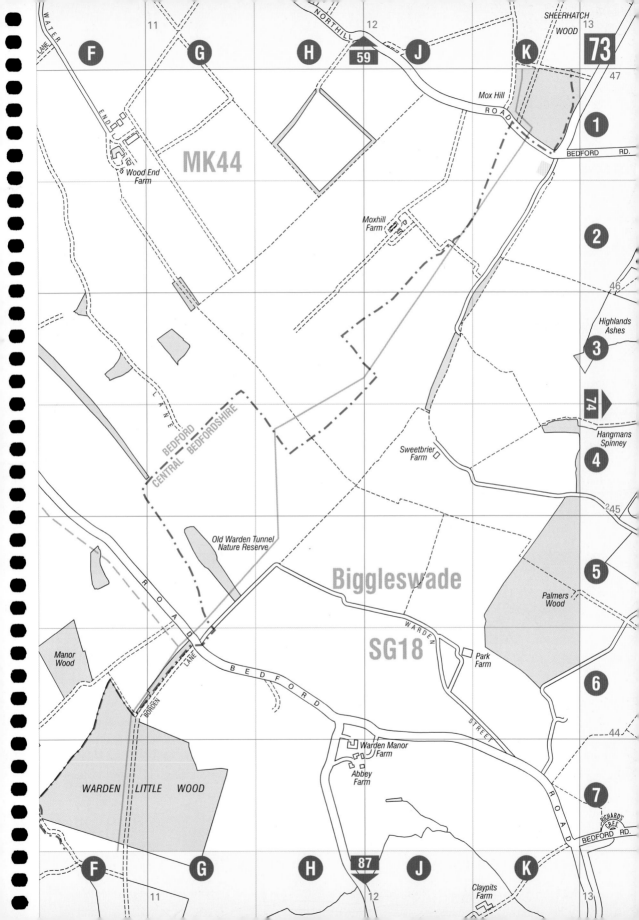

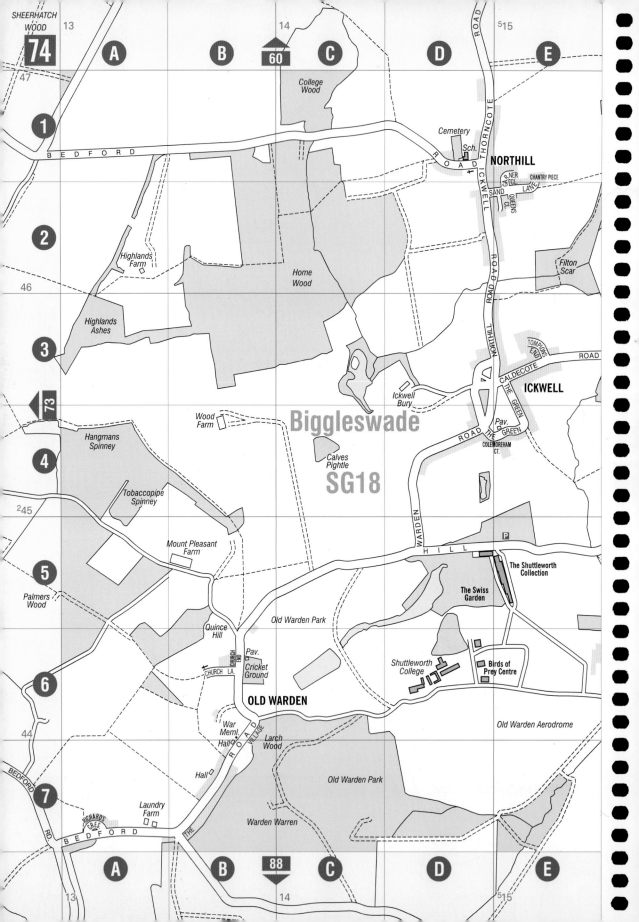

SHEERHATCH WOOD

74

13

47

A

B

60

C

D

5 15

E

College Wood

1

BEDFORD

Cemetery

Sch.

ROAD

ICKWELL

THORNCOTE

ROAD

NORTHILL

GARNER CL.

SAND

QUEENS CL.

LANE

CHANTRY PIECE

2

46

Highlands Farm

Home Wood

Filton Scar

NORTHILL

ROAD

3

Highlands Ashes

Ickwell Bury

ICKWELL

TOMPIONS END

CALDECOTE

THE GREEN

ROAD

73

Hangmans Spinney

Wood Farm

Biggleswade

Pav.

THE GREEN

COLEMOREHAM CT.

ROAD

4

Calves Pightle

SG18

2 45

Tobaccopipe Spinney

Mount Pleasant Farm

WARDEN

P

The Shuttleworth Collection

5

Palmers Wood

HILL

The Swiss Garden

Quince Hill

Old Warden Park

Shuttleworth College

Birds of Prey Centre

6

CHURCH END

Pav.

Cricket Ground

CHURCH LA.

OLD WARDEN

44

War Meml. Hall

ROAD

VILLAGE

Larch Wood

Old Warden Aerodrome

Hall

Old Warden Park

7

BEDFORD

RD.

RICHARDS CRES.

Laundry Farm

THE

BEDFORD

Warden Warren

A

B

88

C

D

E

13

14

5 15

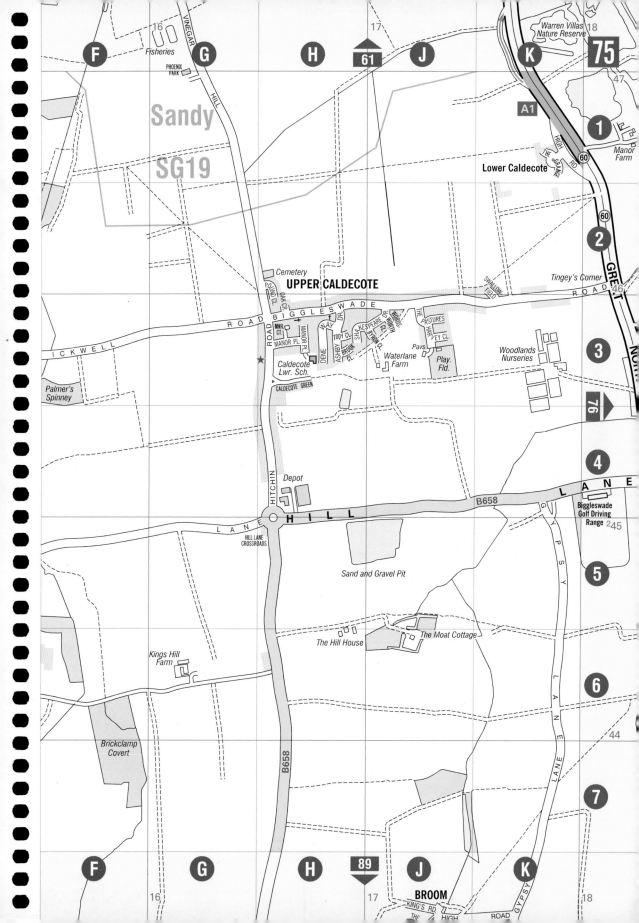

F   G   H   **61**   J   K

16   VINEGAR HILL   17   Warren Villas Nature Reserve   18

Fisheries

PHOENIX PARK

Sandy

SG19

A1

47

1

THE GRANGE   HIGH RD.   60   Manor Farm

Lower Caldecote

60

2

Cemetery

UPPER CALDECOTE

Tingey's Corner

SWALLOW FIELD

ROAD   46

GREAT

NORTH

OAK CR.   PINE CL.

BIGGLESWADE

ROAD

ICKWELL

MNR. CT.

MANOR PL.

DENE

WAY

TIDDY CL.

ASHBY CL.

BROOK

SHAKESPEARE DR.

MANOR DR.

WOODS

WORTH CL.

THE HARVEY CL.

THE PASTURES

Pavs.

Play. Fld.

Woodlands Nurseries

Caldecote Lwr. Sch.

CALDECOTE GREEN

Waterlane Farm

3

Palmer's Spinney

76

4

HITCHIN

Depot

HILL

B658

Biggleswade Golf Driving Range   245

LANE

LANE

HILL LANE CROSSROADS

Sand and Gravel Pit

GYPSY

LANE

5

The Hill House

The Moat Cottage

6

Kings Hill Farm

B658

44

Brickclamp Covert

7

F   G   H   **89**   J   K

16   17   **BROOM**   18

KING'S RD.   THE HIGH   GYPSY   ROAD

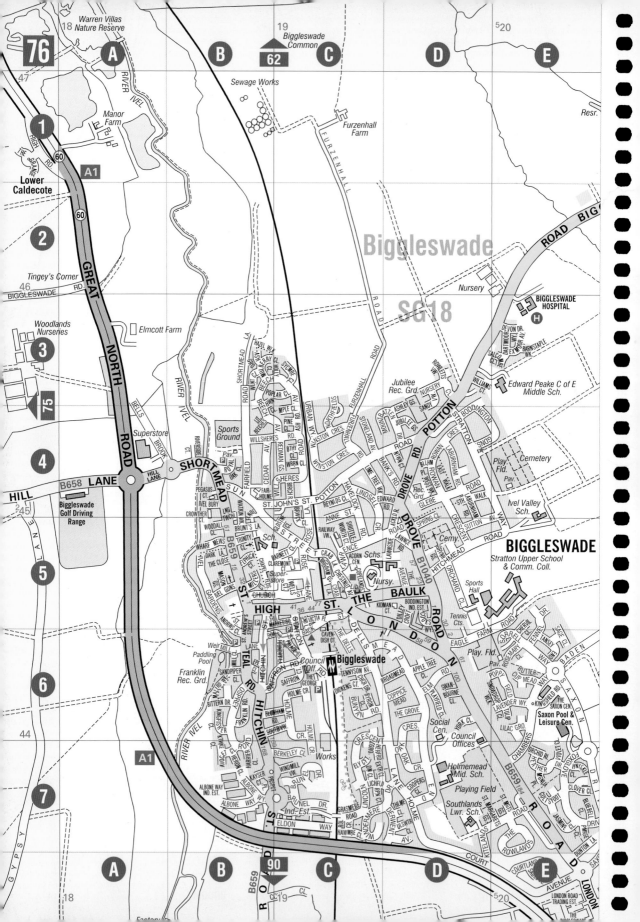

Biggleswade

SG18

76

A **B** **C** **D** **E**

Warren Villas Nature Reserve — 18

19 Biggleswade Common **62**

20

Sewage Works

Furzenhall Farm

RIVER IVEL

Manor Farm

1

47

THE SPINNEY HIGH RD. **60**

A1 **60**

Lower Caldecote

2

Tingey's Corner

46 BIGGLESWADE RD.

Nursery

BIGGLESWADE HOSPITAL **H**

Resr.

Woodlands Nurseries

3

Elmcott Farm

RIVER IVEL

BELLS BROOK

Superstore

75

Jubilee Rec. Grd.

Edward Peake C of E Middle Sch.

DEVON DR. DARTMOOR BARNSTAPLE WK. SALCOMBE CL.

Sports Ground

Cemetery

Play. Fld. Pav.

Ivel Valley Sch.

4

B658 LANE HILL LANE SHORTMEAD

Biggleswade Golf Driving Range

HILL 45

BIGGLESWADE

Stratton Upper School & Comm. Coll.

POTTON RD. DROVE RD.

5

ST. B659 IVEL GARDENS

Sports Hall

Tennis Cts.

B1040 HITCHMEAD ROAD THE BAULK

44

A1

RIVER IVEL

HIGH ST. LONDON

Biggleswade **M**

Franklin Rec. Grd.

Paddling Pool

Weir Mill

TEAL RD. HITCHIN RD. SAFFRON RD. Council Off.

Tennyson Av.

Saxon Pool & Leisure Cen.

6

Holmemead Mid. Sch.

Playing Field

Southlands Lwr. Sch.

Council Offices

Social Cen.

7

A1

Albone Way Ind. Est.

ALBONE WAY

B659 ROAD

Brunel Ind. Est.

GYPSY LANE 18

ELDON WAY

90

B659 ROAD CC 19 CL.

London Road Trading Est.

20

A **B** **C** **D** **E**

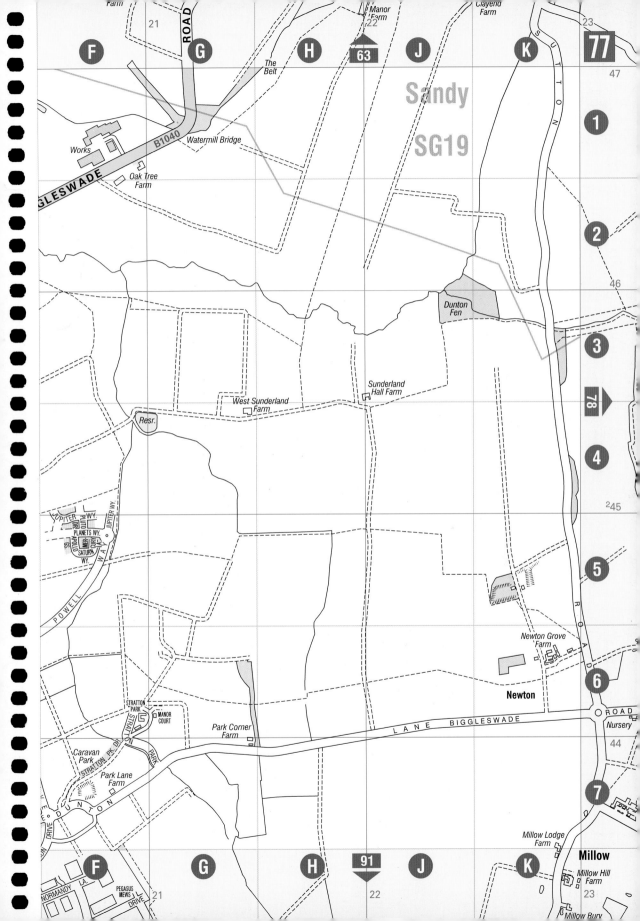

F **G** ROAD **H** **63** **J** **K** **77**

47

Manor Farm

Clayend Farm

The Belt

Sandy

SG19

1

Works

B1040

Watermill Bridge

GLESWADE

Oak Tree Farm

2

46

Dunton Fen

3

Resr.

West Sunderland Farm

Sunderland Hall Farm

78

4

245

JUPITER WY.
PLUTO DR.
PLANETS WY.
JUPITER WY.
SATURN WY.
APOLLO
MERCURY
DR.
POWELL WAY

5

Newton Grove Farm

6

Newton

STRATTON PARK

MANOR COURT

Park Corner Farm

LANE BIGGLESWADE

ROAD

Nursery

44

Caravan Park

STRATTON PK. DR.

PARK

Park Lane Farm

DUNTON DRIVE

7

Millow Lodge Farm

Millow

F **G** **H** **91** **J** **K** Millow Hill Farm

NORMANDY LA.

PEGASUS MEWS

DRIVE

21

22

23

Millow Bury

78

A B ⌂ 64 C D E

1

SUTTON ROAD

23 24 ⁵25

47

Manor Farm

Havannah Farm

2

Sandy

SG19

46

3

Eyeworth

SUTTON RD

STREET EYEWORTH

Manor Farm

Hall

ROAD HIGH

77

Church Farm

4

²45

Biggleswade

SG18

5

Newton Grove Farm

Rec. Grd.

GREENFIELD WAY

BOOT CL

KINGS

POND CL

CAMB RIDGE

YEW CL

Middlesex Farm

HORSESHOE CL

LANE

MAGDAL-ENE CL

CHURCH ST

Dunton Lower School

Church Farm

6

BIGGLESWADE

ROAD

HALLSIDE

CHAPEL CL

LIME

TREE DR

FOX CL

SPRINGFIELD ROAD HIGH

44

Nursery

Nursery

DUNTON

7

Millow Hall Farm

Millow Lodge Farm

Millow

A B ▲ 161 ▼ C D E

Millow Hill Farm

0 23 24 ⁵25

Millow Bury

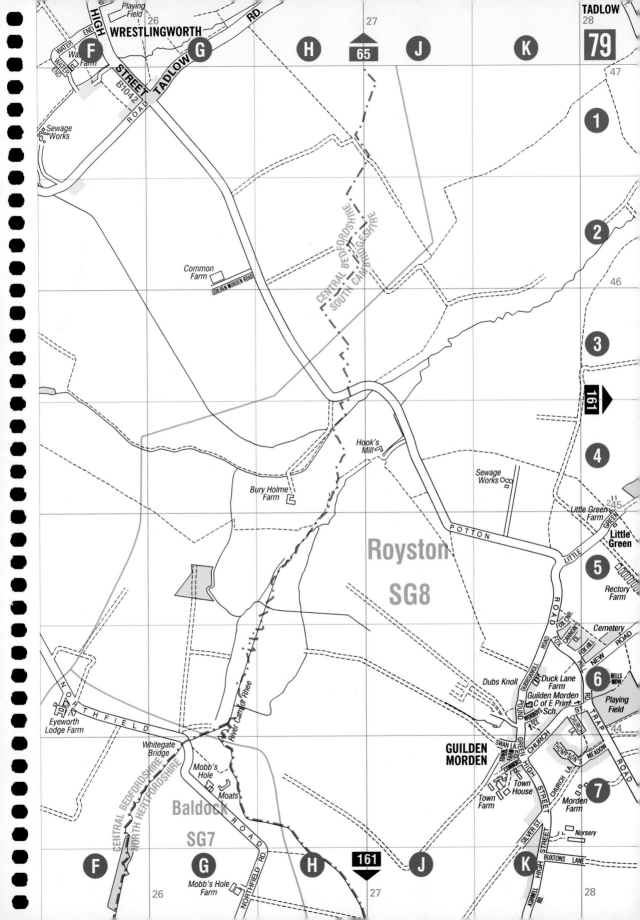

Playing Field

26

WRESTLINGWORTH

WATER END

HIGH END

F

G

H

65

J

K

27

47

Water Farm

STREET

B1042

TADLOW ROAD

Sewage Works

1

2

46

Common Farm

GUILDEN MORDEN ROAD

CENTRAL BEDFORDSHIRE
SOUTH CAMBRIDGESHIRE

3

161

4

Hook's Mill

Sewage Works

Little Green Farm

245

Little Green

Bury Holme Farm

POTTON

Royston

SG8

LITTLE GREEN ROAD

Rectory Farm

5

FOX HILL

FOX CNR.

Cemetery

CANNON'S CL.

NEW ROAD

6

BELLS MDW.

River Cam or Rhee

Dubs Knoll

DUBBSKNOLL RD

POUND

Duck Lane Farm

Guilden Morden C of E Prim. Sch.

Playing Field

WORBOYS'

44

NORTHFIELD

Eyeworth Lodge Farm

Whitegate Bridge

SWAN LA.

GREEN END

TRAP ROAD

GUILDEN MORDEN

Mobb's Hole

COMMONS

TOWN FARM CL.

CHURCH ST.

THOMPSON'S CL.

CHURCH LA.

MEADOW

Moats

Baldock

SG7

NORTHFIELD RD.

CENTRAL BEDFORDSHIRE
NORTH HERTFORDSHIRE

Town Farm

HIGH STREET

Town House

7

Morden Farm

Nursery

SILVER ST.

F

G

Mobb's Hole Farm

26

H

161

J

K

ASHWELL RD.

BUXTONS LANE

27

28

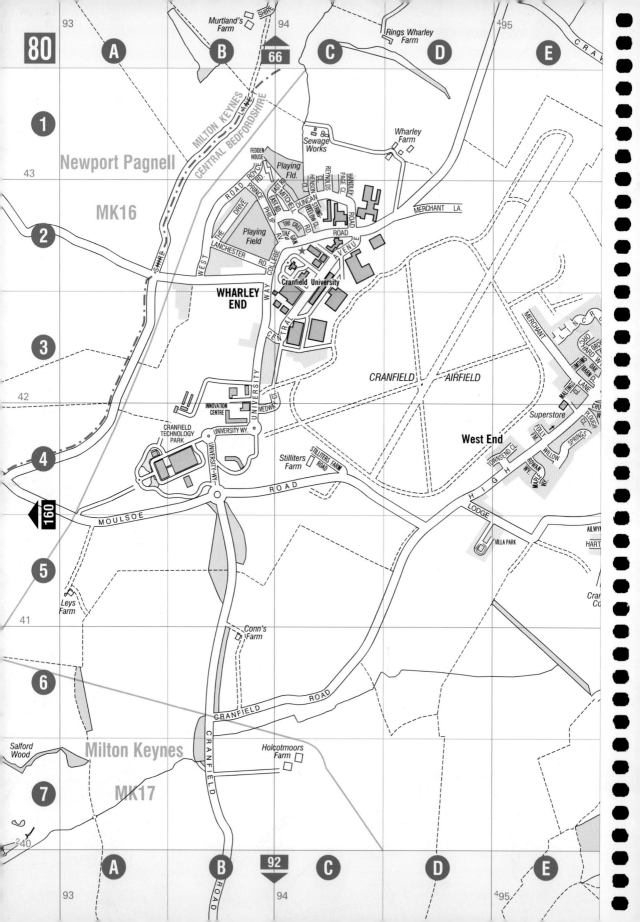

A B 66 C D E

1

Murtland's Farm

Rings Wharley Farm

Newport Pagnell

43

MILTON KEYNES LANE

CENTRAL BEDFORDSHIRE

SHIRE

Sewage Works

Wharley Farm

FEDDEN HOUSE

Playing Fld.

MK16

2

FEDDEN HOUSE

ROYCE RD.

THE PRINCE PHILIP DRIVE

EAST MITCHELL

HENSON CL.

DUNCAN

STRING CL.

THE FELLOW CL.

REYNOLDS CL.

HANDLEY

PAGE CL.

MERCHANT LA.

THE LANCHESTER RD.

WEST ROAD

COLLEGE ROAD

Playing Field

THE GRN.

THE GRN.

ROAD

AVENUE

Cranfield University

WHARLEY END

CENTRAL WAY

3

42

CRANFIELD   AIRFIELD

MERCHANT

LINCR

ORCH CL.

CHARD W.

SIMONS BARN CL.

OAK

MALTINGS CL.

UNIVERSITY WY.

MEDWAY

INNOVATION CENTRE

CRANFIELD TECHNOLOGY PARK

UNIVERSITY WY.

UNIVERSITY-WY-1

Superstore

West End

CHU

PLOUGH CL.

FOLLY WAY

WILLOW

SPRINGS CL.

4

160

MOULSOE

ROAD

Stilliters Farm

STILLITERS FARM ROAD

TOWNSEND CL.

HIGH

MARPLE WY.

ROWAN WY.

AILWY

HART

LODGE

Villa Park

Cran Co

5

41

Leys Farm

6

Conn's Farm

Salford Wood

Milton Keynes

Holcotmoors Farm

CRANFIELD ROAD

CRANFIELD ROAD

MK17

7

240

A B 92 C D E

93 94 495

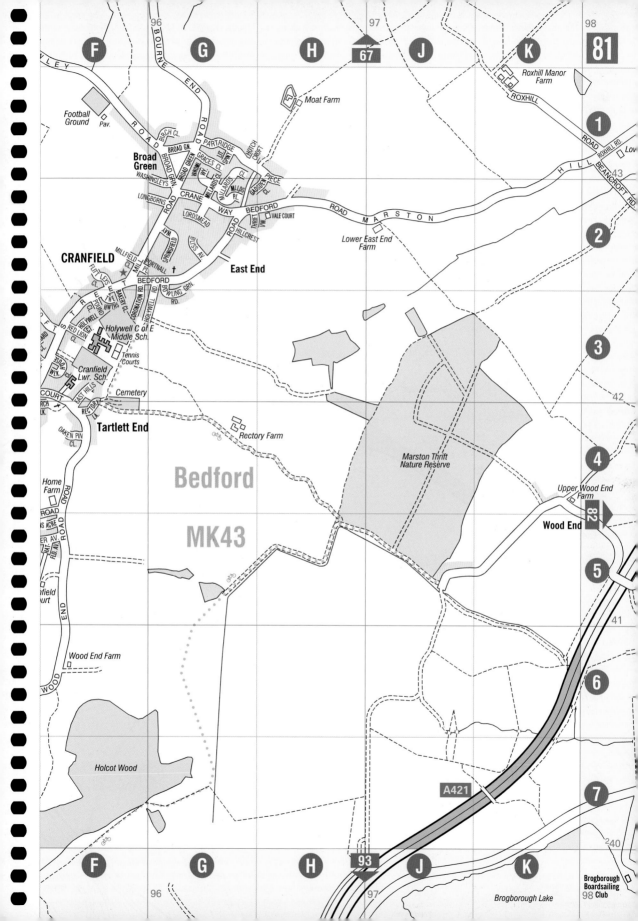

1

Roxhill Manor Farm

ROXHILL

Moat Farm

Football Ground
Pav.

BIRCH CL.
BROAD GN.
PARTRIDGE
GRACES CL.
CROTCH CROFT
Broad Green
BROAD GREEN GRN.
WASHINGLEYS
WILLARDS CL.
GADSDEN CL.
PIECE
LONGBORNS
CRANE
WAY
BEDFORD
VALE COURT
HILLCREST
LORDSMEAD
THRIFT VW.

ROAD MARSTON

43

2

Lower East End Farm

CRANFIELD
MILLFIELD CL.
CORTNALL
SPRINGFIELD
BUSS AV.
FLITT LEYS CL.
MILL
BEDFORD
BOWLING GRN.
RD.
HOLYWELL
CORONATION RD.

East End

3

Holywell C of E Middle Sch.
Tennis Courts
RED LION CL.
Cranfield Lwr. Sch.
EAST HILLS
ROSE WLK.

Cemetery
RECTORY LA.

42

Tartlett End
OAKEN PIN CL.
CHURCH WLK.

Rectory Farm

Marston Thrift
Nature Reserve

4

Upper Wood End Farm

82

Bedford

Home Farm
ROAD
WOOD END
ACRE
HALL FD. AV.
KIER AV.
Cranfield Court

Wood End

5

41

MK43

Wood End Farm

6

Holcot Wood

A421

7

240

Brogborough Boardsailing Club

96   97   98   Brogborough Lake

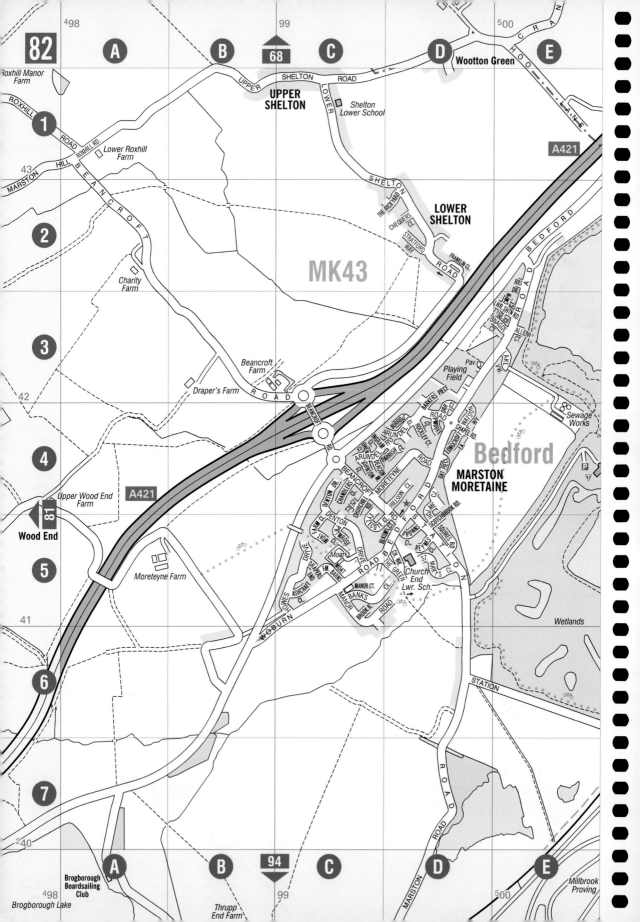

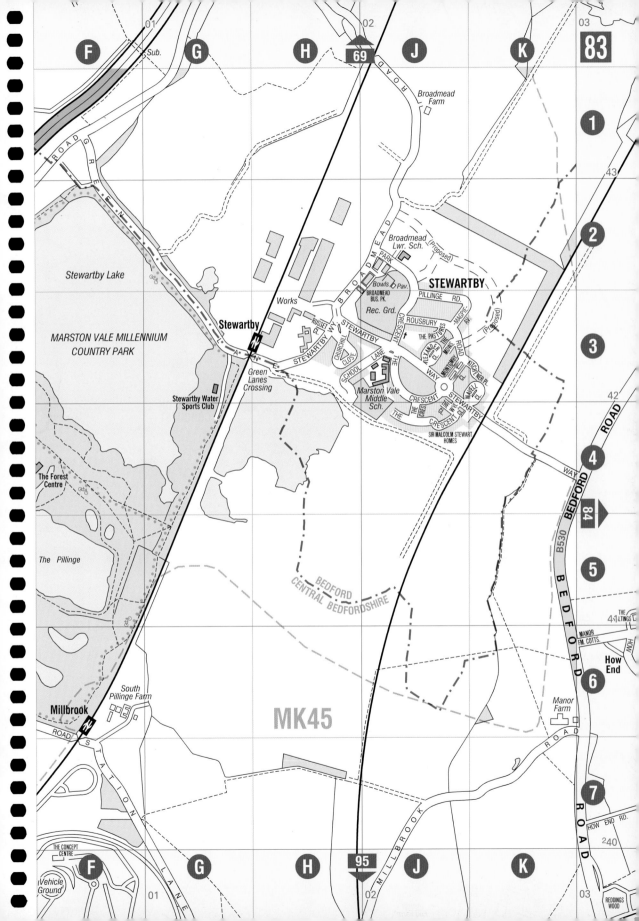

01   02   03

Sub.

Broadmead
Farm

1

43

2

Stewartby Lake

Broadmead Lwr. Sch.
(Proposed)

Works

STEWARTBY

Broadmead Park

BROADMEAD BUS. PK.
Bowls Pav.

Rec. Grd.

PILLINGE RD.

MAGPIE AV.

(Proposed)

RUSSET CL.

STEWARTBY WY.

STEWARTBY

ROUSBURY

THE PASTURES

ALEXANDER CL.

MONTGOMERY CL.

ROAD

KITCHENER PL.

MARSTON VALE MILLENNIUM
COUNTRY PARK

Stewartby

Green
Lanes
Crossing

Stewartby Water
Sports Club

CHURCHILL
CLOSE

SCHOOL
LANE

THE

Marston Vale
Middle Sch.

THE
CRESCENT

THE CRES.

STEWARTBY

WAY

WAVELL
CL.

THE WY.

3

SIR MALCOLM STEWART
HOMES

42

WAY

4

The Forest
Centre

BEDFORD ROAD

B530

84 ▶

The Pillinge

5

THE MALTINGS

HOW

MANOR
FM. COTTS.

**How
End**

South
Pillinge Farm

Millbrook

ROAD

STATION

Manor
Farm

6

BEDFORD ROAD

MK45

7

HOW END RD.

ROAD

THE CONCEPT
CENTRE

MILLBROOK ROAD

40

Vehicle
Ground

01   02   03

BEDFORD
CENTRAL BEDFORDSHIRE

REDDINGS
WOOD

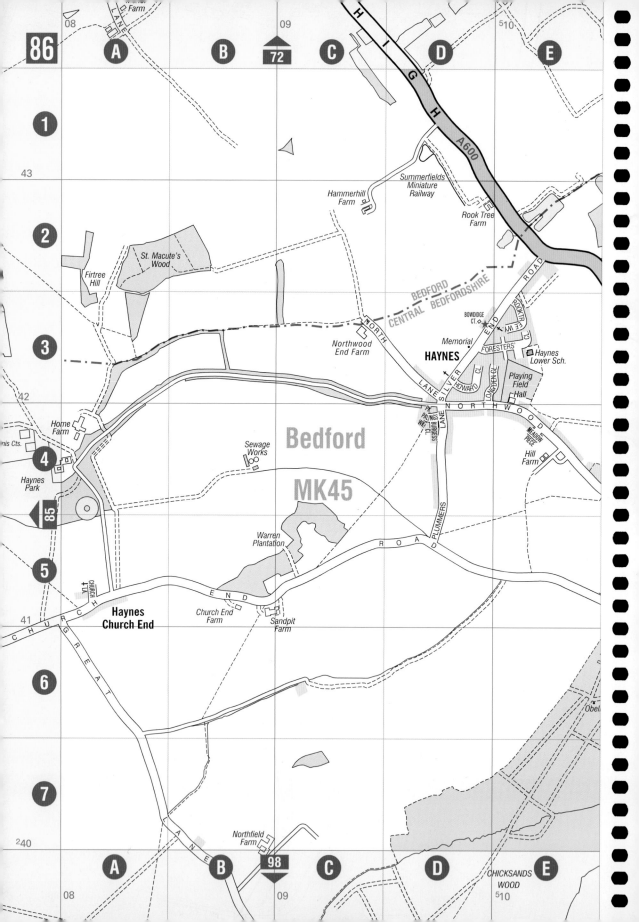

86

A B **72** C D E

08 09 510

1

43

2

Firtree Hill

St. Macute's Wood

Hammerhill Farm

Summerfields Miniature Railway

Rook Tree Farm

3

North Lane

Northwood End Farm

BEDFORD

CENTRAL BEDFORDSHIRE

Memorial

HAYNES

BOWDIDGE CT.

Haynes Lower Sch.

FORESTERS'

Playing Field Hall

42

Home Farm

nis Cts.

4

Haynes Park

85

Sewage Works

Bedford

MK45

SILVER LANE

HOWARD CL

LONGDEN CL

NORTHWOOD

MEADOW PIECE

Hill Farm

PALINGS WK.

BURGESS

PLUMMERS

5

CHURCH LA.

Haynes Church End

Warren Plantation

Church End Farm

Sandpit Farm

END

ROA D

41

CHURCH

GREAT

6

Obel

7

240

Northfield Farm

LANE

A B **98** C D E

CHICKSANDS WOOD

08 09 510

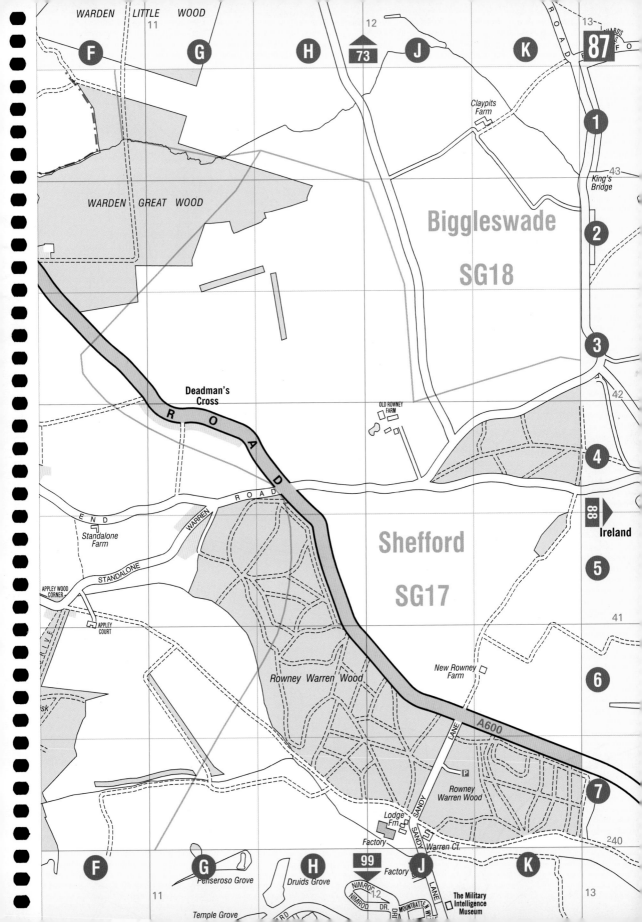

WARDEN LITTLE WOOD

F **G** **H** 73 **J** **K** **87**

12 13

WARDEN GREAT WOOD

Claypits Farm

1

King's Bridge 43

Biggleswade

SG18

2

3

42

Deadman's Cross

OLD ROWNEY FARM

4

ROAD

END

WARREN ROAD

Standalone Farm

STANDALONE

88 Ireland

Shefford

SG17

APPLEY WOOD CORNER

APPLEY COURT

DRIVE

5

41

Rowney Warren Wood

New Rowney Farm

6

A600 LANE

P

Rowney Warren Wood

7

240

Lodge Fm.

Factory

SANDY LANE

Warren Ct.

F **G** 99 **H** **J** **K**

11 Penseroso Grove Druids Grove Factory 13

NIMROD 12

NIMROD DR.

MOUNTBATTEN WY.

The Military Intelligence Museum

Temple Grove

88

BEDFORD **A** RICHARD'S CRES. 13 Laundry Farm THE ROAD VILLAGE **B** Warden Warren 74 **C** Old Warden Park **D** **E** 515

1

43 King's Bridge

2

3 Round Basin Warden Abbey Vineyard Cemy. Southill Lwr. Sch. Play. Fld. CHAPEL LANE

42 SOUTHILL PARK Playing Field SCHOOL LANE HIGH HOWARD'S CL. **SOUTHILL**

4

87 **Ireland** Ireland Spinney Moorhall Covert

5

41

Shefford

6

SG17 Stanfordbury Farm

7 A600 Rowney Warren Wood Collin's Grove Cockshoothill Grove Bury Spinney

240 **A** BEDFORD RD B658 **B** **100** 14 **C** **D** 515 **E** 13

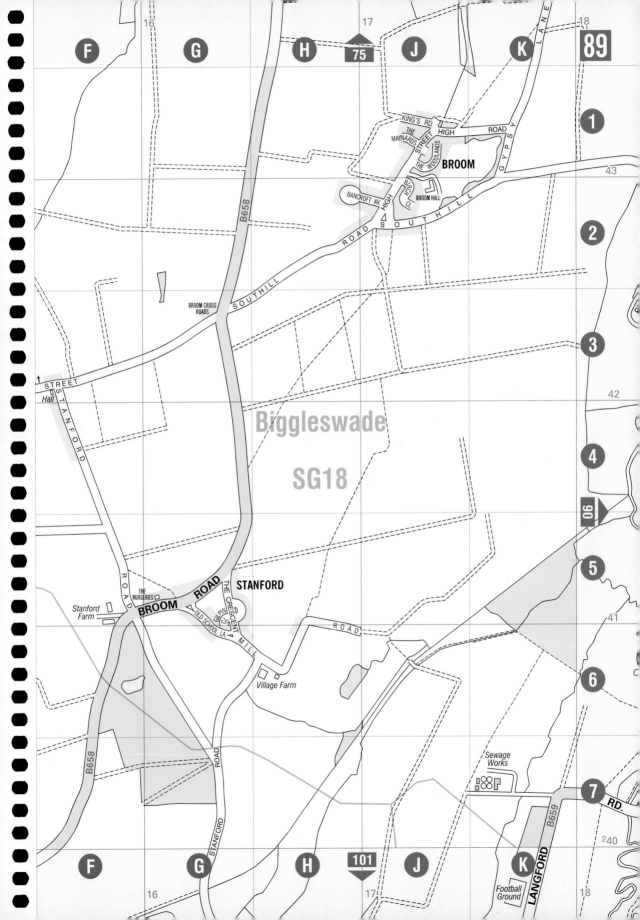

16

17

18

1

43

2

3

42

4

90

5

41

6

7 RD.

240

KING'S RD

THE MAYNARDS

STREET

HIGH

ROAD

THE WOODLANDS

BROOM

BROOM HALL

BANCROFT AV

BIRCH CL

HIGH

ROAD

SOUTHILL

GYPSY LANE

B658

SOUTHILL

BROOM CROSS ROADS

STREET

Hall

STANFORD

Biggleswade

SG18

THE NURSERIES

Stanford Farm

BROOM **ROAD**

STANFORD

ROAD

OLD SCHOOL LA.

THE CRESCENT

MILL

ROAD

Village Farm

B658

STANFORD ROAD

Sewage Works

B659

LANGFORD

Football Ground

16

17

18

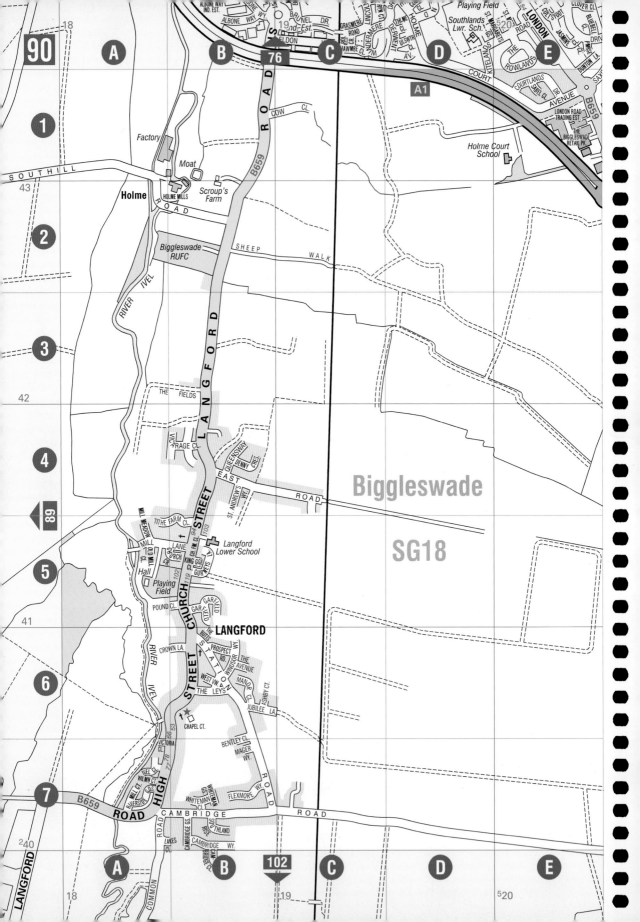

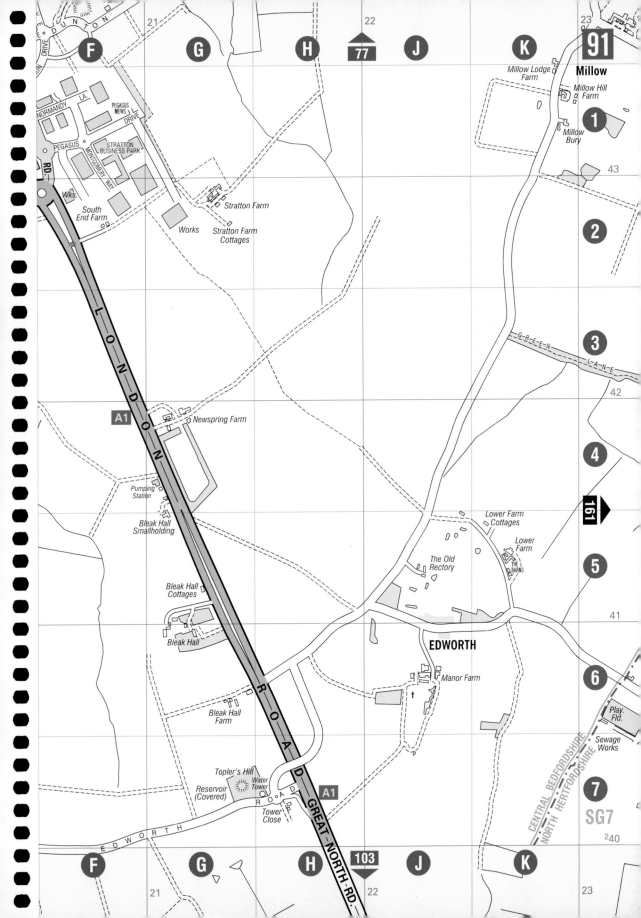

F G H J K

Millow

Edworth

SG7

NORMANDY LA.
PEGASUS MEWS
PEGASUS DRIVE
MONTGOMERY WAY
STRATTON BUSINESS PARK
RD.
Wks.
South End Farm
Works
Stratton Farm
Stratton Farm Cottages

D U N T O N

L O N D O N

R O A D

A1

Newspring Farm

Pumping Station

Bleak Hall Smallholding

Bleak Hall Cottages

Bleak Hall

Bleak Hall Farm

Topler's Hill
Reservoir (Covered)
Water Tower
ROAD
Tower Close
EDWORTH

GREAT NORTH RD.

A1

Millow Lodge Farm
Millow Hill Farm
Millow Bury

43

42

41

40

G R E E N L A N E

161

Lower Farm Cottages
Lower Farm
THE BARNS

The Old Rectory

EDWORTH

Manor Farm

Play. Fld.

Sewage Works

CENTRAL BEDFORDSHIRE
NORTH HERTFORDSHIRE

21 22 23

77

103

1
2
3
4
5
6
7

F G H J K

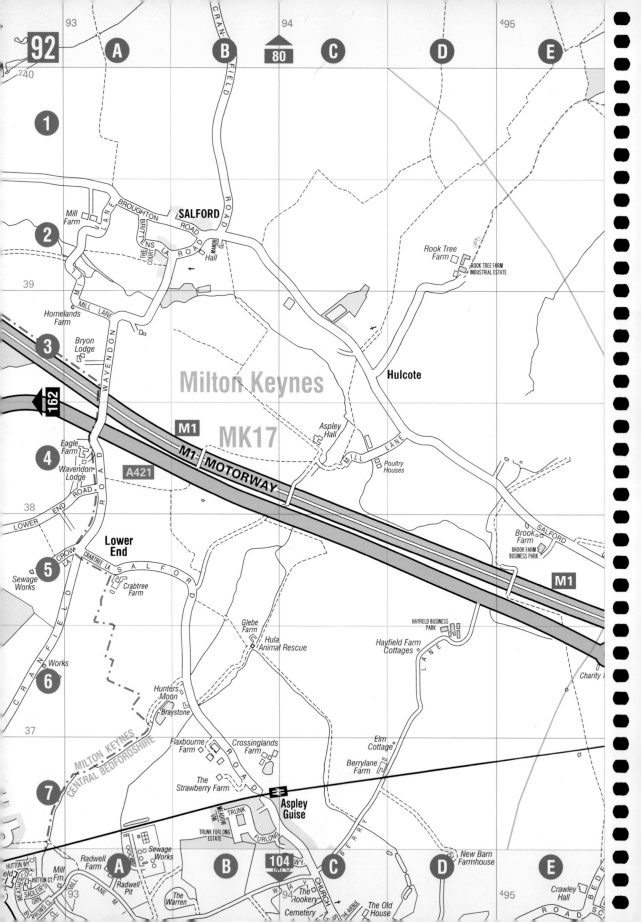

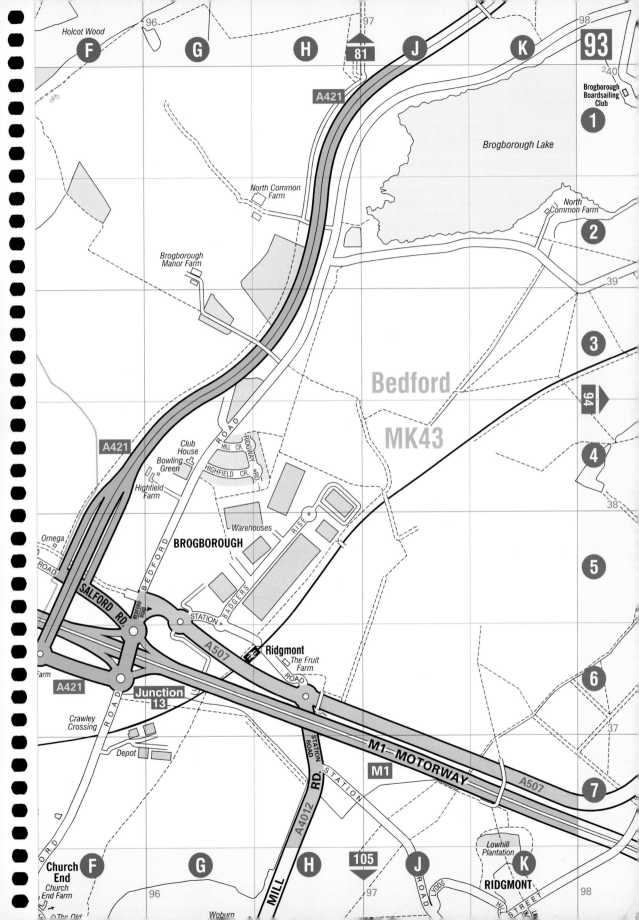

93

F G H J K

81

240

Holcot Wood

96 97 98

Brogborough
Boardsailing
Club

1

Brogborough Lake

North Common
Farm

*North
Common Farm*

2

39

Brogborough
Manor Farm

A421

Bedford

3

94

MK43

A421

Club
House
Bowling
Green

HILL CR.

RIDGWAY RD.

HIGHFIELD CR.

4

38

Highfield
Farm

Warehouses

RISE

5

Omega

ROAD

BEDFORD ROAD

BEDFORD ROAD

BROGBOROUGH

BADGERS

SALFORD RD.

STATION

A507

Ridgmont

*The Fruit
Farm*

ROAD

6

37

A421

**Junction
13**

ROAD

Crawley
Crossing

Depot

STATION ROAD

A4012

STATION ROAD

M1

M1 — MOTORWAY

A507

7

Farm

*Lowhill
Plantation*

**Church
End**
*Church
End Farm*

F G H J K

105

RIDGMONT

ROAD

MILL RD.

WOODS

HILL STREET

96 97 98

Woburn

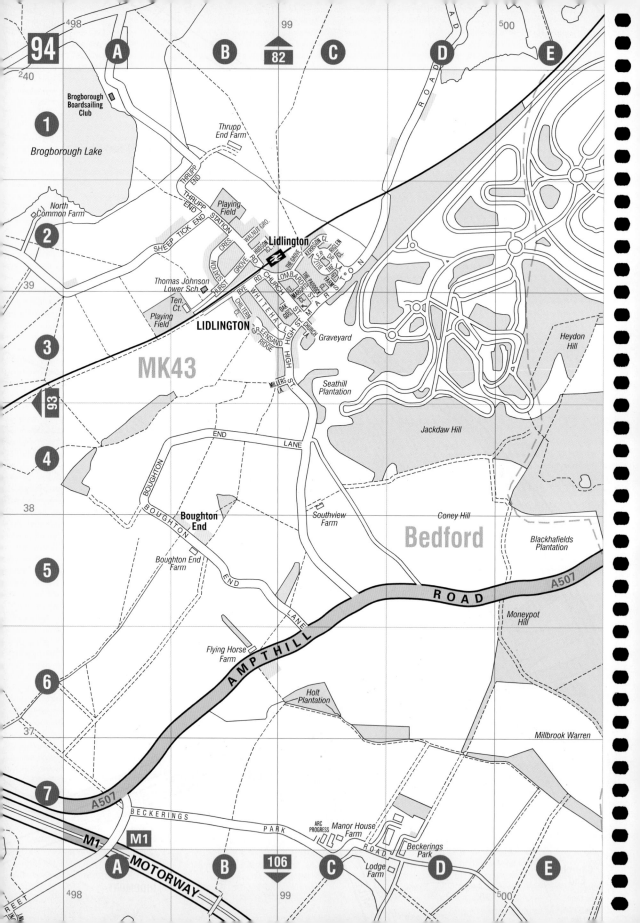

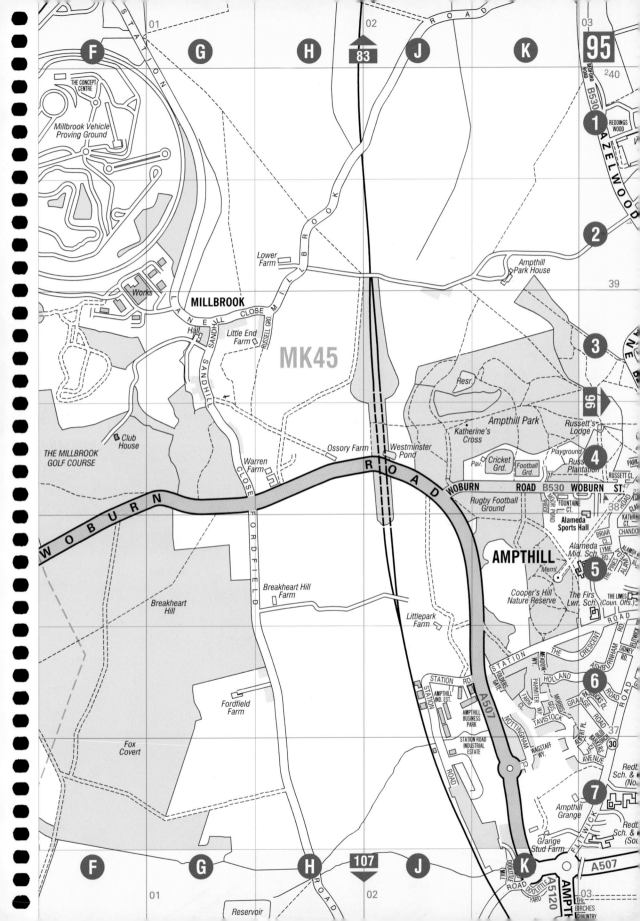

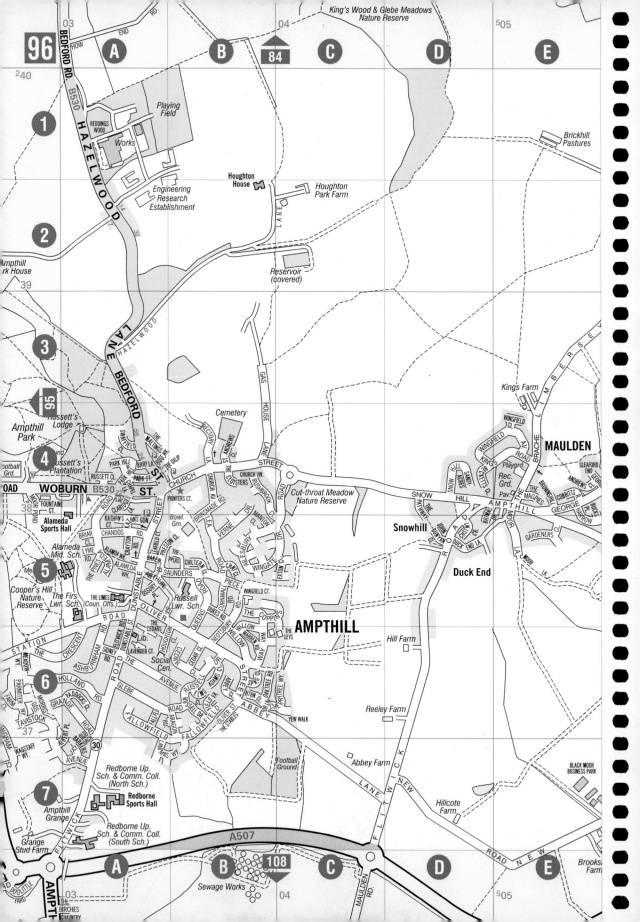

240

A **B** **C** **D** **E**

1
2
3
4
5
6
7

King's Wood & Glebe Meadows
Nature Reserve

03 04 505

84

Playing
Field

REDDINGS
WOOD

Works

Engineering
Research
Establishment

Houghton
House

Houghton
Park Farm

Brickhill
Pastures

HAZELWOOD

BEDFORD RD.

HOW

END RD.

B530

Ampthill
Park House

Reservoir
(covered)

LANE

39

HAZELWOOD

BEDFORD

LANE

GAS HOUSE LANE

56

Russett's
Lodge

Ampthill
Park

Russett's
Plantation

Football
Grd.

Cemetery

RECTORY LA.

ST.MONICA'S ST.

CHURCH AV.

THE CLOISTERS

RUSHBROOK

STREET

Cut-throat Meadow
Nature Reserve

Kings Farm

WINGFIELD CL.

WINGFIELD
ROAD

KING'S CROFTS CL.

Playgrd.

Rec.
Grd.

Pav.

LIMBERSEY

THE BRACHE

MAULDEN

Sleaford
END

ANDREWS CL.

BROWNSHILL

THE MAGPIES

CORBITTS CL.

HARROW

BUCKS CL.

GEORGE

GARDENER'S CL.

WOBURN B530

ST.

CHURCH ST.

Printers Ct.

Bowl. Grn.

Alameda
Sports Hall

FOUNTAINE CT.

MAYOR POND

38

Alameda
Mid. Sch.

Me

Cooper's Hill
Nature
Reserve

The Firs
Lwr. Sch.

The Lines
(Coun. Offs.)

Russell
Lwr. Sch.

DUNSTABLE ST.

OLIVER

QUEENS

The Cedars

Lib.

LAVENDER CT.

Social
Cen.

HOUGHTON CL.

CEDAR CL.

ABBEY

RUSSELL

ADAMS CL.

S. STREET

YEW WALK

WILLOW

WARREN RD.

WINGFIELD CT.

THE COPPINS

THE LEYS

AMPTHILL

Hill Farm

Snowhill

SNOW HILL

THE PATHWAY

JOHN BUNYAN CT.

DUCK END LA.

Duck End

BRANS

AMPTHILL MOOR

MOOR LA.

Reeley Farm

STATION

MEADOW WY.

THE CRESCENT

ASHB

GLEBE ROAD

HOLLAND RD.

GRANGE

PADDOCKS CL.

BARNERS

30

AVENUE

FALLOWFIELD

ALBERT PL.

WAGSTAFF WY.

AVENUE

Ampthill
Grange

Redborne Up.
Sch. & Comm. Coll.
(North Sch.)

Redborne
Sports Hall

Redborne Up.
Sch. & Comm. Coll.
(South Sch.)

Grange
Stud Farm

Football
Ground

Abbey Farm

Hillcote
Farm

BLACK MOOR
BUSINESS PARK

FLITWICK

LANE

NEW

FLITWICK

A507

A **B** **C** **D** **E**

108

Sewage Works

MAULDEN RD.

ROAD NEW

Brooks
Farm

03 04 505

AMPT.

THE BIRCHES
CHAUNTRY

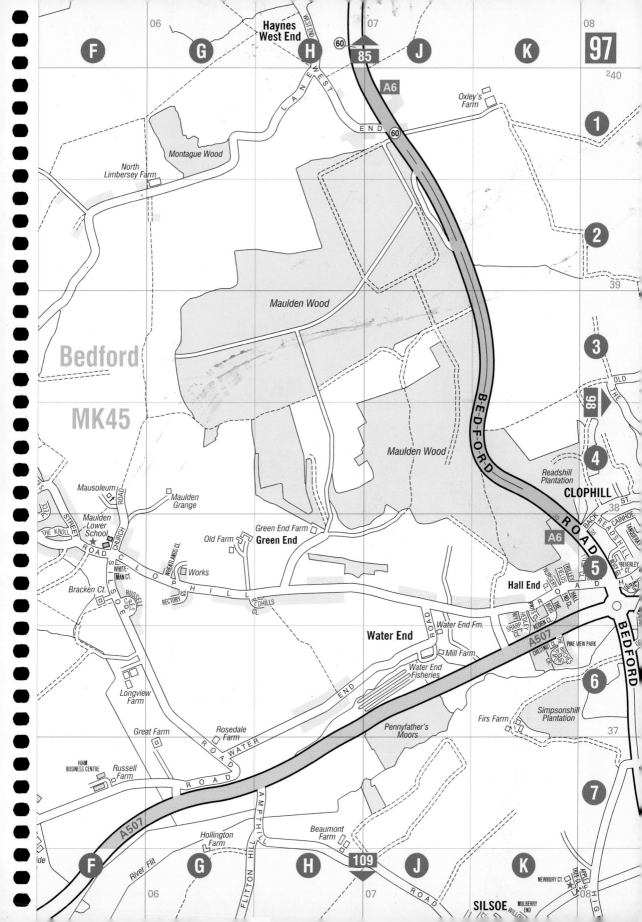

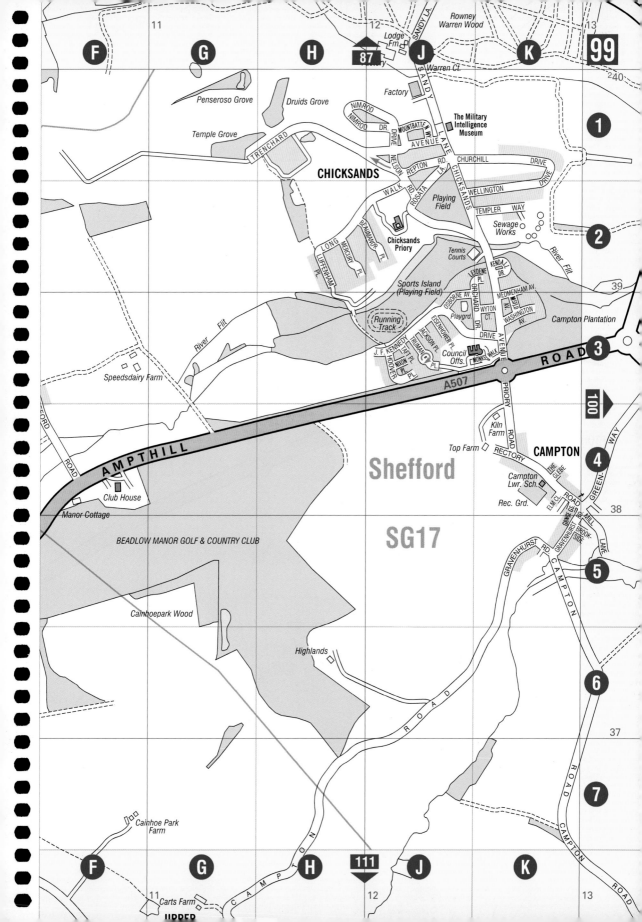

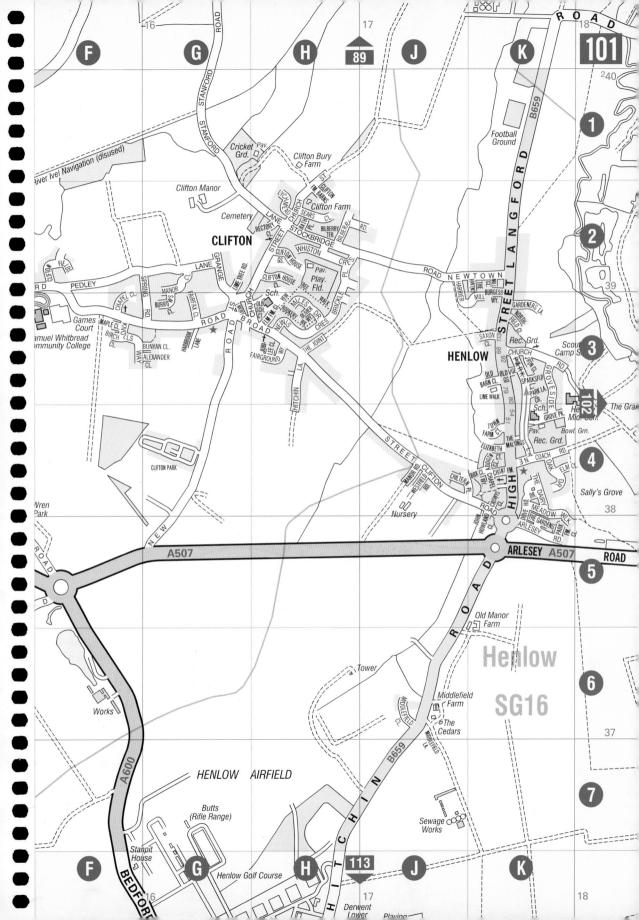

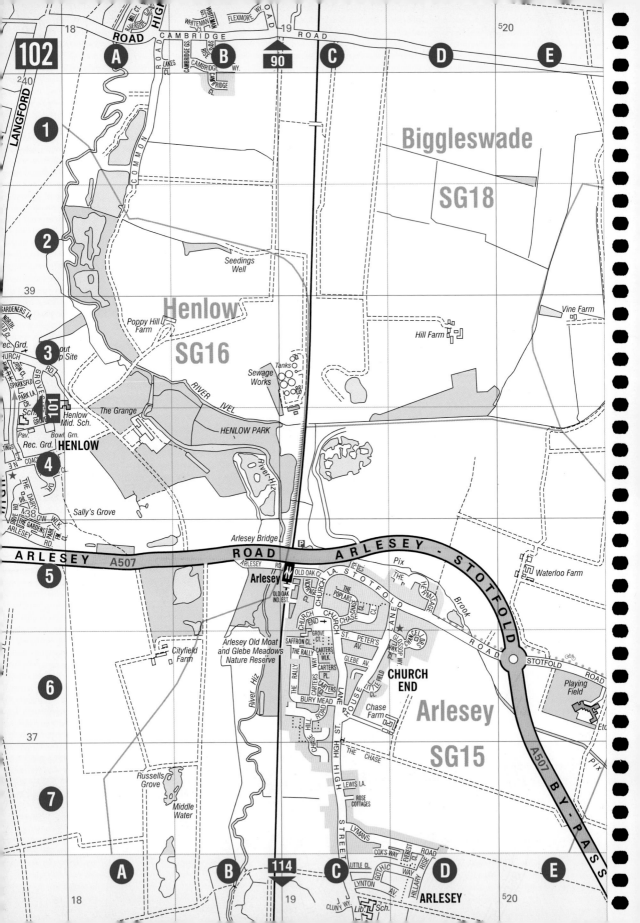

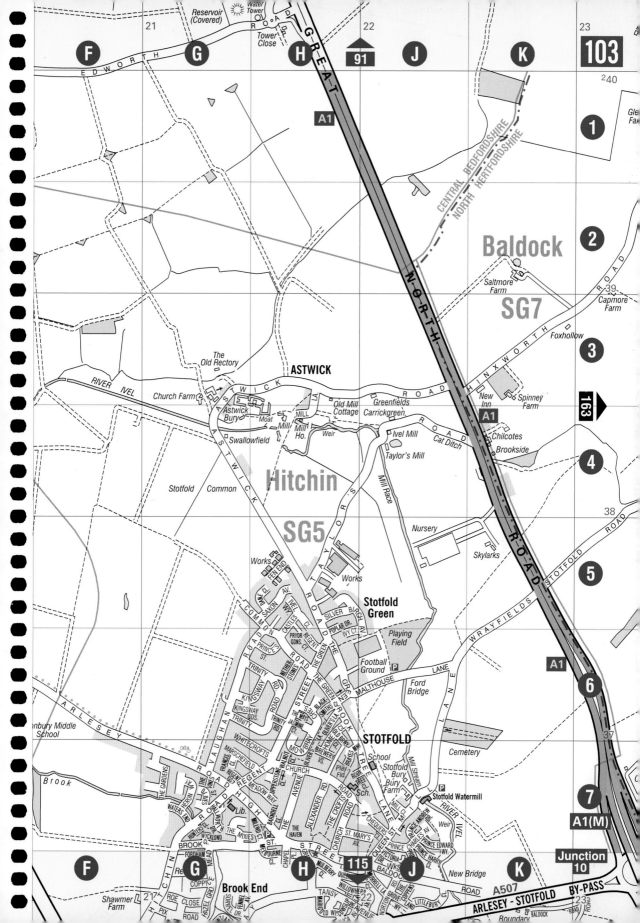

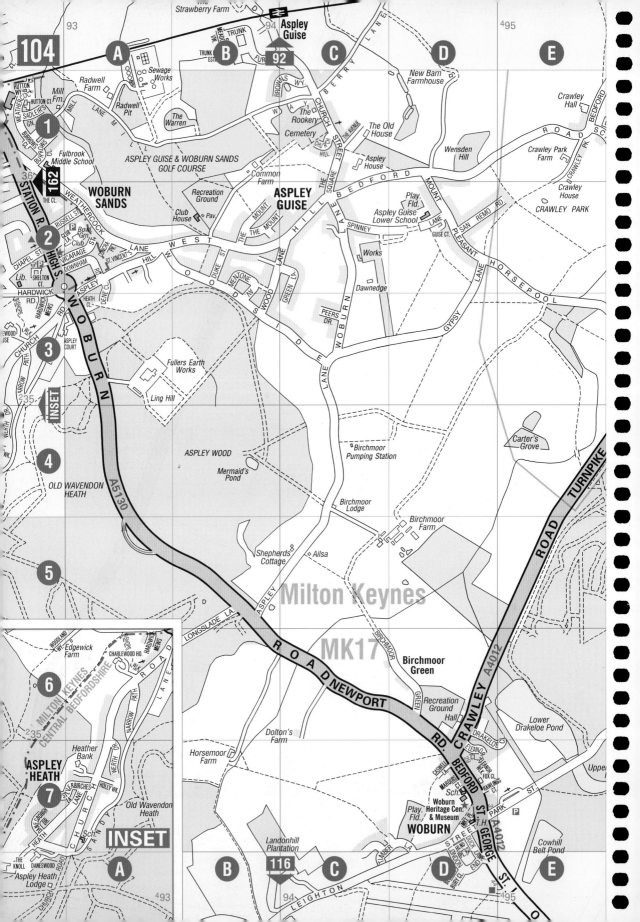

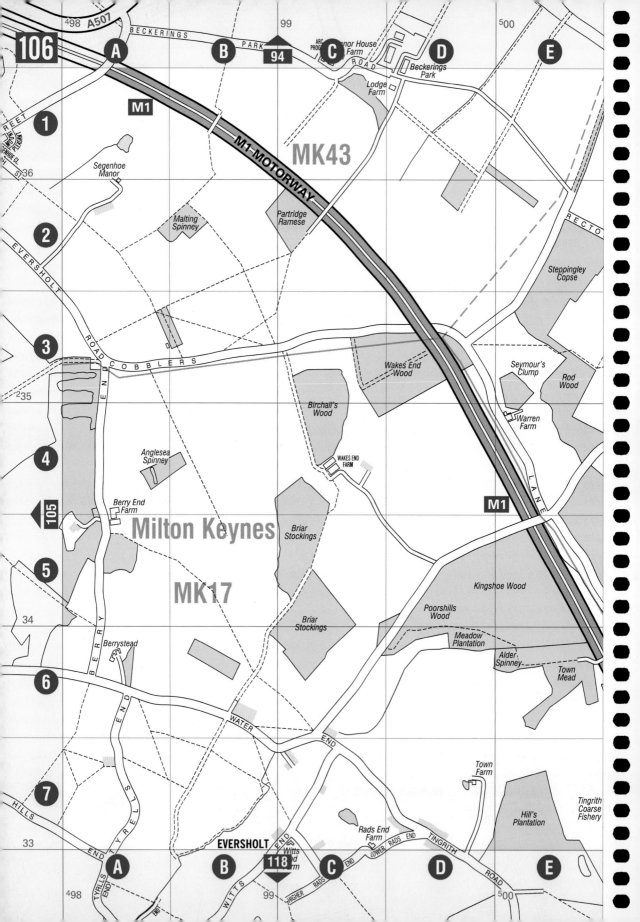

F **G** **H** **95** **J** **K**

01 02 03

Grange

Redb. & (Sou

A507

A507

Grange Stud Farm

1

THE MEADOWS

Reservoir

Froghall

Tennis Courts

ROAD STEPPINGLEY ROAD FROGHALL

Ash Spinney

The Rufus Centre

Kiln Farm

Flitwick Leisure Centre

FLITWICK

MK45

2

HIGH

36

TRAFALGAR

CHAUNTRY WY.

AMPTHILL A5120 RD.

COMMON FARM LA.

MILLWRIGHT WAY

THE THINNINGS

BEAUMONT CL.

BEAUMONT MEWS

3

235

STEPPINGLEY

Rec. Grd.

ROAD CHURCH END

FLITWICK END

EVERSHOLT

PEAKES END

Park Farm

Bedford

Flitwick Plantation

Wood Farm

Flitwick Local Nature Reserve

DICKENS RD.

MILTON BYRON CR.

TENNYSON RD.

KEATS RD.

CHAUCER RD.

BYRON

BLUEBELL

ROSEBAY

CLOVER CL.

PRIMROSE CL.

Lwr. Sch.

Woodland Middle Sch.

Super-store

4

108

PIPIT CL.

WINDM

KEND. CL.

DERWENT

CONISTON

WAY

5

34

The Mount

CHURCH

Old Farm

6

Ckt. Grd. Pav.

7

A5120

Warren Farm

CHURCH

M1-MOTORWAY

M1

STEPPINGLEY

Home Farm

Priestley Planation

Priestley Farm

F **G** **H** **119** Mo... Plantation **J** **K** **WESTONING**

33

HIGH

CHURCH

Cemetery

MANOR

High Thatch

01 02 03

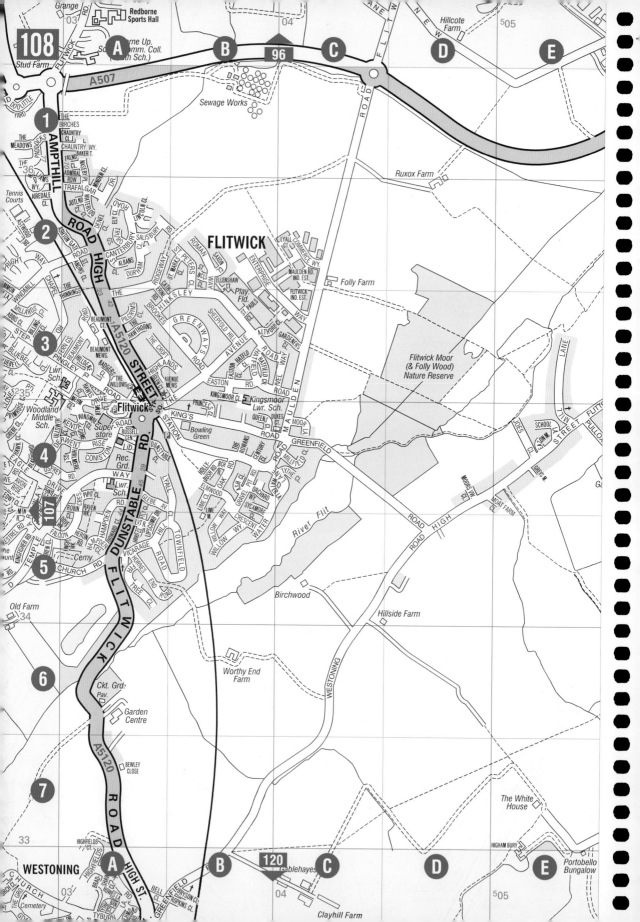

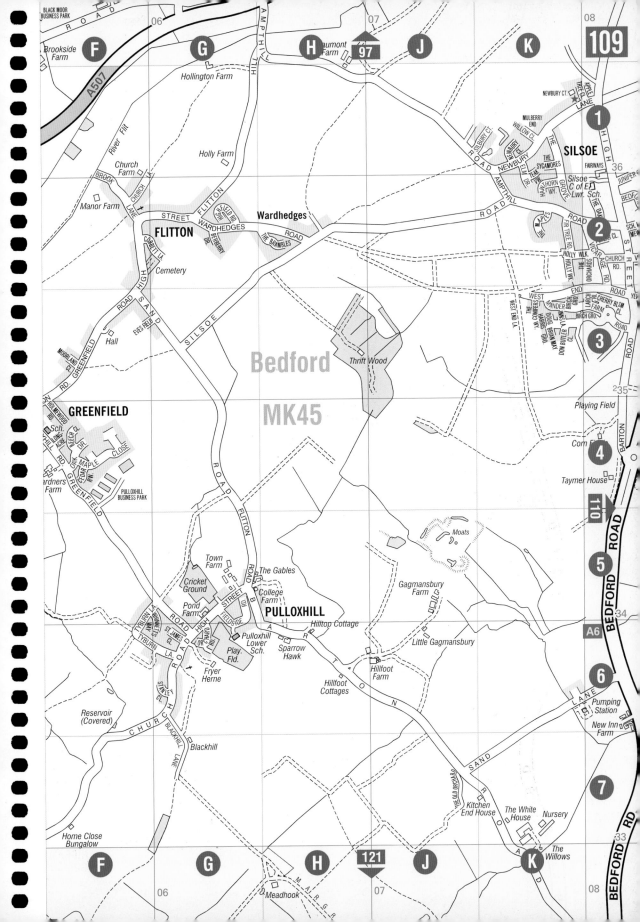

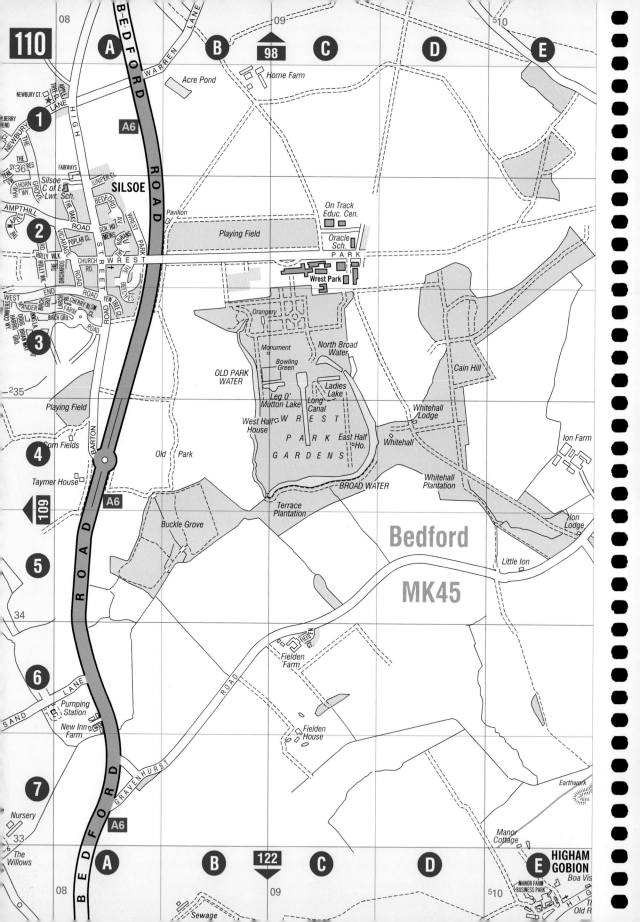

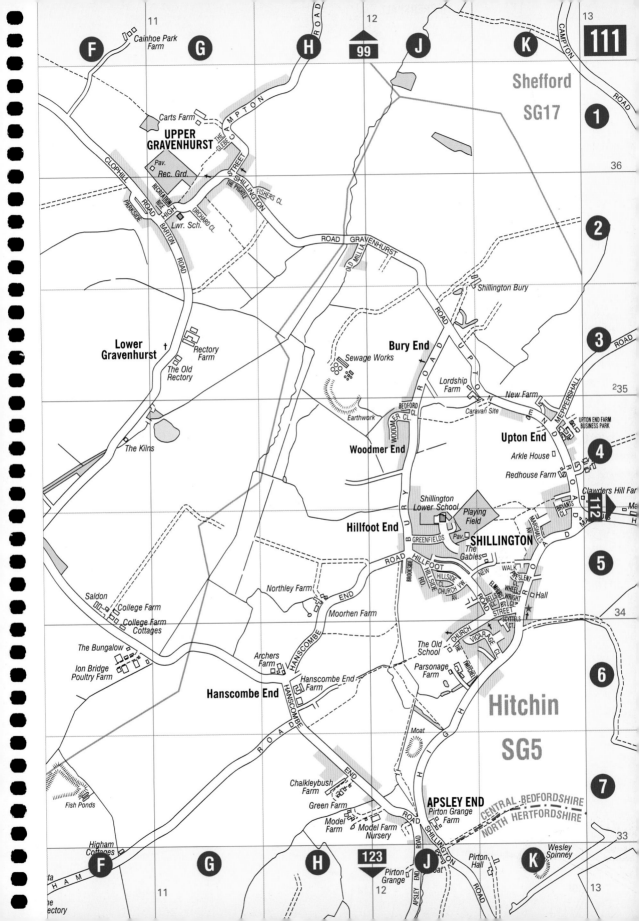

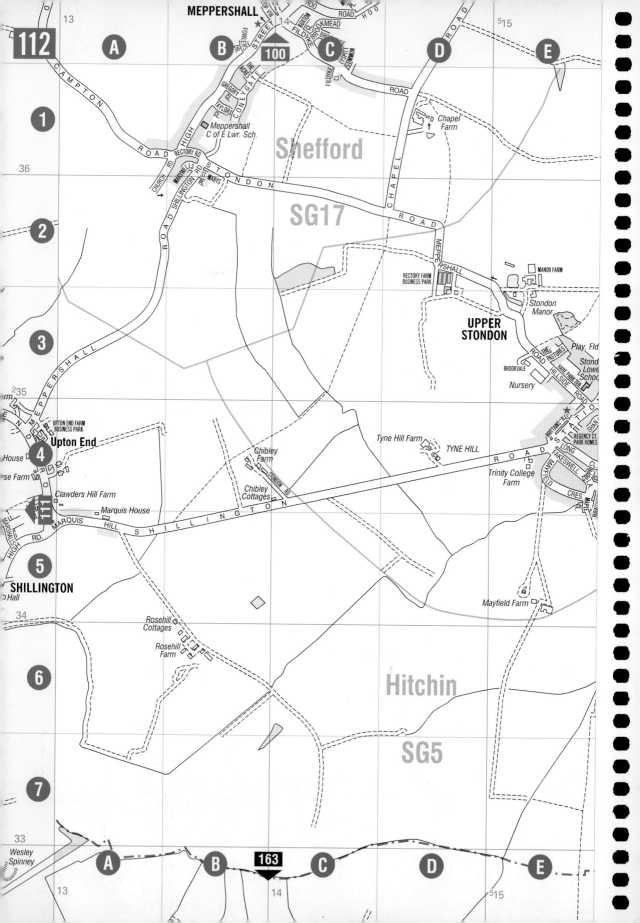

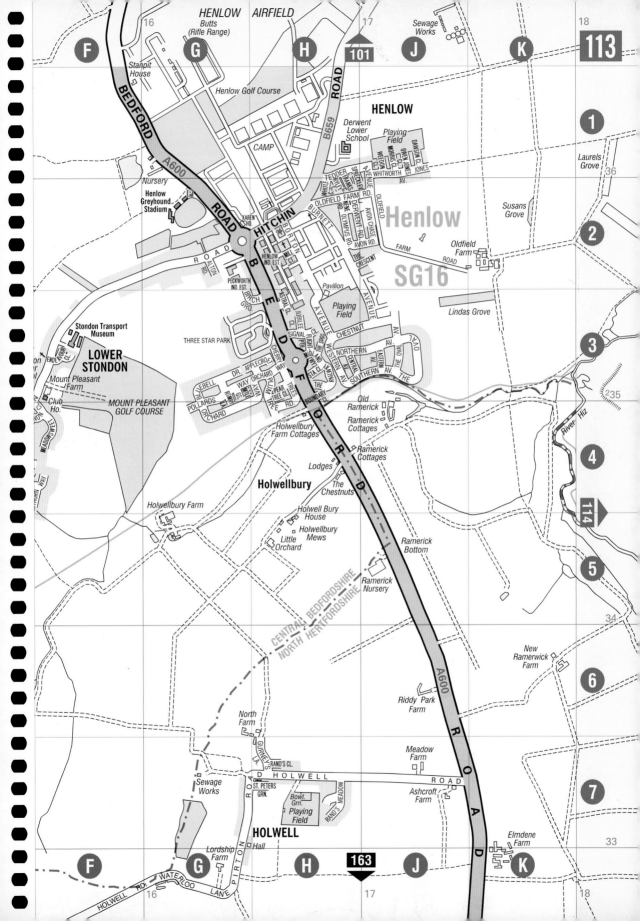

HENLOW AIRFIELD
Butts (Rifle Range)

F G H 101 J K

16 17 18

Sewage Works

Stanpit House

BEDFORD ROAD A600

Henlow Golf Course

HENLOW

B659

Derwent Lower School

Playing Field

DAWSON CL.
OWEN JONES
NORRIS CL.
WEEDON
JONES

Nursery

Henlow Greyhound Stadium

P

KAREN'S HO.

HITCHIN ROAD

CAMP

ALTON RD.
PECKWORTH IND. EST.

HENLOW IND. EST.

BIRCH GRO.

Henlow

Laurels Grove

36

Susans Grove

Oldfield Farm

OLDFIELD FARM RD.
DERWENT RD.
OLYMPUS RD.
AVON CHASE
AVON RD.
FARM

SG16

Lindas Grove

Stondon Transport Museum

LOWER STONDON

Mount Pleasant Farm

Club Ho.

MEADOWSWEET

ENDEAVOUR CL.

THREE STAR PARK

ASTRAL CL.
JUBILEE
SIGNAL
RIGHT WAY
CHERRY WAY
DR. APPLECROFT
ORCHARD WAY
JEBELL
PLUM TREE RD.
POLLARDS ORCHARD
PEAR TREE RD.

BEDFORD ROAD

Pavilion

Playing Field

THE CRESCENT

AVENUE
CHESTNUT AV.
WESTERN AV.
NORTHERN AV.
MID. AV.
CENTRAL AV.
SOUTHERN AV.
EASTERN AV.
THE OVAL
THE OVAL

STA. CL.

Old Ramerick

Ramerick Cottages

Ramerick Cottages

River Hiz

235

MOUNT PLEASANT GOLF COURSE

Holwellbury Farm Cottages

Lodges

The Chestnuts

Holwellbury

Holwellbury Farm

Holwell Bury House

Holwellbury Mews

Little Orchard

Ramerick Bottom

Ramerick Nursery

A600 ROAD

CENTRAL BEDFORDSHIRE
NORTH HERTFORDSHIRE

34

New Ramerwick Farm

North Farm

GURNEYS
RAND'S CL.
D HOLWELL
ST. PETERS GRN.
PIRTON ROAD
RAND'S MEADOW

Bowl. Grn.
Playing Field

Riddy Park Farm

Meadow Farm

ROAD

Ashcroft Farm

Sewage Works

HOLWELL
Hall

Lordship Farm

Elmdene Farm

33

F G H 163 J K

HOLWELL RD. WATERLOO LANE

16 17 18

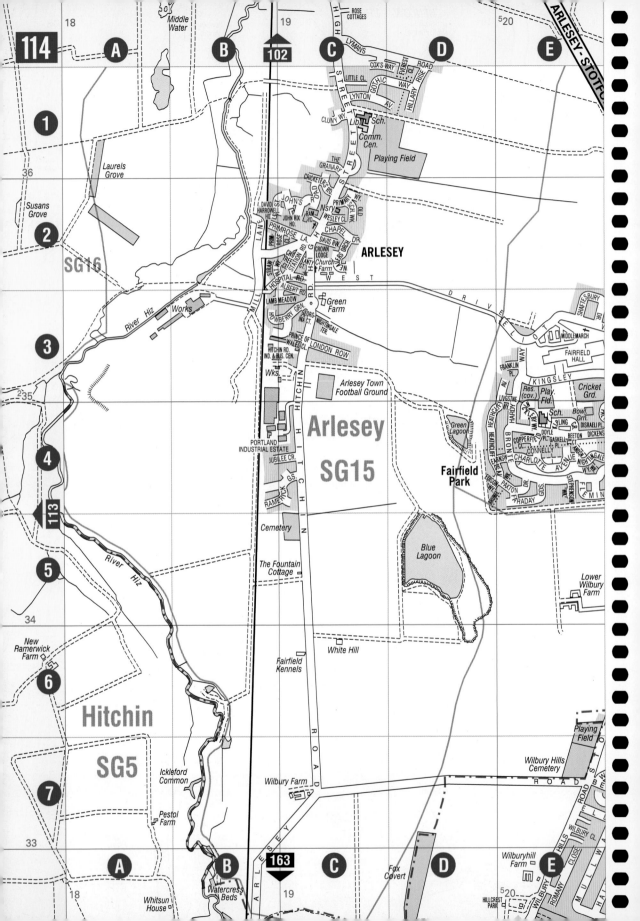

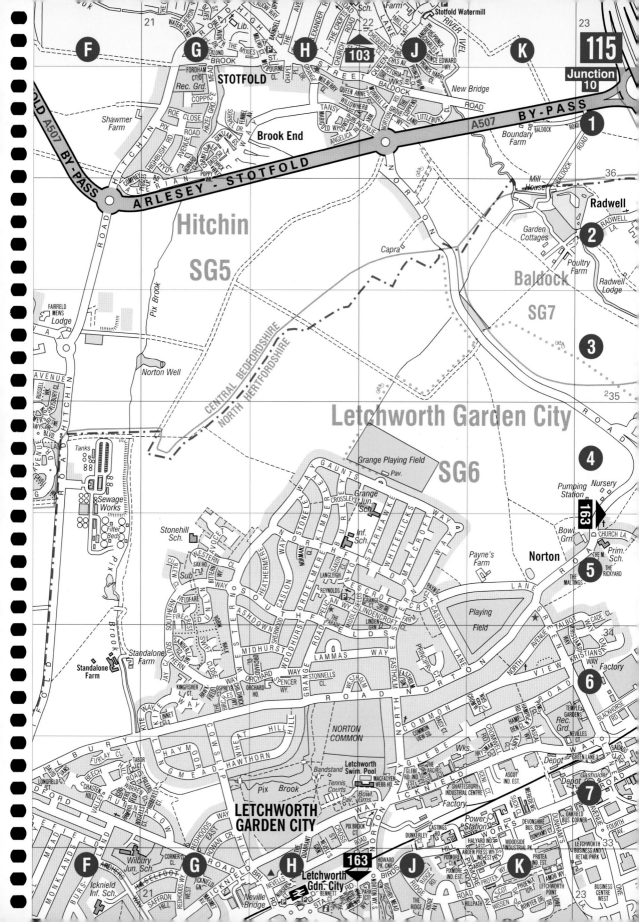

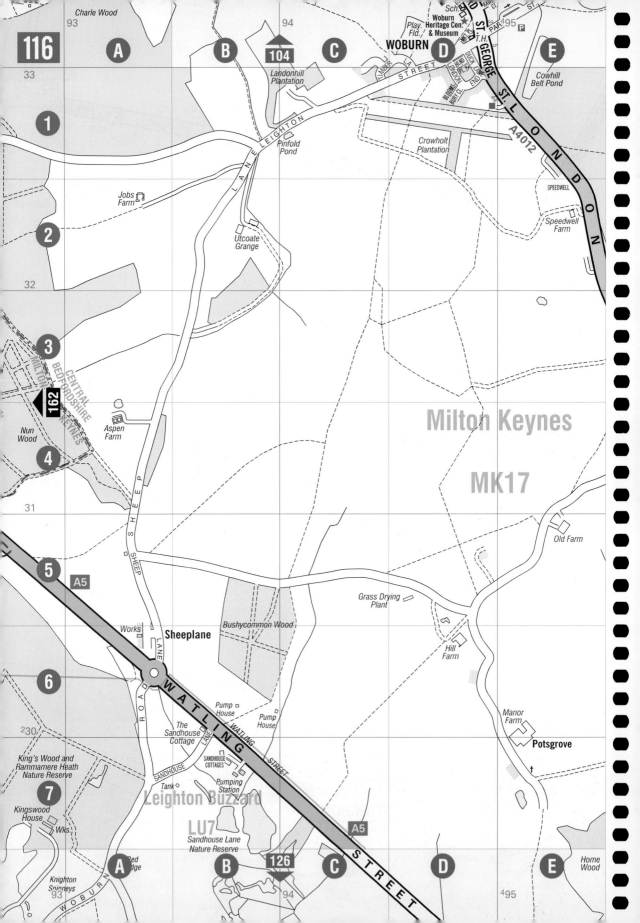

116

A   B   104   C   WOBURN   D   E

Charle Wood
93
33
94
95

Woburn Heritage Cen. & Museum
Play. Fld.
Sch.

Landonhill Plantation
Cowhill Belt Pond

1

LEIGHTON LANE

Pinfold Pond

Crowholt Plantation

SPEEDWELL

Jobs Farm

2

Utcoate Grange

Speedwell Farm

32

3

CENTRAL BEDFORDSHIRE

MILTON KEYNES

162

Aspen Farm

Nun Wood

4

Milton Keynes

MK17

31

Old Farm

5   A5

SHEEP LANE

Grass Drying Plant

Works

Sheeplane

Bushycommon Wood

Hill Farm

6

Manor Farm

WATLING ROAD

Pump House

Pump House

Potsgrove

230

King's Wood and Rammamere Heath Nature Reserve

The Sandhouse Cottage

WATLING STREET

SANDHOUSE LANE

SANDHOUSE COTTAGES

7

Kingswood House

Tank

Pumping Station

Leighton Buzzard

Wks

LU7

Sandhouse Lane Nature Reserve

A5

A   B   126   C   STREET   D   E

Red Lodge

WOBURN

Knighton Sninneys
93

94

Home Wood

495

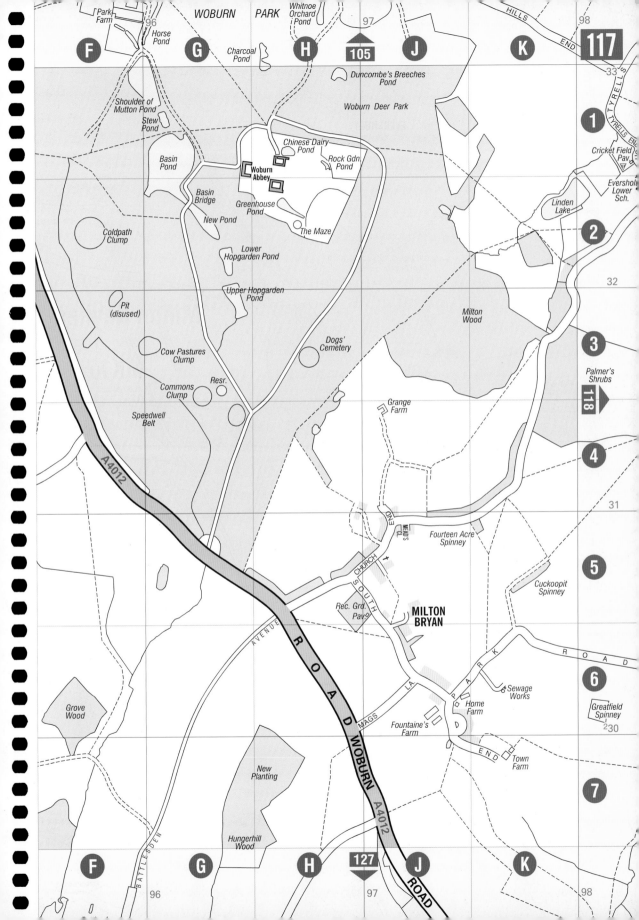

WOBURN PARK

Park Farm

Horse Pond

Whitnoe Orchard Pond

Charcoal Pond

Duncombe's Breeches Pond

Woburn Deer Park

HILLS END

33

TYRELLS END

Cricket Field Pav.

Eversholt Lower Sch.

Shoulder of Mutton Pond

Stew Pond

Basin Pond

Chinese Dairy Pond

Woburn Abbey

Rock Gdn. Pond

Linden Lake

32

Basin Bridge

Greenhouse Pond

New Pond

The Maze

Coldpath Clump

Lower Hopgarden Pond

Upper Hopgarden Pond

Milton Wood

Pit (disused)

Dogs' Cemetery

Palmer's Shrubs

118

Cow Pastures Clump

Resr.

Commons Clump

Grange Farm

31

Speedwell Belt

A4012

Fourteen Acre Spinney

MEAD'S CL.

Cuckoopit Spinney

CHURCH

SOUTH

Rec. Grd. Pav.

MILTON BRYAN

AVENUE

ROAD

ROAD

Grove Wood

MAGS

LA.

PARK

Home Farm

Sewage Works

Greatfield Spinney

30

Fountaine's Farm

END

Town Farm

New Planting

WOBURN

A4012

127

Hungerhill Wood

BATTLESDEN

ROAD

96

97

98

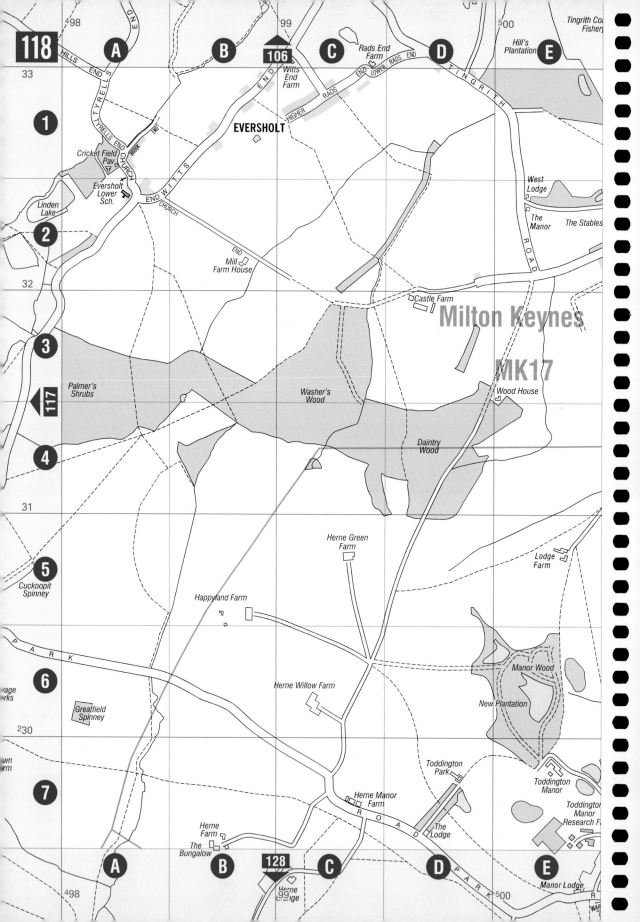

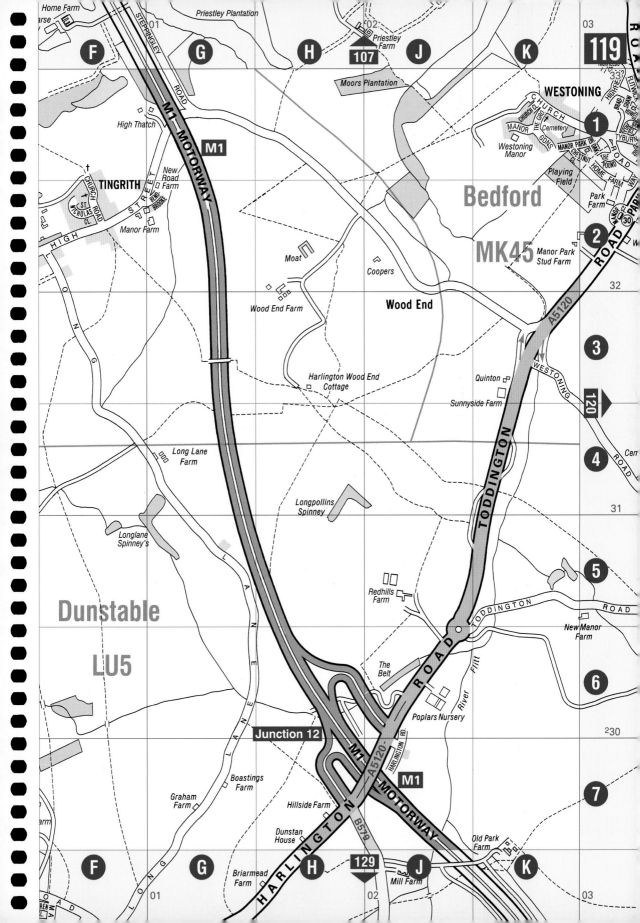

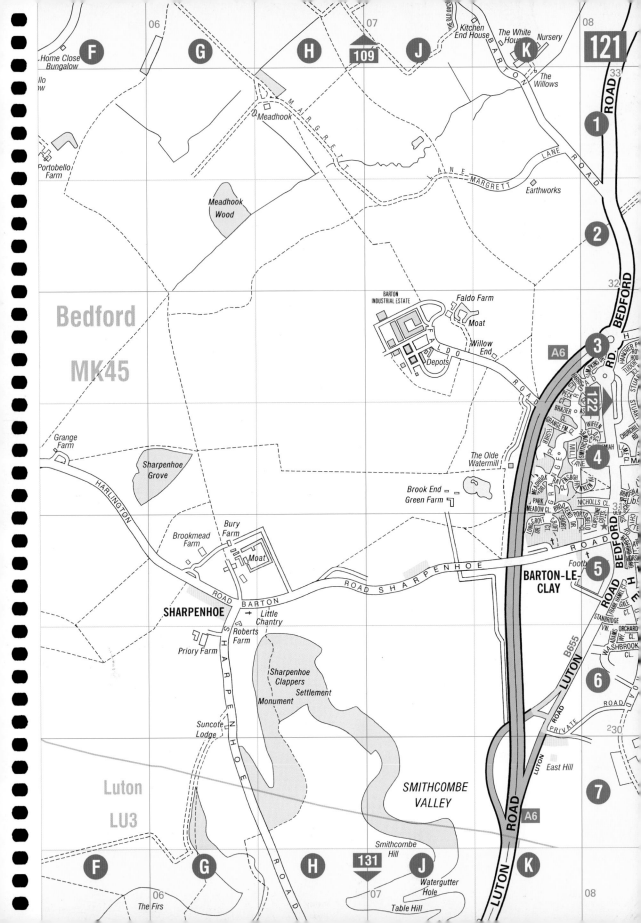

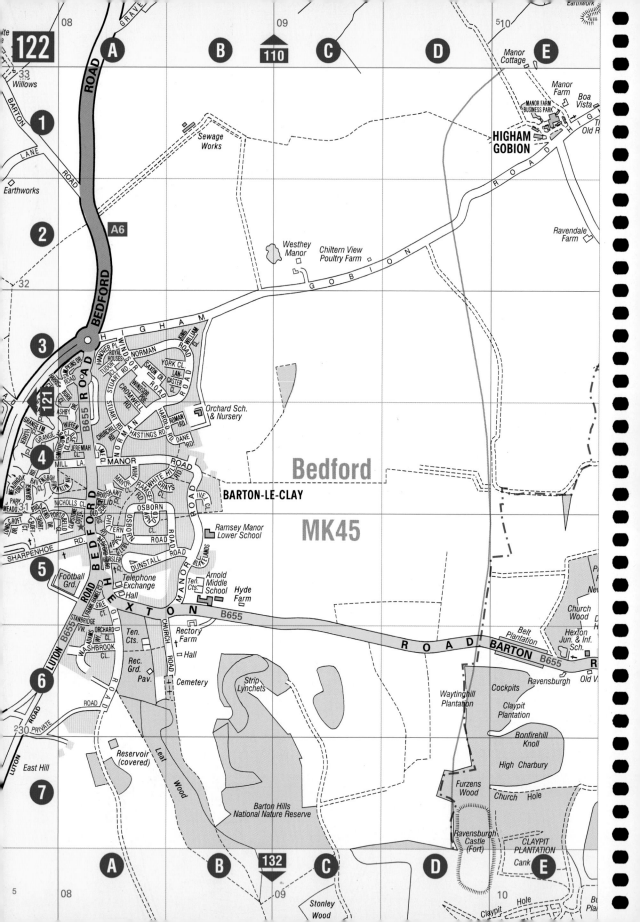

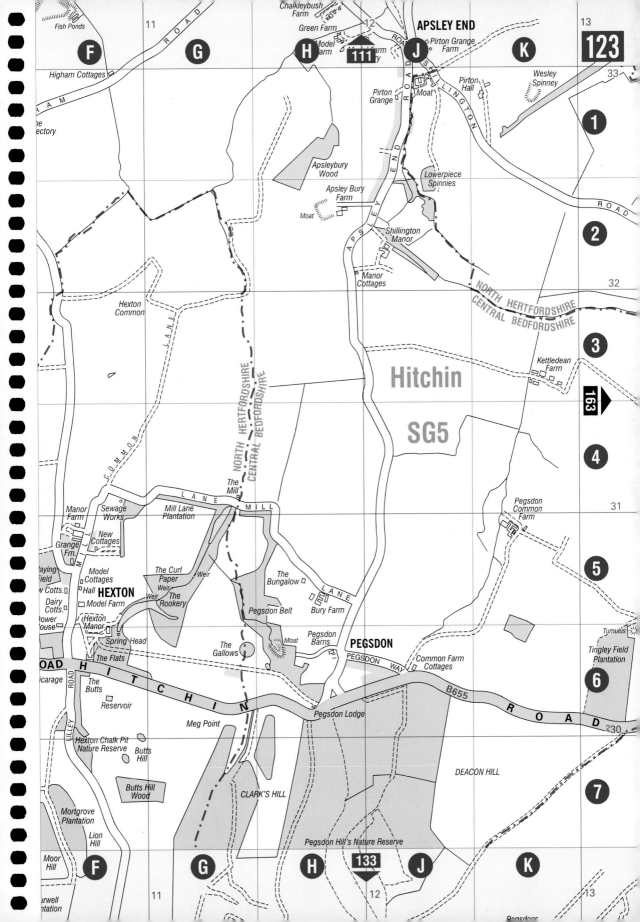

F **G** **H** **J** **K**

111

1
33

2
32

3

163

4

5
31

6
230

7

F **G** **H** **J** **K**

133

11 12 13

Fish Ponds
Chalkleybush Farm
Green Farm
Model Farm
Pirton Grange Farm
Wesley Spinney

Higham Cottages
Pirton Grange
Moat
Pirton Hall

Rectory

Apsleybury Wood
Apsley Bury Farm
Moat
Lowerpiece Spinnies

Shillington Manor

Hexton Common
Manor Cottages

NORTH HERTFORDSHIRE
CENTRAL BEDFORDSHIRE

Hitchin

SG5

Kettledean Farm

LANE

NORTH HERTFORDSHIRE
CENTRAL BEDFORDSHIRE

The Mill
MILL LANE
Pegsdon Common Farm

Manor Farm
Sewage Works
Mill Lane Plantation

New Cottages
Grange Fm.
Model Cottages
The Curl Paper
Weir
The Bungalow
LANE

Playing Field
New Cotts.
Hall
HEXTON
Weir
Weir
The Rookery
Bury Farm

Dairy Cotts.
Model Farm
Pegsdon Belt

Lower House
Hexton Manor
Moat
Pegsdon Barns

Tumulus

Spring Head
The Gallows
PEGSDON
Common Farm Cottages
Tingley Field Plantation

The Flats
Vicarage
ROAD HITCHIN
PEGSDON WAY
B655 ROAD

The Butts
Reservoir
Meg Point
Pegsdon Lodge

Hexton Chalk Pit Nature Reserve
Butts Hill

DEACON HILL

Mortgrove Plantation
CLARK'S HILL
Butts Hill Wood

Lion Hill

Moor Hill

Pegsdon Hill's Nature Reserve

LILLEY ROAD

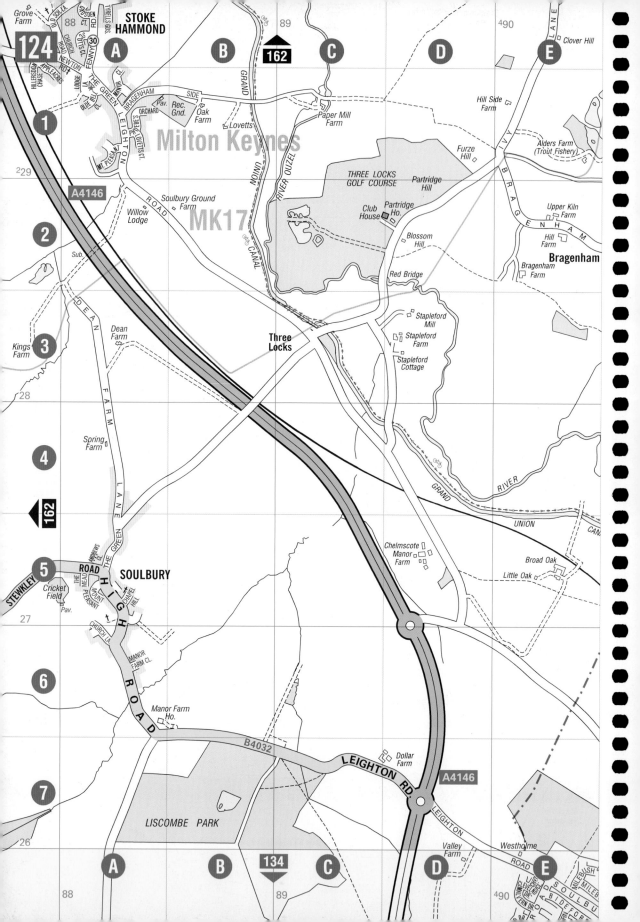

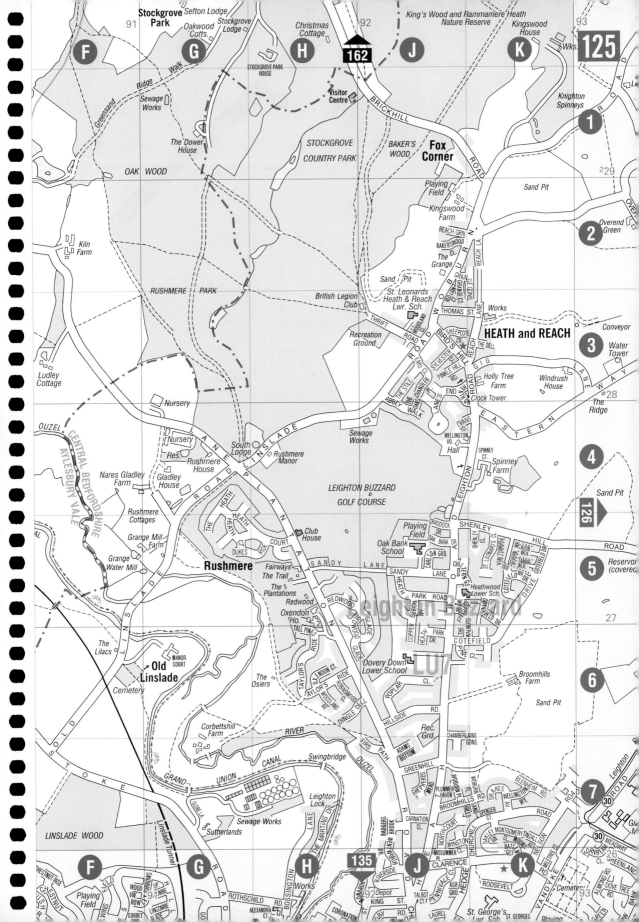

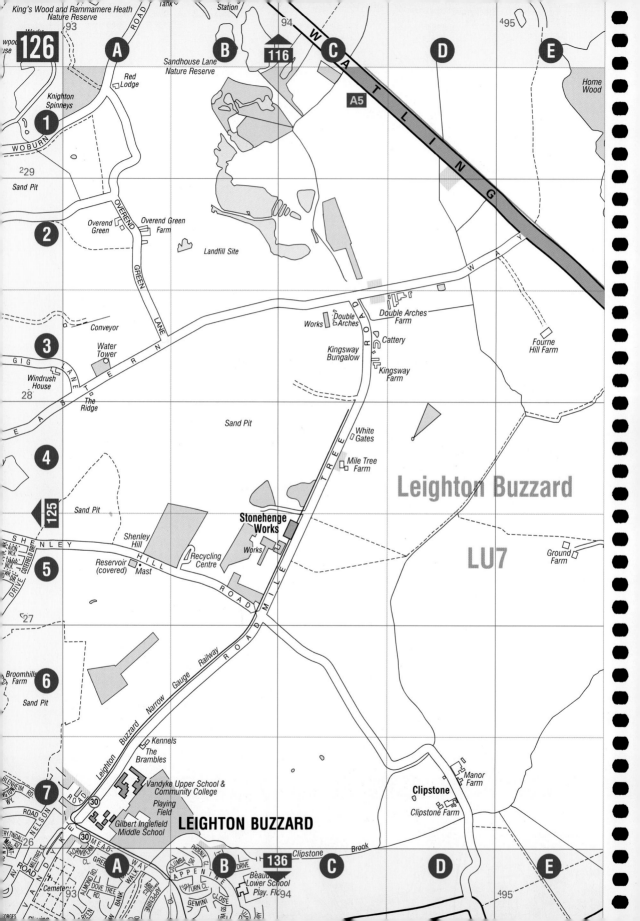

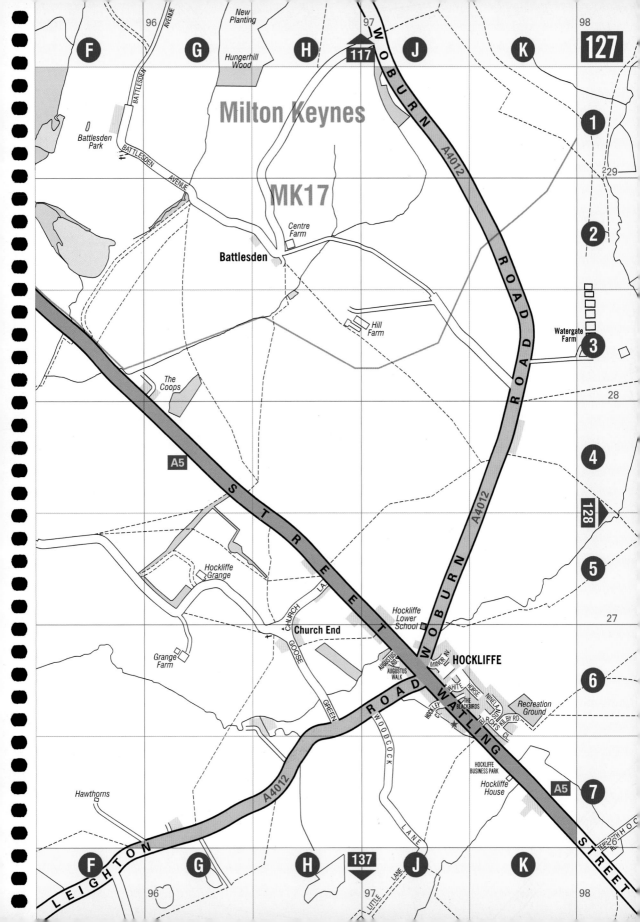

127

F G H 117 J K

Milton Keynes

MK17

Battlesden Park

New Planting

Hungerhill Wood

Battlesden

Centre Farm

Hill Farm

The Coops

A5

Hockliffe Grange

Church End

Grange Farm

Hawthorns

Hockliffe Lower School

Augustus Walk

Church Lane

Goose Lane

Green Lane

Woodcock Lane

A4012

Woburn Road

A4012

Watergate Farm

Hockliffe

The Blackbirds

Recreation Ground

Hockliffe Business Park

Hockliffe House

A5

Leighton Road

Watling Street

Road Watling

1

2

3

4

128

5

27

6

7

229

28

26

F G H 137 J K

96 97 98

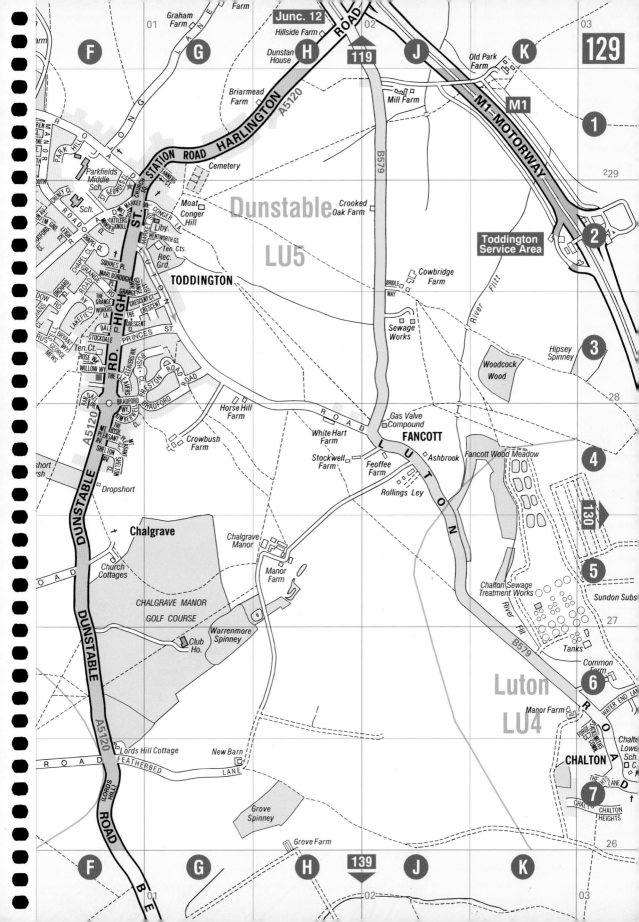

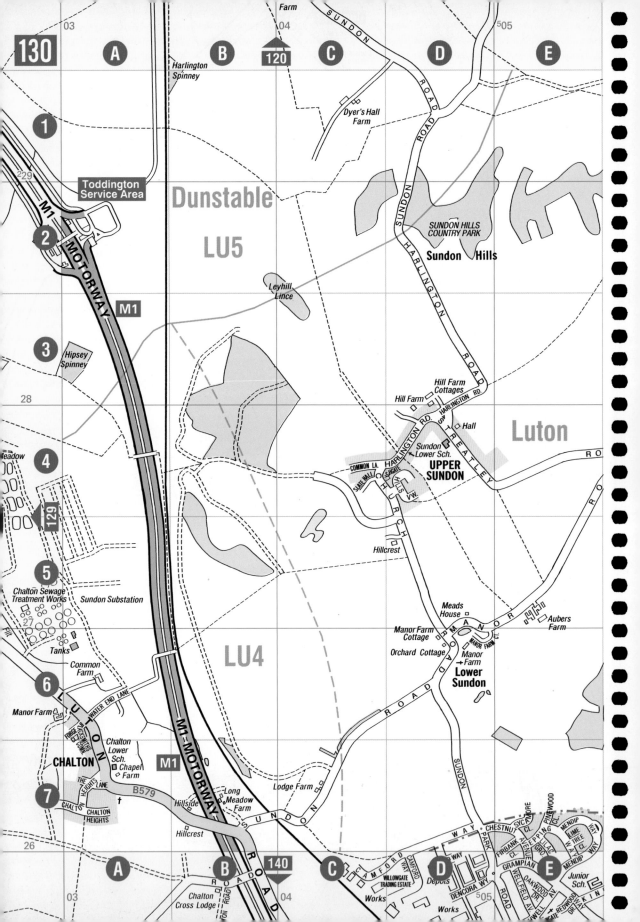

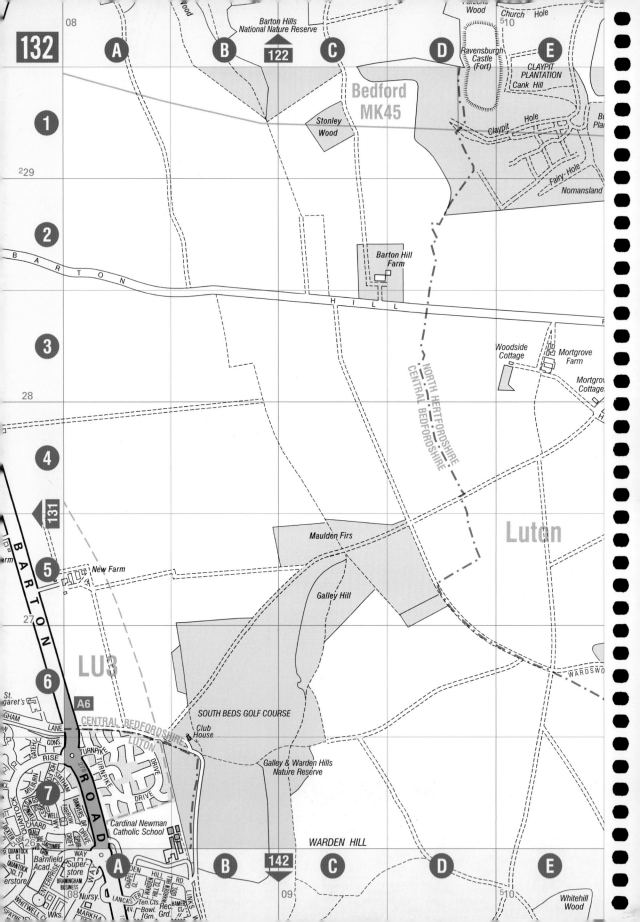

132

08

A   **B**   **122**   **C**   **D**   **E**

Barton Hills
National Nature Reserve

Parsons
Wood

Church   Hole
510

Ravensburgh
Castle (Fort)

CLAYPIT
PLANTATION
Cank Hill

1

Stonley
Wood

**Bedford
MK45**

Claypit   Hole

Bu
Plan

229

Fairy-Hole

Nomansland

2

B   A   R   T   O   N

Barton Hill
Farm

H   I   L   L

3

Woodside
Cottage

Mortgrove
Farm

28

Mortgrov
Cottages

H

NORTH HERTFORDSHIRE
CENTRAL BEDFORDSHIRE

4

Luton

131

5

New Farm

Maulden Firs

Galley Hill

27

6

LU3

St.
argaret's

GHAM

LANE

A6

CENTRAL BEDFORDSHIRE
LUTON

SOUTH BEDS GOLF COURSE

Club
House

WARDSWO

7

26

Cardinal Newman
Catholic School

Galley & Warden Hills
Nature Reserve

A   **B**   **142**   **C**   **D**   **E**

WARDEN   HILL

08

09

510

Whitehill
Wood

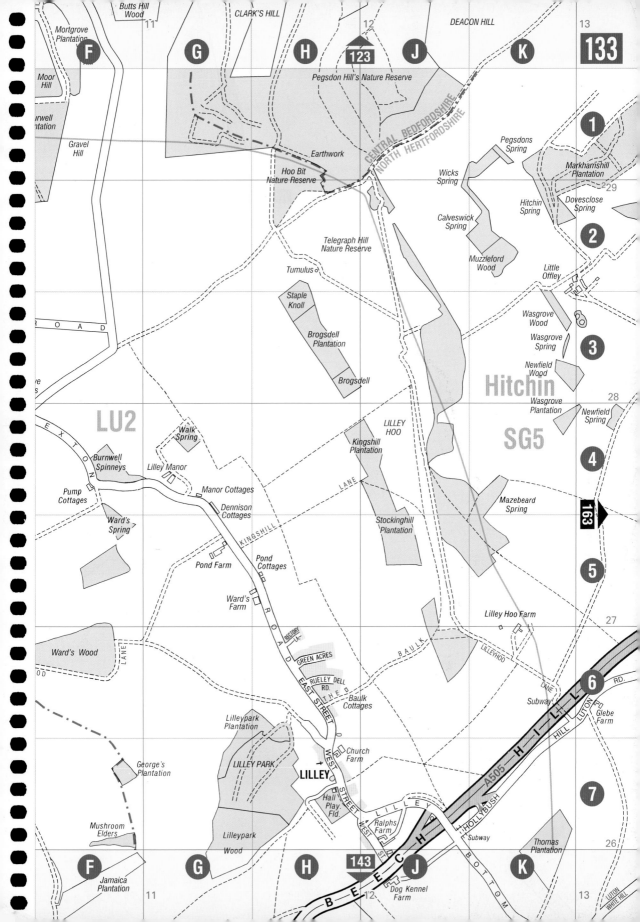

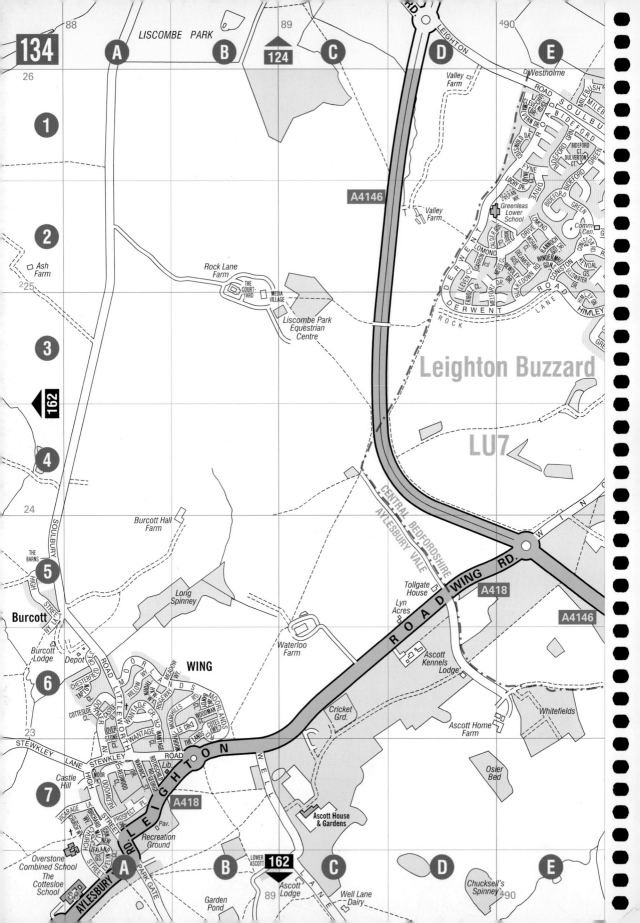

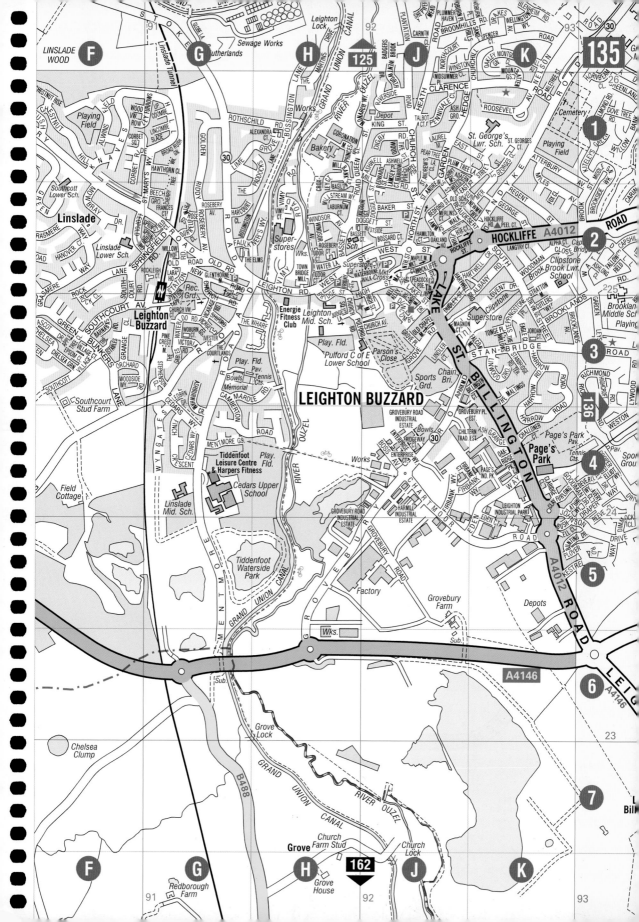

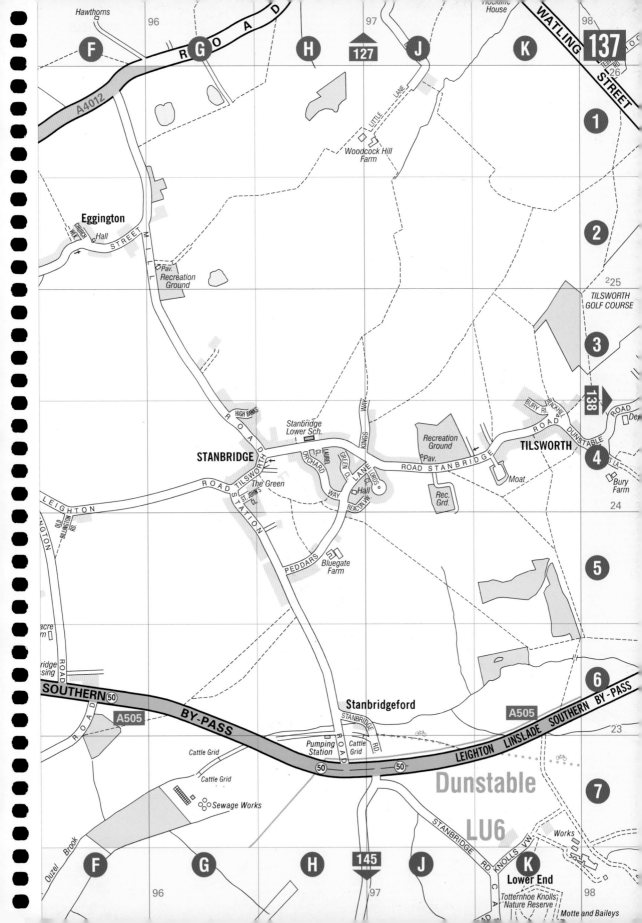

F **R G O A D** **H** 127 **J** **K** WATLING STREET

Hawthorns

96 97 98

A4012

1

Eggington

Hall

CHURCH WK STREET MILL

+

Pav.
Recreation
Ground

2

225

TILSWORTH
GOLF COURSE

3

Woodcock Hill
Farm

LITTLE LANE

HIGH BANKS

ROAD TILSWORTH

Stanbridge
Lower Sch.

KINGS WAY

BURY RD BACKHILL

138 ROAD

Dep

Recreation
Ground

Pav.

ROAD DUNSTABLE

STANBRIDGE

ORCHARD
LAUREL CL

GREEN CL LANE

ROAD STANBRIDGE

TILSWORTH

4

S LA

Bury
Farm

The Green

ST. JOHN'S CL

WAY

BEACON VW

Hall

Moat

Rec.
Grd.

24

LEIGHTON

ngton

OLD BILLINGTON RD

PEDDARS

Bluegate
Farm

5

acre
m

ridge
ssing

ROAD

6

SOUTHERN 50 **BY-PASS**

A505

Stanbridgeford

STANBRIDGE RD

Pumping
Station

Cattle
Grid

A505

LEIGHTON LINSLADE SOUTHERN BY-PASS

23

50 50

Cattle Grid

Cattle Grid

Sewage Works

Dunstable

LU6

7

STANBRIDGE RD KNOLLS VW

Works

F **G** **H** 145 **J** **K**

Lower End

Ouzel Brook

96 97 98

Totternhoe Knolls
Nature Reserve

Motte and Baileys

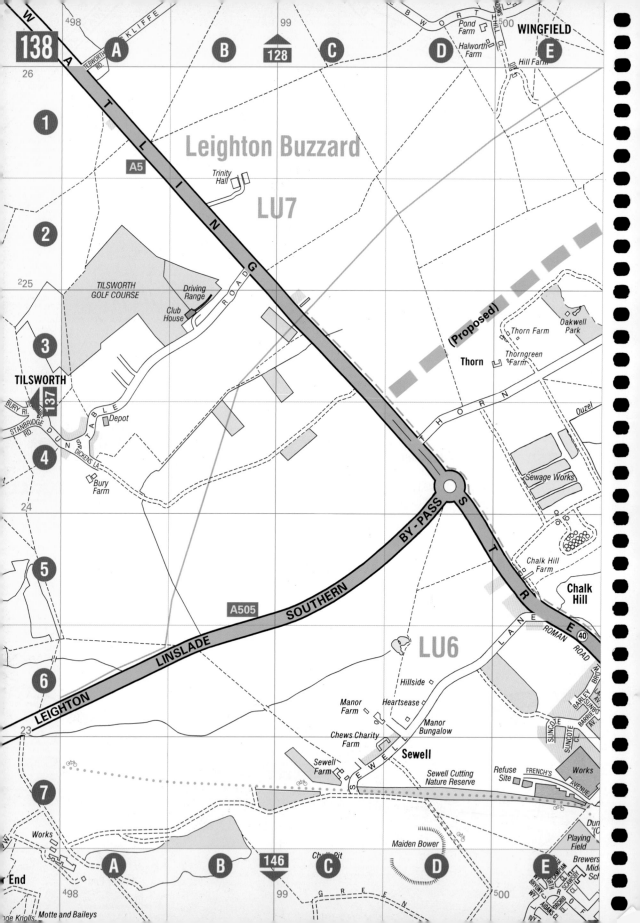

138

W A TERWORTH RD.

A SKLIFFE

26

498

99

B

128

C

D

WORTH

Pond Farm

Halworth Farm

500

WINGFIELD

Hill Farm

E

1

Leighton Buzzard

LU7

A5

Trinity Hall

2

225

TILSWORTH GOLF COURSE

Driving Range

Club House

(Proposed)

Thorn Farm

Oakwell Park

3

TILSWORTH

137

Thorn

Thorngreen Farm

Ouzel

BURY RD.
STANBRIDGE RD.

DUNSTABLE

DICKENS LA.

Depot

THORN

Sewage Works

4

Bury Farm

24

Chalk Hill Farm

5

Chalk Hill

A505

SOUTHERN

BY-PASS

LU6

ROMAN ROAD

40

LINSLADE

Hillside

Heartsease

SEWELL LANE

SUNCOTE CL.

6

LEIGHTON

23

Manor Farm

Chews Charity Farm

Manor Bungalow

Sewell

FRENCH'S AVENUE

Works

7

Works

Sewell Farm

Sewell Cutting Nature Reserve

Refuse Site

Maiden Bower

Playing Field

Brewers

End

498

A

B

146

99

C

GREEN

Chalk Pit

D

500

E

Motte and Baileys

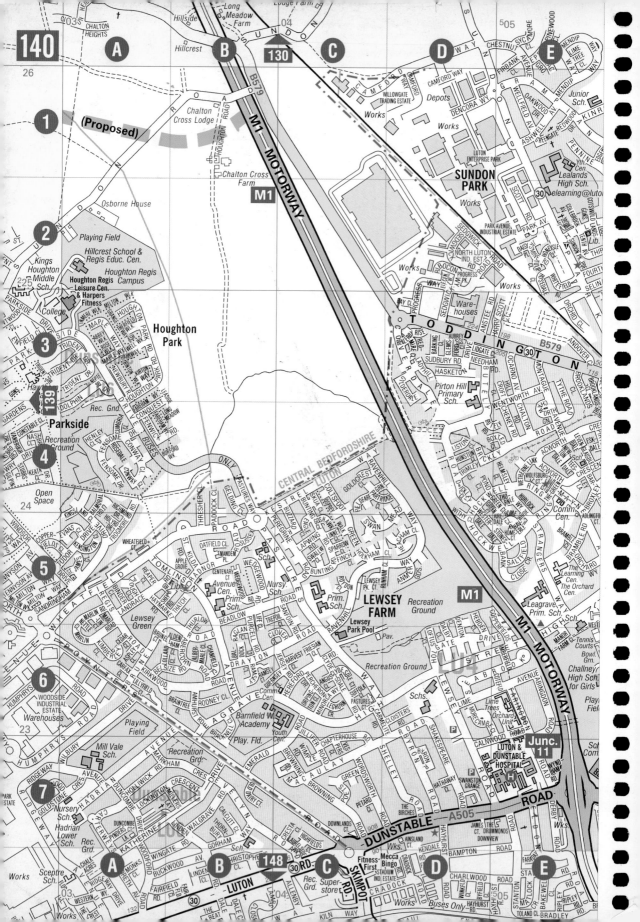

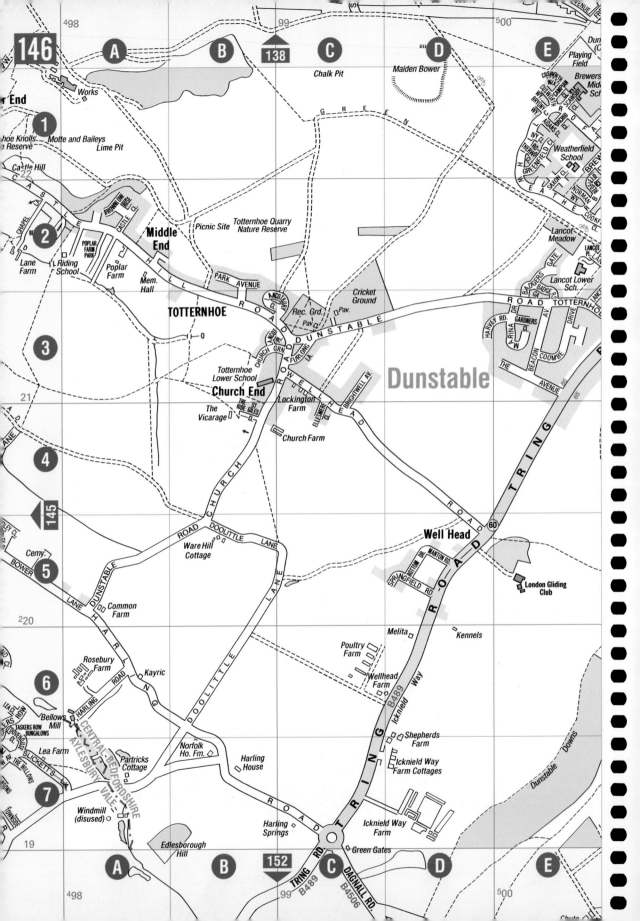

146

498   99   500

A   B   138   C   Maiden Bower   D   E   Playing Field

r End   Works   Chalk Pit   Dun (C

Brewers Mid Sch

CUSWORTH WLK
AIDANS CL   Weatherfield School

1   hoe Knolls e Reserve   Motte and Baileys   Lime Pit

Castle Hill   22

CHAPEL   2   Lane Farm   Riding School   POPLAR FARM PARK   BROWNLOW RISE   CASTLE HILL ROAD   Poplar Farm   Picnic Site   Totternhoe Quarry Nature Reserve   Lancot Meadow   LANCOT PL

Middle End   Mem. Hall   PARK AVENUE   Cricket Ground   Lancot Lower Sch.   BADGERS GATE

3   TOTTERNHOE   LANCOT   Rec. Grd.   Pav.   ROAD   TOTTERNHO   HARTLEY RD.   GARDNERS   DRIVE   THE BEACON   COOMBE   AVENUE

21   Totternhoe Lower School   CHURCH GRN   Pav.   DUNSTABLE   Dunstable

Church End   ST. GILES   Lockington Farm   BRIGHTWELL AV.   ELLESMERE CL   ROWELL   LEAD

The Vicarage   THE RIDE   Church Farm

4   ROAD   CHURCH

145   ROAD   Well Head   60

5   Cemy.   DUNSTABLE   ROAD   DOOLITTLE   LANE   Ware Hill Cottage   London Gliding Club

BOWER   LANE   HARLING   Common Farm   SPRINGFIELD RD   MANTON RD.   NOTTOM DR.   ROAD

220   Melita   Kennels

6   Rosebury Farm   Kayric   Poultry Farm   Wellhead Farm   B489   Icknield Way

Bellows Mill   HARLING ROAD   Shepherds Farm

TASKERS ROW   CENTRAL   BEDFORDSHIRE   Norfolk Ho. Fm.   Harling House   Icknield Way Farm Cottages   Dunstable Downs

Lea Farm   SLICKETT'S LA.   DOOLITTLE   ROAD   TRING

7   THE WILLOWS   AYLESBURY VALE   Partricks Cottage   Icknield Way Farm

Windmill (disused)   Harling Springs   Green Gates

19   Edlesborough Hill

A   B   152   C   D   E
TRING RD.
498   99   B489   DAGNALL RD.   500
B4506

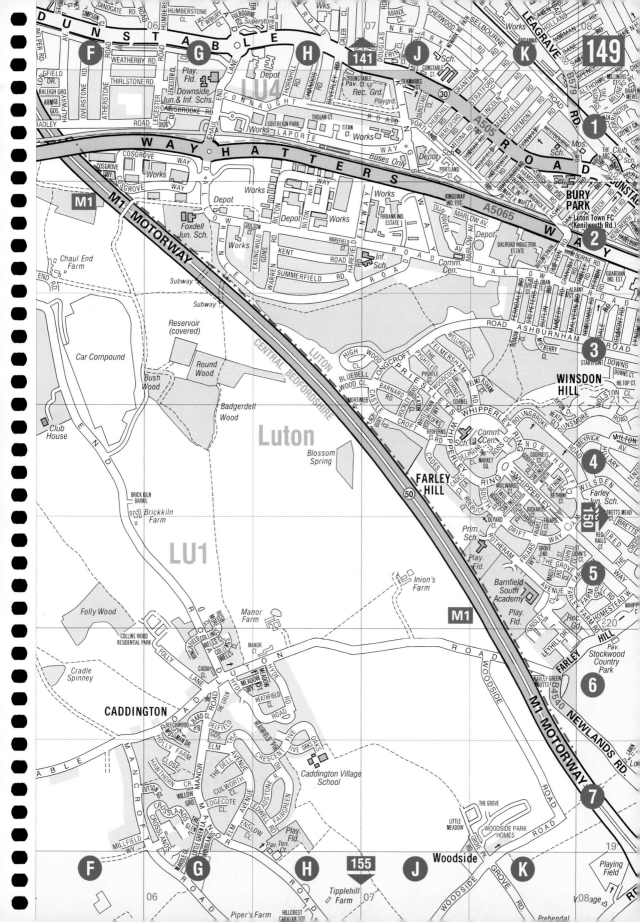

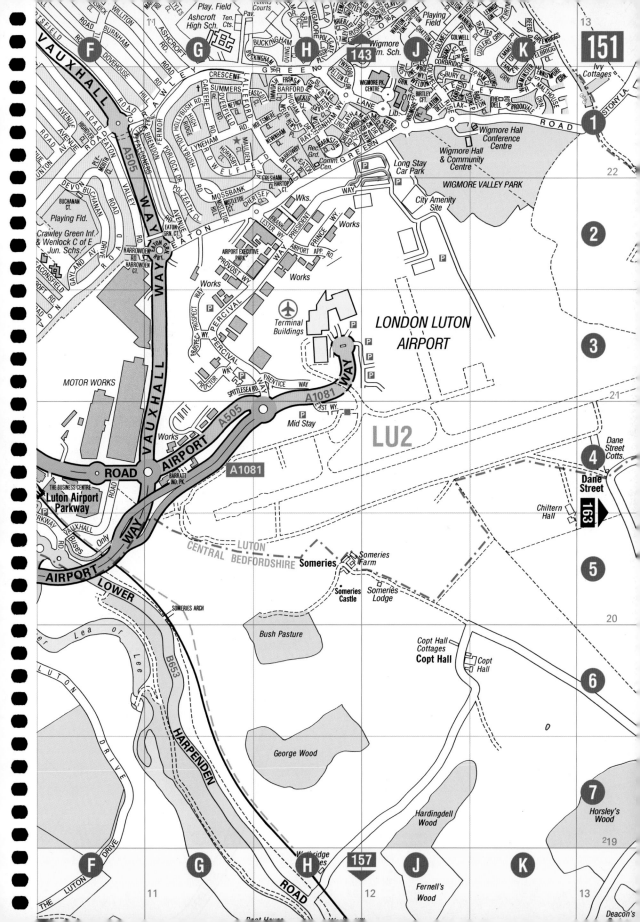

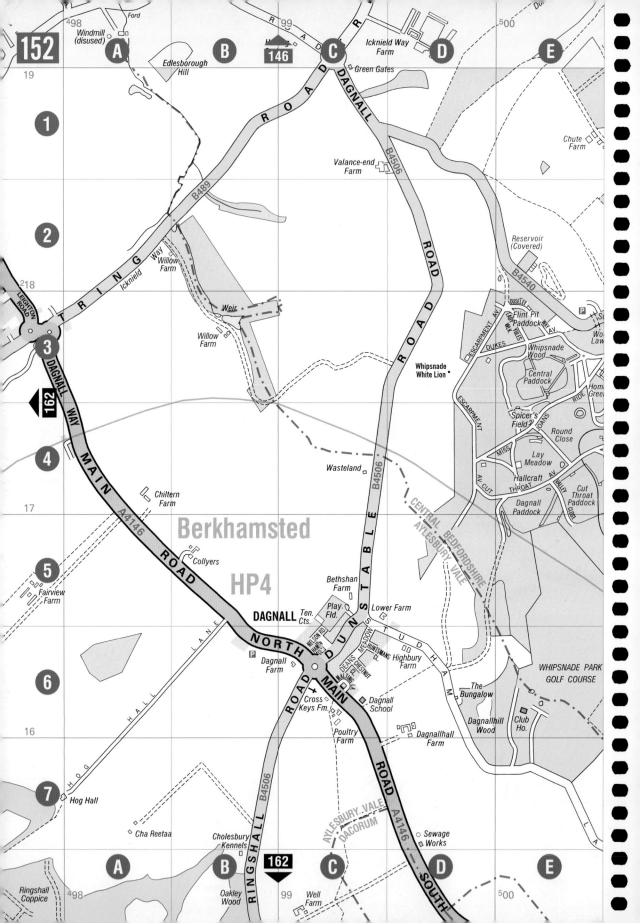

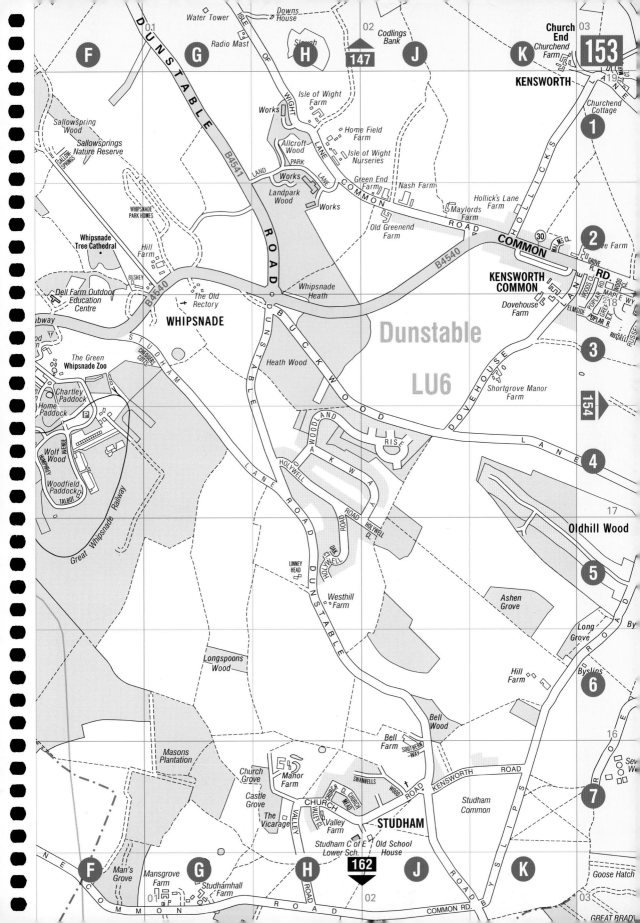

F | G | H | J | K

01 | 02 | 03

DUNSTABLE

Water Tower
Downs House
ISLE OF WIGHT LANE
Radio Mast
Slough
Codlings Bank

Church End
Churchend Farm
Churchend Cottage
KENSWORTH

Works
Isle of Wight Farm
Home Field Farm
Isle of Wight Nurseries

1

Sallowspring Wood
Sallowsprings Nature Reserve
SALLOW SPRINGS
B4541
LAND LANE
Allcroft Wood
PARK
Works
Green End Farm
Nash Farm
Hollick's Lane Farm
Maylords Farm
HOLLICK'S LANE

Whipsnade Park Homes
Landpark Wood
Works
Works
Old Greenend Farm
COMMON ROAD
COMMON
30
KENSWORTH COMMON
MALMS CL.
GROVE PL.
WOODS CL.
POPLAR R.
ELMSIDE
RUSSELL
MAPLE WY
WOOD
18
219
MARKYATE

2
ve Farm

Whipsnade Tree Cathedral
Hill Farm
BUSHEY
B4540
ROAD
The Old Rectory
Whipsnade Heath
Dovehouse Farm
DOVEHOUSE
RD.

Dell Farm Outdoor Education Centre
WHIPSNADE
Whipsnade Heath

Dunstable
LU6
Shortgrove Manor Farm
LANE

3

ailway
STUDHAM
CHECKERS COTTS.
BUCKWOOD
Heath Wood
RISE
154

4

The Green
Whipsnade Zoo
Chartley Paddock
Home Paddock
P
Wolf Wood
HUMPHREY AVENUE
Woodfield Paddock
TALBOT
Great Whipsnade Railway

WOODLAND
BUCKWAY
HOLYWELL ROAD
OAK ROAD
HOLYWELL CL.
Oldhill Wood
17

5

LANE ROAD DUNSTABLE
Linney Head
Westhill Farm
Ashen Grove
Long Grove
Byslins

6

Longspoons Wood
Hill Farm

16

Masons Plantation
Bell Wood
Bell Farm
SOUTHERN WAY
KENSWORTH ROAD
Studham Common

7

NE COMMON
Church Grove
Manor Farm
SWANWELLS
CHURCH CL.
CHURCH MEAD
Castle Grove
The Vicarage
VALLEY CL.
CHURCH
VALLEY
Valley Farm
STUDHAM
WOOD ROAD
BYSLIPS ROAD

Man's Grove
Mansgrove Farm
Studhamhall Farm
Studham C of E Lower Sch.
Old School House
Goose Hatch
Sev W

F | G | H | J | K

147
162

01 | COMMON | 02 | COMMON RD. | 03
ROAD
GREAT BRADL

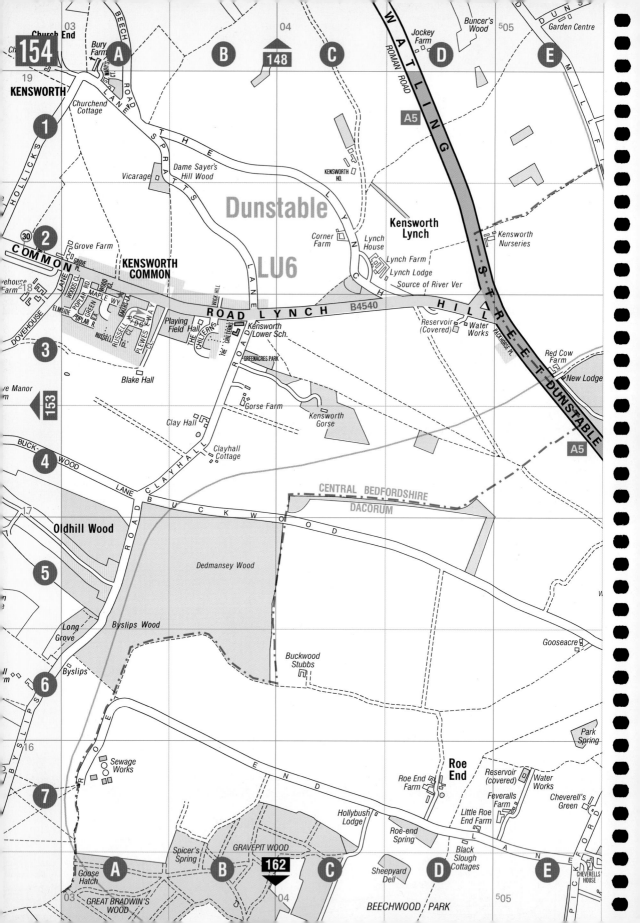

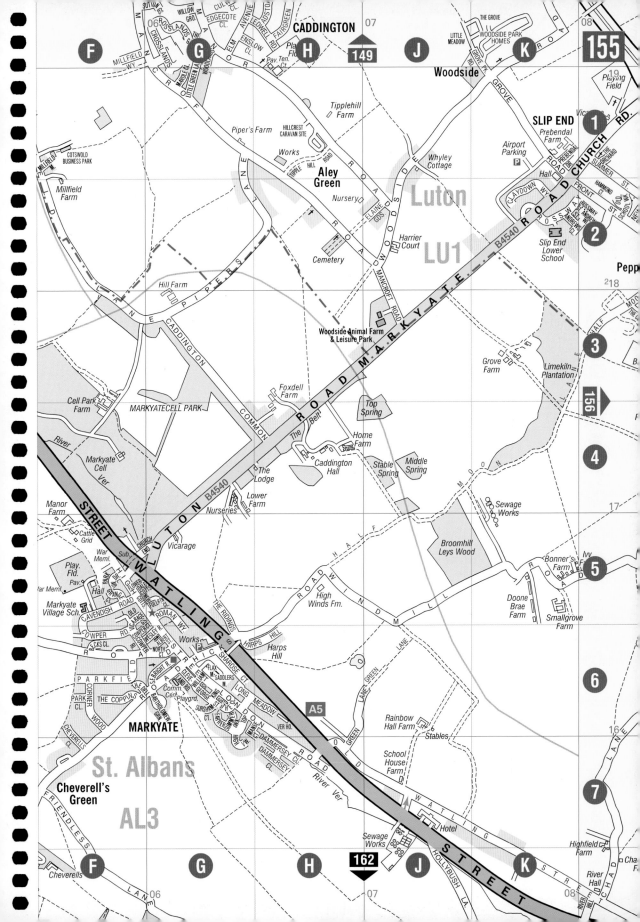

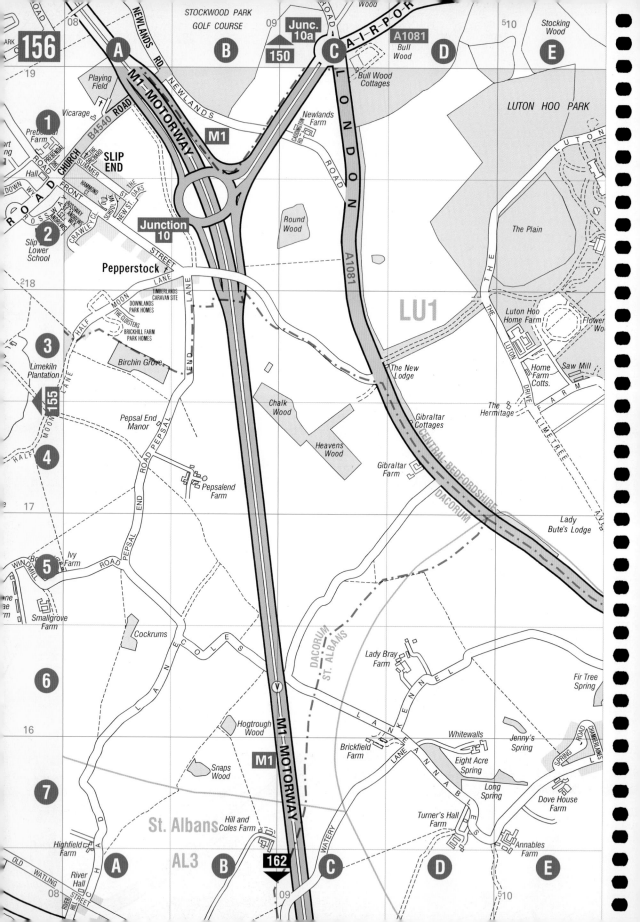

156

STOCKWOOD PARK
GOLF COURSE

Junc. 10a

150

A1081
Bull
Wood

Stocking
Wood

08

09

510

19

Playing
Field

Vicarage

LUTON HOO PARK

1

Prebendal
Farm

Hall

Bull Wood
Cottages

Newlands
Farm

M1

**SLIP
END**

The Plain

2

Slip
Lower
School

**Junction
10**

Pepperstock

Round
Wood

LU1

Luton Hoo
Home Farm

Saw Mill

The New
Lodge

The
Hermitage

Home
Farm
Cotts.

Flower
Wood

218

TIMBERLANDS
CARAVAN SITE

DOWNLANDS
PARK HOMES

THE CLOISTERS

BRICKHILL FARM
PARK HOMES

3

Limekiln
Plantation

Birchin Grove

155

Pepsal End
Manor

Chalk
Wood

Gibraltar
Cottages

4

Pepsalend
Farm

Heavens
Wood

Gibraltar
Farm

17

Lady
Bute's Lodge

5

Ivy
Farm

Bottom

WINDMILL

Smallgrove
Farm

Cockrums

DACORUM
ST. ALBANS

Lady Bray
Farm

Fir Tree
Spring

6

16

Hogtrough
Wood

Brickfield
Farm

Whitewalls

Jenny's
Spring

Eight Acre
Spring

M1 - MOTORWAY

7

Snaps
Wood

Long
Spring

Dove House
Farm

Turner's Hall
Farm

Annables
Farm

Highfield
Farm

St. Albans

Hill and
Coles Farm

AL3

162

River
Hall

OLD WATLING

08

09

510

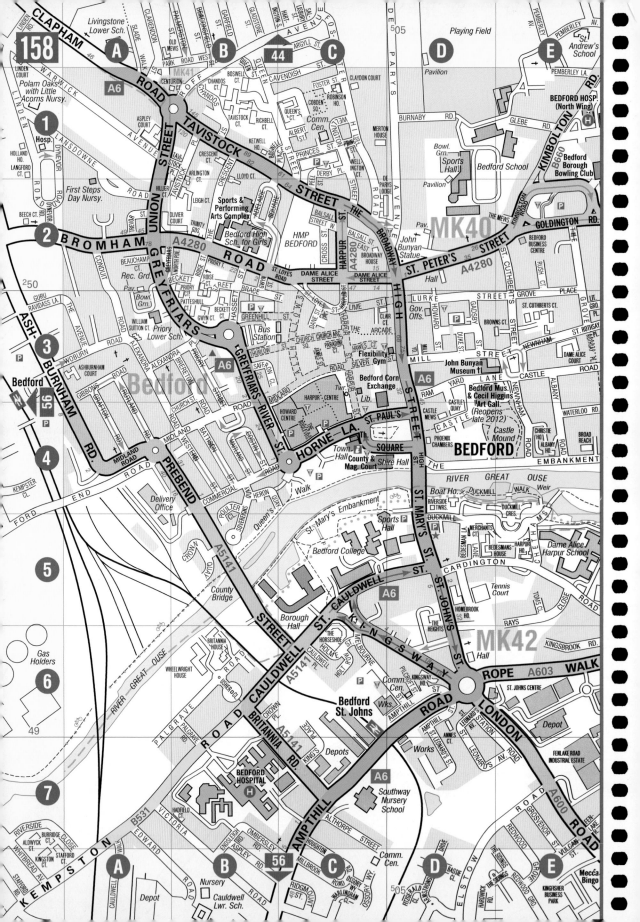

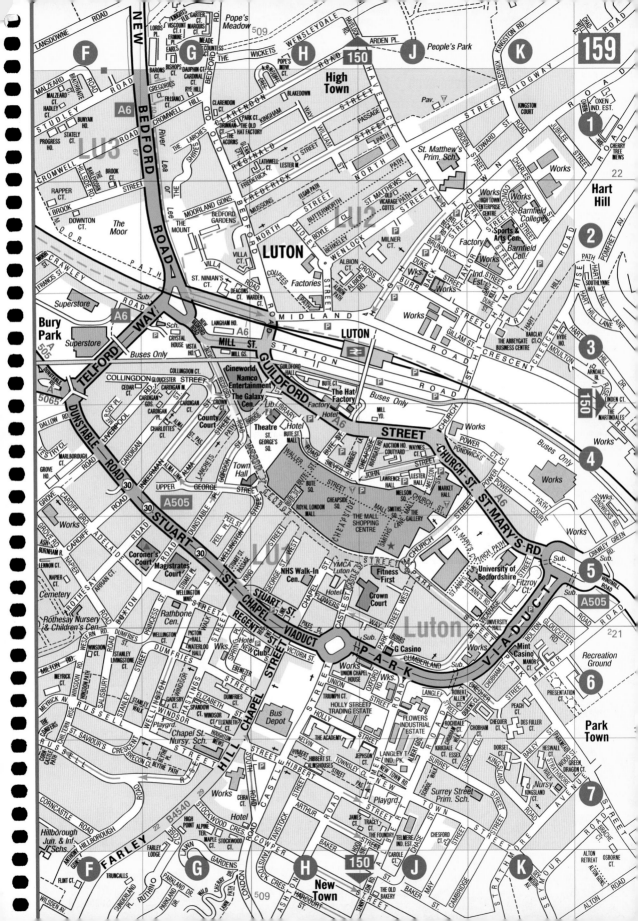

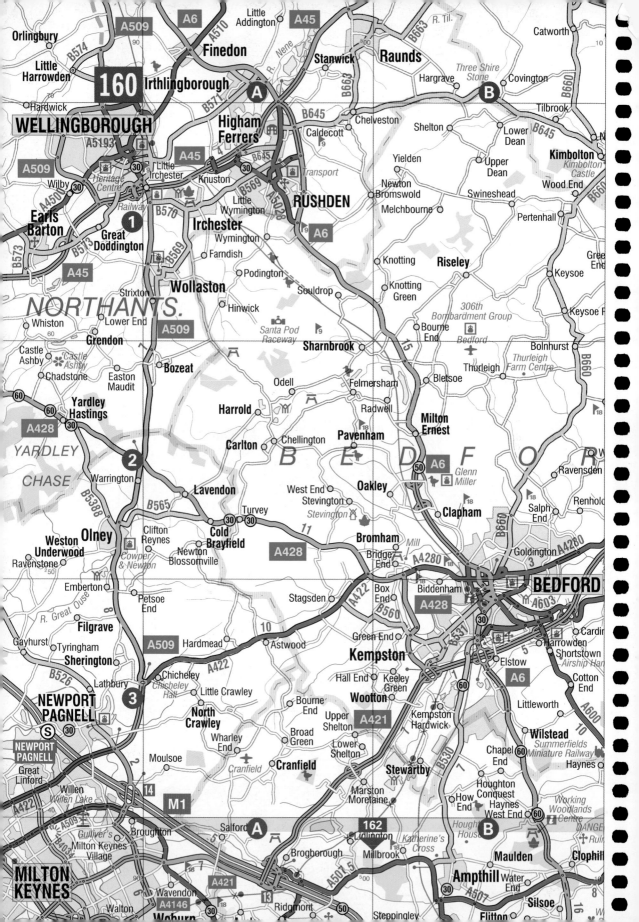

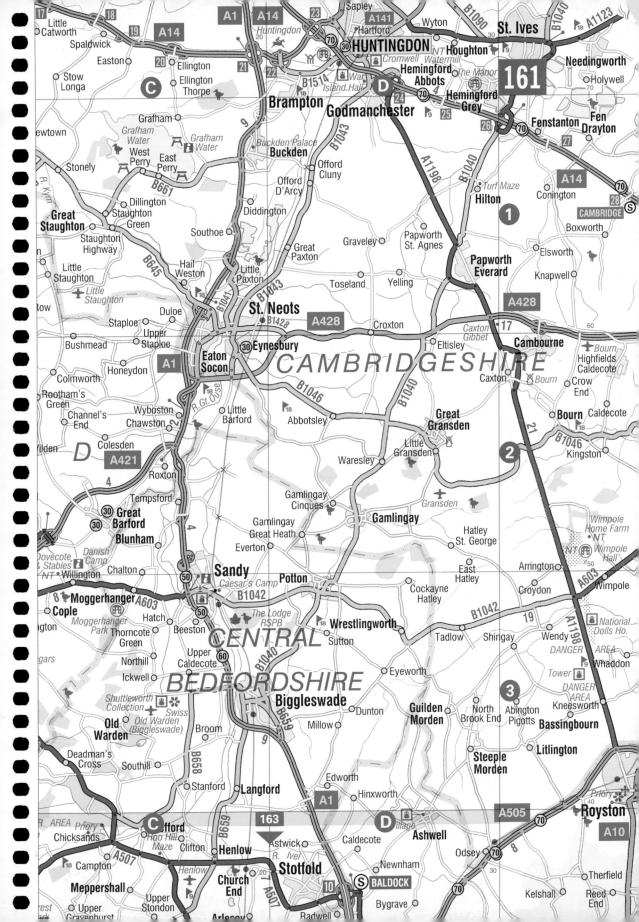

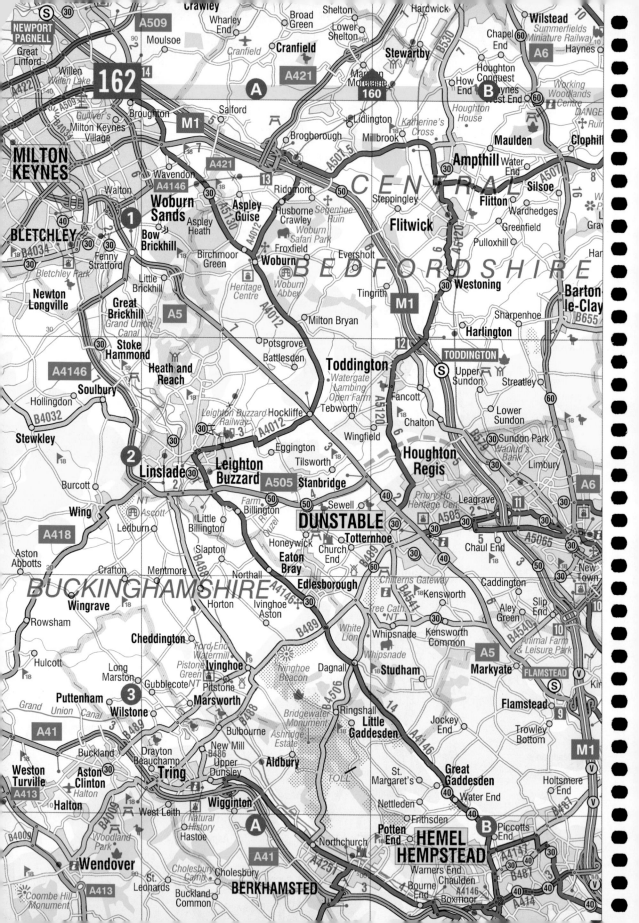

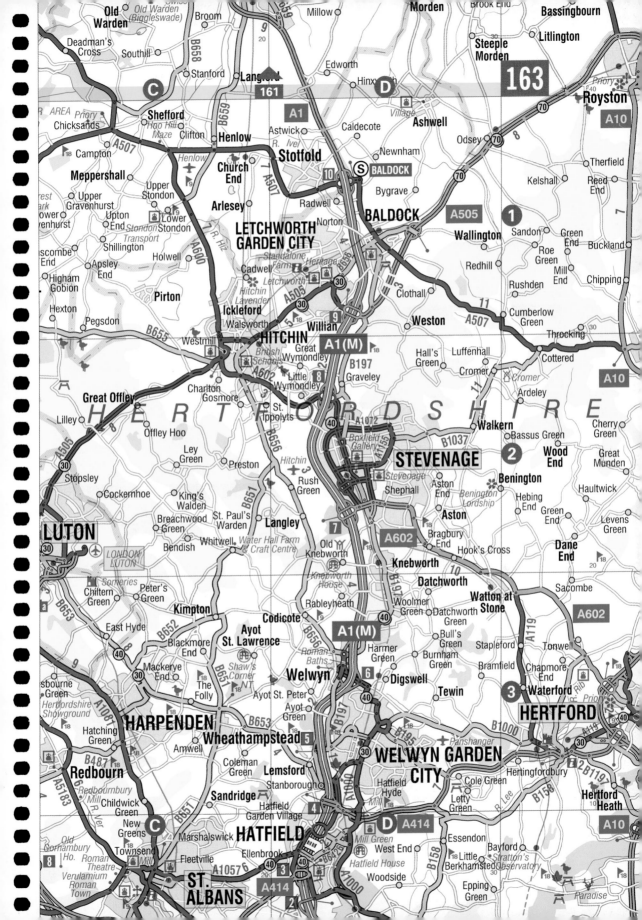

INDEX

Including Streets, Places & Areas, Industrial Estates,
Selected Flats & Walkways, Service Areas, Stations and Selected Places of Interest.

HOW TO USE THIS INDEX

1. Each street name is followed by its Postcode District, then by its Locality abbreviation(s) and then by its map reference;
   e.g. **Abbots Wood Rd.** LU2: Lut . . . .1E **150** is in the LU2 Postcode District and the Luton Locality and is to be found in square 1E on page **150**. The page number is shown in bold type.

2. A strict alphabetical order is followed in which Av., Rd., St., etc. (though abbreviated) are read in full and as part of the street name;
   e.g. **Blue Bells** appears after **Bluebell Dr.** but before **Bluebell Wood Cl.**

3. Streets and a selection of flats and walkways that cannot be shown on street map pages **4-159**, appear in the index with the thoroughfare to which they are connected shown in brackets; e.g. **Abbots Wlk.** SG18: Bigg . . . . 5C **76** (off High St.)

4. Addresses that are in more than one part are referred to as not continuous.

5. Places and areas are shown in the index in BLUE TYPE and the map reference is to the actual map square in which the town centre or area is located and not to the place name shown on the map. Map references for entries that appear on street map pages **4-159** are shown first, with references to road map pages **160-163** shown in brackets;
   e.g. AMPTHILL 5A 96 (1B 162)

6. An example of a selected place of interest is Stondon Transport Mus. 3F 113

7. An example of a station is Arlesey Station (Rail) . . . . 5C 102, also included is Park & Ride.
   e.g. Elstow (Park & Ride) 7C 56

8. Service Areas are shown in the index in BOLD CAPITAL TYPE; e.g. TODDINGTON SERVICE AREA 2A 130

9. Map references for entries that appear on large scale pages **158** & **159** are shown first, with small scale map references shown in brackets;
   e.g. Adelaide Sq. MK40: Bed 2B **158** (1D **56**)

GENERAL ABBREVIATIONS

All. : Alley	**Cft.** : Croft	**La.** : Lane	**Shop.** : Shopping
App. : Approach	**Dr.** : Drive	**Lit.** : Little	**Sth.** : South
Arc. : Arcade	**E.** : East	**Lwr.** : Lower	**Sq.** : Square
Av. : Avenue	**Ent.** : Enterprise	**Mnr.** : Manor	**St.** : Street
Blvd. : Boulevard	**Est.** : Estate	**Mdw.** : Meadow	**Ter.** : Terrace
Bri. : Bridge	**Fld.** : Field	**Mdws.** : Meadows	**Twr.** : Tower
Bungs. : Bungalows	**Flds.** : Fields	**M.** : Mews	**Trad.** : Trading
Bus. : Business	**Gdn.** : Garden	**Mt.** : Mount	**Up.** : Upper
C'way. : Causeway	**Gdns.** : Gardens	**Mus.** : Museum	**Va.** : Vale
Cen. : Centre	**Ga.** : Gate	**Nth.** : North	**Vw.** : View
Chu. : Church	**Grn.** : Green	**Pde.** : Parade	**Vs.** : Villas
Cl. : Close	**Gro.** : Grove	**Pk.** : Park	**Vis.** : Visitors
Comn. : Common	**Hgts.** : Heights	**Pas.** : Passage	**Wlk.** : Walk
Cnr. : Corner	**Ho.** : House	**Pl.** : Place	**W.** : West
Cott. : Cottage	**Ho's.** : Houses	**Res.** : Residential	**Yd.** : Yard
Cotts. : Cottages	**Ind.** : Industrial	**Ri.** : Rise	
Ct. : Court	**Info.** : Information	**Rd.** : Road	
Cres. : Crescent		**Rdbt.** : Roundabout	

LOCALITY ABBREVIATIONS

Abbot : **Abbotsley**	Cople : **Cople**	Hen : **Henlow**	Mogg : **Moggerhanger**
Aley G : **Aley Green**	C End : **Cotton End**	Hex : **Hexton**	N'all : **Northall**
Amp : **Ampthill**	Cov : **Covington**	High G : **Higham Gobion**	Nth C : **North Crawley**
Arl : **Arlesey**	Cran : **Cranfield**	Hin : **Hinwick**	North : **Northill**
Ash : **Ashwell**	Dag : **Dagnall**	Hinx : **Hinxworth**	Nort : **Norton**
Asp G : **Aspley Guise**	Duloe : **Duloe**	Hitc : **Hitchin**	Oak : **Oakley**
Asp H : **Aspley Heath**	Duns : **Dunstable**	Hock : **Hockliffe**	Odell : **Odell**
Astw : **Astwick**	Dunt : **Dunton**	Holme : **Holme**	Old W : **Old Warden**
Ast : **Astwood**	E Hat : **East Hatley**	Hol : **Holwell**	Pave : **Pavenham**
Bar C : **Barton-le-Clay**	E Hyde : **East Hyde**	Honey : **Honeydon**	Peg : **Pegsdon**
Batt : **Battlesden**	Eat B : **Eaton Bray**	Hou C : **Houghton Conquest**	Pep : **Pepperstock**
Bead : **Beadlow**	Eat F : **Eaton Ford**	Hou R : **Houghton Regis**	Per : **Pertenhall**
Bed : **Bedford**	Eat S : **Eaton Socon**	Hulc : **Hulcote**	Pirt : **Pirton**
Bee : **Beeston**	Edles : **Edlesborough**	Hus C : **Husborne Crawley**	Pod : **Podington**
Bidd : **Biddenham**	Edw : **Edworth**	Ickle : **Ickleford**	Pott : **Potton**
Bid : **Bidwell**	Egg : **Eggington**	Ickw : **Ickwell**	Pull : **Pulloxhill**
Bigg : **Biggleswade**	Els : **Elstow**	Kemp : **Kempston**	Rad : **Radwell**
Bill : **Billington**	Ever : **Eversholt**	Kemp H : **Kempston Hardwick**	Rav : **Ravensden**
Blet : **Bletsoe**	Eve : **Everton**	Kens : **Kensworth**	Ren : **Renhold**
Blun : **Blunham**	Eye : **Eyeworth**	Keysoe : **Keysoe**	Ridg : **Ridgmont**
Boln : **Bolnhurst**	Eynes : **Eynesbury**	Kimb : **Kimbolton**	Ring : **Ringshall**
B End : **Bourne End**	Eynes H : **Eynesbury Hardwicke**	Knot : **Knotting**	Rise : **Riseley**
Boz : **Bozeat**	Felm : **Felmersham**	Lang : **Langford**	Rox : **Roxton**
Brag : **Bragenham**	Flam : **Flamstead**	Laven : **Lavendon**	Rush : **Rushden**
Brog : **Brogborough**	Flitt : **Flitton**	Led : **Ledburn**	St N : **St Neots**
Brom : **Bromham**	Flitw : **Flitwick**	Lei Buz : **Leighton Buzzard**	Salf : **Salford**
Broom : **Broom**	Gam : **Gamlingay**	Let C : **Letchworth Garden City**	Sandy : **Sandy**
Bur : **Burcott**	Grav : **Gravenhurst**	Lidl : **Lidlington**	Sew : **Sewell**
Cad : **Caddington**	Gt Bar : **Great Barford**	Lill : **Lilley**	Sharn : **Sharnbrook**
Cald : **Caldecote**	Gt Bri : **Great Brickhill**	Lit Bar : **Little Barford**	Shar : **Sharpenhoe**
Camp : **Campton**	Gt O : **Great Offley**	Lit Bil : **Little Billington**	Shef : **Shefford**
Card : **Cardington**	Gt S : **Great Staughton**	Lit S : **Little Staughton**	Shill : **Shillington**
Carlt : **Carlton**	G'fld : **Greenfield**	Lwr C : **Lower Caldecote**	Short : **Shortstown**
Chalg : **Chalgrave**	Guil M : **Guilden Morden**	Lwr D : **Lower Dean**	Sils : **Silsoe**
Chalt : **Chalton**	Hail W : **Hail Weston**	Lwr Sto : **Lower Stondon**	Slapt : **Slapton**
Chaw : **Chawston**	Hard : **Hardmead**	Lwr Sun : **Lower Sundon**	Slip E : **Slip End**
Chich : **Chicheley**	Harg : **Hargrave**	Lut : **Luton**	Soulb : **Soulbury**
Chic : **Chicksands**	Harl : **Harlington**	Mark : **Markyate**	Sould : **Souldrop**
Clap : **Clapham**	Harp : **Harpenden**	Mars M : **Marston Moretaine**	S'hill : **Southill**
Clif : **Clifton**	Harr : **Harrold**	Maul : **Maulden**	Stag : **Stagsden**
Clop : **Clophill**	Harrow : **Harrowden**	Melch : **Melchbourne**	Stanb : **Stanbridge**
C Hat : **Cockayne Hatley**	Hat : **Hatch**	Mep : **Meppershall**	Stan : **Stanford**
C'hoe : **Cockernhoe**	H Geor : **Hatley St George**	Millb : **Millbrook**	Stap : **Staploe**
Cold B : **Cold Brayfield**	Hay : **Haynes**	Mil B : **Milton Bryan**	Step : **Steppingley**
Colm : **Colmworth**	Heat R : **Heath and Reach**	Mil E : **Milton Ernest**	Stev : **Stevington**

306th Bombardment Group Mus.—Ascott House & Gardens

Stew : Stewartby
Sto H : Stoke Hammond
Stone : Stonely
Stot : Stotfold
Stre : Streatley
Stud : Studham
Sutt : Sutton
Swin : Swineshead
Tad : Tadlow
Tea G : Tea Green
Teb : Tebworth
Temp : Tempsford
Tet : Tetworth
Thor : Thorn
Thur : Thurleigh
Tilb : Tilbrook
Tils : Tilsworth
Ting : Tingrith
Todd : Toddington
Tott : Totternhoe
Turv : Turvey
Up C : Upper Caldecote
Up D : Upper Dean
Up Sto : Upper Stondon
Up Sun : Upper Sundon
Wan E : Wandon End
Wave : Wavendon
West : Westoning
Whar E : Wharley End
Whip : Whipsnade
Wild : Wilden
Will : Willington
Wils : Wilstead
Wing : Wing
Wingf : Wingfield
Wob : Woburn
Wob S : Woburn Sands
Wood : Woodside
Woo : Wootton
Wrest : Wrestlingworth
Wybo : Wyboston
Wym : Wymington
Yeld : Yelden

306th Bombardment Group Mus. . . . 1B 22

A

Abbey Cl. MK41: Ren . . . 2K 45
MK42: Els . . . 7D 56
MK45: Amp . . . 6B 96
Abbey Dr. LU2: Lut . . . 1E 150
Abbey Flds. MK42: Bed, Els . . . 7D 56
Abbeygate Bus. Cen., The
LU2: Lut . . . 3K 159
Abbey Gro. SG19: Sandy . . . 2J 61
Abbey La. MK45: Amp . . . 6B 96
Abbey M. LU6: Duns . . . 4J 147
Abbey Rd. MK41: Bed . . . 7J 45
Abbey Sq. MK43: Turv . . . 4C 40
Abbey Wlk. LU5: Hou R . . . 3A 140
LU7: Heat R . . . 3J 125
Abbey Way NN10: Rush . . . 1A 10
Abbis Cl. MK45: Flitw . . . 3K 107
Abbots Ct. LU2: Lut . . . 1E 150
ABBOTSLEY . . . 3K 39 (2D 161)
Abbotsley & Cromwell Golf Courses . . . 2F 39
Abbotsley Country Homes
PE19: Eynes H . . . 2E 38
Abbots Wlk. *SG18: Bigg* . . . *5C 76*
(off High St.)
Abbots Wood Pde. LU2: Lut . . . 1E 150
Abbots Wood Rd. LU2: Lut . . . 1E 150
Abbott Cres. MK42: Kemp . . . 1K 69
Abercorn Rd. LU4: Lut . . . 6B 140
Abigail Cl. LU3: Lut . . . 6B 142
Abigail Ct. LU3: Lut . . . 6B 142
Abingdon Rd. LU4: Lut . . . 6E 140
ABINGTON PIGOTTS . . . 3D 161
Abrahams Cl. MK40: Bed . . . 1G 57
Acacia Cl. LU7: Lei Buz . . . 3C 136
Acacia Rd. MK42: Bed . . . 5F 57
Acacia Vs. *LU6: Duns* . . . *2H 147*
(off Icknield St.)
Academy, The LU1: Lut . . . 6H 159
Ackerman Gdns. PE19: Eat S . . . 5J 27
Ackerman St. PE19: Eat S . . . 5J 27
Acorn Cen. SG18: Bigg . . . 5C 76
Acorn Cl. LU2: Lut . . . 6D 142
MK45: Maul . . . 5K 97
Acorn Ho. *SG18: Bigg* . . . *4B 76*
(off Sun St.)
Acorn M. SG19: Pott . . . 3J 63
Acorns, The LU2: Lut . . . 1G 159
Acorn Way MK42: Bed . . . 5F 57
Acres, The SG17: Mep . . . 1B 112
Acworth Ct. *LU4: Lut* . . . *4E 140*
(off Acworth Cres.)
Acworth Cres. LU4: Lut . . . 4E 140
Adaern Cl. LU7: Lei Buz . . . 1J 135
Adams Bottom LU7: Lei Buz . . . 7J 125
Adams Cl. MK42: Kemp . . . 2A 70
MK45: Amp . . . 6B 96
Adamson Ct. *MK42: Kemp* . . . *5K 55*
(off Hillgrounds Rd.)
Adamson Wlk. *MK42: Kemp* . . . *5K 55*
(off Hillgrounds Rd.)
Adastral Av. LU7: Lei Buz . . . 3B 136
Addington Cl. MK41: Bed . . . 1J 57
SG16: Hen . . . 4K 101
Addingtons Rd. MK44: Gt Bar . . . 4A 48
Addington Wlk. PE19: Eat S . . . 5J 27
Addington Way LU4: Lut . . . 6F 141
Addison Cl. MK42: Kemp . . . 6B 56
Addison Howard Pk. . . . 5A 56
Adelaide Cl. MK45: Hou C . . . 4D 84
Adelaide Sq.
MK40: Bed . . . 2B 158 (1D 56)
Adelaide St. LU1: Lut . . . 5F 159 (3B 150)
Adlington Ct. LU4: Lut . . . 4E 140
Admiral Row MK45: Flitw . . . 1A 108
Admirals Way PE19: Eat S . . . 5G 27
Adstone Rd. LU1: Cad . . . 7H 149
Aelfric Ct. *MK41: Bed* . . . *4E 44*
(off Dearne Wlk.)
Aidans Cl. LU6: Duns . . . 1E 146
Ailesbury Rd. MK45: Amp . . . 5B 96
Ailsworth Rd. LU3: Lut . . . 3H 141
Ailwyns Acre MK43: Cran . . . 5E 80
Ainsland Ct. LU4: Lut . . . 7D 140
Airedale LU4: Lut . . . 5E 140
Airedale Cl. MK45: Flitw . . . 2K 107
Aire Wlk. MK41: Bed . . . 2E 44
Airfield Ind. Est. MK44: Lit S . . . 6J 17
(not continuous)
Airfield Rd. NN29: Hin . . . 1D 18
Airport App. Rd. LU2: Lut . . . 2H 151
Airport Executive Pk.
LU2: Lut . . . 2G 151
Airport Way LU1: Lut . . . 7C 150
(not continuous)
LU2: Lut . . . 4G 151
Alameda Rd. MK45: Amp . . . 5A 96
Alameda Sports Hall . . . 5K 95
Alameda Wlk. MK45: Amp . . . 5A 96
Alamein Av. MK42: Bed . . . 4G 57
Alamein Cl. SG17: Shef . . . 4C 100
Alamein Ct. PE19: Eat F . . . 2J 27
Albany Ct. LU1: Lut . . . 2K 149
Albany Ho. MK40: Bed . . . 4E 158
Albany Rd. LU7: Lei Buz . . . 2K 135
MK40: Bed . . . 3E 158 (2E 56)
Albermarle Cl. LU4: Lut . . . 6B 140
Albert Ct. LU6: Duns . . . 3J 147
Albert Gdns. LU1: Lut . . . 7J 159 (4C 150)
Albert Pl. MK45: Amp . . . 7A 96
MK45: Hou C . . . 4D 84
Albert Rd. LU1: Lut . . . 7J 159 (4C 150)
SG15: Arl . . . 2C 114
Albert St. AL3: Mark . . . 6G 155
MK40: Bed . . . 1C 158 (1D 56)
Albion Ct. LU2: Lut . . . 2H 159 (2C 150)
LU6: Duns . . . 2H 147
SG19: Sandy . . . 3J 61
Albion M. LU6: Duns . . . 2H 147
Albion Path LU2: Lut . . . 2H 159
(not continuous)
Albion Rd. LU2: Lut . . . 2H 159 (2C 150)
Albion St. LU6: Duns . . . 2H 147
Albone Way SG18: Bigg . . . 7B 76
Albone Way Ind. Est. SG18: Bigg . . . 7B 76
Alburgh Cl. MK42: Bed . . . 5H 57
Albury Cl. LU3: Lut . . . 7J 131
Aldbanks LU6: Duns . . . 1F 147
ALDBURY . . . 3A 162
Aldenham Cl. LU4: Lut . . . 6B 140
MK41: Bed . . . 2K 57
Aldens Mead MK41: Bed . . . 5H 45
Alder Cl. PE19: Eat F . . . 2H 27
Alder Ct. LU3: Lut . . . 6K 141
Alder Cres. LU3: Lut . . . 5J 141
Alders, The MK42: Kemp . . . 7A 56
Alderton Cl. LU2: Lut . . . 1H 151
Aldgate Cl. SG19: Pott . . . 3K 63
Aldhous Cl. LU3: Lut . . . 4K 141
Aldwyck Ct. MK42: Bed . . . 7A 158
Aldwyck Ho. LU5: Duns . . . 7G 139
Alesia Rd. LU3: Lut . . . 3G 141
Alexa Ct. MK42: Bed . . . 5J 57
Alexander Cl. MK43: Stew . . . 3J 83
SG17: Clif . . . 3G 101
Alexander Rd. SG5: Stot . . . 7H 103
SG19: Wrest . . . 6F 65
Alexander Sports Centre, The . . . 7B 44
Alexandra Av. LU3: Lut . . . 6A 142
Alexandra Cotts. *MK40: Bed* . . . *1B 158*
(off Tavistock Pl.)
Alexandra Ct. LU7: Lei Buz . . . 1H 135
Alexandra Pl.
MK40: Bed . . . 3A 158 (2C 56)
Alexandra Rd.
MK40: Bed . . . 3A 158 (2C 56)
ALEY GREEN . . . 1H 155 (3B 162)
Alfred Cope Rd. SG19: Sandy . . . 2J 61
Alfred St. LU5: Duns . . . 2J 147
Alfriston Cl. LU2: Lut . . . 6G 143
Alington Rd. PE19: Lit Bar . . . 1J 39
Allenby Av. LU5: Duns . . . 1C 148
Allen Cl. LU5: Duns . . . 2K 147
MK40: Bed . . . 3B 56
Allen Ct. MK43: Mars M . . . 3E 82
Allendale LU3: Lut . . . 7J 131
Allen Pk. . . . 3A 56
Allhallows MK40: Bed . . . 3C 158 (2D 56)
SG19: Sandy . . . 2H 61
All Saints Rd. LU5: Hou R . . . 4H 139
MK40: Bed . . . 2B 56
MK44: Cople . . . 3E 58
All Saints Way SG19: Sandy . . . 2H 61
Alma Farm Rd. LU5: Todd . . . 2E 128
Alma Link LU1: Lut . . . 4G 159 (3B 150)
(not continuous)
Alma St. LU1: Lut . . . 4G 159 (3B 150)
Alma St. Pas. LU1: Lut . . . 4G 159
Almer's Cl. MK45: Hou C . . . 4D 84
Almond Cl. LU3: Lut . . . 5K 141
(Carolyn Ct.)
LU3: Lut . . . 4J 141
(Lonsdale Cl.)
Almond Cres. MK45: Maul . . . 6K 97
Almond Rd. LU7: Lei Buz . . . 1A 136
Almonds, The MK42: Kemp . . . 7C 56
Alnwick Cl. SG19: Sandy . . . 2J 61
Alpha Ct. LU7: Lei Buz . . . 2K 135
Alpha Dr. PE19: Eat S . . . 6H 27
Alpine Ter. LU1: Lut . . . 7G 159
Alpine Way LU3: Lut . . . 1F 141
Alsop Cl. LU5: Hou R . . . 4H 139
Althorp Cl. MK45: Flitw . . . 3B 108
Althorpe St.
MK42: Bed . . . 7C 158 (4D 56)
Althorp Rd. LU3: Lut . . . 1A 150
Alton Gdns. LU1: Lut . . . 7K 159 (5D 150)
Alton Retreat LU1: Lut . . . 7K 159
Alton Rd. LU1: Lut . . . 7K 159 (5D 150)
SG16: Lwr Sto . . . 2G 113
Alwen Wlk. *MK41: Bed* . . . *4E 44*
(off Wansbeck Rd.)
Alwins Fld. LU7: Lei Buz . . . 1F 135
Alwyn Cl. LU2: Lut . . . 7C 142
Amberley Cl. LU2: Lut . . . 5H 143
Amberley Gdns. MK40: Bed . . . 7F 45
Ambleside LU3: Lut . . . 4H 141
Ambrose La. AL5: Harp . . . 7K 157
Ambuscade Rd. PE19: Eat S . . . 6J 27
Ames Cl. LU3: Lut . . . 7H 131
Amhurst Rd. LU4: Lut . . . 6B 140
Amor Way SG6: Let C . . . 7K 115
AMPTHILL . . . 5A 96 (1B 162)
Ampthill Bus. Pk. MK45: Amp . . . 6J 95
Ampthill Ind. Est. MK45: Amp . . . 6J 95
Ampthill Pk. . . . 4K 95
Ampthill Rd.
MK42: Bed, Kemp . . . 7C 158 (3B 70)
MK43: Lidl . . . 6B 94
MK45: Flitw . . . 1K 107
MK45: Kemp H . . . 6B 70
MK45: Maul . . . 4E 96
MK45: Sils . . . 7H 97
SG17: Bead, Camp, Shef . . . 4F 99
Ampthill St. MK42: Bed . . . 6D 158 (3E 56)
(not continuous)
AMWELL . . . 3C 163
Anderson Wlk. SG5: Stot . . . 4E 114
Andover Cl. LU4: Lut . . . 3E 140
Andrew Rd. PE19: Eynes . . . 1K 39
Andrews Cl. LU7: Soulb . . . 5A 124
MK45: Maul . . . 4E 96
Angel Cl. LU4: Lut . . . 6F 141
Angelica Av. SG5: Stot . . . 1H 115
Angels La. LU5: Hou R . . . 4H 139
Angel Vw. MK42: Bed . . . 4E 56
Angus Cl. LU4: Lut . . . 6C 140
Anmer Gdns. LU4: Lut . . . 5D 140
Annables La. AL5: Harp . . . 7D 156
Annes Ct. MK42: Bed . . . 6D 158
Anne St. SG18: Bigg . . . 4C 76
Anson Pl. PE19: Eat S . . . 5G 27
Anstee Rd. LU4: Lut . . . 3D 140
Anthony Gdns.
LU1: Lut . . . 7F 159 (5B 150)
Anvil Ct. LU3: Lut . . . 4G 141
Apex Bus. Cen. LU5: Duns . . . 7J 139
Apollo Cl. LU5: Duns . . . 3K 147
Apollo Gdns. SG18: Bigg . . . 5F 77
Appenine Way LU7: Lei Buz . . . 1B 136
Appleacres MK17: Sto H . . . 1A 124
Appleby Gdns. LU6: Duns . . . 3H 147
Applecroft SG16: Lwr Sto . . . 3H 113
Applecroft Rd. LU2: Lut . . . 5G 143
Applecross Wlk. MK41: Bed . . . 6K 45
Appledore Rd. MK40: Bed . . . 1F 57
Apple Glebe MK45: Bar C . . . 5A 122
Apple Gro. LU4: Lut . . . 5B 140
PE19: Eat F . . . 3J 27
Apple Tree Cl. LU7: Lei Buz . . . 3F 135
MK45: Sils . . . 1A 110
SG18: Bigg . . . 6D 76
Applewood Cl. AL5: Harp . . . 7J 157
Appley Ct. MK45: Hay . . . 5F 87
Appley Wood Cnr. MK45: Hay . . . 5F 87
APSLEY END . . . 7J 111 (1C 163)
Apsley End Rd. SG5: Shill . . . 2H 123
Apsley Guise & Woburn Sands
Golf Course . . . 2B 104
Aquila Rd. LU7: Lei Buz . . . 1B 136
Aragon Pk. LU5: Hou R . . . 6H 139
Aragon Rd. MK45: Amp . . . 6B 96
Arbour Cl. LU3: Lut . . . 7J 131
Arbroath Rd. LU3: Lut . . . 7F 131
Arcade, The LU4: Lut . . . 1A 150
MK40: Bed . . . 3C 158 (2D 56)
SG6: Let C . . . 7H 115
Archers Way SG6: Let C . . . 7F 115
Arches, The SG6: Let C . . . 7J 115
Archway Pde. LU3: Lut . . . 5H 141
Archway Rd. LU3: Lut . . . 5G 141
Arc Progress MK43: Lidl . . . 7C 94
ARDELEY . . . 2D 163
Arden Pl. LU2: Lut . . . 1J 159 (1C 150)
Arden Press Way SG6: Let C . . . 7K 115
Arden Press Way Ind. Est.
SG6: Let C . . . 7K 115
Arden Wlk. MK41: Bed . . . 6K 45
Ardleigh Grn. LU2: Lut . . . 1H 151
Ardley Cl. LU6: Duns . . . 5J 147
Arenson Way LU5: Duns . . . 7H 139
Argyll Av. LU3: Lut . . . 7A 142
Argyll St. MK40: Bed . . . 1C 158 (7D 44)
Arianne Bus. Cen. LU5: Hou R . . . 6H 139
Aries Ct. LU7: Lei Buz . . . 1A 136
Arkwright Rd. MK42: Bed . . . 5J 57
MK44: Mil E . . . 3H 31
Arkwright Rd. Ind. Est.
MK42: Bed . . . 5J 57
ARLESEY . . . 2C 114 (1C 163)
Arlesey Ho. *SG15: Arl* . . . *5C 102*
(off Church End)
Arlesey Old Moat Nature Reserve . . . 6B 102
Arlesey Rd. SG5: Stot . . . 6F 103
SG6: Let C . . . 7B 114
SG15: Arl . . . 7B 114
SG16: Hen . . . 5K 101
(not continuous)
Arlesey Station (Rail) . . . 5C 102
Arlesey-Stotfold By-Pass
SG5: Stot . . . 2G 115
SG15: Arl . . . 5C 102
Arlington Ct. MK40: Bed . . . 1B 158
Armitage Gdns. LU4: Lut . . . 1F 149
Armstrong Cl. MK45: Wils . . . 1H 85
Armstrong Dr.
MK42: Bed . . . 7D 158 (4E 56)
Arnald Way LU5: Hou R . . . 5G 139
Arncliffe Cres.
LU2: Lut . . . 1H 159 (1C 150)
Arndale Ri. LU2: Lut . . . 3K 159
Arnhem Cl. PE19: Eat F . . . 2J 27
Arnhem Pl. SG17: Shef . . . 3C 100
Arnold Cl. LU2: Lut . . . 6E 142
MK45: Bar C . . . 5A 122
Arran Cl. SG19: Sandy . . . 2H 61
Arran Ct. LU1: Lut . . . 5F 159 (3B 150)
ARRINGTON . . . 2D 161
Arrow Cl. LU3: Lut . . . 3G 141
Arrow Leys MK41: Bed . . . 5H 45
Arthur St. LU1: Lut . . . 7H 159 (4C 150)
MK45: Amp . . . 5A 96
Arun Cl. MK41: Bed . . . 4F 45
Arundel Cl. MK45: Flitw . . . 5K 107
Arundel Ct. NN10: Rush . . . 1A 10
Arundel Cres. PE19: Eynes . . . 1J 39
Arundel Dr. MK41: Bed . . . 5J 45
Arundel Rd. LU4: Lut . . . 6J 141
MK43: Mars M . . . 4C 82
Ascot Dr. LU7: Lei Buz . . . 3F 135
SG6: Let C . . . 7K 115
Ascot Ind. Est. SG6: Let C . . . 7K 115
Ascot Rd. LU3: Lut . . . 7K 141
Ascott House & Gardens . . . 7C 134

Asgard Dr.—Bedford Rd.

Asgard Dr. MK41: Bed 5B 46
Ashburnham Ct.
MK40: Bed 3A 158 (2C 56)
Ashburnham Cres. LU7: Lei Buz . . .3G 135
Ashburnham Rd.
LU1: Lut 5F 159 (3K 149)
MK40: Bed 3A 158 (1C 56)
MK45: Amp 6A 96
Ashby Ct. SG18: Lang 6B 90
Ashby Dr. MK45: Bar C 4A 122
NN10: Rush 1A 10
SG18: Up C 3H 75
Ash Cl. MK45: Flitw 4B 108
SG19: Bee 4H 61
Ashcraft Cl. MK43: Mars M 5C 82
Ashcroft LU6: Duns 1F 147
Ashcroft Rd. LU2: Lut 5F 143
Ashdale Av. MK42: Kemp 6B 56
Ashdale Gdns. LU3: Lut 7J 131
Ashdown SG6: Let C 5G 115
Ashdown Rd. SG17: Shef 2E 100
Ashfield PE28: Kimb 1J 9
Ashfield Way LU3: Lut 3J 141
Ash Grange LU7: Lei Buz 4K 135
Ash Gro. LU5: Duns 2K 147
LU7: Lei Buz 1J 135
MK45: Wils 2H 85
SG18: Bigg 3B 76
Ashington Ct. *SG17: Clif* *3H 101*
(off Broad St.)
Ashley Gdns. AL5: Harp 7H 157
SG18: Bigg 4D 76
Ashlong Cl. LU7: Lei Buz 2A 136
Ashmead Rd. MK41: Bed 2E 44
Ashridge Cl. NN10: Rush 1A 10
Ashridge Dr. MK41: Bed 5A 46
Ash Rd. LU4: Lut 2K 149
SG18: Bigg 4C 76
Ashton Ga. MK45: Flitw 2A 108
Ashton Rd. LU1: Lut 7H 159 (5C 150)
LU6: Duns 1H 147
Ashton Sq. LU6: Duns 2H 147
Ash Tree Rd. LU5: Hou R 3H 139
Ash Wlk. MK42: Kemp 7C 56
ASHWELL 1D 163
Ashwell Av. LU3: Lut 1E 140
Ashwell Pde. *LU3: Lut* *1E 140*
(off Ashwell Av.)
Ashwell Rd. SG8: Guil M 7K 79
Ashwell St. LU7: Lei Buz 1J 135
Ashwell Wlk. LU5: Hou R 3A 140
Ashwood Gdns. MK44: Wybo 2E 36
Aspects Leisure Pk. MK41: Bed 2H 57
Aspen Av. MK41: Bed 5G 45
Aspley Cl. LU4: Lut 6A 140
Aspley Ct. MK17: Asp H 3A 104
MK40: Bed 1A 158 (1C 56)
ASPLEY GUISE 1C 104 (1A 162)
Aspley Guise Station (Rail) 7B 92
ASPLEY HEATH 7A 104 (1A 162)
Aspley Hill MK17: Wob S 2A 104
Aspley La. MK17: Wob 5B 104
Aspley Rd. MK42: Bed 7B 158 (4D 56)
Astley Grn. LU2: Lut 7H 143
ASTON 2D 163
ASTON ABBOTTS 2A 162
ASTON CLINTON 3A 162
Aston Ct. *LU3: Lut* *5H 141*
(off Sarum Rd.)
ASTON END 2D 163
Aston Rd. MK42: Bed 5J 57
Astra Ct. LU2: Lut 7D 142
Astral Cl. SG16: Hen 3H 113
Astrey Cl. LU5: Harl 5B 120
ASTWICK 3G 103 (1D 163)
Astwick Rd. SG5: Astw, Stot 3G 103
ASTWOOD 7E 52 (3A 160)
Astwood Cl. SG19: Pott 2J 63
Astwood Dr. MK45: Flitw 2K 107
Astwood Rd. MK43: B End 3G 67
Atherstone Abbey MK41: Bed 2K 57
Atherstone Rd. LU4: Lut 1F 149
Atholl Cl. LU3: Lut 1F 141
Atholl Wlk. MK41: Bed 5K 45
Attadale Wlk. *MK41: Bed* *5K 45*
(off Milburn Rd.)
Atterbury Av. LU7: Lei Buz 1K 135
Aubrey Gdns. LU4: Lut 3D 140
Auckland Rd. SG18: Bigg 5D 76
Auction Ho. Courtyard LU1: Lut 4J 159
Audley Pl. LU2: Lut 1E 150
Audreys Ct. PE19: Eat S 5H 27
Augustus Rd. LU7: Hock 6J 127
Augustus Wlk. LU7: Hock 6J 127
Austin Canons MK42: Kemp 4B 56
Austin Rd. LU3: Lut 5K 141
Avebury Av. LU2: Lut 5B 142
Aveline Ct. *LU7: Lei Buz* *3J 135*
(off Lake St.)
Avenue, The LU4: Lut 4F 141
LU6: Duns 3E 146
Avenue, The MK17: Asp G 1C 104
MK40: Bed 3A 158 (2C 56)
MK44: Blet 6J 21
MK44: Blun 7D 48
MK44: Mogg 3A 60
MK45: Amp 6A 96
MK45: Flitw 3B 108
SG5: Stot 7H 103
SG18: Bigg 5D 76
SG18: Lang 6B 90
SG19: Sandy 3H 61
Avenue Farm La. MK44: Wild 7B 34
Avenue Grimaldi LU3: Lut 6J 141
Avenue M. MK45: Flitw 3A 108
Avenue One SG6: Let C 7K 115
Avenue Rd. NN10: Rush 2J 11
Avery Cl. LU7: Lei Buz 4A 136
Aviary Wlk. MK41: Bed 4E 44
Avocet SG6: Let C 5G 115
Avocet Cl. SG18: Bigg 7B 76
SG19: Sandy 1H 61
Avon Chase SG16: Hen 2J 113
Avon Ct. *LU1: Lut* *2A 150*
(off Avondale Rd.)
PE19: Eat S 4J 27
Avondale Rd. LU1: Lut 2A 150
Avon Dr. MK41: Bed 4E 44
(not continuous)
Avon Ri. MK45: Flitw 4K 107
Avon Rd. SG16: Hen 2J 113
Avon Wlk. LU7: Lei Buz 5K 125
Axe Cl. LU3: Lut 3G 141
Axis Way PE19: Eat S 2H 27
Aydon Rd. LU3: Lut 3K 141
Aylesbury Ct. *MK41: Bed* *1H 57*
(off Aylesbury Rd.)
Aylesbury Rd. LU7: Wing 7A 134
MK41: Bed 1H 57
Aylott Cl. PE28: Up D 1J 7
Aynscombe Cl. LU6: Duns 2F 147
AYOT GREEN 3D 163
AYOT ST LAWRENCE 3C 163
AYOT ST PETER 3D 163

B

Back La. MK44: Sould 6A 12
Back St. LU2: Lut 2J 159 (2C 150)
MK45: Clop 5A 98
SG18: Bigg 6C 76
Baden Powell Way SG18: Bigg 6E 76
Badgers Brook LU7: Lei Buz 7J 125
Badgers Cl. MK45: Flitw 3A 108
Badgers Ga. LU6: Duns 2E 146
Badgers Ri. MK43: Ridg 5G 93
Bagwicks Cl. LU3: Lut 2G 141
Bailey Hill Ct. *LU1: Lut* *5C 150*
(off Farley Hill)
Bailey St. LU1: Lut 7K 159 (4D 150)
Bailey's Vs. MK43: Felm 7C 20
Baker Av. SG19: Pott 3J 63
Bakers Cl. MK43: Turv 4B 40
Bakers La. LU6: Kens 3A 154
SG19: Temp 1H 49
Bakers Link PE19: Eynes 1J 39
Baker St. LU1: Lut 7H 159 (5C 150)
(not continuous)
LU7: Lei Buz 2J 135
MK45: Amp 5A 96
Bakerswood Cl. LU7: Heat R 2J 125
Baker Ter. MK45: Flitw 1A 108
Bakery, The MK43: Stev 2B 42
Bakery Cl. MK43: Cran 3F 81
Bakewell Cl. LU4: Lut 1E 148
Balcombe Cl. LU2: Lut 5G 143
Balcony MK45: West 1A 120
BALDOCK 1D 163
Baldock Cl. LU4: Lut 6B 140
Baldock Rd. SG5: Stot 1J 115
(not continuous)
Baldur Cl. MK41: Bed 6B 46
Balfour Ho. *LU1: Lut* *3H 159*
(off Guildford St.)
Ballinghall Cl. MK41: Bed 7J 45
Balliol Rd. MK42: Kemp 7J 55
Balls La. MK44: Will 2F 59
Balmoral Av. MK40: Bed 7F 45
Balmoral Cl. *MK45: Flitw* *5K 107*
(off Manor Way)
SG19: Sandy 1H 61
Balmoral Rd. LU5: Hou R 4A 140
Balmoral Way PE19: Eynes 1K 39
Balmore Wood LU3: Lut 7K 131
Balsall St. E. MK40: Bed . . .2C 158 (1D 56)
Balsall St. W.
MK40: Bed 2C 158 (1D 56)
Bamburgh Dr. MK41: Bed 5J 45
Bamford Rd. MK42: Bed 5H 57
Bamfords La. MK43: Turv 3C 40
Bamfords Yd. MK43: Turv 4C 40
Bampton Rd. LU4: Lut 1D 148
Banbury Cl. LU4: Lut 5H 141
Bancroft Av. SG18: Broom 2H 89
Bancroft Rd. LU3: Lut 4K 141
Bank Cl. LU4: Lut 5E 140
Banks Cl. MK43: Mars M 5C 82
Banks Ct. PE19: Eynes 1J 39
Banks Dr. SG19: Sandy 3H 61
Bankside Cl. LU5: Bid 4G 139
Banks Rd. SG18: Bigg 4D 76
Bannatyne's Health Club
Luton .6H 159
Barber End SG17: Shef 2D 100
Barbers La. LU1: Lut 4H 159
Barclay Ct. LU2: Lut 3K 159 (2D 150)
Barford Av. MK42: Bed 4F 57
Barford Ri. LU2: Lut 1H 151
Barford Rd. MK44: Blun, Will 2H 59
MK44: Gt Bar, Wild 5E 34
PE19: Eynes 1J 39
PE19: Lit Bar 2J 39
Barker Dr. MK43: Brom 7D 42
Barkers Cl. MK45: Amp 7A 96
Barker's La. MK41: Bed 2H 57
Barkers Piece MK43: Mars M 4D 82
Barking Cl. LU4: Lut 3D 140
Barley Brow LU6: Duns 6E 138
Barleycorn, The LU3: Lut 1F 159
Barleycorn Cl. LU7: Lei Buz 2B 136
Barleyfield Way LU5: Hou R 5G 139
Barley Kiln La. MK43: Harr 2E 28
Barley La. LU4: Lut 4E 140
Barley Rd. PE19: Eat S 4J 27
Barleyvale LU3: Lut 1J 141
Barley Way MK41: Bed 6J 45
Barnabas Rd. LU7: Lei Buz 3F 135
Barnard Av. MK42: Kemp 7J 55
Barnard Cl. PE19: Eynes 1J 39
Barnard Rd. LU1: Lut 3J 149
Barncroft MK43: Turv 3C 40
Barndell Cl. SG5: Stot 7H 103
Barnes Rd. MK43: Woo 5F 69
Barnett Cl. SG18: Bigg 5C 76
Barnfield Av. LU2: Lut 4B 142
Barnhill MK41: Bed 7J 45
Barns, The LU7: Bur 5A 134
MK44: Rise 4C 14
SG18: Edw 5K 91
Barnstaple Rd. MK40: Bed 7G 45
Barnstaple Wlk. SG18: Bigg 3E 76
Barnston Cl. LU2: Lut 1H 151
Barnwell Dr. NN10: Rush 1A 10
Barnwell Ri. SG19: Pott 4K 63
Baron Ct. PE19: Eat S 3H 27
Barons Ct. LU3: Lut 1G 159
Barratt Ind. Pk. LU2: Lut 4G 151
Barrie Av. LU6: Duns 6E 138
Barrowby Cl. LU2: Lut 1H 151
Barrow Path LU7: Lei Buz 1J 135
Bartholomew Grn. AL3: Mark 6G 155
Barton & Royle Homes
MK43: Turv 4G 41
Barton Av. LU5: Duns 2K 147
Barton Hill Rd. LU2: Stre 2K 131
Barton Hills National Nature Reserve
. . . . .7B 122
Barton Ind. Est. MK45: Bar C 3J 121
BARTON-LE-CLAY 5A 122 (1B 162)
Barton Rd. LU3: Lut, Stre 2J 131
LU5: Harl 5B 120
MK42: Bed 5H 57
MK45: Grav 2G 111
MK45: Pull, Sils 6H 109
MK45: Shar 5G 121
MK45: Sils 4A 110
SG5: Hex 6E 122
Bartram Ct. *MK42: Kemp* *7J 55*
(off High St.)
Bartrum Cl. MK42: Kemp 7J 55
Basen Cl. MK42: Kemp 7H 55
Basildon Ct. LU7: Lei Buz 2H 135
Basmead Mnr. La. PE19: Stap 1C 26
Bassett Ct. LU7: Lei Buz 2H 135
Bassett Rd. LU7: Lei Buz 2H 135
Bassie Cl. MK42: Bed 7D 158 (4E 56)
BASSINGBOURN 3D 161
BASSUS GREEN 2D 163
Batcheldor Gdns. MK43: Brom 1E 54
Bath Abbey MK41: Bed 1K 57
Bath Pl. SG17: Clif 2H 101
Bath Rd. LU3: Lut 7B 142
Battison St. MK40: Bed . . .4B 158 (2D 56)
Battle Abbey MK41: Bed 1K 57
BATTLESDEN 2G 127 (2A 162)
Battlesden Av. MK17: Batt, Mil B . . .1F 127
Baulk, The LU2: Lill 6H 133
MK41: Clap 2A 44
SG18: Bigg 5C 76
SG19: Bee 5H 61
SG19: Pott 4A 64
Baxter Dr. PE19: Eynes 1J 39
Bay Cl. LU4: Lut 3D 140
BAYFORD 3D 163
Bayham Cl. MK42: Els 7F 57
Baylam Dell LU2: Lut 1J 151
Beachampstead Rd. PE19: Gt S 1K 17
Beacon Av. LU6: Duns 3E 146
Beaconsfield LU2: Lut 2F 151
Beaconsfield St.
MK41: Bed 1B 158 (7D 44)
Beacon Vw. LU6: N'all 6F 145
LU7: Stanb 4H 137
Beadlow Manor Golf Course &
Country Club 4F 99
Beadlow Rd. LU4: Lut 5B 140
Beale St. LU6: Duns 1G 147
Beamish Cl. SG19: Sandy 7J 49
Beancroft Rd. MK43: Mars M 1A 82
Beanfield Cl. MK44: Rise 4B 14
Beanley Cl. LU2: Lut 7J 143
Beatrice St. MK42: Kemp 5C 56
Beatty Rd. PE19: Eat S 5H 27
Beauchamp Cl. PE19: Eat S 4H 27
Beauchamp Ct.
MK40: Bed 2A 158 (1C 56)
Beauchamp Pl. MK44: Will 2G 59
Beauchamp Rd. MK43: Woo 4G 69
Beaudesert LU7: Lei Buz 2J 135
Beaufort Way MK41: Bed 3E 44
Beaulieu Wlk. MK41: Bed 4G 45
Beaulieu Way MK41: Bed 4G 45
Beaumanor Pl. SG17: Chic 2H 99
Beaumont Ct. MK45: Flitw 3A 108
Beaumont Gdns. *MK42: Kemp* *7A 56*
(off Chantry Rd.)
Beaumont Ho. MK40: Bed 7C 44
Beaumont M. MK45: Flitw 3A 108
Beaumont Rd. LU3: Lut 7K 141
MK45: Flitw 3A 108
Beauvaise Av. MK42: Short 7K 57
Beauvaise Sq. MK42: Short 7K 57
Beaver Cl. PE19: Eat S 2H 27
Becher Cl. MK41: Ren 4E 46
Beckbury Cl. LU2: Lut 7J 143
Beckerings Pk. Rd. MK43: Lidl 7A 94
Beckett Ct. MK40: Bed 3B 158
Becketts Cl. MK45: Maul 4D 96
Beckett St. MK40: Bed 2B 158 (1D 56)
Beckham Cl. LU2: Lut 2B 142
Becks Cl. AL3: Mark 6F 155
Bec Rd. PE19: St N 2K 27
Bedesman La.
MK42: Bed 5D 158 (3E 56)
Bedesmans Ho. MK42: Bed 5D 158
BEDFORD 4C 158 (3B 160)
Bedford & County Badminton Club
. . . .*1F 57*
(off Bradgate Rd.)
Bedford & County Golf Course 2B 44
Bedford Autodrome 2C 22
Bedford Av. MK45: Sils 2A 110
Bedford Blues RUFC 1F 57
Bedford Borough Bowling Club
. . . . .1E 158 (1E 56)
Bedford Bus. Cen. MK40: Bed 2E 158
MK42: Bed 5F 57
Bedford Civic Theatre 4C 158 (2D 56)
Bedford Cl. SG5: Shill 4J 111
Bedford Corn Exchange . . .3C 158 (2E 56)
Bedford Ct. LU5: Hou R 5H 139
Bedford Crematorium MK41: Bed . . .5B 46
Bedford Gdns.
LU3: Lut 2G 159 (2B 150)
Bedford Golf Course, The 3G 55
Bedford Hgts. MK41: Bed 5D 44
Bedford International Athletic Stadium
. . . . .2H 57
Bedford Mus. 3D 158 (2E 56)
Bedford Pk. 6E 44
Bedford Rd.
LU5: Bid, Hou R, Thor 1G 139
MK17: Asp G 2C 104
MK41: Clap 4B 44
MK42: Kemp 6K 55
(not continuous)
MK42: Wils 4E 70
(not continuous)
MK43: Brog, Hus C 1E 104
MK43: Cran 2F 81
MK43: Mars M 5D 82
MK43: Pave 5E 30
MK43: Stag 3A 54
(not continuous)
MK43: Turv 4D 40
MK43: Woo 4F 69
MK44: Card 5A 58
MK44: Cople, Will 3D 58
MK44: Gt Bar 6H 47
MK44: Mil E 4H 31
MK44: Mogg 3K 59
MK44: Per 4H 9
MK44: Rav 1G 45

Bedford Rd. MK44: Rox 7D 36
MK45: Amp, Hou C, Kemp H 7B 70
MK45: Clop, Sils, Bar C 4K 97
MK45: Wils 6F 71
MK46: Cold B 4A 40
NN10: Rush 1H 11
SG5: Hitc, Hol, Ickle 1F 113
SG6: Let C 7F 115
SG16: Hen, Lwr Sto 1F 113
SG17: Shef 1B 100
SG18: North 1K 73
SG18: Old W 6H 73
SG19: Sandy 3H 61
Bedfordshire Golf Course 4B 54
Bedford Sports & Hockey Cen. 2K 55
Bedford Sq. LU5: Hou R 5H 139
Bedford Station (Rail) 3A 158 (2C 56)
Bedford St Johns Station (Rail) 6C 158 (3D 56)
Bedford St. LU7: Lei Buz 2J 135
MK17: Wob 7D 104
MK45: Amp 3A 96
Bedford Town FC 3B 58
Beeby Way MK43: Carlt 5E 28
Beech Av. MK45: Wils 2H 85
SG18: Bigg 3B 76
Beech Cl. LU6: Duns 5A 148
MK45: Pull 4F 109
Beech Ct. AL5: Harp 7K 157
MK40: Bed 2A 158
SG19: Pott 2J 63
Beechdale Rd. MK42: Bed 5E 56
Beeches, The MK45: Maul 5K 97
MK45: Sils 2A 110
Beech Grn. LU6: Duns 1F 147
Beech Gro. LU7: Lei Buz 2G 135
Beech Hill LU2: Lill, Lut 2G 143
SG6: Let C 7F 115
Beech Hill Path LU4: Lut 1K 149
Beech Ridge AL5: Harp 6F 157
Beech Rd. LU1: Lut 2A 150
LU6: Duns, Kens 5A 148
MK45: Flitw 4B 108
Beech Tree Way LU5: Hou R 4H 139
Beech Wlk. MK42: Kemp 7B 56
Beechwood Cl. LU6: Duns 3F 147
Beechwood Pk. LU1: Cad 6G 149
Beechwood Ri. SG17: Shef 3C 100
Beechwood Rd. LU4: Lut 5F 141
BEECROFT 1F 147
Beecroft Way LU6: Duns 2F 147
BEESTON 5H 61 (3C 161)
Beeton Ct. SG5: Stot 4E 114
Beezling Cl. PE19: Eat F 1J 27
Begwary Brook Nature Reserve 3H 37
Begwary Cl. PE19: Eat S 2H 27
Belam Way SG19: Sandy 1H 61
Belfry, The LU2: Lut 3C 142
Belfry Cl. MK42: Els 6D 56
Belfry Ct. SG19: Sandy 3J 61
Belgrave Rd. LU4: Lut 4F 141
Bell All. LU7: Lei Buz 2J 135
Bellamy Cl. PE19: Eynes 1J 39
Bellamy Rd. MK43: Woo 5F 69
Bell Cl. MK45: West 1A 120
Bellerby Ri. LU4: Lut 3D 140
Bellevue Cl. SG19: Pott 3H 63
Bellingham Pl. SG18: Bigg 4D 76
Bell La. MK45: C End 4B 72
Bells Brook SG18: Bigg 4A 76
Bells Cl. MK42: Short 7J 57
SG5: Shill 5K 111
Bells Mdw. SG8: Guil M 6K 79
Belmont Rd. LU1: Lut 3A 150
Belper Rd. LU4: Lut 7F 141
Belsham Pl. LU2: Lut 7J 143
Belsize Rd. LU4: Lut 6A 140
Belvedere Rd. LU3: Lut 4K 141
Belvoir Wlk. MK41: Bed 4H 45
Bembridge Gdns. LU3: Lut 2H 141
Bendbrooke MK17: Ting 2G 119
BENDISH 2C 163
BENINGTON 2D 163
Benington Cl. LU2: Lut 4C 142
Bennett Ct. SG6: Let C 7H 115
Bennetts Cl. LU6: Duns 3H 147
MK44: Blet 6J 21
Benning Av. LU6: Duns 2F 147
Benson Cl. LU3: Lut 2H 141
Bentley Cl. SG18: Lang 7B 90
Bentley Ct. LU1: Lut 2A 150
(off Moor St.)
Bentley M. SG17: Shef 3B 100
Bents Cl. MK41: Clap 3K 43
Berberry Dr. MK45: Flitt 2G 109
Bereford Cl. MK44: Gt Bar 4K 47
Beresford Rd. LU4: Lut 1J 149
MK40: Bed 2G 57
Berkeley Av. MK45: Wils 2H 85
Berkeley Cl. MK45: Wils 2H 85
SG18: Bigg 7C 76
Berkeley Path
LU2: Lut 2H 159 (2C 150)
Berkeley Rd. MK42: Bed 6E 56
BERKHAMSTED 3A 162
Bernard Cl. LU5: Duns 1J 147
Berrow Cl. LU2: Lut 7J 143
Berry Dr. MK43: Brom 7E 42
Berry End MK17: Ever 6A 106
Berry La. MK17: Asp G 1C 104
Berry Leys LU3: Lut 2G 141
Bert Collins Ct. LU1: Lut 3A 150
(off Wolston Cl.)
Berwick Way SG19: Sandy 2J 61
Besford Cl. LU2: Lut 7J 143
Bethune Cl. LU1: Lut 4K 149
Bethune Ct. LU1: Lut 4K 149
Betony Wlk. NN10: Rush 1B 10
Beverley Cl. MK45: Clop 5A 98
Beverley Cres. MK40: Bed 1B 56
Beverley Gdns. MK45: Clop 5A 98
Beverley Gro. MK40: Bed 1A 56
Beverley Rd. LU4: Lut 1H 149
Bevery Cl. MK43: Oak 1G 43
Bevington Way PE19: Eynes 1J 39
Bewcastle Cl. MK41: Bed 4J 45
Bewdley Dr. LU7: Lei Buz 2E 134
Bewley Cl. MK45: West 7A 108
Bexhill Rd. LU2: Lut 7H 143
Bibshall Cres. LU6: Duns 4J 147
Bickerdikes Gdns. SG19: Sandy 2H 61
BIDDENHAM 1J 55 (3B 160)
Biddenham Grange
MK40: Bidd 7J 43
Biddenham Turn MK40: Bidd 2K 55
Bideford Ct. LU7: Lei Buz 1E 134
Bideford Gdns. LU3: Lut 5B 142
Bideford Grn. LU7: Lei Buz 1E 134
BIDWELL 3G 139
Bidwell Cl. LU5: Hou R 4H 139
Bidwell Hill LU5: Hou R 4G 139
Bidwell Path LU5: Hou R 5H 139
BIGGLESWADE 5C 76 (3C 161)
Biggleswade Golf Driving Range 4A 76
Biggleswade Retail Pk., The
SG18: Bigg 1E 90
Biggleswade Rd. SG18: Bigg 2E 76
SG18: Dunt 6J 77
SG18: Up C 3H 75
SG19: Pott, Sutt 2E 76
Biggleswade Station (Rail) 6C 76
Bigthan Rd. LU5: Duns 2J 147
Bilberry Cl. PE19: Eat F 2J 27
Bilberry Rd. SG17: Clif 2H 101
Bilberry Ter. SG17: Clif 2H 101
BILLINGTON 7C 136 (2A 162)
Billington Cl. MK45: Flitw 3K 107
Billington Ct. LU7: Lei Buz 3K 135
Billington Rd. LU7: Lei Buz 3K 135
LU7: Stanb 4E 136
Bilton Way LU1: Lut 2H 149
Binder Cl. LU4: Lut 5A 140
Binder Ct. LU4: Lut 5A 140
(off Binder Cl.)
Bindon Abbey MK41: Bed 2J 57
Binham Cl. LU2: Lut 2B 142
Binks Ct. MK42: Short 7J 57
(off Central Av.)
Birbeck Cl. MK41: Clap 2J 43
Birch Cl. MK43: Cran 1G 81
SG17: Clif 3F 101
SG18: Broom 2J 89
Birchdale Av. MK42: Kemp 6B 56
Birchen Gro. LU2: Lut 6D 142
Birches, The LU4: Lut 7D 140
MK45: Flitw 1A 108
MK45: Maul 6K 97
SG6: Let C 6G 115
Birchfield Rd. MK44: Gt Bar 1H 47
Birch Gro. MK45: Sils 3K 109
(not continuous)
SG16: Lwr Sto 3G 113
SG19: Sandy 4H 61
Birch Link LU4: Lut 1A 150
BIRCHMOOR GREEN 104 6C (1A 162)
Birchmoor Grn. MK17: Wob 6C 104
Birch Rd. SG18: Bigg 4C 76
Birch's Cl. LU7: Hock 6K 127
Birch Side LU6: Duns 4K 147
Birchside Path LU6: Duns 4K 147
Bird Ct. MK45: Wils 7G 71
Birds of Prey Cen. 6D 74
Birdsfoot La. LU3: Lut 4K 141
Birds Hill LU7: Heat R 3J 125
SG6: Let C 7J 115
Birkdale Rd. MK41: Bed 4G 45
Birling Dr. LU2: Lut 4G 143
Birse Grn. MK41: Bed 5K 45
Birtley Cft. LU2: Lut 1J 151
BISCOT 7A 142
Biscot Rd. LU3: Lut 6K 141
Bishop Cl. LU7: Lei Buz 3B 136
Bishopscote Rd. LU3: Lut 6K 141
Bishops Ct. LU2: Lut 1G 159
Bishops Rd. MK41: Bed 1K 57
Bishopstone Ct. MK40: Bed 2C 56
Bishops Wlk. MK17: Asp H 3A 104
Bittern Dr. SG18: Bigg 6B 76
Bittern La. MK42: Wils 5F 71
Bittern Way SG6: Let C 5G 115
Blackbird Cl. MK45: Flitw 4K 107
Blackbirds, The LU7: Hock 6J 127
Blackbird St. SG19: Pott 3J 63
Blackburn Cl. MK42: Short 1K 71
Blackburn Rd. LU5: Hou R 6H 139
Black Hat Cl. MK45: Wils 7G 71
Blackhill LU7: Tils 4K 137
Blackhill La. MK45: Pull 6G 109
Blackhorse Rd. SG6: Let C 6K 115
Black Moor Bus. Pk.
MK45: Maul 7E 96
BLACKMORE END 3C 163
Blacksmith Cl. SG19: Eve 6E 50
(off Sandy Rd.)
Blacksmiths Cl. PE19: Abbot 3K 39
SG5: Stot 6H 103
Blacksmiths Comn. LU4: Chalt 6A 130
Blacksmiths Ct. LU6: Duns 2H 147
(off Matthew St.)
MK43: Mars M 5D 82
Blacksmiths La. PE19: Abbot 3K 39
Blacksmiths Row AL3: Mark 6G 155
(off High St.)
Black Swan La. LU3: Lut 4J 141
Blackthorn Dr. LU2: Lut 5G 143
Black Thorn Rd. LU5: Hou R 3J 139
Blackwood Rd. PE19: Eat S 4H 27
Blair Way PE19: Eynes 1J 39
Blakedown LU2: Lut 1H 159 (1C 150)
Blakedown Rd. LU7: Lei Buz 2E 134
Blakelands MK45: Bar C 5B 122
Blakeney Dr. LU2: Lut 2A 142
Blakes Way PE19: Eat S 5H 27
Blandford Av. LU2: Lut 3B 142
Blaydon Rd. LU2: Lut 2E 150
SG19: Sandy 7J 49
Blenheim Cl. PE19: Eat F 3J 27
Blenheim Ct. MK42: Kemp 5B 56
Blenheim Cres. LU3: Lut 7A 142
Blenheim Link MK45: Flitw 5K 107
Blenheim Rd. LU7: Lei Buz 7K 125
MK42: Short 1J 71
BLETCHLEY 1A 162
BLETSOE 6J 21 (2B 160)
Bliss Av. MK43: Cran 2G 81
SG17: Shef 2D 100
Bloomfield Av. LU2: Lut 1E 150
Bloomfield Dr. SG17: Shef 3B 100
Bloomfield Rd. AL5: Harp 7K 157
Bloomsbury Cl. MK17: Wob 1D 116
Bloomsbury Gdns. LU5: Hou R 4K 139
Blow's Downs 2A 148
Blows Rd. LU5: Duns 3K 147
Bluebell Cl. MK42: Bed 6H 57
MK45: Flitw 3K 107
SG18: Bigg 7E 76
Bluebell Dr. SG16: Lwr Sto 3G 113
Blue Bells MK44: Chaw 3E 36
Bluebell Wood Cl. LU1: Lut 3H 149
Bluebird Gdns. MK42: Wils 4F 71
Blue Spruce Cl. MK43: Brom 6C 42
Bluewater Quay MK42: Wils 4E 70
Blundell Pl. MK42: Bed 6E 56
Blundell Rd. LU3: Lut 6J 141
BLUNHAM 6E 48 (2C 161)
Blunham La. SG19: Temp 4G 49
Blunham Rd. MK44: Mogg 3C 60
SG18: Bigg 6B 76
Blythe Cl. MK41: Bed 4E 44
Blythe Path LU1: Lut 7G 159
Blyth Pl. LU1: Lut 4B 150
(off Russell St.)
Boddington Gdns. SG18: Bigg 4D 76
Boddington Ind. Est. SG18: Bigg 5D 76
Bodmin Rd. LU4: Lut 5H 141
Bodyflight & Leisure Cen. 3A 32
Bolingbroke Rd. LU1: Lut 4K 149
Bolney Grn. LU2: Lut 6H 143
BOLNHURST 3B 24 (2B 160)
Bolnhurst Rd. MK44: Colm 2F 25
Bolton Rd. LU1: Lut 6K 159 (3D 150)
Bond Ct. AL5: Harp 7K 157
Bonds La. SG18: Bigg 6B 76
Bonnick Cl. LU1: Lut 4A 150
Boothey Cl. SG18: Bigg 4C 76
Booth Pl. LU6: Eat B 4J 145
Boot La. SG18: Dunt 6B 78
Borden La. SG18: Old W 6G 73
Borders Way LU5: Hou R 3J 139
(off Black Thorn Rd.)
Borough Rd. LU5: Duns 3K 147
Borrowdale Av. LU6: Duns 4J 147
Borton Av. SG16: Hen 2H 113
Boscombe Rd. LU5: Duns 7J 139
Bosmore Rd. LU3: Lut 3H 141
Bossard Ct. LU7: Lei Buz 2J 135
Boss Av. LU7: Lei Buz 4J 135
Bossington La. LU7: Lei Buz 2G 135
Boswell Ct. MK40: Bed 1B 158 (1D 56)
Boswell Pl. MK40: Bed 1B 158 (1D 56)
Boteler Gdns. MK42: Bed 5H 57
Bottom Dr. LU6: Eat B 5D 146
Bottoms, The LU5: Harl 6D 120
Boughton End La. MK43: Lidl 4A 94
Boulevards, The MK40: Bed 4C 158
Boundary, The MK41: Bed 7J 45
Boundary Cl. SG16: Hen 3H 113
BOURN 2D 161
BOURNE END
Bedford, MK43 .... 5G 67 (3A 160)
Bedford, MK44 .... 1H 21 (1B 160)
Hemel Hempstead 3B 162
Bourne End La. MK44: Blet 1H 21
Bourne End Rd.
MK43: B End, Cran 6G 67
MK43: Woo 4K 67
Bourne Rd. MK44: Rise 4B 14
Bourneside MK41: Bed 3F 45
BOW BRICKHILL 1A 162
Bowbrookvale LU2: Lut 1K 151
Bowdidge Ct. MK45: Hay 3D 86
Bower Cl. LU6: Eat B 5K 145
Bower La. LU6: Eat B 5K 145
Bowers Cl. MK44: Rise 3D 14
Bower's La. MK44: Rise 3D 14
Bower St. MK40: Bed 1F 57
Bowhill MK41: Bed 6H 45
Bowland Cres. LU6: Duns 4G 147
Bowles Way LU6: Duns 5K 147
Bowling Grn. La. LU2: Lut 7C 142
Bowling Grn. Rd. MK43: Cran 3G 81
Bowmans Cl. LU6: Duns 3J 147
Bowmans Way LU6: Duns 3J 147
Bowyer Dr. SG6: Let C 7K 115
Boxall Cl. SG19: Pott 3G 63
BOX END 3F 55 (3B 160)
Box End Pk. 4G 55
Box End Rd. MK43: Brom, Kemp 3F 55
Boxgrove Cl. LU2: Lut 4G 143
Boxgrove Priory MK41: Bed 1K 57
BOXMOOR 3B 162
Boxted Cl. LU4: Lut 4E 140
BOXWORTH 1D 161
Boyde Gdns. MK40: Bed 3A 56
Boyle Cl. LU2: Lut 2H 159 (2C 150)
BOZEAT 2A 160
Brabazon Cl. MK42: Short 1J 71
Braceby Cl. LU3: Lut 3H 141
Brace St. MK40: Bed 2B 158 (2D 56)
Brache, The MK45: Maul 4E 96
Brache Ct. LU1: Lut 7K 159 (4D 150)
Brackendale Gro. AL5: Harp 7H 157
LU3: Lut 4J 141
Bracken Pl. MK41: Bed 1K 57
Bracklesham Gdns. LU2: Lut 6H 143
Brackley Rd. MK42: Bed 5E 56
Bracknell Cl. LU4: Lut 6B 140
Bradford Rd. LU5: Todd 4G 129
Bradford Way LU5: Todd 3F 129
Bradgate Rd. MK40: Bed 1F 57
Bradgers Hill Rd. LU2: Lut 5C 142
Bradley Rd. LU4: Lut 1E 148
Bradshaw Cl. MK45: West 1A 120
Bradshaws Cl. MK45: Bar C 4A 122
Bradshaws Ct. PE19: Eat F 3J 27
Braemar Ct. MK40: Bed 2C 56
Braeside MK41: Bed 5H 45
BRAGBURY END 2D 163
BRAGENHAM 2E 124
Bragenham La.
LU7: Brag, Heat R 2E 124
Bragenham Side MK17: Sto H 1A 124
Braggs La. SG19: Wrest 6F 65
Braintree Cl. LU4: Lut 6B 140
Braithwaite Ct.
LU3: Lut 1F 159 (1B 150)
Bramble Cl. LU4: Lut 5E 140
LU7: Lei Buz 3A 136
Bramble Rd. LU4: Lut 5E 140
Brambles MK45: Wils 7H 71
Brambles, The MK44: Gt Bar 4K 47
MK45: Flitt 2H 109
NN10: Wym 1F 11
Brambling Cl. SG19: Sandy 7J 49
Brambling Gdns. MK42: Wils 4E 70
BRAMFIELD 3D 163
Bramhanger Acre LU3: Lut 2F 141
Bramingham Bus. Pk. LU3: Lut 1K 141
Bramingham Rd. LU3: Lut 4G 141
Bramley Cl. SG17: Shef 3B 100
Bramley Ct. LU5: Duns 1K 147
MK43: Harr 2D 28
(off Orchard La.)
Bramley Way MK41: Bed 2E 44

Brampton—Caldecote Grn.

BRAMPTON ... 1D 161
Brampton Cl. MK42: Bed ... 5H 57
Brampton Ri. LU6: Duns ... 4J 147
Brancaster Cl. MK42: Bed ... 6H 57
Brancker Av. MK42: Short ... 1J 71
Brandreth Av. LU5: Duns ... 1A 148
Brandreth Pl. SG19: Sandy ... 4K 61
Brangwyn Gdns. MK41: Bed ... 6D 44
Branton Cl. LU2: Lut ... 7J 143
Brantwood Rd. LU1: Lut ... 3A 150
Braybrook SG19: Sandy ... 2G 61
Braybrooks Dr. SG19: Pott ... 3J 63
Brayes Mnr. SG5: Stot ... 7H 103
Bray's Ct. LU2: Lut ... 6F 143
Brays Rd. LU2: Lut ... 6F 143
Brazier Cl. MK45: Bar C ... 4K 121
BREACHWOOD GREEN ... 2C 163
Breamish Wlk. *MK41: Bed ... 2E 44*
(off Carron Rd.)
Brecon Cl. LU1: Lut ... 7F 159 (4B 150)
Brecon Way MK41: Bed ... 4G 45
Brendon Av. LU2: Lut ... 1G 151
MK41: Bed ... 6G 45
Brentwood Cl. LU5: Hou R ... 3K 139
Brereton Rd. MK40: Bed ... 3B 158 (2D 56)
Brett Dr. MK43: Brom ... 1F 55
Bretts Mead LU1: Lut ... 5A 150
Bretts Mead Ct. LU1: Lut ... 4A 150
Brewers Hill Rd. LU6: Duns ... 1E 146
Brewery La. MK45: Amp ... 4A 96
Brian May Gro. MK45: Sils ... 3K 109
Brian Rd. LU5: Harl ... 5C 120
Briar Bank Pk. MK45: Wils ... 1H 85
Briar Cl. LU2: Lut ... 5G 143
MK45: Amp ... 5A 96
Briars, The MK42: Kemp ... 7B 56
Brickfield Rd. MK41: Ren ... 3K 45
BRICKHILL ... 4F 45
Brickhill Cl. MK44: Blun ... 6E 48
SG19: Sandy ... 3K 61
Brickhill Dr. MK41: Bed ... 6C 44
Brickhill Farm Pk. Homes
LU1: Pep ... 3A 156
Brickhill Rd. LU7: Heat R ... 1J 125
SG19: Sandy ... 2K 61
Brick Kiln Barns LU1: Cad ... 4F 149
Brick Kiln La. LU2: C'hoe, Tea G ... 5K 143
Brickle Pl. SG17: Clif ... 3H 101
Brickly Rd. LU4: Lut ... 4D 140
BRIDGE END ... 7F 43 (2B 160)
Bridge End MK43: Rad ... 1E 30
Bridgeman Dr. LU5: Hou R ... 4K 139
Bridgend MK43: Carlt ... 4F 29
Bridge Rd. MK42: Bed ... 4E 56
SG6: Let C ... 7H 115
Bridge St. LU1: Lut ... 4H 159 (3C 150)
LU7: Lei Buz ... 3H 135
MK43: Turv ... 4B 40
MK46: Cold B ... 4B 40
Bridle Dr. MK41: Clap ... 2J 43
Bridle Way LU5: Todd ... 2J 129
Brierley Cl. LU2: Lut ... 7H 143
LU6: Duns ... 5J 147
Briggington Cotts. LU7: Lei Buz ... 2B 136
Brigham Gdns. SG18: Bigg ... 5C 76
Brightmans Dr. MK45: Maul ... 5D 96
Brightwell Av. LU6: Tott ... 3C 146
Brill Cl. LU2: Lut ... 7H 143
Brimfield Cl. LU2: Lut ... 7H 143
Brindley Cl. SG19: Sandy ... 1H 61
Brinsmade Rd. MK45: Amp ... 5B 96
Bristol Rd. LU3: Lut ... 5J 141
Britain St. LU5: Duns ... 2J 147
Britannia Av. LU3: Lut ... 4K 141
Britannia Est. LU3: Lut ... 7K 141
Britannia Ho.
MK42: Bed ... 6B 158 (3D 56)
Britannia Rd.
MK42: Bed ... 6B 158 (3D 56)
Brittain Cl. PE19: Eynes ... 1J 39
Brittains Ri. SG16: Lwr Sto ... 4E 112
Brittany Ct. LU6: Duns ... 2J 147
Britten Rd. SG17: Shef ... 2D 100
Brittens La. MK17: Salf ... 2A 92
Brittons Cl. MK44: Sharn ... 3E 20
Brive Rd. LU5: Duns ... 3A 148
Brixham Cl. MK40: Bed ... 7G 45
Broadacres LU2: Lut ... 3B 142
Broad Av. MK42: Bed ... 5F 57
BROAD GREEN ... 1G 81 (3A 160)
Broad Grn. MK43: Cran ... 1G 81
Broadhurst Abbey MK41: Bed ... 2J 57
Broad Mead LU3: Lut ... 6J 141
Broadmead SG18: Bigg ... 6D 76
Broadmead Bus. Pk. MK43: Stew ... 3J 83
Broadmead Rd. MK43: Stew ... 3H 83
Broad Oak Ct. *LU2: Lut ... 6H 143*
(off Handcross Rd.)
Broad Reach MK40: Bed ... 4E 158 (2F 57)
Broad Rush Grn. LU7: Lei Buz ... 1G 135
Broad St. SG17: Clif ... 3G 101
Broad Wlk. LU5: Duns ... 1H 147
SG17: Clif ... 3H 101
(off Newis Cres.)
Broadway MK45: Hou C ... 4D 84
Broadway, The
MK40: Bed ... 2C 158 (1D 56)
Broadway Ho. MK40: Bed ... 2C 158
Brocket Ct. LU4: Lut ... 3F 141
Brockton Cl. LU1: Lut ... 3J 149
Brockwell MK43: Oak ... 1G 43
BROGBOROUGH ... 5G 93 (1A 162)
Brogborough Boardsailing Club ... 1A 94
Brogborough Lake ... 1K 93
BROMHAM ... 7E 42 (2B 160)
Bromham Mill & Gallery ... 7F 43
Bromham Pk. ... 6G 43
Bromham Pk. MK43: Brom ... 7F 43
Bromham Rd.
MK40: Bed, Bidd ... 2A 158 (7G 43)
(not continuous)
Bromley Gdns. LU5: Hou R ... 4K 139
(not continuous)
Brompton Cl. LU3: Lut ... 1H 141
Brompton Gdns. LU3: Lut ... 1H 141
Bronte Av. SG5: Stot ... 4E 114
Brook Cl. LU6: Duns ... 1G 147
SG16: Hen ... 4K 101
SG18: Up C ... 3H 75
Brook Ct. LU3: Lut ... 1F 159 (1B 150)
Brook Dr. MK42: Kemp ... 7J 55
BROOK END
Hitchin ... 1G 115
Sandy ... 6G 61
Brook End MK17: Ever ... 1A 118
SG19: Pott ... 3J 63
Brookend Dr. MK45: Bar C ... 4K 121
Brookes Rd. MK45: Flitw ... 3A 108
Brook Farm Bus. Pk. MK17: Hulc ... 5E 92
Brook Farm Cl. NN10: Wym ... 1F 11
Brookfield Av. LU5: Hou R ... 4J 139
Brookfield Pk. LU5: Hou R ... 4J 139
LU6: Tott ... 2K 145
Brookfield Rd. MK41: Bed ... 1H 57
Brookfields MK43: Pave ... 4C 30
SG19: Pott ... 3K 63
Brookfield Wlk. LU5: Hou R ... 5K 139
Brooklands MK42: Kemp ... 1A 70
Brooklands Av. LU7: Lei Buz ... 3K 135
MK42: Wils ... 4E 70
Brooklands Cl. LU4: Lut ... 3E 140
Brooklands Dr. LU7: Lei Buz ... 3K 135
Brooklands Rd. MK44: Rise ... 5B 14
Brook La. MK41: Ren ... 3K 45
MK43: Harr ... 1D 28
MK44: Gt Bar ... 4A 48
MK45: Flitt ... 1F 109
PE28: Up D ... 1J 7
Brookmead SG17: Mep ... 7C 100
Brook Rd. MK43: Mars M ... 5C 82
PE19: Eat F ... 3J 27
Brooks Cl. MK42: Kemp ... 7H 55
Brookside MK41: Ren ... 2K 45
MK44: Gt Bar ... 4A 48
SG5: Shill ... 5J 111
SG17: Camp ... 5K 99
SG17: Mep ... 7C 100
Brookside Pk. Homes
MK43: Brom ... 7D 42
Brookside Wlk. LU7: Lei Buz ... 2A 136
Brook St. LU3: Lut ... 2F 159 (2B 150)
LU6: Edles ... 6K 145
LU7: Lei Buz ... 2A 136
MK42: Bed ... 5F 57
NN9: Harg ... 1C 4
SG5: Stot ... 7G 103
Brookvale SG16: Up Sto ... 3E 112
Brook Way MK43: Brom ... 7E 42
BROOM ... 1J 89 (3C 161)
Broom Cross Roads
SG18: Broom ... 3G 89
Broom Hall SG18: Broom ... 2J 89
Broomhills Rd. LU7: Lei Buz ... 7J 125
Broom Rd. SG18: Stan ... 5G 89
Brooms Rd. LU2: Lut ... 2E 150
Broomstick Ind. Est. *LU6: Edles ... 6K 145*
(off High St.)
BROUGHTON ... 1A 162
Broughton Av. LU3: Lut ... 4A 142
LU5: Todd ... 2E 128
Broughton Rd. MK17: Salf ... 2A 92
Browney Path MK41: Bed ... 2E 44
Browning Cl. MK43: Brom ... 7E 42
Browning Dr. PE19: Eat F ... 1J 27
Browning Rd. LU4: Lut ... 7C 140
Brownlow Av. LU6: Edles ... 7K 145
Brownlow Ri. LU6: Tott ... 2A 146
Browns Cl. LU4: Lut ... 4F 141
MK43: Mars M ... 5D 82
Browns Ct. MK40: Bed ... 3D 158
Browns Cres. LU5: Harl ... 4B 120
Brownshill MK45: Maul ... 4E 96
Browns La. MK43: Woo ... 5F 69
Brownslea LU7: Lei Buz ... 2A 136
Browns Way MK17: Asp G ... 1B 104
Broxley Mead LU4: Lut ... 4E 140
Bruce Rd. MK42: Kemp ... 7K 55
Brunel Ct. LU4: Lut ... 6A 140
Brunel Dr. SG18: Bigg ... 7C 76
Brunel Rd. LU4: Lut ... 6A 140
MK41: Bed ... 2H 57
Brunel Rd. Ind. Est. MK41: Bed ... 2J 57
Brunel Wlk. SG5: Stot ... 4D 114
Brunswick Cl. SG18: Bigg ... 4C 76
Brunswick St. LU2: Lut ... 2J 159 (2C 150)
Brunts La. SG18: Bigg ... 5B 76
Brussels Way LU3: Lut ... 7F 131
Bruthwaite Grn. MK41: Bed ... 5A 46
Bryants Cl. PE28: Up D ... 1J 7
SG5: Shill ... 4K 111
Bryant Way LU5: Todd ... 3F 129
Bryony Cl. MK41: Bed ... 1K 57
Bryony Way LU6: Duns ... 1E 146
Bryson Cl. MK45: West ... 1B 120
Buchanan Ct. LU2: Lut ... 2F 151
Buchanan Dr. LU2: Lut ... 2F 151
BUCKDEN ... 1C 161
Buckfast Av. MK41: Bed ... 4H 45
Buckingham Dr. LU2: Lut ... 7H 143
Buckingham M. MK45: Flitw ... 5K 107
BUCKLAND
Royston ... 1D 163
Tring ... 3A 162
BUCKLAND COMMON ... 3A 162
Buckle Cl. LU3: Lut ... 2H 141
Bucks Cl. MK43: Brom ... 7F 43
Buckwood Av. LU5: Duns ... 1A 148
Buckwood La. LU6: Stud ... 3H 153
Buckwood Rd. AL3: Mark, Stud ... 4B 154
LU6: Stud ... 4B 154
Budna Rd. MK44: Mogg ... 5B 60
SG19: Hat ... 5B 60
Buff La. SG19: E Hat, H Geor ... 1J 65
BULBOURNE ... 3A 162
Bullpond La. LU6: Duns ... 2H 147
BULL'S GREEN ... 3D 163
Bull St. SG19: Pott ... 3J 63
Bunhill Cl. LU6: Duns ... 2F 147
Bunkers Dr. MK45: C End ... 4B 72
Bunkers La. LU7: Lei Buz ... 3F 135
Bunting Dr. LU7: Lei Buz ... 5K 135
Bunting Rd. LU4: Lut ... 4C 140
Buntings, The MK41: Bed ... 5E 44
SG19: Sandy ... 7J 49
Bunyan Cl. MK45: Hou C ... 4C 84
SG17: Clif ... 3G 101
Bunyan Ho. LU3: Lut ... 1F 159 (1B 150)
Bunyan Rd. MK42: Bed ... 5D 56
MK42: Kemp ... 7A 56
MK45: West ... 2A 120
SG18: Bigg ... 6C 76
SG19: Sandy ... 1H 61
Bunyans Cl. LU3: Lut ... 4J 141
Bunyans Mead MK42: Els ... 6E 56
Bunyan Sports Cen. ... 6G 57
Bunyans Wlk. LU5: Harl ... 5B 120
BURCOTT ... 5A 134 (2A 162)
Burdetts Ct. SG19: Pott ... 3J 63
Bure Cl. MK41: Bed ... 3E 44
Burfield Ct. LU2: Lut ... 6H 143
Burford Cl. LU3: Lut ... 7H 131
Burford Wlk. LU5: Hou R ... 4A 140
Burges Cl. LU6: Duns ... 5K 147
Burgess Cl. MK42: Kemp ... 4K 55
MK45: Hay ... 4D 86
Burgess Way SG16: Hen ... 3K 101
Burghley Cl. MK45: Flitw ... 5J 107
Burgoyne Ct. SG19: Pott ... 2H 63
Burleigh Pl. MK43: Oak ... 1G 43
Burley SG6: Let C ... 5H 115
Burnaby Rd. MK40: Bed ... 1D 158 (1E 56)
Burnett Av. SG16: Hen ... 2H 113
BURNHAM GREEN ... 3D 163
Burnham Rd. LU2: Lut ... 7F 143
Burnix Ct. MK44: Colm ... 5F 25
Burns Ct. PE19: Eat F ... 2K 27
Burnt Cl. LU3: Lut ... 2H 141
Burr Cl. MK42: Kemp ... 7H 55
MK45: Bar C ... 3A 122
PE19: Eynes ... 1J 39
Burridge Cl. MK43: Mars M ... 4D 82
Burridge Ct. MK42: Bed ... 7A 158
Burridge's Cl. MK43: Stev ... 2C 42
Burrows Cl. MK17: Wob S ... 1A 104
SG17: Clif ... 3G 101
Burrsholt MK44: Cople ... 5E 58
Burrs Pl. LU1: Lut ... 6J 159 (4C 150)
Burr St. LU2: Lut ... 2J 159 (2C 150)
LU6: Duns ... 2H 147
Bursland SG6: Let C ... 7F 115
Burwell Rd. PE19: Eat F ... 1J 27
Bury, The MK43: Pave ... 4C 30
Bury Cl. LU5: Harl ... 6B 120
Bury Ct. MK41: Bed ... 7K 45
BURY END
Bedford ... 7A 42
Hitchin ... 3J 111
Bury Farm Cl. LU7: Slapt ... 4A 144
Bury Hill SG19: Pott ... 3K 63
Bury La. LU3: Stre ... 3J 131
Bury Mead SG15: Arl ... 6C 102
BURY PARK ... 3F 159 (2A 150)
Bury Pk. Ind. Pk. LU1: Lut ... 1A 150
Bury Pk. Rd. LU1: Lut ... 1A 150
Bury Ri. LU7: Tils ... 4K 137
Bury Rd. SG5: Shill ... 5J 111
SG17: Shef ... 2E 100
Bury Wlk. MK41: Bed ... 7K 45
Bush Cl. LU5: Todd ... 3F 129
Bushell Cl. LU7: Lei Buz ... 5K 135
Bushey Cl. LU6: Whip ... 2F 153
BUSHMEAD ... 2H 25 (1C 161)
Bushmead Av. MK40: Bed ... 1F 57
Bushmead Ct. LU2: Lut ... 3C 142
Bushmead Gdns. PE19: Eat S ... 4H 27
Bushmead Priory ... 1H 25
Bushmead Rd. LU2: Lut ... 4C 142
MK44: Colm ... 2G 25
PE19: Eat S ... 3E 26
Business Centre, The LU2: Lut ... 4F 151
Business Centre West
SG6: Let C ... 7K 115
Butcher's La. SG19: Wrest ... 6F 65
Bute Ct. LU1: Lut ... 3H 159
Butely Rd. LU4: Lut ... 3D 140
Bute Sq. LU1: Lut ... 4H 159 (3C 150)
Bute St. LU1: Lut ... 4H 159 (3C 150)
(not continuous)
Bute St. Mall LU1: Lut ... 4H 159
Butler Dr. MK43: Lidl ... 2C 94
Butler St. MK44: Rav ... 6G 33
(not continuous)
Butler Way MK42: Kemp ... 5A 56
Butlin Rd. LU1: Lut ... 3K 149
Butlin's Path LU1: Lut ... 2K 149
Buttercup Cl. LU6: Duns ... 3G 147
MK42: Bed ... 6G 57
Buttercup La. LU6: Duns ... 4G 147
Buttercup Mead SG18: Bigg ... 6E 76
Butterfield LU2: Lut ... 3F 143
Butterfield Ct. MK44: Mil E ... 3H 31
Butterfield Grn. Rd. LU2: Lut ... 3E 142
Buttermere Av. LU6: Duns ... 4J 147
Buttermere Cl. MK42: Kemp ... 7K 55
MK45: Flitw ... 4A 108
Buttermere Path *SG18: Bigg ... 7C 76*
(off Rydal Cl.)
Butterworth Path
LU2: Lut ... 2H 159 (2C 150)
Butts, The MK44: Rise ... 5A 14
SG18: Lang ... 6B 90
Buxton Cl. SG17: Mep ... 7C 100
Buxton Rd. LU1: Lut ... 5F 159 (3B 150)
Buxtons La. SG8: Guil M ... 7K 79
Buzzard Rd. LU4: Lut ... 5C 140
Byards Grn. SG19: Pott ... 2H 63
Bye Rd. MK43: Lidl ... 2B 94
Byfield Cl. LU4: Lut ... 1D 148
LU5: Todd ... 2E 128
Byford Path LU7: Lei Buz ... 4B 136
Byford Way LU7: Lei Buz ... 4B 136
BYGRAVE ... 1D 163
Byng Cl. PE19: Eat S ... 5H 27
Byrnes M. SG17: Shef ... 2C 100
Byron Cl. SG18: Bigg ... 6C 76
SG18: Up C ... 3J 75
Byron Cres. MK40: Bed ... 7B 44
MK45: Flitw ... 3K 107
Byron Pl. PE19: Eat F ... 1J 27
Byron Rd. LU4: Lut ... 7D 140
Byslips Rd. LU6: Stud ... 7K 153

C

CADDINGTON ... 6G 149 (3B 162)
Caddington Comn. AL3: Mark ... 3G 155
Caddington Golf Course ... 4F 149
Caddington Pk. *LU1: Lut ... 1D 148*
(off Skimpot La.)
Caddington Rd. LU1: Lut ... 1C 156
Cade Cl. SG6: Let C ... 5K 115
Cades Cl. LU1: Lut ... 4J 149
Cades La. LU1: Lut ... 4J 149
Cadia Cl. LU1: Cad ... 6G 149
CADWELL ... 1C 163
Caernarvon Rd. PE19: Eynes ... 1J 39
Cainhoe Rd. MK45: Clop ... 5A 98
Caister Rd. MK41: Bed ... 5K 45
Calcutt Cl. LU5: Duns ... 7B 140
CALDECOTE
Cambourne ... 2D 161
Letchworth Garden City ... 1D 163
Caldecote Grn. SG18: Up C ... 3H 75

Colwell Ri.—Daneswood

Colwell Ri. LU2: Lut . . . 7J 143
Colworth Rd. MK44: Sharn . . . 3B 20
Comet Dr. MK42: Short . . . 1J 71
Comfrey Cl. NN10: Rush . . . 1B 10
Comfrey Rd. SG5: Stot . . . 2F 115
Commerce Way LU7: Lei Buz . . . 3C 136
MK45: Flitw . . . 2C 108
Commerce Way Ind. Est.
LU7: Lei Buz . . . 3C 136
Commercial Rd.
MK40: Bed . . . 4B 158 (2D 56)
Common, The AL5: Harp . . . 7F 157
Common Farm La. MK45: Flitw . . . 2K 107
Common La. LU3: Up Sun . . . 4C 130
SG5: Hex . . . 4F 123
Common Rd. LU6: Kens . . . 2H 153
LU6: Stud . . . 7F 153
SG5: Stot . . . 5H 103
SG18: Lang . . . 1A 102
SG19: Pott . . . 2J 63
Common Vw. SG6: Let C . . . 6J 115
Common Vw. Sq. SG6: Let C . . . 6J 115
Comp, The LU6: Eat B . . . 4J 145
Compass Dr. MK42: Short . . . 7J 57
Comp Ga. LU6: Eat B . . . 4J 145
Compton Av. LU4: Lut . . . 5F 141
Compton Cl. MK45: Flitw . . . 5K 107
Concept Cen., The MK45: Millb . . . 1F 95
Concorde Cl. MK42: Short . . . 1J 71
Concorde St. LU2: Lut . . . 2K 159 (2D 150)
Concord Way LU7: Lei Buz . . . 4C 136
Concra Pk. MK17: Wob S . . . 2A 104
Conduit Rd. MK40: Bed . . . 2A 158 (1C 56)
Coneygate SG19: Mep . . . 1B 112
Coneygeare Ct. PE19: Eynes . . . 3K 27
Conger La. LU5: Todd . . . 2G 129
Conifers, The LU1: Lut . . . 6F 159 (4B 150)
MK45: Sils . . . 3K 109
CONINGTON . . . 1D 161
Coniston Cl. MK42: Kemp . . . 6A 56
Coniston Rd. LU3: Lut . . . 4H 141
LU7: Lei Buz . . . 2E 134
MK45: Flitw . . . 4A 108
Connaught Rd. LU4: Lut . . . 1G 149
Connaught Way MK41: Bed . . . 3F 45
Connelly La. SG5: Stot . . . 4E 114
Connors Cl. SG8: Guil M . . . 7K 79
Conquest Rd. LU5: Hou R . . . 4A 140
MK42: Bed . . . 5E 56
Constable Av. PE19: Eat F . . . 2K 27
Constable Cl. LU5: Hou R . . . 4K 139
Constable Ct. LU4: Lut . . . 7J 141
Constable Hill MK41: Bed . . . 7C 44
Constables Leys PE28: Kimb . . . 1J 9
Conway Cl. LU5: Hou R . . . 4A 140
NN10: Rush . . . 1A 10
Conway Cres. MK41: Bed . . . 4E 44
Conway Dr. MK45: Flitw . . . 5K 107
Conway Rd. LU4: Lut . . . 1K 149
Cook Dr. PE19: Eynes . . . 1J 39
Cookfield Cl. LU6: Duns . . . 2E 146
Cook's Mdw. LU6: Edles . . . 6J 145
Cooks Way SG18: Bigg . . . 5D 76
Coombe Dr. LU6: Duns . . . 3E 146
Coombs Cl. MK42: Bed . . . 4F 57
Cooper Cl. MK44: Wybo . . . 2E 36
SG16: Lwr Sto . . . 4E 112
Cooper Dr. LU7: Lei Buz . . . 4A 136
Coopers Cl. MK40: Bidd . . . 2J 55
MK44: Gt Bar . . . 4J 47
SG18: Bigg . . . 7D 76
SG19: Sandy . . . 4H 61
Coopers Ct. SG17: Shef . . . 3D 100
Coopers Fld. SG6: Let C . . . 7F 115
Cooper's Hill Nature Reserve . . . 5K 95
Coopers Way LU5: Hou R . . . 5G 139
Cooters End La. AL5: Harp . . . 7J 157
LU1: Lut . . . 7J 157
LU2: E Hyde . . . 7J 157
Cooters Hill Barns AL5: Harp . . . 6K 157
(not continuous)
Copelands SG18: Bigg . . . 5C 76
Copeland Wlk. MK41: Bed . . . 6K 45
Copenhagen Cl. LU3: Lut . . . 1F 141
COPLE . . . 4E 58 (3C 161)
Cople Pit's . . . 3E 58
Cople Rd. MK44: Card . . . 6B 58
Coplowe La. MK44: Blet . . . 6J 21
Coppens, The SG5: Stot . . . 1J 115
Copper Beech Way LU7: Lei Buz . . . 6J 125
Copperfield Cl. SG5: Stot . . . 4E 114
Copperfields LU4: Lut . . . 5E 140
Copperfields Cl. LU5: Hou R . . . 5K 139
Coppice Mead SG5: Stot . . . 1G 115
SG18: Bigg . . . 6D 76
Coppins, The AL3: Mark . . . 6F 155
MK45: Amp . . . 5B 96
Copse, The MK41: Bed . . . 7K 45
MK43: Turv . . . 4F 41
Copse Way LU3: Lut . . . 1F 141
COPT HALL . . . 6J 151
Copthorne LU2: Lut . . . 6H 143
Copthorne Cl. MK43: Oak . . . 1G 43
Coral Cl. LU6: Eat B . . . 4J 145
Corbet Ride LU7: Lei Buz . . . 1F 135
Corbet Sq. LU7: Lei Buz . . . 1F 135
Corbridge Dr. LU2: Lut . . . 7J 143
Corby Cl. MK42: Bed . . . 6F 57
Corfe Rd. MK41: Bed . . . 5J 45
Corinium Gdns. LU3: Lut . . . 1J 141
Cormorant Way LU7: Lei Buz . . . 4A 136
Corncastle Path
LU1: Lut . . . 7F 159 (4B 150)
Corncastle Rd.
LU1: Lut . . . 7F 159 (4A 150)
Corncrake Cl. LU2: Lut . . . 4G 143
Cornel Cl. LU1: Lut . . . 3J 149
Cornel Ct. LU1: Lut . . . 3J 149
Corner Cl. NN29: Pod . . . 5C 10
SG6: Let C . . . 7G 115
Corner Wood AL3: Mark . . . 6F 155
Cornflower Cres. SG5: Stot . . . 1G 115
Cornish Cl. SG17: Shef . . . 2C 100
Cornland MK41: Bed . . . 6J 45
Corn Mill Cl. LU7: Wing . . . 7A 134
Cornwall Ct. PE19: Eat S . . . 3J 27
Cornwallis Cl. MK43: Brom . . . 6E 42
Cornwallis Dr. PE19: Eat S . . . 4G 27
Cornwall Rd. MK40: Bed . . . 7F 45
MK45: Amp . . . 5B 96
Coronation Bus. Pk.
MK43: Kemp H . . . 7A 70
Coronation M. LU7: Lei Buz . . . 1H 135
Coronation Rd. MK43: Cran . . . 3F 81
Coroner's Court
Luton . . . 5F 159
Corunna Cl. PE19: Eat F . . . 2J 27
Cosgrove Way LU1: Lut . . . 1F 149
Cosmic Av. MK42: Bed . . . 6C 56
Costin St. MK40: Bed . . . 4B 158 (2D 56)
Cotefield LU4: Lut . . . 6E 140
Cotefield Dr. LU7: Lei Buz . . . 6J 125
(not continuous)
Cotes Way LU7: Wing . . . 6B 134
Cotman Cl. MK41: Bed . . . 6D 44
Cotswold Bus. Pk. LU1: Cad . . . 1F 155
Cotswold Cl. MK41: Bed . . . 6H 45
Cotswold Dr. LU7: Lei Buz . . . 1E 134
Cotswold Gdns. LU3: Lut . . . 2E 140
Cotswold Pl. MK45: Flitw . . . 4K 107
Cottage Rd. SG19: Sandy . . . 1H 61
COTTERED . . . 2D 163
Cottesloe Cl. LU7: Wing . . . 6A 134
COTTON END . . . 4B 72 (3B 160)
Cotton End Rd. MK45: Wils . . . 7H 71
Cottril Way MK42: Bed . . . 4G 57
Coulson Ct. LU1: Lut . . . 2G 149
Countess Cl. PE19: Eat S . . . 3H 27
Countess Ct. LU2: Lut . . . 1G 159
Countess Gdns. MK42: Kemp . . . 7K 55
County Court
Bedford . . . 4C 158 (2D 56)
Luton . . . 4G 159
Coupees Path LU2: Lut . . . 2H 159 (2C 150)
Court, The MK17: Salf . . . 2A 92
Court Dr. LU5: Duns . . . 1H 147
Courtlands, The LU7: Lei Buz . . . 3G 135
Courtlands Dr. SG18: Bigg . . . 1E 90
Court La. MK43: Stev . . . 1B 42
Court Rd. MK43: Cran . . . 3F 81
Court Yard, The LU7: Soulb . . . 2B 134
Covent Gdn. Cl. LU4: Lut . . . 6H 141
Coventry Rd. MK40: Bed . . . 2B 56
Coverdale LU4: Lut . . . 3D 140
COVINGTON . . . 2H 5 (1B 160)
Covington Rd. PE28: Cov . . . 3H 5
Cow Cl. SG18: Holme . . . 1C 90
Cowdray Cl. LU2: Lut . . . 6G 143
Cow La. LU6: Edles . . . 5H 145
Cowper Ct. AL3: Mark . . . 6F 155
PE19: Eat F . . . 1K 27
Cowper Ri. AL3: Mark . . . 6F 155
Cowper Rd. AL3: Mark . . . 6F 155
MK40: Bed . . . 7B 44
Cowper St. LU1: Lut . . . 7H 159 (5C 150)
Cowridge Cres. LU2: Lut . . . 1E 150
Cowslip Dr. SG5: Stot . . . 1H 115
Cowslip Hill SG6: Let C . . . 7G 115
Cox's Cl. MK40: Bed . . . 3B 56
MK44: Sharn . . . 3B 20
Cox's Way SG15: Arl . . . 7C 102
Coyney Grn. LU3: Lut . . . 1A 150
Crab La. SG18: Bigg . . . 5C 76
(not continuous)
Crabtree La. MK17: Wave . . . 5A 92
Crabtree Way LU6: Duns . . . 1H 147
Crackle Hill Rd. SG17: Mep . . . 7C 100
Craddock Dr. LU7: Lei Buz . . . 5J 125
Cradock Rd. LU4: Lut . . . 1C 148
CRAFTON . . . 3A 162
Cranborne Cl. MK41: Bed . . . 5K 45
Cranbrook Dr. LU3: Lut . . . 1F 141
Crancott Cl. MK45: Hou C . . . 4D 84
Cranes Cl. MK43: Turv . . . 4B 40
Crane Way MK43: Cran . . . 2G 81
CRANFIELD . . . 2F 81 (3A 160)
Cranfield Airfield . . . 3C 80
Cranfield Rd. MK16: Ast . . . 7E 52
MK17: Salf . . . 7B 80
MK17: Wave, Wob S . . . 6A 92
MK43: Cran . . . 6B 80
MK43: Woo . . . 7E 68
Cranfield Technology Pk.
MK43: Cran . . . 4B 80
Cranfield University . . . 2C 80
Cranleigh Gdns. LU3: Lut . . . 6A 142
Crawley Cl. LU1: Slip E . . . 2A 156
Crawley Crossing MK43: Hus C . . . 6F 93
Crawley Grn. Rd.
LU1: Lut . . . 5K 159 (3D 150)
LU2: Lut . . . 1G 151
Crawley Pk. MK43: Hus C . . . 1E 104
Crawley Rd. LU1: Lut . . . 2F 159 (2B 150)
MK17: Wob . . . 6D 104
MK43: Cran . . . 7E 66
Crayton Rd. MK45: Amp . . . 5A 96
Creasey Pk. Dr. LU6: Duns . . . 7F 139
Crecy Ct. PE19: Eat F . . . 2J 27
Crediton Cl. MK40: Bed . . . 7G 45
Creran Wlk. LU7: Lei Buz . . . 2E 134
Crescent, The LU1: Cad . . . 6G 149
LU5: Todd . . . 3F 129
MK40: Bed . . . 2B 158 (1D 56)
MK42: Short . . . 7J 57
MK43: Stew . . . 3J 83
MK43: Whar E . . . 2C 80
MK44: Mogg . . . 3C 60
MK45: Amp . . . 6K 95
MK45: C End . . . 4B 72
PE19: Eat S . . . 4J 27
SG16: Hen . . . 2J 113
SG18: Stan . . . 5G 89
SG19: Bee . . . 5H 61
Crescent Cl. LU5: Todd . . . 3F 129
Crescent Ct. LU5: Todd . . . 3F 129
MK40: Bed . . . 1B 158
Crescent Ri. LU2: Lut . . . 3K 159 (2D 150)
Crescent Rd. LU2: Lut . . . 3K 159 (2D 150)
Crescent Vw. MK44: Mogg . . . 2C 60
Cresswell Gdns. LU3: Lut . . . 7K 131
Crest, The LU3: Lut . . . 2K 141
LU5: Duns . . . 1A 148
Cresta Cl. LU5: Duns . . . 7C 140
Criccieth Way PE19: Eynes . . . 1K 39
Cricket Cl. MK41: Bed . . . 7J 45
Cricketer's Rd. SG15: Arl . . . 2C 114
Cricket La. MK41: Bed . . . 7J 45
Crispin Dr. MK41: Bed . . . 1E 44
(not continuous)
Crocus Way NN10: Rush . . . 1B 10
Croft, The LU3: Lut . . . 1F 141
MK41: Bed . . . 7J 45
MK45: Flitw . . . 3A 108
Croft Grn. LU6: Duns . . . 2F 147
Croft La. SG6: Let C . . . 5J 115
Crofton Cl. MK41: Bed . . . 5F 45
Croft Rd. LU2: Lut . . . 6F 143
Crofts, The MK44: Sharn . . . 3E 20
SG5: Stot . . . 7H 103
CROMER . . . 2D 163
Cromer Way LU2: Lut . . . 2B 142
Cromwell Ct. *MK42: Kemp . . . 6A 56*
(off Farrer St.)
PE28: Kimb . . . 1J 9
Cromwell Grn. SG6: Let C . . . 6K 115
Cromwell Hill LU2: Lut . . . 1G 159 (1B 150)
Cromwell Rd. LU3: Lut . . . 1F 159 (1B 150)
MK40: Bed . . . 3B 56
MK45: Bar C . . . 3A 122
SG6: Let C . . . 6K 115
Crosby Cl. LU4: Lut . . . 7J 141
LU6: Duns . . . 4J 147
Cross End MK44: Thur . . . 6G 23
Cross End La. MK44: Thur . . . 5G 23
Crosshall Rd. PE19: Eat F . . . 1J 27
Cross Keys Mall *PE19: St N . . . 2K 27*
(off High St.)
Crosslands LU1: Cad . . . 7G 149
Crossleys SG6: Let C . . . 4H 115
Crosspaths AL5: Harp . . . 7G 157
Cross St. LU2: Lut . . . 2J 159 (2C 150)
MK40: Bed . . . 2C 158 (1D 56)
PE28: Cov . . . 2H 5
SG6: Let C . . . 7H 115
Cross St. Nth. LU6: Duns . . . 1G 147
Crossway LU7: Lei Buz . . . 2B 136
Crossway, The LU1: Lut . . . 5A 150
Crossways LU5: Hou R . . . 4J 139
Crossways Cl. SG16: Hen . . . 4K 101
CROW END . . . 2D 161
Crowe Rd. MK40: Bed . . . 2B 56
Crow Hill SG19: Sandy . . . 7H 49
Crowland Rd. LU2: Lut . . . 4G 143
Crow La. MK17: Wave . . . 5A 92
MK43: Hus C . . . 2F 105
Crown Court
Luton . . . 5J 159 (3C 150)
Crown Ct. LU1: Lut . . . 3G 159
Crown La. SG18: Lang . . . 6B 90
Crown Lodge SG15: Arl . . . 2C 114
Crown Pl. MK42: Bed . . . 6B 158 (3D 56)
Crown Quay MK40: Bed . . . 5B 158 (3D 56)
Crown Wlk. PE19: Eat S . . . 3H 27
Crowsley Rd. MK42: Kemp . . . 7H 55
Crowther Ct. SG18: Bigg . . . 4B 76
Croxden Way MK42: Els . . . 7E 56
Croxley Ct. LU7: Lei Buz . . . 2H 135
CROXTON . . . 1D 161
Croxton Cl. LU3: Lut . . . 2J 141
CROYDON . . . 3D 161
Croyland Dr. MK42: Els . . . 7F 57
Cryselco Cl. MK42: Kemp . . . 7K 55
Crystal Ho. LU1: Lut . . . 3G 159 (2B 150)
Cubbington Cl. LU3: Lut . . . 2J 141
Cuckoo Cl. SG19: Sandy . . . 7H 49
Cuckoo's Nest LU2: Lut . . . 3E 150
Cuffley Cl. LU3: Lut . . . 5H 141
Cullen Cl. LU3: Lut . . . 6A 142
Culloden Cl. PE19: Eat F . . . 2J 27
Culver Ho. *MK40: Bed . . . 7C 44*
(off Linden Rd.)
Culverhouse Rd. LU3: Lut . . . 5A 142
Culworth Cl. LU1: Cad . . . 7G 149
Cumberland St.
LU1: Lut . . . 6J 159 (4C 150)
LU5: Hou R . . . 5H 139
Cumberland Way PE19: Eynes . . . 1K 39
CUMBERLOW GREEN . . . 1D 163
Cumbria Cl. LU5: Hou R . . . 4A 140
Cunningham Way PE19: Eat S . . . 5G 27
Curlew Cl. SG6: Let C . . . 5G 115
Curlew Cres. MK41: Bed . . . 5D 44
Curlew Rd. LU2: Lut . . . 4G 143
Curzon Rd. LU3: Lut . . . 1A 150
Cussen Pl. LU3: Lut . . . 2F 141
Cusworth Wlk. LU6: Duns . . . 1E 146
Cusworth Way LU6: Duns . . . 1E 146
Cutcliffe Gdns. MK40: Bed . . . 2B 56
Cutcliffe Gro. MK40: Bed . . . 1B 56
Cutcliffe Pl. MK40: Bed . . . 2B 56
Cutenhoe Rd. LU1: Lut . . . 6C 150
Cutlers Grn. LU2: Lut . . . 7K 143
Cutlers Way LU7: Lei Buz . . . 3K 135
Cut Throat Av. LU6: Whip . . . 4D 152
Cut Throat La. MK41: Bed . . . 7B 44
Cut-throat Meadow Nature Reserve
. . . 4C 96
Cygnus Dr. LU7: Lei Buz . . . 1B 136
Cynthia Ct. MK43: Woo . . . 5G 69

D

Daffodil Dr. NN10: Rush . . . 1B 10
Dag La. MK44: Rise . . . 4B 14
DAGNALL . . . 6C 152 (3A 162)
Dagnall Rd. LU6: Duns, Whip . . . 1C 152
Dagnall Way LU6: Edles . . . 3A 152
Dahl Cl. MK42: Bed . . . 6E 56
Dahlia Cl. LU2: Lut . . . 6F 143
Daimler Dr. LU6: Duns . . . 7F 139
Dairy, The SG16: Hen . . . 4K 101
Daisy Ct. SG6: Let C . . . 6J 115
Daisy La. SG5: Stot . . . 1G 115
Daisy Pl. LU3: Lut . . . 2E 140
Dalby Cl. LU4: Lut . . . 6D 140
Dale Cl. LU5: Duns . . . 1B 148
LU5: Todd . . . 3F 129
MK41: Bed . . . 6J 45
Dale Rd. LU1: Lut . . . 3A 150
LU5: Duns . . . 1B 148
Dallas Rd. MK42: Bed . . . 4C 56
Dalling Dr. LU5: Hou R . . . 4J 139
Dallow Rd. LU1: Lut . . . 4F 159 (2G 149)
Dalroad Ind. Est. LU1: Lut . . . 2K 149
Dalton Cl. LU3: Lut . . . 7K 131
Dame Alice Ct.
MK40: Bed . . . 3E 158 (2E 56)
Dame Alice St.
MK40: Bed . . . 2C 158 (1D 56)
Dammersey Cl. AL3: Mark . . . 7H 155
Dane Cl. SG5: Stot . . . 5H 103
DANE END . . . 2D 163
Dane La. MK42: Wils . . . 6E 70
MK45: Wils . . . 6E 70
Dane Rd. LU3: Lut . . . 7K 141
MK45: Bar C . . . 4B 122
Danesborough Dr.
MK17: Asp H . . . 7A 104
Danescroft SG6: Let C . . . 5H 115
DANE STREET . . . 4K 151
Dane St. MK40: Bed . . . 3C 158 (2D 56)
Danes Way LU7: Lei Buz . . . 2B 136
Daneswood MK17: Asp H . . . 7A 104

Danish Camp Riverside Vis. Cen.—Eaton Pk.

Danish Camp Riverside Vis. Cen. 1G 59
Danvers Dr. LU3: Lut 7A 132
Dapifer Dr. SG19: Sandy 2J 61
Dark La. SG18: Bigg 5B 76
Darlington Cl. SG19: Sandy 1K 61
Darlow Dr. MK40: Bidd 2K 55
Darrington Cl. PE19: Eat S 4H 27
Dartmoor Way SG18: Bigg 3E 76
Dartmouth M. LU4: Lut 6F 141
Dart Rd. MK41: Bed 4E 44
Darwin Rd. MK42: Bed 5E 56
DATCHWORTH 3D 163
DATCHWORTH GREEN 3D 163
Daubeney Cl. LU5: Harl 5B 120
Dauphin Ct. LU2: Lut 1G 159
Davey Ct. PE19: Eat F 3J 27
David Evans Ct. SG6: Let C 7F 115
David Harrowell Ho. SG15: Arl 2B 114
David Lloyd Leisure
Luton 5D 150
Davies Gdns. MK44: Rise 4C 14
Davis Cl. MK42: Bed 5E 56
Davis Row SG15: Arl 2C 114
Dawlish Dr. MK40: Bed 1G 57
Dawlish Rd. LU4: Lut 6H 141
Dawson Cl. SG16: Hen 1J 113
Daysfield MK45: Hou C 4D 84
Day's La. MK40: Bidd 1J 55
Deacon Av. MK42: Kemp 1J 69
Deacon M. MK43: Mars M 4C 82
Deacons Ct. LU2: Lut 2G 159
DEADMAN'S CROSS 3G 87 (3C 161)
Dean Cl. NN10: Rush 1A 10
Dean Farm La. LU7: Soulb 3A 124
Deans Mdw. HP4: Dag 6C 152
Dean St. MK40: Bed 1H 57
Dearmans Cl. MK45: Clop 4A 98
Dearne Wlk. MK41: Bed 4E 44
DEEPDALE 3F 63
Deep Denes LU2: Lut 7E 142
Deep Spinney MK40: Bidd 1H 55
Deeside MK41: Bed 4F 45
De Havilland Av. MK42: Short 1J 71
Delamere Cl. SG19: Sandy 1H 61
Delamere Gdns. LU7: Lei Buz 2E 134
Delamere Wlk. MK41: Bed 6K 45
Delco Way LU6: Duns 7F 139
Delfield Gdns. LU1: Cad 6G 149
Dell, The AL3: Mark 6F 155
LU1: Cad 7G 149
LU2: Lut 1K 151
LU7: Heat R 3K 125
MK42: Kemp 1H 69
Dellcot Cl. LU2: Lut 4F 143
Dell Farm Outdoor Education Cen. 2F 153
Dellfield Ct. LU2: Lut 7H 143
Dellmont Rd. LU5: Hou R 4H 139
Dell Rd. LU5: Hou R 4H 139
Dells, The SG18: Bigg 6C 76
Dells La. SG18: Bigg 6C 76
Delphine Cl. LU1: Lut 4J 149
De Montfort Ct. *LU5: Todd* *4F 129* *(off Mt. Pleasant Av.)*
Denbigh Cl. MK43: Mars M 4D 82
Denbigh Rd. LU3: Lut 7K 141
Denbigh Way MK41: Bed 5J 45
Dencora Way LU3: Lut 1D 140
Dene Cl. MK17: Wob S 3A 104
Denel Cl. MK45: Flitw 2A 108
Dene Way SG18: Up C 3H 75
Denham Cl. LU3: Lut 1G 141 (not continuous)
Denmark Cl. LU3: Lut 7G 131
Denmark St. MK40: Bed 1G 57
Dennis Cl. MK41: Clap 2J 43
Dennis Ct. MK42: Kemp 1K 69
Dennis Grn. SG19: Gam 4K 51
Dennis Rd. MK42: Kemp 1J 69
Denny Cres. SG18: Lang 4B 90
Denton Cl. LU4: Lut 5D 140
MK42: Kemp 4K 55
Denton Dr. MK43: Mars M 4C 82
Dents Rd. MK42: Bed 4F 57
De Parys Av. MK40: Bed 1D 158 (7E 44)
De Parys Lodge MK40: Bed 2C 158
Derby Pl. MK40: Bed 1C 158 (1D 56)
Derby Rd. LU4: Lut 7E 140
Derwent Av. LU3: Lut 2K 141
SG18: Bigg 7D 76
Derwent Cotts. MK43: Pave 5B 30
Derwent Dr. LU6: Duns 5J 147
Derwent Pl. MK42: Bed 4D 56
Derwent Ri. MK45: Flitw 4K 107
Derwent Rd. AL5: Harp 7G 157
LU2: Lut 2E 150
LU7: Lei Buz 2D 134
SG16: Hen 2H 113
Des Fuller Ct. LU1: Lut 6K 159
Deverell Way LU7: Lei Buz 4A 136
Devizes Av. MK41: Bed 4J 45
Devon Dr. SG18: Bigg 3E 76
Devon Rd. LU2: Lut 2F 151
MK40: Bed 1F 57
Devonshire Bus. Cen.
SG6: Let C 7K 115
Dewlands MK43: Oak 2F 43
Dew Pond Rd. MK45: Flitw 5K 107
Dewsbury Rd. LU3: Lut 3K 141
Dexter Cl. LU3: Lut 7K 131
Diamond Ct. SG19: Pott 3J 63
Dickens Blvd. SG5: Stot 4E 114
Dickens Cl. MK43: Harr 2D 28
Dickens Ct. SG18: Bigg 6C 76
Dickens La. LU7: Tils 4A 138
Dickens Rd. MK45: Flitw 3J 107
DIDDINGTON 1C 161
Digby Cl. LU4: Lut 1G 149
Digby Ct. PE19: Eat S 4H 27
Digby Rd. LU7: Lei Buz 1J 135
DIGSWELL 3D 163
Digswell Cl. SG17: Shef 3D 100
Dilley Cft. SG18: Bigg 5D 76
DILLINGTON 1C 161
Dillock La. MK43: Woo 2C 68
Dimmock Cl. LU7: Lei Buz 5A 136
Dimmock Rd. MK43: Woo 4F 69
Dines Cl. MK45: Wils 7G 71
Dingle Dell LU7: Lei Buz 6H 125
Disraeli Pl. SG5: Stot 4E 114
Ditchling Cl. LU2: Lut 6G 143
Ditmas Av. MK42: Kemp 1H 69
Ditton Grn. LU2: Lut 6J 143
Dodds Cl. MK44: Rise 3D 14
Doggett St. LU7: Lei Buz 2H 135
Dolcey Way MK44: Sharn 4B 20
Dolmans Pl. LU6: Duns 2H 147
Dolphin Dr. LU5: Hou R 4A 140
Don Butler Cl. MK45: Sils 3K 109
Donnelly Dr. MK41: Bed 1J 57
Doolittle La. LU6: Tott 5B 146
Doolittle Mill MK45: Amp 1K 107
Doolittle Yd. MK45: Flitw 1K 107
Dorchester Cl. LU5: Duns 1H 147
Dorchester Ho. *SG6: Let C* *7H 115* *(off Station Rd.)*
Dorchester Way MK42: Els 7E 56
Dordans Rd. LU4: Lut 5G 141
Dorel Cl. LU2: Lut 7D 142
Dormer Av. LU7: Wing 6A 134
Dornan Ct. LU1: Lut 5C 150
Dorrington Cl. LU3: Lut 1A 150
Dorset Ct. LU1: Lut 7K 159
Dorsey Dr. MK42: Bed 5D 56
Dothans Cl. MK44: Gt Bar 4K 47
Doug Harris Way MK45: Sils 3K 109
Douglas Cres. LU5: Hou R 6G 139
Douglas Pl. LU5: Hou R 7G 139
Douglas Rd. LU4: Lut 7J 141
MK41: Bed 3F 45
Dove Cl. SG19: Sandy 7J 49
Dovedale LU2: Lut 3C 142
Dovehouse Cl. LU6: Edles 6K 145
MK43: Brom 7F 43
Dove Ho. Dr. SG16: Hen 4K 101
Dovehouse Hill LU2: Lut 7F 143
Dovehouse La. LU6: Kens 4J 153
Dove La. MK42: Wils 5E 70
MK43: Harr 2E 28
Dover Cl. LU3: Lut 6J 141
Dover Cres. MK41: Bed 4J 45
Dove Rd. MK41: Bed 5F 45
Dove Tree Rd. LU7: Lei Buz 1A 136
Dove Wlk. MK45: Flitw 5A 108
Downfield Way MK42: Kemp 5A 56
Downham Rd. MK17: Wob S 2A 104
Downlands LU3: Lut 2E 140
Downlands Ct. LU4: Lut 7C 140
Downlands Pk. Homes LU1: Pep 3A 156
Downs Ct. LU1: Lut 3A 150
DOWNSIDE 3K 147
Downside MK41: Bed 6J 45
Downside Gdns. SG19: Pott 2J 63
Downs Rd. LU1: Lut 3A 150
LU5: Duns 2K 147
Downs Vw. LU4: Lut 5F 141
LU5: Duns 3K 147
Downton Ct. LU3: Lut 2F 159 (2B 150)
Downview LU4: Lut 7D 140
Doyle Pl. SG5: Stot 4E 114
Drakeloe Cl. MK17: Wob 6D 104
Drake Rd. PE19: Eat S 5H 27
Drakes Av. LU7: Lei Buz 7K 125
Drapers End MK43: Mars M 5C 82
Drapers M. LU3: Lut 1A 150
Draper Way LU7: Lei Buz 4A 136
DRAYTON BEAUCHAMP 3A 162
Drayton Rd. LU4: Lut 6B 140
MK42: Kemp 1K 69
Drewels La. PE19: Eynes H 1D 38 (not continuous)
Drinnan Ct. LU2: Lut 1G 159
Drive, The MK43: Oak 2F 43
MK43: Whar E 2B 80
MK44: Sharn 3C 20
Drivers Ct. LU7: Lei Buz 2B 136
Dropshort Marsh 4E 128
Drove Rd. SG18: Bigg 4D 76
SG19: Gam 5H 51
Drovers Way LU6: Duns 2F 147
Drummonds, The LU4: Lut 7E 140
Drury Cl. LU5: Hou R 4J 139
Drury La. LU5: Hou R 4J 139
Dubbs Knoll Rd. SG8: Guil M 6K 79
Duchess Cl. PE19: Eat S 4G 27
Duchess Ct. *LU5: Duns* *1J 147* *(off The Mall)*
Duchess Rd. MK42: Bed 6H 57
Duchess Wlk., The PE28: Kimb 1J 9
DUCK END
Bedford, MK43 3A 42
MK45, Maulden 5D 96
MK45, Wilstead 6G 71
Duck End Cl. MK45: Hou C 3C 84
Duck End La. MK40: Bidd 1H 55
MK45: Maul 5D 96
MK45: Wils 6G 71
Duck La. MK17: Wob 7D 104
SG17: Shef *2C 100* *(off High St.)*
Duckmill Cres.
MK42: Bed 4E 158 (2E 56)
Duckmill La.
MK42: Bed 5D 158 (3E 56)
Duckmill Wlk.
MK40: Bed 4D 158 (2E 56)
Dudley Cl. MK42: Kemp 7A 56
Dudley St. LU2: Lut 2H 159 (2C 150)
LU7: Lei Buz 3J 135
MK40: Bed 1G 57
Duke Dr. MK41: Clap 2K 43
Dukeminster Est. LU5: Duns 1J 147
Dukes Av. LU6: Whip 3E 152
Dukes Ct. *LU5: Duns* *1J 147* *(off The Mall)*
MK45: Flitw 4C 108
Dukes Ride LU2: Lut 1B 150
LU7: Lei Buz 5G 125
Dukes Rd. MK45: Amp 5B 96
PE19: Eat S 3H 27
Dukes Row PE28: Kimb 1J 9
Duke St. LU2: Lut 2J 159 (2C 150) (not continuous)
MK17: Asp G 2B 104
MK40: Bed 3D 158 (2E 56)
DULOE 1F 27 (1C 161)
Duloe Brook PE19: Eat S 3H 27
DULOE BUTTS 2F 27
Duloe Rd. PE19: Eat S 2H 27
Dulverton Ct. LU7: Lei Buz 1E 134
Dumfries Ct. LU1: Lut 6G 159
Dumfries St. LU1: Lut 6F 159 (4B 150) (not continuous)
Duncan Rd. MK43: Whar E 2C 80
Duncombe Cl. LU3: Lut 3A 142
Duncombe Ct. LU5: Duns 7A 140
Duncombe Dr. LU5: Duns 7A 140
LU7: Lei Buz 3J 135
Duncombe St. MK42: Kemp 6B 56
Dungee Rd. MK43: Odell 2A 18
NN29: Boz 2A 18
Dunham Cl. MK42: Bed 5H 57
Dunhams Ct. SG6: Let C 7K 115
Dunham's La. SG6: Let C 7K 115
Dunkerley Ct. SG6: Let C 7J 115
Dunkirk Cl. MK42: Kemp 5C 56
Dunlin SG6: Let C 5G 115
Dunmow Ct. LU3: Lut 7B 142
Dunraven Av. LU1: Lut 2J 149
Dunsby Rd. LU3: Lut 3J 141
Dunsmore Rd. LU1: Lut 4K 149
DUNSTABLE 2H 147 (2B 162)
Dunstable Cl. LU4: Lut 1J 149
MK45: Flitw 4A 108
Dunstable Ct. LU4: Lut 1H 149
Dunstable Downs 7E 146
Dunstable Downs Golf Course 5F 147
Dunstable Leisure Cen. & Harpers Fitness 1H 147
Dunstable Pl. LU1: Lut 5G 159 (3B 150)
Dunstable Rd. HP4: Dag 6C 152
LU1: Cad 5B 148
LU1: Lut 7F 141
LU4: Lut 3F 159 (7C 140)
LU5: Chalg, Todd 5F 129
LU5: Hou R 5H 139
LU6: Duns, Tott 3C 146
LU6: Eat B, Tott 5A 146
LU6: Kens, Stud 6F 147
LU6: Whip 6C 152
LU7: Tils 4K 137
MK45: Flitw 5A 108
Dunstable St. AL3: Mark 3E 154
MK45: Amp 6A 96
Dunstall Rd. MK45: Bar C 5A 122
Dunster Gdns. MK41: Bed 4K 45
Dunster Way PE19: Eynes 1K 39
DUNTON 6B 78 (3D 161)
Dunton La. SG18: Bigg 7E 76 (not continuous)
Dunvegan Way MK41: Bed 4H 45
Dunville Rd. MK40: Bed 2B 56
Durbar Rd. LU4: Lut 1J 149
Durham Cl. MK45: Flitw 2A 108
SG18: Bigg 7C 76
Durham Rd. LU2: Lut 2E 150
Durler Av. MK42: Kemp 1H 69
Durler Gdns. LU1: Lut 5B 150
Durrell Cl. LU7: Lei Buz 2G 135
Duxford Cl. LU3: Lut 2K 141
Dyers Rd. LU6: Eat B 3J 145
Dylan Ct. LU5: Hou R 4J 139
Dynes Pl. MK44: Mogg 3C 60
Dynevor Cl. MK43: Brom 7E 42
Dynevor Rd. MK40: Bed 1A 158 (1C 56)

E

Eagle Cen. Way LU4: Lut 2D 140
Eagle Cl. LU4: Lut 5C 140
LU7: Lei Buz 3K 135
Eagle Dr. MK45: Flitw 4K 107
Eagle Farm Rd. SG18: Bigg 6D 76
Eagle Gdns. MK41: Bed 6D 44
Eagle Way MK43: Harr 2D 28
Earl Cl. PE19: Eat S 3H 27
EARLS BARTON 1A 160
Earls Ct. LU5: Duns 1J 147
Earls Holme MK42: Kemp 4K 55
Earls Meade LU2: Lut 1G 159 (1B 150)
Earnshaw Dr. SG5: Stot 4E 114
Easby Abbey MK41: Bed 2K 57
Easedale Cl. LU6: Duns 4J 147
Easingwold Gdns. LU1: Lut 2H 149
Eastcote MK42: Short 7J 57
Eastcott Cl. LU2: Lut 1H 151
EASTCOTTS 6H 57
Eastcotts Pk. MK42: Bed 5J 57
Eastcotts Rd. MK42: Bed 5H 57
East Ct. MK41: Bed 7J 45
Eastdale Cl. MK42: Kemp 6C 56
EAST END
Bedford 2G 81
Newport Pagnell 5D 66
East End LU5: Hou R 4J 139
MK43: Pave 5F 31
East End La. MK44: Wild 5F 35
Eastern Av. LU5: Duns 2K 147
SG16: Hen 3J 113
Eastern Av. Ind. Est. LU5: Duns 2K 147
Eastern Way LU7: Heat R 4K 125
SG6: Let C 6J 115
Eastfield Cl. LU2: Lut 5G 143
EAST HATLEY 2D 161
East Hill LU3: Lut 3K 141
Easthill Rd. LU5: Hou R 4J 139
East Hills MK43: Cran 3F 81
Eastholm SG6: Let C 6J 115
Eastholm Grn. SG6: Let C 6J 115
EAST HYDE 4K 157 (3C 163)
East La. SG19: Gam 3K 51
Eastnor Gdns. *MK41: Bed* *5J 45* *(off Dover Cres.)*
EASTON 1C 161
Easton Cl. MK45: Flitw 3B 108
Easton Grn. Ct. LU2: Lut 2G 151
EASTON MAUDIT 2A 160
Easton Rd. MK45: Flitw 3B 108
EAST PERRY 1C 161
East Rd. MK43: Whar E 2B 80
SG18: Lang 4B 90
SG19: Sandy 2H 61
East Side SG19: Bee 5J 61
East Sq. MK42: Short 7J 57
East St. LU2: Lill 6H 133
LU7: Lei Buz 1J 135
PE28: Kimb 1K 9
Eastville Rd. MK42: Bed 5D 56
East Wlk. SG18: Bigg 4D 76
Easy Way LU2: Lut 4H 151
EATON BRAY 4J 145 (2A 162)
Eaton Bray Rd. LU6: N'all 6G 145
LU6: Tott 2J 145
Eaton Ct. Rd. PE19: Eat S 6H 27
EATON FORD 1K 27
Eaton Ford Grn. PE19: Eat F 2K 27
Eatongate Cl. LU6: Eat B 6J 145
Eaton Grn. Rd. LU2: Lut 2G 151 (not continuous)
Eaton Grn. Rdbt. LU2: Lut 2G 151
Eaton M. MK45: G'fld 4E 108
Eaton Pk. LU6: Eat B 4K 145

172 A-Z Bedfordshire Atlas

Flitton Hill—Grange La.

Flitton Hill MK45: Flitt ... 2G 109
Flitton Rd. MK45: G'fld ... 4E 108
MK45: Pull ... 5G 109
FLITWICK ... 2A 108 (1B 162)
Flitwick Ind. Est. MK45: Flitw ... 3C 108
Flitwick Leisure Cen. ... 2K 107
Flitwick Local Nature Reserve ... 4J 107
Flitwick Moor (& Folly Wood)
Nature Reserve ... 3D 108
Flitwick Rd. MK45: Amp ... 7A 96
(not continuous)
MK45: Flitw, West ... 5A 108
MK45: Maul ... 7C 96
MK45: Step ... 3G 107
MK45: West ... 1A 120
Flitwick Station (Rail) ... 3A 108
Florence Av. LU3: Lut ... 2F 141
Florence Cl. LU5: Duns ... 1A 148
Flowerdale Cotts. AL3: Mark ... 5F 155
Flowerdale Wlk. MK41: Bed ... 5K 45
Flowers Ind. Est.
LU1: Lut ... 6J 159 (4C 150)
Flowers Way LU1: Lut ... 5H 159 (3C 150)
Folders Ga. MK45: Amp ... 6K 95
Folly Farm MK43: Cran ... 4E 80
Folly La. LU1: Cad ... 6G 149
Folly Pk. MK41: Clap ... 3K 43
FOLLY, THE ... 3C 163
Fontwell Cl. MK40: Bed ... 1F 57
Ford, The MK41: Clap ... 4A 44
Ford Cl. PE19: Eat F ... 2K 27
Ford End Rd. MK40: Bed ... 5A 158 (3B 56)
Fordfield Rd. MK45: Millb, Step ... 5G 95
Fordham Courtyard SG5: Stot ... 1G 115
Ford La. MK44: Rox ... 7E 36
Forest Centre, The ... 4F 83
Foresters' Cl. MK45: Hay ... 3D 86
Forge Cl. LU4: Chalt ... 6A 130
PE19: Eat S ... 5H 27
Forge Gdns. MK44: Yeld ... 2B 6
Forrest Cres. LU2: Lut ... 6E 142
Forty Foot La.
MK44: Sharn, Sould ... 7G 11
NN29: Hin ... 3A 18
Foster Av. LU5: Duns ... 6J 139
Foster Gro. SG19: Sandy ... 3J 61
Foster Hill Rd.
MK40: Bed ... 1C 158 (7D 44)
MK41: Bed ... 7D 44
Foster Pl. MK42: Kemp ... 6A 56
Foster Rd. LU5: Harl ... 5B 120
MK42: Kemp ... 5K 55
MK43: Woo ... 3F 69
Foster St. MK40: Bed ... 1C 158 (1D 56)
Foster Way MK43: Woo ... 3F 69
Foston Cl. LU3: Lut ... 3H 141
Foundry, The LU1: Lut ... 7J 159
Foundry La. SG18: Bigg ... 6C 76
Foundry Way PE19: Eat S ... 6H 27
Fountaine Ct. MK45: Amp ... 4K 95
Fountain Gro. MK42: Kemp ... 5K 55
Fountains Rd. LU3: Lut ... 6A 142
MK41: Bed ... 4G 45
Fourth Av. LU3: Lut ... 2E 140
SG6: Let C ... 7K 115
Fowler Cl. MK42: Kemp ... 5K 55
Fowlers Dr. SG17: Mep ... 7B 100
Foxbrook MK43: Stev ... 2C 42
Foxbury Cl. LU2: Lut ... 3B 142
Fox Cl. MK17: Wob ... 7D 104
MK41: Clap ... 2J 43
SG18: Dunt ... 6B 78
FOX CORNER ... 1J 125
Fox Cnr. SG8: Guil M ... 6K 79
Foxdells LU6: Duns ... 5J 147
Foxglove Cl. PE19: Eat F ... 2J 27
Foxglove Dr. SG18: Bigg ... 7E 76
Foxglove Way LU3: Lut ... 7B 142
MK42: Bed ... 6G 57
Fox Hedge Way MK44: Sharn ... 4B 20
Fox Hill SG8: Guil M ... 6K 79
Foxhill LU2: Lut ... 4C 142
Fox Hill Rd. SG8: Guil M ... 6K 79
Foxlease MK41: Bed ... 4G 45
Frampton Ct. MK41: Bed ... 4E 44
(off Severn Way)
Frances Ashton Ho. LU6: Duns ... 2H 147
(off Bullpond La.)
Frances Ct. LU7: Lei Buz ... 2G 135
Francis Cl. SG5: Stot ... 7G 103
Francis Groves Cl. MK41: Bed ... 5F 45
Francis St. LU1: Lut ... 2F 159 (2A 150)
Frank Hamel Ct. MK45: Bar C ... 5A 122
Frank Lester Way LU2: Lut ... 2H 151
Franklin Av. MK45: Bar C ... 4K 121
Franklin Cl. MK43: Mars M ... 2D 82
Franklin Pl. SG5: Stot ... 3E 114
Franklin Rd. LU6: Duns ... 2F 147
SG18: Bigg ... 6B 76
Franklyn Gdns. MK40: Bidd ... 1J 55
Franks Cl. SG16: Hen ... 2H 113
Fraser Rd. MK44: Bed ... 4A 58
Frederick St. LU2: Lut ... 2H 159 (2C 150)
Frederick St. Pas.
LU2: Lut ... 2G 159 (1C 150)
Freeman Av. LU3: Lut ... 1K 141
Freemans Cl. LU5: Hou R ... 5G 139
Freemantle Ct. PE19: Eat S ... 4H 27
Frenchmans Cl. LU5: Todd ... 3E 128
French's Av. LU6: Duns ... 7E 138
French's Ga. LU6: Duns ... 7F 139
Freshwater Cl. LU3: Lut ... 2H 141
Friars Cl. LU1: Lut ... 5K 149
Friars Ct. LU1: Lut ... 5K 149
Friars Wlk. LU6: Duns ... 3H 147
SG19: Sandy ... 2J 61
Friars Way LU1: Lut ... 5K 149
Friary Fld. LU6: Duns ... 2H 147
Friday St. LU7: Lei Buz ... 2H 135
Friendless La. AL3: Flam, Mark ... 7F 155
Friesian Cl. LU4: Lut ... 6C 140
Friston Grn. LU2: Lut ... 1H 151
FRITHSDEN ... 3B 162
Froghall Rd. MK45: Amp, Step ... 2J 107
Frogmore Rd. LU5: Hou R ... 5A 140
Frome Cl. LU4: Lut ... 5G 141
MK41: Bed ... 4E 44
Front St. LU1: Slip E ... 2A 156
FROXFIELD ... 7J 105 (1A 162)
Fuchsia Way NN10: Rush ... 1B 10
Fulbourne Cl. LU4: Lut ... 7G 141
Fullers Ct. SG6: Let C ... 7G 115
Fullerton Cl. AL3: Mark ... 5G 155
Fulmar Rd. MK41: Bed ... 5F 45
Furlay Cl. SG6: Let C ... 7F 115
Furlong, The MK41: Bed ... 5H 45
MK43: Oak ... 7G 31
Furlong La. LU6: Tott ... 3C 146
Furmston Ct. SG6: Let C ... 7J 115
Furness Av. LU6: Duns ... 3J 147
Furness Cl. MK41: Bed ... 4H 45
Furrows, The LU3: Lut ... 2K 141
Furze Cl. LU2: Lut ... 2B 142
Furzefield MK41: Bed ... 6H 45
Furzen Cl. LU6: Duns ... 5J 147
Furzenhall Rd. SG18: Bigg ... 1C 76
Fyne Dr. LU7: Lei Buz ... 1E 134

G

Gables, The LU7: Lei Buz ... 3G 135
Gable Way LU5: Hou R ... 3K 139
Gaddesden Turn LU7: Bill ... 7C 136
Gadsby Ct. LU1: Lut ... 6G 159
Gadsby St. MK40: Bed ... 3D 158 (2E 56)
Gadsden Cl. MK43: Cran ... 2G 81
Gadsden Ct. MK17: Sto H ... 1A 124
Gainsborough Av. PE19: Eat F ... 2J 27
Gainsborough Ct. LU2: Lut ... 7D 142
Gainsborough Dr. LU5: Hou R ... 4K 139
Gainsborough Ri. MK41: Bed ... 6D 44
Gaitskill Ter. LU2: Lut ... 3K 159 (2D 150)
Gala Cl. MK41: Bed ... 2E 44
Galaxy Centre, The ... 3G 159 (2B 150)
Gale Ct. MK45: Bar C ... 5A 122
Gales Pl. MK45: C End ... 4B 72
Gallery, The LU1: Lut ... 4J 159
SG6: Let C ... 7H 115
(off Openshaw Way)
Galley & Warden Hills Nature Reserve
... 7B 132
Galliard Cl. LU3: Lut ... 5K 141
Galloway Cl. MK42: Kemp ... 7J 55
Galston Rd. LU3: Lut ... 1F 141
GAMLINGAY ... 4K 51 (2D 161)
GAMLINGAY CINQUES ... 3K 51 (2D 161)
GAMLINGAY GREAT HEATH
... 5G 51 (2D 161)
Gamlingay Rd. SG19: Gam, Pott ... 2K 63
Garden Cl. MK42: Kemp ... 5K 55
Garden Ct. LU3: Lut ... 5J 141
Gardener Pl. MK40: Bidd ... 1J 55
Gardeners Cl. MK45: Flitw ... 3C 108
MK45: Maul ... 5E 96
Gardeners La. SG16: Hen ... 3K 101
Garden Flds. LU2: C'hoe ... 6J 143
SG19: Pott ... 2H 63
Garden Hedge LU7: Lei Buz ... 1J 135
Gardenia Av. LU3: Lut ... 5H 141
Gardenia Av. Pas. LU3: Lut ... 5J 141
Garden Leys LU7: Lei Buz ... 3A 136
Garden Rd. LU6: Duns ... 3J 147
Gardens, The SG5: Stot ... 7G 103
SG16: Hen ... 5K 101
Gardens End LU5: Hou R ... 4J 139
Gardner Ct. LU1: Lut ... 6C 150
Gardners Cl. LU6: Duns ... 3E 146
Garfield SG18: Lang ... 5B 90
Garfield Ct. LU2: Lut ... 6H 143
Garfield St. MK41: Bed ... 1B 158 (7D 44)
Garland Way LU7: Lei Buz ... 4A 136
Garner Cl. SG18: North ... 1E 74
Garnith Cl. MK42: Kemp ... 6B 56
Garrett Cl. LU6: Duns ... 5K 147
Garretts Mead LU2: Lut ... 6F 143
Garter Ct. LU2: Lut ... 1G 159
Gas Ho. La. MK45: Amp ... 3B 96
Gaskell Pl. SG5: Stot ... 4E 114
Gatehill Gdns. LU3: Lut ... 7K 131
Gateshead Cl. SG19: Sandy ... 1J 61
Gaunts Way SG6: Let C ... 4H 115
GAYHURST ... 3A 160
Gayland Av. LU2: Lut ... 2F 151
Gayton Cl. LU3: Lut ... 5K 141
Gazelle Cl. PE19: Eat S ... 2H 27
G Casino
Luton ... 6J 159
Gelding Cl. LU4: Lut ... 4B 140
Gelt, The MK41: Bed ... 2E 44
(off The Wharfe)
Gemini Cl. LU7: Lei Buz ... 1B 136
Generation Bus. Pk. PE19: Lit Bar ... 2K 39
Gentian Gdns. SG5: Stot ... 1G 115
George, The SG18: Bigg ... 6C 76
George Pl. PE19: Eynes ... 1K 39
George St. AL3: Mark ... 6G 155
LU1: Lut ... 4H 159 (3C 150)
LU6: Duns ... 1H 147
LU7: Lei Buz ... 2K 135
LU7: Wing ... 7A 134
MK17: Wob ... 7D 104
MK40: Bed ... 1G 57
MK41: Clap ... 3J 43
(not continuous)
MK45: Maul ... 4E 96
SG17: Shef ... 3B 100
George St. West
LU1: Lut ... 5H 159 (3C 150)
Georgetown Cotts. SG19: Sandy ... 1G 61
Georgetown Rd. SG19: Sandy ... 1G 61
(not continuous)
Georgina Ct. SG15: Arl ... 3C 114
Gerald Ct. MK40: Bed ... 2B 56
Gery Ct. PE19: Eat S ... 2J 27
Gibbards Cl. MK44: Sharn ... 3B 20
Gibbons Rd. MK40: Bed ... 3A 158 (2C 56)
GIBRALTAR ... 1F 69
Gibson Dr. LU7: Lei Buz ... 4A 136
Gifford Pl. MK44: Wybo ... 2F 37
Gifford Rd. MK42: Bed ... 4F 57
Gig La. LU7: Heat R ... 3K 125
Gilbert Cl. MK42: Kemp ... 4K 55
Gilbert M. LU7: Lei Buz ... 1J 135
Gilded Acre LU6: Duns ... 5J 147
Gilder Cl. LU3: Lut ... 1J 141
Gilderdale LU4: Lut ... 3D 140
Gillam St. LU2: Lut ... 3J 159 (2C 150)
Gillan Way LU5: Hou R ... 4A 140
(off Houghton Pk. Rd.)
Gillespie Cl. MK42: Bed ... 4E 56
Gilpin Cl. LU5: Hou R ... 4K 139
SG18: Stan ... 5G 89
Gilpin St. LU6: Duns ... 7G 139
Gilwell Cl. MK41: Bed ... 4G 45
Gipping Cl. MK41: Bed ... 2F 45
Gipsey La. LU7: Lit Bil ... 2A 144
Gipsy La. LU1: Lut ... 4E 150
Girtford Bri. SG19: Sandy ... 4G 61
Girtford Cres. SG19: Sandy ... 3H 61
Glade, The MK43: Brom ... 6C 42
Gladstone Av. LU1: Lut ... 3A 150
Gladstone Cl. SG18: Bigg ... 5C 76
Gladstone Dr. SG5: Stot ... 4F 115
Gladstone St.
MK41: Bed ... 1B 158 (7D 44)
Glaisdale LU4: Lut ... 4E 140
Glamis Ct. PE19: Eynes ... 1J 39
Glamis Wlk. MK41: Bed ... 5J 45
Glastonbury Abbey MK41: Bed ... 2K 57
Glebe, The MK41: Clap ... 2J 43
MK45: Grav ... 1G 111
SG17: Camp ... 4K 99
Glebe Av. MK45: Flitw ... 4A 108
SG15: Arl ... 6C 102
Glebe Cl. MK44: Thur ... 5E 22
SG19: Sandy ... 2H 61
Glebe Gdns. LU5: Harl ... 5B 120
Glebe Ho. MK40: Bed ... 7E 44
Glebe Meadows Nature Reserve
... 6B 102
Glebe Ri. MK44: Sharn ... 3C 20
Glebe Rd. MK40: Bed ... 1E 158 (1E 56)
MK45: Amp ... 6A 96
SG6: Let C ... 7J 115
SG18: Bigg ... 4D 76
SG19: Sandy ... 2J 61
Glebe Rd. Ind. Est. SG6: Let C ... 7J 115
Glebe Way MK45: Hou C ... 5C 84
Glemsford Cl. LU4: Lut ... 3D 140
Glen, The LU1: Cad ... 7G 149
MK42: Kemp ... 7K 55
Glenavon Rd. MK41: Bed ... 5A 46
Glen Ct. MK45: Flitw ... 3A 108
Gleneagles Cl. MK40: Bidd ... 3J 55
Gleneagles Dr. LU2: Lut ... 3C 142
Glenfield Rd. LU3: Lut ... 3A 142
Glen Miller & Twinwood Airfield Mus.
... 6B 32
Glenrose Av. MK41: Bed ... 3G 45
Glenthorne M. LU7: Lei Buz ... 2G 135
Globe La. LU7: Lei Buz ... 7G 125
Glossop Way SG15: Arl ... 6D 102
Gloucester Ct. MK45: Amp ... 5A 96
(off Flitwick Rd.)
Gloucester Rd.
LU1: Lut ... 5K 159 (4D 150)
MK42: Bed ... 5E 56
Gloucester Ter. LU1: Lut ... 3G 159
Go Ape
Woburn Safari Pk. ... 4F 105
Go Bowling ... 1H 147
Godfrey La. MK44: Sharn ... 3E 20
Godfreys Cl. LU1: Lut ... 4K 149
Godfreys Ct. LU1: Lut ... 4K 149
GODMANCHESTER ... 1D 161
Godso Cl. MK41: Bed ... 5H 45
Godwin Cl. MK43: Brom ... 7F 43
Godwin Way MK43: Brom ... 7F 43
Goldcrest Cl. LU4: Lut ... 4C 140
Goldcrest Way MK41: Bed ... 5D 44
Golden Miller Ct. LU7: Wing ... 7A 134
(off High St.)
Golden Riddy LU7: Lei Buz ... 1G 135
Goldfinch Cl. MK42: Wils ... 6F 71
Goldfinch Dr. SG19: Sandy ... 7H 49
GOLDINGTON ... 7J 45 (2B 160)
Goldington Av. MK40: Bed ... 7F 45
Goldington Grn. MK41: Bed ... 7J 45
Goldington Rd.
MK40: Bed ... 2E 158 (1F 57)
MK41: Bed ... 7A 46
Gold La. MK40: Bidd ... 1H 55
Gold's Gym
Bedford ... 7A 46
Goldstone Cres. LU5: Duns ... 7K 139
Gold St. MK44: Rise ... 4B 14
NN29: Pod ... 4C 10
Goodhall Cres. MK45: Clop ... 5A 98
Good Intent LU6: Edles ... 6J 145
Goodman Dr. LU7: Lei Buz ... 4K 135
Goodman Rd. MK42: Bed ... 5D 56
Goodmayes Cl. MK42: Bed ... 4H 57
Goodrich Av. MK41: Bed ... 5J 45
Goodwick Dr. MK44: Honey ... 5B 26
Goodwins Yd. MK44: Gt Bar ... 4A 48
Goodwood Cl. MK45: Clop ... 6A 98
Gooseberry Hill LU3: Lut ... 3K 141
Goose Grn. LU7: Hock ... 6H 127
Goosey Lodge Est. NN10: Wym ... 2G 11
Gordon St. LU1: Lut ... 4G 159 (3B 150)
Gorham Pl. PE19: Eat F ... 3K 27
Gorham Way LU5: Duns ... 7B 140
Gosforth Cl. SG19: Sandy ... 7J 49
Goshawk Cl. LU4: Lut ... 5C 140
GOSMORE ... 2C 163
Gostwick Pl. MK44: Will ... 2G 59
Gostwick Rd. MK42: Bed ... 6E 56
GOSWELL END ... 4B 120
Goswell End Rd. LU5: Harl ... 4B 120
Gothic Way SG15: Arl ... 1C 114
Gower Dr. MK40: Bidd ... 1J 55
G Park MK42: Bed ... 5K 57
Graces Cl. MK43: Cran ... 1G 81
GRAFHAM ... 1C 161
Grafton Rd. MK40: Bed ... 3A 158 (2C 56)
Graham Gdns. LU3: Lut ... 5A 142
Graham Rd. LU5: Duns ... 3A 148
Grahams Gdns. MK44: Rise ... 4C 14
Grampian Way LU3: Lut ... 1E 140
Granary, The MK42: Kemp ... 6J 55
SG15: Arl ... 1C 114
Granby Rd. LU4: Lut ... 6F 141
Granet Cl. MK40: Bed ... 1B 56
Grange, The LU5: Todd ... 3F 129
MK42: Kemp ... 5A 56
SG18: Lwr C ... 1K 75
Grange Av. LU4: Lut ... 5F 141
Grange Cl. AL3: Mark ... 5F 155
LU7: Lei Buz ... 3F 135
MK43: Oak ... 1G 43
MK45: Hou C ... 5C 84
Grange Ct. LU7: Heat R ... 2J 125
MK43: Brom ... 6E 42
SG6: Let C ... 5J 115
Grange Dr. SG5: Stot ... 1H 115
Grange Farm Cl. MK45: Bar C ... 4K 121
Grange Gdns. LU5: Todd ... 2F 129
LU7: Heat R ... 2J 125
MK44: Sharn ... 3C 20
SG17: Camp ... 5K 99
SG19: Bee ... 5H 61
Grange La. MK43: Brom ... 6E 42
MK44: Cople ... 5D 58

Hart Hill—Hiltop Ct.

HART HILL ... 2K 159 (1F 151)
Hart Hill Dr. LU2: Lut ... 3K 159 (2D 150)
Hart Hill La. LU2: Lut ... 2K 159 (2D 150)
Hart Hill Path LU2: Lut ... 3K 159 (2D 150)
Hartington St.
MK41: Bed ... 1B 158 (7D 44)
Hartland Av. MK40: Bed ... 1G 57
Hart La. LU2: Lut ... 1E 150
Hartley Rd. LU2: Lut ... 3K 159 (2D 150)
Hartop Cl. MK41: Bed ... 5H 45
Hartop Ct. LU2: Lut ... 2H 151
Hartsfield Rd. LU2: Lut ... 7E 142
Hartshill MK41: Bed ... 6G 45
Hart Wlk. LU2: Lut ... 1E 150
Hartwell Cres. LU7: Lei Buz ... 2J 135
Hartwell Dr. MK42: Kemp ... 4A 56
Hartwell Gro. LU7: Lei Buz ... 2J 135
Hartwood *LU2: Lut ... 2D 150*
(off Hart Hill Dr.)
Harvest Cl. LU4: Lut ... 6C 140
Harvester Ct. LU7: Lei Buz ... 2B 136
Harvey Cl. SG18: Up C ... 3J 75
Harveycombe M. *LU7: Lei Buz ... 2G 135*
(off Old Rd.)
Harvey Ct. SG19: Sandy ... 3H 61
Harvey Rd. LU6: Duns ... 3D 146
MK41: Bed ... 7J 45
NN10: Rush ... 1B 10
Harvey's Hill LU2: Lut ... 4D 142
Haselfoot SG6: Let C ... 7G 115
Hasketon Dr. LU4: Lut ... 3D 140
Hassett St. MK40: Bed ... 3B 158 (2D 56)
Hastings Rd. MK42: Kemp ... 1K 69
MK45: Bar C ... 4A 122
Hastings St. LU1: Lut ... 6G 159 (4B 150)
HASTOE ... 3A 162
HATCH ... 6F 61 (3C 161)
Hatch Common SG19: Hat ... 6F 61
HATCH END ... 7J 15
Hatchet La. PE19: Stone ... 2K 9
HATCHING GREEN ... 3C 163
Hatch La. MK44: Keysoe ... 1J 23
Hat Factory, The ... 3H 159
HATFIELD ... 3D 163
Hatfield Av. MK43: Cran ... 5F 81
Hatfield Cl. MK45: Flitw ... 3B 108
Hatfield Cres. MK41: Bed ... 1H 57
MK45: Flitw ... 3B 108
HATFIELD GARDEN VILLAGE ... 3D 163
HATFIELD HYDE ... 3D 163
Hatfield Rd. MK45: Flitw ... 3B 108
Hathaway Cl. LU4: Lut ... 7D 140
PE19: Eat S ... 4J 27
Hatherley Chase LU2: Lut ... 7C 142
Hatley Pk. ... 1J 65
Hatley Rd.
SG19: C Hat, Pott, Wrest ... 3K 63
HATLEY ST GEORGE ... 2D 161
Hatters Way LU1: Lut ... 1D 148
HAULTWICK ... 2D 163
Havelock Cl. SG19: Sandy ... 1H 61
Havelock Ri. LU2: Lut ... 1C 150
Havelock Rd. LU2: Lut ... 1H 159 (1C 150)
SG18: Bigg ... 4C 76
Havelock St. MK40: Bed ... 3C 56
Haven, The SG5: Stot ... 7H 103
Haverdale LU4: Lut ... 5E 140
Hawes Cl. MK45: Flitw ... 3A 108
Hawes Ct. MK40: Bed ... 3C 158 (2D 56)
Hawesmere Cl. SG18: Bigg ... 7C 76
Hawk Cl. MK45: Flitw ... 4K 107
Hawk Dr. MK41: Bed, Clap ... 3C 44
SG19: Sandy ... 7H 49
Hawker Cl. LU7: Lei Buz ... 4B 136
Hawkfield SG6: Let C ... 6G 115
Hawkfields LU2: Lut ... 3C 142
Hawkins Rd. MK42: Bed ... 5E 56
Hawthorn Av. LU2: Lut ... 5F 143
Hawthorn Cl. LU6: Duns ... 3J 147
LU7: Lei Buz ... 1G 135
MK43: Turv ... 3C 40
MK45: Amp ... 6B 96
SG18: Bigg ... 3B 76
SG19: Pott ... 2J 63
Hawthorn Cres. LU1: Cad ... 7G 149
Hawthorne Av. MK40: Bed ... 3A 56
Hawthorne Cl. MK45: Clop ... 4C 98
Hawthorne Dr. MK45: Wils ... 1G 85
Hawthorn Hill SG6: Let C ... 7G 115
Hawthorns, The MK43: Cran ... 3F 81
MK45: Flitw ... 3A 108
SG16: Hen ... 2K 101
Hawthorn Ter. MK43: Brom ... 7D 42
Hawthorn Way LU7: Wing ... 6A 134
MK45: Sils ... 2K 109
SG16: Lwr Sto ... 4E 112
Haycroft LU2: Lut ... 3C 142
MK43: Woo ... 5G 69
Hayes Cl. LU2: Lut ... 4F 143
Hayfield Bus. Pk. MK17: Asp G ... 5D 92
Hayhurst Rd. LU4: Lut ... 7D 140
Haylands Way MK41: Bed ... 7H 45
Hay La. MK43: Kemp, Stag ... 5K 53
Hayley Ct. LU5: Hou R ... 3J 139
Hayling Dr. LU2: Lut ... 6H 143
Haylock Cl. MK42: Kemp ... 1J 69
Haymarket Rd. LU4: Lut ... 5A 140
Haymoor SG6: Let C ... 7G 115
HAYNES ... 3D 86 (3B 160)
HAYNES CHURCH END ... 5A 86
Haynes Pk. ... 4K 85
Haynes Rd. MK42: Bed ... 5E 56
HAYNES WEST END ... 7H 85 (3B 160)
Haysman Cl. SG6: Let C ... 7K 115
Hayton Cl. LU3: Lut ... 6K 131
Hazelbury Ct. *LU1: Lut ... 2A 150*
(off Hazelbury Cres.)
Hazelbury Cres. LU1: Lut ... 2A 150
Hazel Cl. SG17: Shef ... 3B 100
Hazel Gro. SG5: Stot ... 1G 115
Hazel Wlk. SG18: Bigg ... 3B 76
Hazelwood Cl. LU2: Lut ... 5F 143
Hazelwood La. MK45: Amp ... 1A 96
Hazelwood Rd. MK42: Bed ... 5F 57
Heacham Cl. LU4: Lut ... 5D 140
HEATH, THE ... 6G 51
Heath, The LU7: Lei Buz ... 5G 125
HEATH AND REACH ... 3J 125 (2A 162)
Heathcliff Av. SG5: Stot ... 4D 114
Heath Cl. LU1: Lut ... 4K 149
MK17: Wob S ... 3A 104
Heath Ct. LU7: Lei Buz ... 5G 125
Heather Dr. SG18: Bigg ... 7E 76
Heather Gdns. MK41: Bed ... 1K 57
Heather Mead LU6: Eat B ... 5J 145
Heathermere SG6: Let C ... 5H 115
Heathfield MK41: Bed ... 6J 45
Heathfield Cl. LU1: Cad ... 6H 149
Heathfield Path LU1: Cad ... 6H 149
Heathfield Rd. LU3: Lut ... 5A 142
Heath Grn. LU7: Heat R ... 3J 125
Heath La. MK17: Asp H ... 7A 104
Heath Pk. Dr. LU7: Lei Buz ... 6J 125
Heath Pk. Rd. LU7: Lei Buz ... 5J 125
Heath Rd. LU7: Lei Buz ... 1J 135
SG19: Gam ... 5H 51
Heathwood Cl. LU7: Lei Buz ... 5J 125
Heaton Dell LU2: Lut ... 1J 151
Hebden Cl. LU4: Lut ... 5D 140
HEBING END ... 2D 163
Hedgerow, The LU4: Lut ... 4E 140
Hedley Ri. LU2: Lut ... 7J 143
Hedley Way MK45: Maul ... 5K 97
Heights, The *LU3: Lut ... 4G 141*
(off Marsh Rd.)
MK42: Bed ... 5D 158 (3E 56)
Helford Cl. MK41: Bed ... 3F 45
Helmsley Av. MK41: Bed ... 4J 45
Helmsley Cl. LU4: Lut ... 4E 140
HEMEL HEMPSTEAD ... 3B 162
HEMINGFORD ABBOTS ... 1D 161
Hemingford Dr. LU2: Lut ... 3B 142
HEMINGFORD GREY ... 1D 161
Hempsals PE19: Eat F ... 1J 27
Henderson Way MK42: Kemp ... 6B 56
Henge Way LU3: Lut ... 2F 141
Henley Cl. LU5: Hou R ... 4A 140
Henley Rd. MK40: Bed ... 2C 56
HENLOW ... 3K 101 (1C 163)
Henlow Airfield ... 7G 101
Henlow Greyhound Stadium ... 2G 113
Henlow Ind. Est. SG16: Hen ... 2H 113
Henry Ct. LU6: Duns ... 2G 147
Hensman Cl. MK43: Felm ... 7C 20
Henson Cl. MK43: Whar E ... 2C 80
Henstead Pl. LU2: Lut ... 1H 151
Herbrand Rd. MK42: Bed ... 6H 57
Hercules Cl. LU7: Lei Buz ... 1A 136
Hereford Gro. SG18: Bigg ... 7C 76
Hereford Rd. LU4: Lut ... 6C 140
MK42: Bed ... 6G 57
Hermitage, The SG15: Arl ... 5D 102
Hermitage Gdns. MK45: C End ... 4B 72
Herne Cl. LU5: Todd ... 1F 129
Heron Cl. SG17: Shef ... 3C 100
SG18: Bigg ... 7B 76
SG19: Sandy ... 4H 61
Heron Dr. LU2: Lut ... 3C 142
Heron Gdns. MK42: Wils ... 5E 70
Heron Hgts. *MK41: Bed ... 7J 45*
(off Goldington Grn.)
Heron Quay MK40: Bed ... 4B 158 (2D 56)
Heron Rd. MK45: Flitw ... 5A 108
Heronscroft MK41: Bed ... 6H 45
Heronslee SG17: Shef ... 2D 100
Herons Mead MK43: Brom ... 7F 43
Heron Way SG5: Stot ... 7G 103
HERTFORD ... 3D 163
HERTFORD HEATH ... 3D 163
HERTINGFORDBURY ... 3D 163
Heswall Ct. LU1: Lut ... 7K 159
Hewlett Path LU3: Lut ... 5G 141
Hewlett Rd. LU3: Lut ... 4G 141
HEXTON ... 5F 123 (1C 163)
Hexton Chalk Pit Nature Reserve
... 7F 123
Hexton Rd. LU2: Lill ... 4F 133
MK45: Bar C ... 5A 122
Heywood Dr. LU2: Lut ... 7D 142
Hiam Bus. Cen. MK45: Maul ... 7F 97
Hibberts Ct. SG6: Let C ... 7G 115
Hibbert St. LU1: Lut ... 7H 159 (4C 150)
Hibbert St. Almshouses
LU1: Lut ... 7H 159
Hibbert St. Pas. LU1: Lut ... 7H 159
Hickling Cl. LU2: Lut ... 1H 151
MK40: Bed ... 3A 56
Hickman Ct. LU3: Lut ... 1F 141
Hicks Rd. AL3: Mark ... 6G 155
Higham Bury MK45: Pull ... 1E 120
Higham Dr. LU2: Lut ... 1H 151
HIGHAM FERRERS ... 1A 160
HIGHAM GOBION ... 1E 122 (1C 163)
Higham Gobion Rd. MK45: Bar C ... 3A 122
SG5: High G ... 3A 122
Higham Pk. Rd. NN10: Rush ... 1A 12
Higham Rd. SG5: High G, Shill ... 1E 122
High Banks LU7: Stanb ... 4G 137
High Beech Rd. LU3: Lut ... 2F 141
Highbury Gro. MK41: Clap ... 2K 43
Highbury Rd. LU3: Lut ... 1A 150
Highbush Rd. SG5: Stot ... 1G 115
Highcroft LU7: Lei Buz ... 3A 136
High Elms MK43: Carlt ... 7E 28
Higher Rads End MK17: Ever ... 1C 118
Highfield Cres. MK43: Brog ... 4G 93
Highfield Oval AL5: Harp ... 7K 157
Highfield Rd. LU4: Lut ... 1K 149
LU7: Lei Buz ... 2A 136
MK41: Clap ... 7G 31
MK42: Kemp ... 7A 56
MK43: Oak ... 7G 31
MK45: Flitt ... 2G 109
Highfields MK45: West ... 1A 120
HIGHFIELDS CALDECOTE ... 2D 161
Highfields Cl. LU5: Duns ... 7C 140
Highfields Ct. MK45: West ... 7A 108
High Green PE19: Abbot ... 3K 39
Highlands MK45: Flitw ... 3A 108
High Mead LU3: Lut ... 6J 141
Highover Cl. LU2: Lut ... 1F 151
High Point LU1: Lut ... 7G 159
High Ridge AL5: Harp ... 7J 157
LU2: Lut ... 1G 151
High Rd. LU7: Soulb ... 5A 124
MK42: Short ... 1K 71
MK45: C End ... 5A 72
SG5: Shill ... 7J 111
SG17: Shef ... 5A 72
SG18: Broom ... 1J 89
SG18: Lwr C ... 1K 75
SG19: Bee ... 4H 61
High Rd., The MK42: Bed, Harrow ... 6J 57
MK43: Felm ... 7C 20
High St. AL3: Mark ... 5F 155
LU4: Lut ... 6E 140
LU5: Hou R ... 5H 139
LU5: Todd ... 3F 129
LU6: Eat B ... 4H 145
LU6: Edles ... 7J 145
LU7: Bur ... 5A 134
LU7: Egg ... 2E 136
LU7: Lei Buz ... 2H 135
LU7: Wing ... 7A 134
MK16: Nth C ... 5A 66
MK17: Ting ... 2F 119
MK17: Wob S ... 2A 104
MK40: Bed ... 3D 158 (2E 56)
MK41: Clap ... 3K 43
MK42: Els ... 6D 56
MK42: Kemp ... 7J 55
MK43: Carlt ... 5E 28
MK43: Cran ... 4D 80
MK43: Harr ... 2D 28
MK43: Lidl ... 3C 94
MK43: Oak ... 1F 43
MK43: Odell ... 1F 29
MK43: Pave ... 5K 29
MK43: Ridg ... 2J 105
MK43: Stag ... 4A 54
MK43: Turv ... 4C 40
MK44: Blun ... 6E 48
MK44: Gt Bar ... 4K 47
MK44: Lit S ... 4E 16
MK44: Rise ... 5B 14
MK44: Rox ... 6E 36
MK44: Sharn ... 3C 20
MK44: Sould ... 6A 12
MK44: Swin ... 5K 7
MK44: Thur ... 5E 22
MK44: Wild ... 5C 34
MK44: Yeld ... 3B 6
MK45: Clop ... 5A 98
High St. MK45: Flitt ... 2F 109
MK45: Flitw ... 2A 108
MK45: G'fld ... 5D 108
MK45: Grav ... 2G 111
MK45: Hou C ... 4D 84
MK45: Pull ... 6G 109
MK45: Sils ... 1A 110
MK45: West ... 1A 120
NN10: Wym ... 1F 11
NN29: Pod ... 4C 10
PE19: St N ... 2K 27
PE28: Kimb ... 1J 9
PE28: Lwr D, Tilb ... 5K 5
PE28: Lwr D, Up D ... 5G 5
SG5: Stot ... 7G 103
SG8: Guil M ... 7K 79
SG8: Tad ... 7K 65
SG15: Arl ... 7C 102
SG16: Hen ... 4K 101
SG17: Mep ... 1B 112
SG17: Shef ... 2C 100
SG18: Bigg ... 5B 76
SG18: Broom ... 2J 89
SG18: Dunt ... 6B 78
SG18: Lang ... 7A 90
SG18: S'hill ... 4D 88
SG19: Eye ... 3D 78
SG19: Sandy ... 3J 61
SG19: Sutt ... 7J 63
SG19: Wrest ... 6F 65
High St. M. LU7: Lei Buz ... 3J 135
High St. Nth. LU6: Duns ... 7F 139
High St. Sth. LU6: Duns ... 2H 147
High Top Barns MK44: Yeld ... 3B 6
HIGH TOWN ... 2J 159 (2C 150)
Hightown Community Sports & Arts Cen.
... 2K 159 (2D 150)
High Town Ent. Cen. LU2: Lut ... 2K 159
High Town Rd.
LU2: Lut ... 3J 159 (2C 150)
High Vw. AL3: Mark ... 7G 155
MK41: Bed ... 6J 45
Highway, The
MK42: Harrow, Short ... 7J 57
PE19: Gt S ... 1K 17
High Wood Cl. LU1: Lut ... 3H 149
Hilbre Grange MK40: Bed ... 7C 44
Hill, The MK44: Blun ... 6D 48
Hillary Cl. LU3: Lut ... 2F 141
Hillary Cres. LU1: Lut ... 4A 150
Hillary Ri. SG15: Arl ... 1D 114
Hillborough Cres. LU5: Hou R ... 2J 139
Hillborough Rd.
LU1: Lut ... 7F 159 (4B 150)
Hill Cl. LU3: Lut ... 2A 142
LU7: Wingf ... 7E 128
Hill Cres. MK43: Brog ... 4G 93
Hillcrest MK43: Cran ... 2G 81
Hillcrest Av. LU2: Lut ... 1A 142
Hillcrest Caravan Site
LU1: Wood ... 1H 155
Hillcrest Pk. SG6: Let C ... 7D 114
Hillcroft LU6: Duns ... 1E 146
Hillcroft Cl. LU4: Lut ... 3E 140
Hilldene Cl. MK45: Flitw ... 3A 108
Hillersdon Chase MK17: Sto H ... 1A 124
Hillesden Av. MK42: Els ... 6D 56
Hill Farm La. MK43: Stag ... 4G 53
HILLFOOT END ... 5J 111
Hillfoot Rd. SG5: Shill ... 5J 111
Hillgrounds Rd. MK42: Kemp ... 4K 55
Hillier Ct. MK40: Bed ... 2A 158
Hill La. SG18: Bigg, Up C ... 5H 75
Hill La. Crossroads SG18: Old W ... 5G 75
Hillpath SG6: Let C ... 7K 115
Hill Plantation *MK43: Brom ... 1E 54*
(off Brookside Mobile Home Pk.)
Hill Ri. LU3: Lut ... 2E 140
MK41: Bed ... 6D 44
MK42: Kemp ... 1H 69
Hill Rd. SG18: Old W, Up C ... 5D 74
Hills Cl. MK44: Rox ... 7E 36
Hills End MK17: Ever ... 7K 105
Hillside LU5: Hou R ... 4H 139
Hillside Cl. SG5: Shill ... 5J 111
Hillside Rd. AL5: Harp ... 7K 157
LU3: Lut ... 1F 159 (1B 150)
LU5: Duns ... 3K 147
LU7: Lei Buz ... 6J 125
SG5: Shill ... 5J 111
SG16: Lwr Sto, Up Sto ... 3E 112
Hillson Cl. MK43: Mars M ... 4D 82
Hills Vw. LU3: Up Sun ... 4D 130
Hilltop Vw. SG17: Mep ... 7B 100
Hill Vw. SG19: Bee ... 5J 61
Hillview Cres. LU2: Lut ... 2A 142
Hillview La. LU7: Bill ... 7B 136
Hillyfields LU6: Duns ... 4J 147
HILTON ... 1D 161
Hilton Av. LU6: Duns ... 4H 147
Hiltop Ct. LU1: Lut ... 3A 150

Layham Dr.—Lucas Ct.

Layham Dr. LU2: Lut 1H 151
Leabank *LU3: Lut* *3G 141*
(off Penhill)
Lea Bank Ct. LU3: Lut 3G 141
LEA BRIDGE CORNER 4K 157
Leafield LU3: Lut 3G 141
(Five Springs)
LU3: Lut 5H 141
(Thorneycroft Cl.)
Leafield Ct. MK45: Amp 5A 96
Leafields LU5: Hou R 3J 139
Leaf Rd. LU5: Hou R 3H 139
LEAGRAVE 4E 140 (2B 162)
Leagrave High St. LU4: Lut 6B 140
Leagrave Rd. LU3: Lut 6J 141
LU4: Lut 6J 141
Leagrave Station (Rail) 4G 141
Lea Manor Recreation Cen. 1H 141
Leamington Rd. LU3: Lut 2J 141
Lea Rd. MK45: Amp 5B 96
Learoyd Way LU7: Lei Buz 3B 136
Leaside LU5: Hou R 3A 140
Leasway MK41: Bed 6H 45
Leathwaite Cl. LU3: Lut 3H 141
Leck Ho. *LU7: Lei Buz* *2J 135*
(off Lake St.)
LEDBURN 2A 162
Ledburn Gro. LU7: Lei Buz 3G 135
Ledwell Rd. LU1: Cad 7H 149
Lee Cl. MK40: Bidd 1J 55
LEEDON 2B 136
Leedon Furlong LU7: Lei Buz 2A 136
Leeds Smith Dr. SG19: Sandy 2J 61
Lee Farm Cotts. MK44: Sharn 1J 19
Lees Cl. SG18: Dunt 6B 78
Leghorn Cres. LU4: Lut 6C 140
Leicester Cl. LU4: Lut 1G 149
Leicester Rd. LU4: Lut 1G 149
Leigh Cl. LU5: Todd 2F 129
Leigh Ct. MK40: Bed 2B 158
Leighfield Cl. MK41: Bed 6A 46
LEIGHTON BUZZARD 2J 135 (2A 162)
Leighton Buzzard Golf Course . . .5H 125
Leighton Buzzard Narrow Gauge Railway
Page's Park Station 4K 135
Stonehenge Works Station . . .5C 126
Leighton Buzzard Station (Rail) . . .2G 135
Leighton Buzzard Theatre 2J 135
Leighton Ct. LU6: Duns 2G 147
MK41: Bed 4E 44
Leighton Ind. Pk. LU7: Lei Buz 4K 135
Leighton Linslade Southern By-Pass
LU6: Sew, Tott 7J 137
LU7: Bill 6C 136
Leighton Rd. LU5: Todd 3E 128
LU6: Edles, N'all . . . .3D 144 & 3A 152
LU7: Bill 6A 136
LU7: Egg 2E 136
LU7: Egg, Lei Buz 1C 136
LU7: Heat R 4J 125
LU7: Lei Buz 2H 135
LU7: Lei Buz, Stanb, Bill 3C 136
LU7: Soulb 7C 124
LU7: Wing 7A 134
MK17: Sto H 1A 124
Leighton St. MK17: Wob 1B 116
Leiston Cl. MK42: Bed 5G 57
Leith Rd. MK42: Bed 5H 57
Lely Cl. MK41: Bed 6C 44
LEMSFORD 3D 163
Lennon Ct. LU1: Lut 5F 159 (3A 150)
Lennox Grn. LU2: Lut 7K 143
Leopold Rd. LU7: Lei Buz 2F 135
Lesbury Cl. LU2: Lut 1J 151
Leslie Sell Scout Activity Centre, The
. . . . .5E 42
Lester Hall LU1: Lut 4J 159
Lester M. LU2: Lut 1H 159
Leston Cl. LU6: Duns 5K 147
Letchworth Arts Cen. *7H 115*
(off The Arcade)
Letchworth Bus. & Retail Pk.
SG6: Let C 7K 115
LETCHWORTH GARDEN CITY
. . . . .7H 115 (1D 163)
Letchworth Garden City Station (Rail)
. . . . .7H 115
Letchworth Point SG6: Let C 7K 115
Letchworth Rd. LU3: Lut 5J 141
Letchworth Swimming Pool 7H 115
LETTY GREEN 3D 163
Leven Cl. LU7: Lei Buz 2D 134
Levendale LU4: Lut 4E 140
LEVENS GREEN 2D 163
Leven Wlk. MK41: Bed 2E 44
Lewens Cft. MK16: Ast 7E 52
Lewes Gdns. MK41: Bed 4J 45
Lewis La. SG15: Arl 7C 102
LEWSEY FARM 5B 140
Lewsey Pk. Ct. LU4: Lut 5C 140
Lewsey Pk. Pool 5C 140
Lewsey Rd. LU4: Lut 6D 140
Leyburne Rd. LU3: Lut 3K 141
Leydene Pl. SG17: Chic 2K 99
LEY GREEN 2C 163
Leygreen Cl. LU2: Lut 2E 150
Leyhill Dr. LU1: Lut 6K 149
Leyland Rd. LU6: Duns 7F 139
Leys, The MK45: Amp 6C 96
SG18: Lang 6B 90
Leyside MK43: Brom 7F 43
Library Rd. LU1: Lut 4H 159 (3C 150)
Library Wlk. *MK41: Bed* *5H 45*
(off Putnoe St.)
Lichfield SG18: Bigg 7C 76
Lichfield Cl. MK42: Kemp 5A 56
Liddel Cl. LU3: Lut 6J 141
Liddell Way LU7: Lei Buz 4B 136
Lidgate Cl. LU4: Lut 3D 140
LIDLINGTON 3C 94 (1A 162)
Lidlington Station (Rail) 2B 94
Life Cl. LU4: Lut 5B 140
Lifelines Fitness Studio *5E 150*
(within Vauxhall Recreation Club)
Lighthorne Ri. LU3: Lut 1J 141
Lilac Av. MK45: Wils 2H 85
Lilac Gro. LU3: Lut 7E 130
NN10: Rush 1B 10
SG18: Bigg 6E 76
Lilac Wlk. MK42: Kemp 7B 56
Lilleshall Dr. MK42: Els 7E 56
LILLEY 7H 133 (2C 163)
Lilley Bottom LU2: Lill 7J 133
Lilleyhoo La. LU2: Lill 6K 133
Lilley Rd. SG5: Hex 6F 123
Lillyfield Cl. LU4: Lut 6A 140
Lily Cl. MK42: Bed 6H 57
Lily Wlk. *SG16: Lwr Sto* *3G 113*
(off Orchard Way)
Limbersey La. MK45: Maul 4E 96
LIMBURY 5H 141 (2B 162)
Limbury Mead LU3: Lut 3H 141
Limbury Rd. LU3: Lut 5H 141
Lime Av. LU4: Lut 6D 140
SG19: Bee 4H 61
Lime Cl. MK43: Brom 1E 54
MK45: Bar C 4A 122
MK45: Flitw 4B 108
Lime Gro. LU7: Lei Buz 1G 135
Lime M. MK45: Flitw 4B 108
Limes, The *LU1: Lut* *5C 150*
(off London Rd.)
MK40: Bed 1C 56
MK45: Amp 5A 96
Lime St. MK40: Bed 3C 158 (2D 56)
Limetree Av. LU1: Lut 4E 156
Lime Tree Cl. LU3: Lut 7E 130
Lime Tree Dr. SG18: Dunt 6B 78
Lime Tree Rd. SG17: Clif 2G 101
Lime Tree Wlk. SG18: Bigg 4C 76
Lime Wlk. LU5: Duns 2K 147
SG16: Hen 3K 101
Linacres LU4: Lut 5F 141
Linbridge Way LU2: Lut 7J 143
Linclare Pl. PE19: Eat F 3J 27
Lincoln Cl. LU5: Duns 4A 148
MK45: Flitw 2A 108
Lincoln Ct. *MK40: Bed* *2G 57*
(off Tennyson Rd.)
Lincoln Cres. SG18: Bigg 7C 76
Lincoln Rd. LU4: Lut 1K 149
MK42: Kemp 1K 69
MK42: Short 1J 71
Lincoln Way LU5: Harl 5B 120
Lincombe Slade LU7: Lei Buz 1G 135
Lincroft MK43: Cran 3E 80
MK43: Oak 1G 43
Linden Cl. LU5: Duns 1B 148
Linden Ct. LU2: Lut 3K 159
LU5: Hou R 5H 139
MK40: Bed 1A 158 (7C 44)
Lindencroft SG6: Let C 5J 115
Linden Grn. SG6: Let C 5J 115
Linden Rd. LU4: Lut 5F 141
(not continuous)
LU5: Duns 7B 140
MK40: Bed 1A 158 (1C 56)
Lindens, The LU5: Hou R 5H 139
Lindisfarne Cl. PE19: Eynes 1K 39
SG19: Sandy 2J 61
Lindisfarne Priory MK41: Bed 2K 57
Lindler Ct. LU7: Lei Buz 3J 135
Lindsell Cres. SG18: Bigg 4C 76
Lindsey Cl. MK40: Bidd 4J 55
Lindsey Rd. LU2: Lut 1H 151
Link, The LU5: Hou R 4H 139
SG6: Let C 5J 115
Link Rd. NN10: Rush 1B 10
Links, The MK42: Kemp 7A 56
Links Way LU2: Lut 1B 142
Linkway MK41: Bed 7J 45
SG17: Clif 3G 101
Linley Dell LU2: Lut 7H 143
Linmere Wlk. LU5: Hou R 3A 140
Linnet Cl. LU4: Lut 5C 140
SG6: Let C 6G 115
SG19: Sandy 7J 49
Linnet La. MK42: Wils 6E 70
Linnet Way MK41: Bed 5E 44
Linney Head LU6: Stud 5H 153
LINSLADE 2E 134 (2A 162)
Linslade Rd. LU7: Heat R 4H 125
Linton Cl. PE19: Eat S 4G 27
Linwood Gro. LU7: Lei Buz 3K 135
Lippitts Hill LU2: Lut 4C 142
Lipscomb Dr. MK45: Flitw 5A 108
Liscombe Pk. 7A 124
Liscombe Pk. Equestrian Cen. 3C 134
Liscombe Rd. LU5: Duns 1A 148
Liston Cl. LU4: Lut 4D 140
Litchfield MK44: Rise 4C 14
LITLINGTON 3D 161
LITTLE ADDINGTON 1A 160
Lit. America Ind. Est. PE19: Gt S . . .7K 17
LITTLE BARFORD 2K 37 (2C 161)
Little Beeches SG18: Bigg 4B 76
LITTLE BERKHAMSTED 3D 163
Little Berries LU3: Lut 2G 141
LITTLE BILLINGTON 7A 136 (2A 162)
LITTLE BRICKHILL 1A 162
Littlebury Cl. SG5: Stot 1J 115
LITTLE CATWORTH 1C 161
Little Causeway MK42: Wils 4E 70
Lit. Church Rd. LU2: Lut 6F 143
Little Cl. SG15: Arl 1C 114
LITTLE CRAWLEY 3A 160
Littledale St. MK42: Kemp 5B 56
Little End Rd. PE19: Eat S 5H 27
Little End Rd. Ind. Est.
PE19: Eat S 5H 27
Little Fld. Cl. SG15: Arl 6C 102
Littlefield Rd. LU2: Lut 6F 143
LITTLE GADDESDEN 3A 162
LITTLE GRANSDEN 2D 161
LITTLE GREEN 4K 79
Little Green SG8: Guil M 5K 79
Lit. Green La. LU1: Cad 1G 155
Little Gro. Pl.
MK40: Bed 3E 158 (2E 56)
LITTLE HARROWDEN 1A 160
Little Headlands MK41: Bed 5H 45
LITTLE HEATH 5K 51
Little Heath SG19: Gam 5K 51
Little Hill LU7: Bill 7C 136
LITTLE IRCHESTER 1A 160
Little La. LU7: Hock 1J 137
MK45: Clop 4B 98
Little Mdw. LU1: Wood 7J 149
LITTLE PAXTON 1C 161
Little Portway MK40: Bidd 4H 55
Little Spinney MK43: Cran 1G 81
LITTLE STAUGHTON 4E 16 (1C 161)
Little Staughton Airfield 6H 17
Lit. Staughton Rd. MK44: Colm 5F 25
MK44: Lit S, Per 5G 9
Little Theatre, The
Dunstable 2J 147
Lit. Townsend Cl. MK42: Els 6D 56
Lit. Wood Cft. LU3: Lut 2G 141
LITTLEWORTH 6K 71 (3B 160)
Littleworth LU7: Wing 6A 134
LITTLE WYMINGTON 1A 10 (1A 160)
LITTLE WYMONDLEY 2D 163
Liverpool Rd. LU1: Lut . . .4F 159 (3B 150)
Livingstone Way SG5: Stot 3E 114
Lloyd Ct. MK40: Bed 1B 158 (1D 56)
Loak Cl. MK41: Clap 2J 43
Lobelia Cotts. PE19: Eat F 3J 27
Locarno Av. LU4: Lut 3E 140
Lochy Dr. LU7: Lei Buz 2E 134
Lockhart Cl. LU6: Duns 4A 148
Lockington Cres. LU5: Duns 7A 140
Lodge, The MK41: Clap 3K 43
Lodge Av. MK42: Kemp 7J 55
Lodge Cl. MK44: Sharn 3C 20
Lodge La. MK17: Sto H 1A 124
Lodge Nature Reserve, The (RSPB)
. . . . .5A 62
Lodge Nature Reserve Visitor Centre, The
. . . . .5C 62
Lodge Rd. MK43: Cran 4D 80
MK44: Sharn 3B 20
NN10: Rush 1A 10
Loftus Cl. LU4: Lut 6D 140
Lollard Cl. LU4: Lut 6A 140
Lombard St. MK43: Lidl 2C 94
Lombardy Cl. MK41: Bed 5G 45
Lomond Dr. LU7: Lei Buz 2D 134
LONDON END 6C 16
London End MK17: Wob 1D 116
MK44: Mil E 4H 31
London Gliding Club 5E 146
London La. MK45: Hay, Hou C 4D 84
LONDON LUTON AIRPORT
. . . . .3H 151 (2C 163)
London Rd. AL3: Mark 6G 155
AL5: Harp 5B 150
LU1: Cad 4K 147
LU1: Lut 7G 159 (5B 150)
LU6: Duns 4K 147
MK17: Mil B, Wob 1E 116
MK42: Bed 6D 158 (4E 56)
PE28: Kimb 1K 9
SG18: Bigg 5C 76
SG18: Bigg, Edw 3F 91
SG19: Sandy 1H 61
London Rd. Trad. Est. SG18: Bigg . . .1E 90
London Row SG15: Arl 3C 114
Longacre MK41: Bed 5G 45
MK45: Pull 4F 109
Longborns MK43: Cran 2F 81
Longbrooke LU5: Hou R 5K 139
Long Cl. LU2: Lut 6G 143
SG16: Lwr Sto 4E 112
Longcroft Dr. MK45: Bar C 5K 121
Longcroft La. MK43: Mars M 4D 82
Longcroft Rd. LU1: Lut 3J 149
Longden Cl. MK45: Hay 3D 86
Long Dr. MK45: Clop, Hay 2C 98
Longfellow Pl. PE19: Eat F 2K 27
Longfield Ct. SG6: Let C 7F 115
Longfield Dr. LU4: Lut 1F 149
Longfield Rd. SG19: Sandy 2H 61
Long Hedge LU5: Duns 2K 147
Longholme Way MK40: Bed 3F 57
Long La. LU5: Todd 1F 129
MK17: Ting, Todd 2F 119
Longleat MK41: Bed 1A 58
Longleat Cl. MK45: Flitw 5K 107
LONG MARSTON 3A 162
Long Mead LU5: Hou R 3H 139
Longmead SG6: Let C 7G 115
Long Meadow AL3: Mark 6G 155
LU5: Hou R 4A 140
LU6: Duns 2G 147
Longmeadow Dr. MK45: Wils 1G 85
Long Riding SG19: Sandy 4C 62
Long Row MK43: Pave 4B 30
Longslade La. MK17: Wob 6B 104
Long Twitchell SG18: Bigg 4B 76
Long Wlk. SG17: Chic 2H 99
Lonsdale Cl. LU3: Lut 4J 141
Lords Cl. LU7: Stanb 4J 137
Lords Hill LU5: Chalg 7F 129
Lords Mead LU6: Eat B 4J 145
Lordsmead MK43: Cran 2G 81
Lords Pl. LU2: Lut 1G 159 (1B 150)
Lords Ter. *LU6: Eat B* *4J 145*
(off High St.)
Lorimer Cl. LU2: Lut 3C 142
Loring Rd. LU6: Duns 1F 147
MK44: Sharn 3B 20
Lorraine Rd. MK43: Woo 4E 68
Lothair Rd. LU2: Lut 5E 142
Lottings Way PE19: Eat F 1J 27
Lovat Wlk. MK42: Kemp 7A 56
Lovell Homes MK43: Oak 3G 43
Lovell Rd. MK42: Bed 4H 57
MK43: Oak 2G 43
Lovent Dr. LU7: Lei Buz 2K 135
Loveridge Av. MK42: Kemp 4K 55
Lovers Wlk. LU5: Duns 2J 147
Lovet Rd. MK45: Flitw 5A 108
Lovett Grn. MK45: Shar 4E 120
Lovett Way LU5: Duns 6K 139
Lowe Dr. SG6: Let C 7K 115
Lower Ascott LU7: Wing 7B 134
LOWER CALDECOTE 1K 75
LOWER DEAN 5G 5 (1B 160)
LOWER END
Dunstable 1K 145
Milton Keynes 5A 92
Wellingborough 1A 160
Lower End Rd. MK17: Wave 5A 92
Lwr. Farm Rd. MK43: Brom 5G 43
LOWER GRAVENHURST
. . . . .3F 111 (1C 163)
Lwr. Harpenden Rd.
LU1: E Hyde, Lut 5F 151
LU2: E Hyde 5F 151
Lwr. Rads End MK17: Ever 1C 118
Lower Rd. SG8: Tad 6K 65
LOWER SHELTON 2D 82 (3A 160)
Lwr. Shelton Rd. MK43: Mars M 1C 82
(not continuous)
LOWER STONDON 3F 113 (1C 163)
LOWER SUNDON 6D 130 (2B 162)
Lowry Dr. LU5: Hou R 4K 139
Lowry Rd. PE19: Eat F 1J 27
Lowsdon La. MK44: Rise 5B 14
Lowther Rd. LU6: Duns 4J 147
MK41: Bed 4G 45
Loyne Cl. LU7: Lei Buz 1E 134
Lucas Ct. MK40: Bidd 1J 55

Lucas Gdns.—Medley Cl.

Lucas Gdns. LU3: Lut 1K **141**
Lucas Way SG17: Shef 1C **100**
Lucerne Way LU3: Lut 5A **142**
Ludlow Av. LU1: Lut 6C **150**
Ludlow Wlk. MK41: Bed 5J **45**
Ludun Cl. LU5: Duns 2A **148**
LUFFENHALL 2D **163**
Luffenham Pl. SG17: Chic 2H **99**
Luke Pl. MK42: Bed 6E **56**
Lullington Cl. LU2: Lut 6G **143**
Lunedale Cl. MK42: Kemp 7A **56**
Lune Wlk. MK41: Bed 4E **44**
Lurke St. MK40: Bed 3D **158** (2E **56**)
LUTON 4H **159** (2B **162**)
Luton Airport Parkway (Rail) 4F **151**
Luton & Vauxhall Tennis Club 5E **150**
Luton Dr., The LU1: Lut 5E **150**
Luton Ent. Pk. LU3: Lut 1D **140**
LUTON HOO ESTATE 3F **157**
Luton Library Theatre 4H **159** (3C **150**)
LONDON LUTON AIRPORT 3H **151** (2C **163**)
Luton Regional Sports Cen. 4D **142**
Luton Rd. AL3: Mark 5G **155**
AL5: Harp 6H **157**
LU1: Cad 6G **149**
LU2: C'hoe 6J **143**
LU3: Stre 2J **131**
LU4: Chalt 2G **129**
LU5: Duns 1K **147**
LU5: Todd 2G **129**
MK45: Bar C 7K **121**
MK45: Wils 7G **71**
SG5: Gt O 6K **133**
Luton Station (Rail) 3H **159** (2C **150**)
Luton Town FC 2A **150**
Luton White Hill SG5: Gt O 1K **143**
Luxembourg Cl. LU3: Lut 1F **141**
Lyall Cl. MK45: Flitw 4A **108**
Lyall Ct. MK45: Flitw 2C **108**
Lychgate LU3: Up Sun 4D **130**
Lychmead SG17: Clif 2H **101**
Lydds Hill MK43: Ridg 1J **105**
Lydford Cl. MK40: Bed 1G **57**
Lygetun Dr. LU3: Lut 3G **141**
Lymans Rd. SG15: Arl 7C **102**
Lyme Rd. MK45: Amp 5A **96**
Lymington Gdns. *MK41: Bed 5A 46 (off Ashridge Dr.)*
Lynch, The LU6: Kens 1B **154**
Lynch Hill LU6: Kens 3C **154**
Lyndhurst Rd. LU1: Lut 3A **150**
Lyneham Rd. LU2: Lut 1G **151**
Lynford Way NN10: Rush 1A **10**
Lynn Cl. MK42: Els 1E **70**
Lynton Av. SG15: Arl 1C **114**
Lynton Gro. MK42: Bed 6D **56**
Lynwood Av. LU2: Lut 6D **142**
Lynwood Lodge LU6: Duns 1G **147**
Lyon Cl. MK42: Kemp 1A **70**
Lyra Gdns. LU7: Lei Buz 1B **136**
Lyspitt Comn. SG17: Mep 7C **100**
Lytham Pl. MK40: Bidd 4H **55**
Lywood Rd. LU7: Lei Buz 3A **136**

M

Mabel Rd. MK42: Bed 5D **56**
Macaulay Rd. LU4: Lut 7C **140**
Macfadyen Webb Ho. SG6: Let C 7J **115**
MACKERYE END 3C **163**
McNish Ct. PE19: Eat S 5H **27**
Magdalene Cl. SG18: Dunt 6B **78**
Mager Way SG18: Lang 7B **90**
Magistrates' Court
Bedford 4C **158** (2D **56**)
Luton & South Bedfordshire 5G **159** (3B **150**)
Magnolia Cl. MK42: Kemp 1B **70**
Magnolia Dr. NN10: Rush 1B **10**
Magnolia Pl. SG18: Bigg 7E **76**
Magnon Ct. LU7: Lei Buz 3J **135**
Magpie Av. MK43: Stew 3J **83**
Magpie Gdns. MK42: Wils 5E **70**
Magpies, The LU2: Lut 3B **142**
MK45: Maul 4E **96**
Mags La. MK17: Mil B 6J **117**
Mahew Ct. *MK42: Kemp 5K 55 (off Emmerton Rd.)*
Maia Cl. MK41: Bed 2J **57**
Maidenbower Av. LU6: Duns 1F **147**
Maidenhall Rd. LU4: Lut 7J **141**
Main Rd. MK16: Ast 7E **52**
MK40: Bidd 2J **55**
PE19: Stone 1K **9**
Main Rd. Nth. HP4: Dag 4A **152**
Main Rd. Sth. HP4: Dag 6C **152**
Maitland St. MK40: Bed 4B **158** (2D **56**)
Malakand Rd. MK42: Kemp 5C **56**
Malaunay Pl. SG19: Sandy 3J **61**
Malcote Cl. MK40: Bidd 1J **55**
Malden Way PE19: Eynes 5K **27**
Malham Cl. LU4: Lut 6H **141**
MK45: Flitw 4A **108**
Mall, The LU5: Duns 1J **147**
Mallard Cl. SG17: Shef 3C **100**
Mallard Ct. MK42: Wils 4F **71**
Mallard Gdns. LU3: Lut 4J **141**
Mallard Hill MK41: Bed 5D **44**
Mallard Wlk. SG18: Bigg 6B **76**
Mallow, The LU3: Lut 6H **141**
Mall Shop. Cen., The LU1: Lut 5H **159** (3C **150**)
Malmesbury Abbey MK41: Bed 2J **57**
Malms Cl. LU6: Kens 2K **153**
Malthouse Grn. LU2: Lut 1K **151**
Malthouse La. SG5: Stot 6J **103**
Malting La. HP4: Dag 6C **152**
Maltings, The LU6: Duns 1G **147**
LU7: Lei Buz 3K **135**
MK45: Amp 4A **96**
MK45: Hou C 5A **84**
PE19: Eat S 2J **27**
SG6: Nort 5K **115**
SG16: Hen 4K **101**
SG17: Shef 2C **100**
Maltings Cl. MK43: Cran 3E **80**
Maltings Way MK44: Gt Bar 4A **48**
Malvern Av. MK41: Bed 7H **45**
Malvern Cl. MK45: Flitw 4J **107**
Malvern Dr. LU7: Lei Buz 1E **134**
Malvern Rd. LU1: Lut 3K **149**
Malzeard Ct. LU3: Lut 1F **159**
Malzeard Rd. LU3: Lut 1F **159** (1A **150**)
Manchester Pl. LU6: Duns 1H **147**
Manchester St. LU1: Lut 4H **159** (3C **150**)
Mancroft Rd. LU1: Aley G, Cad 7F **149**
Mandem Pl. LU4: Lut 5B **140**
Mander Cl. LU5: Todd 2F **129**
Mander Farm Rd. MK45: Sils 3K **109**
Mandrell Cl. LU5: Duns 7G **139**
MANGROVE GREEN 5K **143**
Mangrove Rd. LU2: C'hoe 5J **143**
LU2: Lut 6G **143**
Manning Ct. LU5: Hou R 4J **139**
Manning Pl. LU2: Lut 7J **143**
Mannock Way LU7: Lei Buz 4B **136**
Manor, The SG19: Pott 2K **63**
Manor Av. LU7: Hock 6J **127**
Manorbier Rd. MK41: Bed 4H **45**
Manor Cl. LU5: Harl 5B **120**
LU5: Hou R 5H **139**
LU7: Bill 1C **144**
MK17: Salf 2B **92**
MK17: Sto H 1A **124**
MK42: Kemp 6K **55**
MK43: Brom 5G **43**
MK43: Carlt 5E **28**
MK44: Wild 5D **34**
MK45: West 2A **120**
SG17: Clif 2G **101**
SG18: Lang 6B **90**
Manor Ct. LU1: Cad 6H **149**
LU1: Lut 6K **159** (4D **150**)
LU7: Heat R 6G **125**
MK43: Mars M 5C **82**
MK44: Blun 6E **48**
SG18: Bigg 6G **77**
SG18: Up C 3H **75**
Manor Dr. MK42: Kemp 6K **55**
Manor Farm SG16: Up Sto 2E **112**
Mnr. Farm Bus. Pk. SG5: High G 1E **122**
Mnr. Farm Cl. LU4: Lut 6E **140**
LU7: Soulb 6A **124**
MK45: Bar C 4A **122**
Mnr. Farm Cotts. MK45: Hou C 6A **84**
Mnr. Farm Ct. LU3: Lwr Sun 6D **130**
Mnr. Farm Rd. PE19: Abbot 4J **39**
Mnr. Farm Way MK44: Sharn 4C **20**
Manor Gdns. MK45: West 1K **119**
SG19: Pott 2K **63**
Manor Ho. Cl. PE19: Eat S 5J **27**
Manor La. NN10: Wym 1E **10**
Manor Lodge MK42: Kemp 6K **55**
Manor Pk. LU5: Hou R 5H **139**
MK42: Bed 5F **57**
Manor Pk. Dr. MK45: West 1K **119**
Manor Pl. SG18: Up C 3H **75**
Manor Rd. LU1: Cad, Wood 7G **149**
LU1: Lut 6K **159** (4D **150**)
LU3: Lwr Sun 5D **130**
LU5: Todd 1F **129**
MK40: Bidd 2H **55**
MK41: Bed 7J **45**
MK43: Kemp H 4J **69**
MK43: Mars M 5C **82**
MK43: Woo 4G **69**
MK45: Bar C 4A **122**
NN10: Rush 1B **10**
Manor Rd. SG16: Hen 4J **101**
SG19: Sandy 2H **61**
Manor Way MK45: C End 4B **72**
MK45: Flitw 4K **107**
SG19: Pott 2K **63**
Manse Ct. AL3: Mark 6G **155**
Mansfield Rd. LU4: Lut 1K **149**
Manshead Ct. LU5: Duns 4K **147**
Mansion La. MK43: Harr 2D **28**
Manton Cen. MK41: Bed 6C **44**
Manton Cen., The MK41: Bed 6C **44**
Manton Cl. MK45: Amp 5B **96**
Manton Dr. LU2: Lut 5B **142**
Manton Ind. Est. MK41: Bed 5C **44**
Manton La. MK41: Bed 5C **44**
Manton Rd. LU6: Eat B 5D **146**
Manx Cl. LU4: Lut 7J **141**
Manyweathers Ct. *MK45: Amp 5A 96 (off Dunstable St.)*
Maple Cl. MK45: Pull 4F **109**
MK45: Wils 1H **85**
SG16: Lwr Sto 4E **112**
SG17: Clif 3F **101**
SG18: Bigg 4C **76**
Maple Ct. LU1: Lut 7G **159**
Maple Dr. SG17: Shef 3E **100**
Maple Flats AL5: Harp 7K **157**
Maple Gdns. MK44: Rise 3C **14**
Maple M. LU7: Lei Buz 2J **135**
Maple Rd. SG19: Sandy 1J **61**
Maple Rd. E. LU4: Lut 2K **149**
Maple Rd. W. LU4: Lut 2K **149**
Maples, The MK42: Kemp 7A **56** (not continuous)
MK45: Sils 2K **109**
Maple Way LU5: Hou R 3A **140**
LU6: Kens 3A **154**
MK43: Cran 4E **80**
Maple Wood NN10: Rush 1B **10**
Marbury Pl. LU3: Lut 4H **141**
Marchioness Way PE19: Eat S 3H **27**
Mardale Av. LU6: Duns 4J **147**
Mardale Cl. MK42: Kemp 6A **56**
Mardle Cl. LU1: Cad 1G **155**
Mardle Rd. LU7: Lei Buz 3G **135**
Maree Cl. LU7: Lei Buz 2E **134**
Maresfield Av. SG17: Chic 3K **99**
Mareth Rd. MK42: Bed 4G **57**
Margetts Rd. MK42: Kemp 6B **56**
Margil Rd. MK41: Bed 2F **45**
Margrett La. MK45: Bar C, Pull 1H **121**
Marigold Way MK42: Bed 6G **57**
SG5: Stot 1H **115**
Marina Ct. MK42: Bed 4C **56**
Marina Dr. LU6: Duns 3E **146**
Market Ct. LU7: Lei Buz 2J **135**
Market Hall LU1: Lut 4J **159** (3C **150**)
Market Pl. LU6: Eat B 4H **145**
MK17: Wob 7D **104**
Market Sq. LU1: Lut 4K **149**
LU5: Todd 2F **129**
LU6: Eat B 4H **145**
LU7: Lei Buz 2J **135**
PE19: St N 2K **27**
SG18: Bigg 5C **76**
SG19: Pott 3J **63**
SG19: Sandy 3J **61**
Markfield Cl. LU3: Lut 3A **142**
Markham Cres. LU5: Duns 7A **140**
Markham Rd. LU3: Lut 1A **142**
Mark Rutherford Rd. MK42: Bed 4F **57**
MARKYATE 5G **155** (3B **162**)
Markyate Rd. LU1: Slip E 3J **155**
Marlborough Ct. LU1: Lut 4F **159**
Marlborough Footpath LU3: Lut 1B **150**
Marlborough Pk. MK42: Kemp 4B **56**
Marlborough Pl. LU5: Todd 2F **129**
Marlborough Rd. LU3: Lut 1A **150**
MK40: Bed 2B **56**
PE19: Eat S 6J **27**
Marley Flds. LU7: Lei Buz 3B **136**
Marlin Ct. LU4: Lut 5A **140**
Marlin Rd. LU4: Lut 5A **140**
Marlow Av. LU1: Lut 2J **149**
Marlowe Ct. PE19: Eat F 1K **27**
Marlow Way MK41: Bed 3E **44**
Marmet Av. SG6: Let C 7G **115**
Marne St. MK42: Kemp 5C **56**
Marquis Cl. PE19: Eat S 3H **27**
Marquis Ct. LU2: Lut 1G **159**
MK17: Wob 7D **104**
Marquis Hill SG5: Shill 5A **112**
Marriott Rd. LU3: Lut 3K **141**
Marriotts Cl. MK43: Felm 7C **20**
Marschefield SG5: Stot 7G **103**
Marsh, The MK43: Carlt 5D **28**
Marshall Cl. MK42: Kemp 5K **55**
Marshall Ct. MK41: Bed 1J **57**
Marshall Rd. LU2: Lut 7G **143**
Marshalls Av. SG5: Shill 5K **111**
MARSHALSWICK 3C **163**
MARSH FARM 2G **141**
Marsh Ho. LU3: Lut 5H **141**
Marsh La. MK44: Mil E 3H **31**
Marsh Leys MK43: Kemp 3K **69**
Marsh Rd. LU3: Lut 4G **141**
Marsom Gro. LU3: Lut 1K **141**
Marston Gdns. LU2: Lut 5B **142**
Marston Hill MK43: Mars M 2J **81**
MARSTON MORETAINE 4D **82** (3A **160**)
Marston Rd. MK43: Lidl 3C **94**
Marston Thrift Nature Reserve 4J **81**
Marston Vale Millennium Country Pk. 3F **83**
MARSWORTH 3A **162**
Martell Dr. MK42: Kemp 7H **55**
Martham Cl. MK40: Bed 3K **55**
Martin Cl. MK41: Bed 5F **45**
Martindales, The LU2: Lut 4K **159**
Martin Rd. MK45: Flitw 5K **107**
Martins Dr., The LU7: Lei Buz 1H **135**
Mary Brash Ct. LU2: Lut 6G **143**
Maryport Rd. LU4: Lut 7J **141**
Maryville Rd. MK42: Bed 5D **56**
Marywells SG17: Mep 1B **112**
Masefield Av. PE19: Eat F 1J **27**
Maskell Dr. MK41: Bed 4A **46**
Massey Cl. MK42: Kemp 6A **56**
Masters Cl. LU1: Lut 5K **149**
MK40: Bidd 3J **55**
Matlock Cres. LU4: Lut 1E **148**
Matthew St. LU6: Duns 2H **147**
MAULDEN 5F **97** (1B **162**)
Maulden Cl. LU2: Lut 1G **151**
Maulden Rd. MK45: Flitw 4C **108**
Maulden Rd. Ind. Est. MK45: Flitw 2C **108**
Maule Cl. PE19: Eynes 1J **39**
Maundsey Cl. LU6: Duns 5J **147**
May Cl. LU6: Eat B 4J **145**
Maycroft SG6: Let C 5J **115**
Mayer Way LU5: Hou R 6H **139**
Mayes Cl. MK44: Wild 6D **34**
Mayfield Cl. AL5: Harp 7J **157**
MK42: Kemp 5A **56**
Mayfield Ct. SG19: Sandy 3H **61**
Mayfield Cres. SG16: Lwr Sto 4E **112**
Mayfield Rd. LU2: Lut 5F **143**
LU5: Duns 4K **147**
Mayfields SG17: Shef 2D **100**
Mayhew Cl. MK43: Brom 1E **54**
Maynards, The SG18: Broom 1J **89**
Mayne Av. LU4: Lut 4E **140**
May Rd. MK43: Turv 3C **40**
Mayston Cl. SG19: Pott 3G **63**
May St. LU1: Lut 7J **159** (5C **150**)
Mead, The LU7: Soulb 5A **124**
Mead End SG18: Bigg 6D **76**
Meadhook Dr. MK45: Bar C 4K **121**
Mead Open Farm 6E **136**
Meadow Cl. SG19: Bee 5H **61**
Meadow Cft. LU1: Cad 6H **149**
Meadow La. LU5: Hou R 4H **139**
MK44: Card 3B **58**
Meadow Piece MK45: Hay 4E **86**
Meadow Rd. LU3: Lut 5K **141**
LU5: Todd 3E **128**
Meadows, The LU7: Wingf 7E **128**
MK43: Stew 3J **83**
MK45: Flitw 1K **107**
Meadowsweet PE19: Eat F 2H **27**
SG16: Lwr Sto 4F **113**
Meadowsweet Dr. MK42: Bed 6G **57**
Meadow Vw. LU2: Lut 7C **142**
MK17: Asp G 7B **92**
Meadowview Rd. MK42: Kemp 7J **55**
Meadow Wlk. SG16: Hen 4K **101**
Meadow Way LU1: Cad 6G **149**
LU7: Lei Buz 2B **136**
LU7: Wing 6A **134**
MK45: Amp 6K **95**
SG5: Stot 7H **103**
Meads, The LU3: Lut 6J **141**
LU6: Eat B 5J **145**
Meads Cl. LU5: Hou R 4H **139**
MK17: Mil B 5J **117**
Meadway LU6: Duns 3F **147**
LU7: Lei Buz 2A **136** (Clipstone Cres.)
LU7: Lei Buz 7A **126** (Hornbeam Cl.)
MK41: Bed 7J **45**
MK43: Harr 1E **28**
Meadway Ct. LU6: Duns 3F **147**
Mecca Bingo
Bedford 7E **158** (4E **56**)
Luton 1D **148**
Mecury La. SG18: Bigg 5F **77**
Medbury La. MK42: Els 1E **70**
Media Village LU7: Soulb 3B **134**
Medina Rd. LU4: Lut 1J **149**
Medley Cl. LU6: Eat B 5K **145**

180 A-Z Bedfordshire Atlas

Medmenham Av.—Needwood Rd.

Medmenham Av. SG17: Chic 3K 99
Medusa Way SG19: Sandy 1H 61
Medway Cl. MK45: Flitw 4K 107
Medway Ct. MK43: Cran 4B 80
Mees Cl. LU3: Lut 7H 131
Meeting Cl. MK45: C End 4B 72
Meeting La. SG19: Pott 3J 63
Melbourne Cl. SG5: Stot 7H 103
Melbourne St.
MK42: Bed 6C 158 (3D 56)
MELCHBOURNE 5E 6 (1B 160)
Melchbourne Pk. MK44: Melch 6E 6
Melchbourne Rd. MK44: Knot 2E 12
Melford Cl. LU2: Lut 1H 151
Melfort Dr. LU7: Lei Buz 3D 134
Melrose Dr. MK42: Els 7E 56
Melson Sq. LU1: Lut 4J 159
Melson St. LU1: Lut 4J 159 (3C 150)
Melton Ct. LU6: Duns 3F 147
Melton Wlk. LU5: Hou R 3A 140
Memorial Ct. LU3: Lut 5H 141
Memorial La. MK43: Felm 7C 20
MK44: Blet 6J 21
Memorial Rd. LU3: Lut 5H 141
Mendham Way MK45: Clop 5A 98
Mendip Cl. MK45: Flitw 4J 107
Mendip Cres. MK41: Bed 7G 45
Mendip Way LU3: Lut 7E 130
MENTMORE 3A 162
Mentmore Cl. MK40: Bidd 4H 55
Mentmore Cres. LU6: Duns 5J 147
Mentmore Gdns. LU7: Lei Buz 4G 135
Mentmore Rd. LU7: Lei Buz 5G 135
Mentone Av. MK17: Asp G 2B 104
Mepham Rd. MK43: Woo 3F 69
MEPPERSHALL 7B 100 (1C 163)
Meppershall Rd. SG5: Shill 4K 111
SG16: Up Sto 2D 112
SG17: Mep, Shill 4K 111
Merchant La. MK43: Cran 3E 80
MK43: Whar E 2D 80
Merchants Ct. MK42: Bed 5D 158
Mercia Rd. MK40: Bidd 4H 55
Mercury Pl. SG17: Chic 2H 99
Mercury Way LU7: Lei Buz 1B 136
Meredews SG6: Let C 7K 115
Merlin Dr. SG19: Sandy 7H 49
Merlin Gdns. MK41: Bed 5E 44
Merlins Ct. LU7: Lei Buz 2J 135
Merrils Fld. MK40: Bidd 2J 55
Mersey Cl. MK45: Flitw 4K 107
Mersey Pl. LU1: Lut 4F 159 (3B 150)
Mersey Way *MK41: Bed 4E 44*
(off Wansbeck Rd.)
Merton Ho. MK40: Bed 1C 158 (1D 56)
Merton Rd. MK40: Bed 7F 45
Mews, The MK40: Bed 2E 158 (1E 56)
SG6: Nort 5K 115
Meyrick Av. LU1: Lut 6F 159 (4A 150)
Meyrick Ct. LU1: Lut 6F 159 (4A 150)
MIDDLE END 2K 145
Middlefield Cl. SG16: Hen 6J 101
Middlefield Ind. Est. SG19: Sandy 1J 61
Middlefield La. SG16: Hen 6J 101
Middlefields SG6: Let C 5H 115
Middlefields Ct. *SG6: Let C 5H 115*
(off Middlefields)
Middle Grn. LU7: Lei Buz 1A 136
Middleham Cl. SG19: Sandy 2J 61
Middlemarch SG5: Stot 3E 114
Middleton Rd. LU2: Lut 5H 143
Middleton Way LU7: Lei Buz 4B 136
Midhurst SG6: Let C 6H 115
Midhurst Gdns. LU3: Lut 5A 142
Midland Cl. SG17: Shef 3C 100
Midland Gdns. SG17: Shef 3C 100
Midland Rd. LU2: Lut 3H 159 (2C 150)
MK40: Bed 4A 158 (2C 56)
SG19: Sandy 2H 61
Midland Way SG16: Hen 3H 113
Midsummer Pl. LU7: Lei Buz 1J 135
Midway MK43: Pave 4E 30
Milburn Cl. LU3: Lut 7K 131
Milburn Rd. MK41: Bed 5K 45
Milebush LU7: Lei Buz 1E 134
Mile Rd. MK42: Bed 6E 56
(not continuous)
Miles Av. LU7: Lei Buz 1K 135
Miles Dr. SG17: Clif 3H 101
Milestone Cl. PE19: Eat F 1J 27
Milestones *SG18: Bigg 7E 76*
(off Dunton La.)
Miletree Ct. LU7: Lei Buz 1K 135
Miletree Cres. LU6: Duns 4K 147
Mile Tree Rd. LU7: Heat R 5B 126
Military Intelligence Museum, The
1J 99
Mill, The MK42: Kemp 6J 55
MK43: Turv 4B 40
Millards Cl. MK43: Cran 2G 81
MK45: Flitw 3K 107
Millards Pl. MK43: Cran 2G 81
Millbank LU7: Lei Buz 1H 135
MILLBROOK 3G 95 (1B 162)
Millbrook Cl. MK42: Wils 4E 70
Millbrook Golf Course, The 4F 95
Millbrook Rd.
MK42: Bed 7C 158 (4D 56)
MK45: Amp, Hou C, Millb 2H 95
Millbrook Station (Rail) 6F 83
Millbrook Vehicle Proving Ground
1F 95
Mill Cl. SG5: Stot 7J 103
SG16: Hen 2K 101
SG18: Bigg 6B 76
Mill Cotts. MK42: Kemp 6J 55
Mill Ct. MK44: Mil E 6H 31
MILL END 1D 163
Mill End MK45: Shar 4E 120
Mill End Cl. LU6: Eat B 6K 145
Miller Cl. MK41: Clap 3J 43
Miller Ct. MK42: Bed 6D 56
Miller Rd. MK42: Bed 5D 56
Millers Cl. LU7: Lei Buz 2B 136
Millers Ct. SG18: Bigg 5B 76
Millers La. MK43: Lidl 3B 94
Millers Lay LU5: Duns 7B 140
Millers Way LU5: Hou R 5G 139
Mill Est. NN10: Rush 1B 10
Mill Farm Barns MK45: Hou C 3D 84
Millfield MK43: Brom 7F 43
Millfield Cl. MK43: Cran 2F 81
MK45: Flitw 4C 108
Millfield La. AL3: Mark 7E 148
LU1: Cad 7E 148
Millfield M. LU1: Cad 1F 155
Millfield Rd. LU3: Lut 6J 141
Millfield Way LU1: Cad 7F 149
Mill Gdns. LU1: Lut 3G 159
Mill Grn. MK43: Turv 4B 40
Mill Hill MK44: Keysoe 3K 15
MK44: Thur 6D 22
Mill Hill Rd. PE19: Eat F 2J 27
Milligan Cl. LU4: Lut 5F 141
Milliners Ct. LU3: Lut 1A 150
Milliners Pl. *LU6: Duns 2H 147*
(off Matthew St.)
Milliners Way LU3: Lut 1A 150
Mill La. MK17: Hulc 4C 92
MK17: Salf 2A 92
MK17: Wob S 1A 104
MK42: Kemp 6J 55
MK43: Odell 7H 19
MK43: Pave 5B 30
MK43: Turv 4B 40
MK44: Keysoe 4K 15
MK45: Bar C 4K 121
MK45: Clop 4A 98
MK45: G'fld 4E 108
MK45: Hou C 4D 84
SG5: Astw 4H 103
SG5: Hex, Peg 5F 123
SG5: Stot 7J 103
SG15: Arl 3B 114
SG17: Camp 5A 100
SG18: Bigg 6B 76
SG18: Lang 5A 90
SG19: Eve, Pott 2F 63
SG19: Sandy 3H 61
SG19: Temp 3F 49
Mill Mdw. SG18: Lang 4A 90
MILLOW 1K 91 (3D 161)
Mill Rd. LU5: Hou R 5G 139
LU7: Egg, Stanb 2G 137
LU7: Lei Buz 1J 135
LU7: Slapt 4A 144
MK43: Cran 2F 81
MK43: Hus C 2G 105
MK44: Colm 7E 24
MK44: Sharn 4E 20
MK44: Thur 7D 22
SG18: Stan 6G 89
Millstream Ct. SG17: Shef 2D 100
Millstream Way LU7: Lei Buz 2H 135
Mill St. LU1: Lut 3G 159 (2B 150)
MK40: Bed 3D 158 (2E 56)
Mills Wlk. SG19: Sandy 2J 61
Mill Twr. LU6: Eat B 4J 145
Mill Vw. Ct. PE19: Eat S 5J 27
Mill Way
MK17: Asp G, Wob S 1A 104
Millwood Ct. SG5: Stot 7H 103
Millwright Way MK45: Flitw 2K 107
Mill Yd. LU1: Lut 4J 159
MK40: Bed 3D 158
Milner Ct. LU2: Lut 2J 159 (2C 150)
Milne Row MK40: Bed 1B 56
Milton Av. PE19: Eat F 1J 27
MILTON BRYAN 5J 117 (1A 162)
MILTON ERNEST 3H 31 (2B 160)
MILTON KEYNES 1A 162
MILTON KEYNES VILLAGE 1A 162
Milton Rd. LU1: Lut 6F 159 (4A 150)
MK40: Bed 1B 56
MK41: Clap 7J 31
MK44: Thur 7A 22
MK45: Flitw 3J 107
Milton Wlk. LU5: Hou R 5K 139
Milton Way LU5: Hou R 5K 139
Milverton Grn. LU3: Lut 2J 141
Minden Cl. MK45: Flitw 2A 108
Minden Ct. PE19: Eat F 2J 27
Minorca Way LU4: Lut 6C 140
Mint Casino
Luton 6K 159 (4D 150)
Miss Joans Ride LU6: Whip 4E 152
Mistletoe Ct. LU2: Lut 2G 151
Mistletoe Hill LU2: Lut 2G 151
Mitchell Rd. MK43: Whar E 2C 80
Mitford Cl. MK41: Bed 5J 45
Mitre Cl. MK41: Bed 1K 57
Mixes Hill Ct. LU2: Lut 5D 142
Mixes Hill Rd. LU2: Lut 6D 142
Mixies, The SG5: Stot 7G 103
Moakes, The LU3: Lut 2G 141
Moat Farm Barns MK43: Mars M 5C 82
Moat Farm Cl. MK43: Mars M 5C 82
MK45: G'fld 4E 108
Moat La. LU3: Lut 5K 141
Mobbs Cl. MK42: Kemp 5K 55
Mobley Grn. LU2: Lut 6F 143
MOGGERHANGER 3C 60 (3C 161)
Moggerhanger Pk. 4B 60
Moira Cl. LU3: Lut 2F 141
Molescroft AL5: Harp 7H 157
Molivers La. MK43: Brom 5E 42
Molly Moore Av. MK42: Kemp 7K 55
Monarch Rd. PE19: Eat S 4G 27
Monarch Way LU7: Lei Buz 1H 135
Monklands SG6: Let C 7F 115
Monks Cl. LU5: Duns 1A 148
Monkshill MK41: Bed 6J 45
Monks Row MK43: Pave 5B 30
Monks Wlk. SG17: Chic 3K 99
Monmouth Cl. LU5: Todd 2E 128
MK42: Bed 5F 57
Monmouth Rd. LU5: Harl 5B 120
Monoux Pl. SG19: Sandy 3J 61
Monoux Rd. MK43: Woo 5G 69
Monoworld Bus. Pk.
MK44: Sharn 7E 12
Montague Av. LU4: Lut 3E 140
Montagu Sq. PE19: Eynes 3K 27
Montgomery Av. SG17: Shef 4C 100
Montgomery Cl. LU7: Lei Buz 7K 125
MK43: Stew 3J 83
Montgomery Ct. MK42: Kemp 5C 56
Montgomery Way SG18: Bigg 1F 91
Monton Cl. LU3: Lut 3H 141
Montrose Av. LU3: Lut 6K 141
Montrose Path LU3: Lut 6A 142
Moor, The MK43: Carlt 4E 28
Moor Cotts. NN9: Harg 2D 4
Moore Cres. LU5: Hou R 5J 139
MOOR END 5K 145
Moor End LU6: Eat B 6K 145
Moor End Cl. LU6: Eat B 6K 145
Moor End La. LU6: Eat B 5K 145
MK43: Rad 7E 20
Moor End Rd. MK43: Rad 1F 31
Moores Cl. MK45: Maul 5A 98
Moorhills Cres. LU7: Wing 7B 134
Moorhills Rd. LU7: Wing 6B 134
Moorhouse Path LU7: Lei Buz 4B 136
Moorhouse Way LU7: Lei Buz 4B 136
Moorland Cl. MK42: Wils 4E 70
MK45: Flitt 3F 109
Moorland Gdns.
LU2: Lut 2G 159 (2B 150)
Moorlands LU7: Wing 6A 134
Moorlands Rd. LU7: Wing 6B 134
Moor La. MK42: Bed 6F 57
MK45: Flitw 4C 108
MK45: Maul 5E 96
Moor Pk. LU7: Wing 7A 134
Moor Path LU3: Lut 2F 159 (2B 150)
Moor Pond Piece MK45: Amp 4K 95
Moor Rd. PE19: Gt S 6G 17
Moor St. LU1: Lut 2F 159 (2A 150)
Moors Vw. Cl. MK45: G'fld 4D 108
Moot Hall 6D 56
Morar Cl. LU7: Lei Buz 2E 134
Morcom Rd. LU5: Duns 4A 148
Mordaunt Cl. MK43: Turv 3C 40
Morecambe Cl. LU4: Lut 6D 140
Moreteyne Rd. MK43: Mars M 4C 82
Moreton Rd. Nth. LU2: Lut 7E 142
Moreton Rd. Sth. LU2: Lut 7E 142
Morgan Cl. LU4: Lut 6G 141
Morgans Cl. MK45: Wils 1H 85
Moriston Rd. MK41: Bed 3E 44
Morland Cl. LU6: Duns 4G 147
Morland Way MK41: Bed 6D 44
Morrell Cl. LU3: Lut 2J 141
Morris Cl. LU3: Lut 1G 141
(not continuous)
SG16: Hen 1J 113
Morris Gdns. MK45: Amp 6K 95
Morris Rd. LU6: Duns 7F 139
Morris Wlk. MK44: Wybo 2F 37
Mortimer Cl. LU1: Lut 3H 149
Mortimer Rd. MK42: Kemp 4K 55
Mossbank Av. LU2: Lut 2G 151
Mossdale Ct. *LU4: Lut 4E 140*
(off Glaisdale)
Moss La. MK42: Els 2E 70
Mossman Dr. LU1: Cad 6G 149
Mostyn Rd. LU3: Lut 5G 141
MOULSOE 3A 160
Moulsoe Rd. MK43: Cran 5A 80
Moulton Av. MK42: Bed 4G 57
Moulton Ri. LU2: Lut 3K 159 (2D 150)
Mount, The LU3: Lut 2G 159 (2B 150)
MK17: Asp G 2B 104
Mountbatten Ct. PE19: Eat S 3J 27
Mountbatten Dr. SG18: Bigg 4D 76
Mountbatten Gdns. LU7: Lei Buz 7K 125
Mountbatten Pl. MK41: Bed 1K 57
Mountbatten Way SG17: Chic 1J 99
Mount Dr. MK41: Bed 6J 45
Mountfield Path LU2: Lut 7C 142
Mountfield Rd. LU2: Lut 7C 142
Mountgrace Rd. LU2: Lut 3G 143
Mt. Pleasant LU7: Soulb 5A 124
MK17: Asp G 2D 104
MK17: Sto H 1A 124
MK43: Ridg 1K 105
Mt. Pleasant Av. LU5: Todd 4F 129
Mt. Pleasant Cl. LU5: Todd 4F 129
Mount Pleasant Golf Course 3F 113
Mt. Pleasant Rd. LU3: Lut 4G 141
MK41: Clap 3K 43
Mountview Av. LU5: Duns 4K 147
Mowbray Cl. MK43: Brom 6E 42
Mowbray Cres. SG5: Stot 7H 103
Mowbray Dr. LU7: Lei Buz 2F 135
Mowbray Pl. MK44: Will 1G 59
Mowbray Rd. MK42: Bed 6E 56
Mowbrays, The SG5: Stot 6H 103
Mowhills MK43: Harr 2D 28
Mowsbury Golf & Squash Complex
2G 45
Mowsbury Golf Course 2G 45
Mowsbury Pk. 3G 45
Mowsbury Wlk. MK41: Bed 3F 45
Moxes Wood LU3: Lut 2G 141
Moxhill Gdns. MK44: Will 3G 59
Muirfield LU2: Lut 3C 142
MK40: Bidd 4H 55
Mulberry Cl. LU1: Lut 3K 149
SG5: Stot 1H 115
SG18: Bigg 3B 76
Mulberry End MK45: Sils 1K 109
Mulberry Wlk. MK42: Kemp 7B 56
Mullein Cl. PE19: Eat F 2J 27
Mullion Cl. LU2: Lut 4F 143
Mullway SG6: Let C 7E 114
Muntjac Cl. PE19: Eat S 2H 27
Murdock Rd. MK41: Bed 5C 44
Murrell La. SG5: Stot 1J 115
Mussons Path
LU2: Lut 2H 159 (2C 150)
Muswell Cl. LU3: Lut 3K 141
Muswell Rd. MK42: Bed 5D 56
Mutford Cft. LU2: Lut 1H 151
Myers Rd. SG19: Pott 2H 63
Myrtle Gdns. SG16: Lwr Sto 3G 113
Myrtle Rd. MK42: Bed 5F 57

N

Nags Head La. NN9: Harg 2D 4
Nagshead La. MK44: Wybo 3G 37
Namco Entertainment 3G 159
Napier Ct.
LU1: Lut 5F 159 (3B 150)
Napier Rd. LU1: Lut 5F 159 (3B 150)
MK41: Bed 6B 46
Nappsbury Rd. LU4: Lut 4F 141
Narrow Path MK17: Asp H 3A 104
Naseby Pl. MK45: Flitw 1A 108
Naseby Rd. LU1: Lut 3K 149
Nash Cl. LU5: Hou R 4K 139
Nash Rd. MK42: Bed 4G 57
Nayland Cl. LU2: Lut 1J 151
Naylor Av. MK42: Kemp 1A 70
Neale Rd. MK43: Woo 3F 69
Neale Way MK43: Woo 3F 69
Neath Abbey MK41: Bed 2K 57
Nebular Ct. LU7: Lei Buz 1A 136
Needham Rd. LU4: Lut 3D 140
NEEDINGWORTH 1D 161
Needwood Rd. MK41: Bed 5K 45

Orchard Way—Plane Tree Cl.

Orchard Way MK44: Gt Bar .5A 48
MK45: Flitw .4B 108
SG6: Let C .6H 115
SG16: Lwr Sto .4G 113
Orchid Cl. LU3: Lut .3E 140
LU6: Duns .1E 146
PE19: Eat F .1J 27
Ordelmere SG6: Let C .5H 115
Oregon Way LU3: Lut .1J 141
Orion Way LU7: Lei Buz .1B 136
ORLINGBURY .1A 160
Ormesby Way MK40: Bed .3A 56
Ormsby Cl. LU1: Lut .5C 150
Orpington Cl. LU4: Lut .6C 140
Orwell Cl. MK41: Bed .4E 44
Osborn Cres. SG17: Shef .3C 100
Osborne Av. SG17: Chic .3J 99
Osborne Ct. LU1: Lut .7K 159 (5D 150)
MK42: Bed .4D 56
Osborne Rd. LU1: Lut .4D 150
LU6: Duns .3H 147
Osborn Rd. MK45: Bar C .4A 122
Osier Ct. PE19: Eat F .1J 27
Osier Link MK45: Amp .6B 96
Osprey Cl. MK42: Kemp .1A 70
SG19: Sandy .7H 49
Osprey Ct. SG6: Let C .6G 115
Osprey Rd. MK45: Flitw .4K 107
SG18: Bigg .6B 76
Osprey Wlk. LU4: Lut .4C 140
Ossory Pl. MK45: Amp .5A 96
Ossory Way MK42: Bed .7C 158 (4D 56)
Oswald Cl. MK42: Short .7K 57
Othello Ct. *MK40: Bed .7B 44*
(off Shakespeare Rd.)
Otter Wlk. MK41: Bed .4E 44
Otter Way PE19: Eat S .2H 27
Ouseland Rd. MK40: Bed .3A 56
Ouseley Cl. LU4: Lut .6F 141
Ouseley Way LU6: Whip .3E 152
Ouse Rd. MK41: Bed .7J 45
PE19: Eat F .3J 27
Ouse Valley Golf Course, The .7K 43
Oval, The SG16: Hen .3J 113
Overdale MK41: Bed .6J 45
Overend Grn. La. LU7: Heat R .2A 126
Overfield Rd. LU2: Lut .1G 151
Overlord Cl. SG17: Shef .4C 100
Overstone Cl. LU7: Wing .6A 134
Overstone Rd. LU4: Lut .1F 149
Oving Cl. LU2: Lut .7H 143
Owen Cl. MK42: Kemp .7K 55
MK43: Mars M .4C 82
Owen Jones Cl. SG16: Hen .1J 113
Owlswick MK44: Wild .5D 34
Owlswood SG19: Sandy .7H 49
Oxendon Ct. LU7: Lei Buz .6H 125
Oxen Ind. Est.
LU2: Lut .1K 159 (1D 150)
Oxen Rd. LU2: Lut .1K 159 (1D 150)
Oxford Rd. LU1: Lut .6J 159 (4C 150)
Oxford St. NN10: Wym .1A 10
Oxlip, The MK45: Amp .4B 96

P

Packhorse Pl. LU6: Kens .3E 154
Padbury Ho. MK40: Bed .1C 56
Paddlers Ct. MK40: Bed .3A 56
Paddock, The MK40: Bidd .2K 55
MK43: Lidl .2C 94
Paddock Cl. LU4: Lut .5B 140
MK41: Clap .2J 43
Paddocks, The LU7: Lei Buz .2G 135
MK43: Brom .1F 55
MK45: Flitw .1K 107
PE19: Eat F .3K 27
SG19: Pott .3H 63
Paddocks Chase
SG19: Pott .3H 63
Paddocks Cl. MK45: Amp .6A 96
Paddock Vw. LU2: C'hoe .4J 143
Page's Ind. Pk. LU7: Lei Buz .4K 135
Page's Park Station
Leighton Buzzard
Narrow Gauge Railway .4K 135
Paignton Cl. LU4: Lut .5F 141
Paisley Cl. LU4: Lut .6F 141
Palace St. SG18: Bigg .6C 76
Palgrave Rd.
MK42: Bed .7A 158 (4C 56)
Palma Cl. LU6: Duns .6F 139
Palmer Cl. SG17: Shef .2C 100
Palmer Cres. LU7: Lei Buz .4B 136
Palmer Sport .7D 14
Palmerston St.
MK41: Bed .1B 158 (7D 44)
Palmerston Way SG5: Stot .4E 114
PAPWORTH EVERARD .1D 161
PAPWORTH ST AGNES .1D 161
Parade, The LU3: Lut .2E 140
LU6: Duns .1G 147
SG6: Let C .5H 115
(off Southfields)
Paradine Ct. MK40: Bed .3C 158 (2D 56)
Paradine Rd. MK42: Bed .4F 57
Parish Cl. MK41: Bed .5K 45
Park & Ride
Elstow .7C 56
Park Av. LU3: Lut .2E 140
LU5: Hou R .4J 139
LU6: Tott .2B 146
MK40: Bed .7D 44
Park Av. Ind. Est. LU3: Lut .2D 140
Park Cl. AL3: Mark .6F 155
MK44: Mogg .4B 60
Park Ct. LU2: Lut .1G 159 (1B 150)
SG6: Let C .7J 115
SG19: Sandy .4J 61
Park Cres. MK43: Stew .2J 83
PARK END .3C 42
Parker Cl. PE19: Eynes .1J 39
Park Farm Cl. SG16: Hen .5K 101
Park Farm Ct. MK41: Clap .3B 44
Parkfield AL3: Mark .6F 155
Park Ga. LU7: Wing .7A 134
Park Hill LU5: Todd .1F 129
MK45: Amp .4A 96
Parkland MK43: Brom .6D 42
Parkland Dr. LU1: Lut .7G 159 (5B 150)
Parklands MK41: Bed .7H 45
Parklands, The LU5: Duns .1H 147
Parkland Sq. LU1: Lut .5D 150
Park La. LU6: Eat B .3H 145
MK44: Blun .6E 48
MK44: Card, Cople .1E 72
MK44: Sharn .3D 20
PE19: Stone .2K 9
SG16: Hen .3K 101
SG19: Gam .3J 51
Park La. Cres. SG16: Hen .3K 101
Park Leys LU5: Harl .6B 120
Parkmead LU1: Lut .7K 159
Park Mdw. Cl. MK45: Bar C .4K 121
Park M. LU7: Lei Buz .3J 135
Park Palings Wlk. MK45: Hay .4D 86
Park Ri. AL5: Harp .7J 157
Park Rd. LU5: Duns .3J 147
LU5: Todd .6J 117
MK17: Mil B .6J 117
MK42: Kemp .5B 56
MK43: Stev .2C 42
MK44: Melch .5E 6
MK44: Mogg .3B 60
MK44: Rox .6E 36
MK45: West .2A 120
MK45: Wils .2G 85
SG19: Sandy .3J 61
Park Rd. Nth. LU5: Hou R .4J 139
MK41: Bed .7D 44
Park Rd. W. MK41: Bed .1B 158 (7D 44)
PARKSIDE .4J 139
Parkside MK44: Mil E .3H 31
MK45: Grav .2F 111
Parkside Cl. LU5: Hou R .4K 139
Parkside Dr. LU5: Hou R .3K 139
Parkside Flats LU5: Duns .2J 147
Park Sq. LU1: Lut .5J 159 (3C 150)
Parkstone Cl. MK41: Bed .3G 45
Park St. LU1: Lut .5J 159 (3C 150)
LU6: Duns .1G 147
MK17: Wob .7E 104
MK45: Amp .4A 96
Park St. W. LU1: Lut .6J 159 (4C 150)
PARK TOWN .6K 159 (4C 150)
Park Viaduct LU1: Lut .6J 159 (4C 150)
Park Vw. MK44: Blun .6D 48
Park Vw. Cl. LU3: Lut .3F 141
Park Vw. Ct. PE19: Eat F .2K 27
Park Vw. Dr. AL3: Mark .5F 155
Parkview La. LU7: Teb .6C 128
Parkway LU5: Hou R .3A 140
Parkway Rd. LU1: Lut .5F 151
Parmiter Way MK45: Amp .6K 95
Parrish Cl. MK43: Mars M .4D 82
Parrott Cl. LU5: Duns .1A 148
Parsonage Cl. MK43: Oak .2G 43
Partridge Cl. LU4: Lut .4C 140
Partridge Hill MK17: Gt Bri .1D 124
Partridge La. MK43: Brom .1D 54
Partridge Piece MK43: Cran .1G 81
SG19: Sandy .7H 49
Parys Rd. LU3: Lut .3K 141
Pascal Way SG6: Let C .6K 115
Pascomb Rd. LU6: Duns .2F 147
Pashley Ct. *PE19: Eynes .1J 39*
(off Baxter Dr.)
Pastures, The LU6: Edles .7K 145
MK43: Stew .3J 83
SG16: Up Sto .3E 112
SG18: Up C .3J 75
Pastures Ct. LU4: Lut .6C 140
Pastures Way LU4: Lut .4B 140
Pathway, The MK45: Maul .4D 96
Patterdale Cl. LU6: Duns .3H 147
Patteshull Ct. MK40: Bed .3B 158
Paula Radcliffe Sharnbrook
Community Sports Cen. .4A 20
Paula Radcliffe Way MK41: Bed .3J 43
MK41: Clap .3J 43
MK43: Brom .3J 43
MK43: Clap, Oak .7H 31
Paulsons Cl. MK44: Rise .4C 14
Paul Waller Av. MK44: Card .7K 57
PAVENHAM .4C 30 (2A 160)
Pavenham Mobile Home Pk.
MK43: Pave .4E 30
Pavenham Osier Beds Nature Reserve
.5C 30
Pavenham Pk. Golf Course .4D 30
Pavenham Rd. MK43: Carlt .4F 29
MK43: Felm .7C 20
MK43: Oak .7F 31
Pax Hill MK41: Bed .5G 45
Paxton Dr. SG5: Stot .4E 114
Payne Rd. MK43: Woo .4F 69
Paynes Cl. SG6: Let C .5J 115
Peach Ct. LU1: Lut .6K 159 (4D 150)
Peach's Cl. MK43: Harr .1E 28
Peacock All. *LU7: Lei Buz .2J 135*
(off Hockliffe St.)
Peacock Gdns. MK42: Wils .4F 71
Peacock M. *LU7: Lei Buz .2J 135*
(off Hockliffe St.)
Peacock Pde. LU7: Lei Buz .2J 135
Peacock Rd. MK43: Brom .7D 42
Peacock Yd. *LU7: Lei Buz .2J 135*
(off Hockliffe St.)
Peakes End MK45: Step .3G 107
Pearcey Rd. MK42: Bed .5E 56
Pearmain Cl. MK41: Bed .1H 57
Pearson Cl. PE19: Eynes .1J 39
Pear Tree Cl. MK43: Brom .1D 54
SG16: Lwr Sto .3H 113
Peartree Cl. LU5: Todd .3E 128
SG17: Shef .3E 100
Pear Tree La. LU7: Lei Buz .1J 135
Peartree Rd. LU2: Lut .5G 143
Pear Tree Vw. MK42: Els .1E 70
Peashill La. MK44: Gt Bar .3K 47
Pebblemoor LU6: Edles .7J 145
Peck Ct. MK45: Bar C .3K 121
Peckworth Ind. Est.
SG16: Lwr Sto .2G 113
Peddars La. LU7: Stanb .5H 137
Pedley La. SG17: Clif .2F 101
Pedley Way MK41: Bed .4A 46
Peel Ct. LU7: Lei Buz .2K 135
Peel Pl. LU1: Lut .5G 159 (3B 150)
Peel's Pl. SG19: Sandy .3K 61
Peel St. LU1: Lut .5G 159 (3B 150)
LU5: Hou R .4H 139
MK40: Bed .2C 158 (1D 56)
Peer Rd. PE19: Eat S .3H 27
Peers Dr. MK17: Asp G .3C 104
Pegasus Ct. SG18: Bigg .4B 76
Pegasus Dr. SG18: Bigg .1F 91
Pegasus Ho. *SG18: Bigg .5B 76*
(off High St.)
Pegasus M. SG18: Bigg .1F 91
Pegasus Rd. LU7: Lei Buz .1A 136
Peggles La. SG5: Stot .2G 115
PEGSDON .6H 123 (1C 163)
Pegsdon Cl. LU3: Lut .2K 141
Pegsdon Hill's Nature Reserve .7H 123
Pegsdon Way SG5: Peg .6H 123
Pelican Way SG6: Let C .5H 115
Pemberley Av.
MK40: Bed .1E 158 (7E 44)
Pemberley La.
MK40: Bed .1E 158 (1E 56)
Pembroke Av. LU4: Lut .6G 141
PE19: Eynes .1K 39
Pembroke Cl. MK43: Mars M .4D 82
Pembroke Rd. MK45: Hou C .5D 84
Pembroke St. MK40: Bed .2F 57
Penda Cl. LU3: Lut .3H 141
Pendennis Rd. MK41: Bed .5J 45
Penfold Cl. SG17: Shef .3A 100
Penhill LU3: Lut .3G 141
Penhill Ct. LU3: Lut .3F 141
Penlee Cl. MK41: Bed .1H 57
Pennine Av. LU3: Lut .1E 140
Pennine Ri. MK45: Flitw .4K 107
Pennine Rd. MK41: Bed .6G 45
Pennivale Cl. LU7: Lei Buz .1J 135
Pennyfarthers Cl. MK45: Maul .5K 97
Penrith Av. LU6: Duns .3H 147
Penrwyn Ct. PE19: Eynes .1K 39
Penshurst Cl. AL5: Harp .7H 157
Pentelows, The PE28: Cov .2H 5
Pentland Cl. SG19: Sandy .2H 61
Pentland Ri. MK41: Bed .6G 45
Penwright Cl. MK42: Kemp .5K 55
Penwrights La. MK44: Gt Bar .3K 47
Peppercorn La. PE19: Eat S .5J 27
Peppercorn Pk. MK41: Clap .2B 44
Peppercorn Way LU6: Duns .7F 139
PEPPERSTOCK .2A 156
Peppiatts, The LU6: N'all .5F 145
Pepsal End Rd. LU1: Pep .5A 156
Percheron Dr. LU4: Lut .6C 140
Percival Way LU2: Lut .3G 151
Peregrine Rd. LU4: Lut .5C 140
Periwinkle La. LU6: Duns .3J 147
Periwinkle Ter. *LU6: Duns .3J 147*
(off Periwinkle La.)
Perkins Rd. MK41: Bed .7A 46
Perring Cl. MK44: Sharn .3C 20
Perry Mead LU6: Eat B .5J 145
Perrymead LU2: Lut .7K 143
Pershore Cl. MK41: Bed .4G 45
PERTENHALL .6F 9 (1B 160)
Pertenhall Rd. MK44: Keysoe .3K 15
MK44: Swin .5A 8
PE19: Stone .4H 9
Petard Cl. LU4: Lut .7C 140
Petersfield Gdns. LU3: Lut .7G 131
PETER'S GREEN .3C 163
Petley Cl. MK45: Flitw .5A 108
Petropolis Ho. LU6: Duns .2H 147
PETSOE END .3A 160
Petteril Wlk. *MK41: Bed .2E 44*
(off Carron Rd.)
Petunia Ct. LU3: Lut .1A 150
Pevensey Cl. LU2: Lut .5H 143
Pevensey Gro. MK45: Flitw .5J 107
Pevensey Rd. MK41: Bed .6J 45
Pheasant Gro. MK42: Wils .4F 71
Pheasant Wlk. MK45: Flitw .4K 107
Philip Gdns. PE19: Eynes .1K 39
Phillips Mdws. MK44: Yeld .2A 6
Phillpotts Av. MK40: Bed .1G 57
Phipps Cl. MK45: Wils .1H 85
Phoebe's Orchard MK17: Sto H .1A 124
Phoenix Chambers MK40: Bed .4D 158
Phoenix Cl. LU7: Lei Buz .1B 136
Phoenix Dr. SG6: Let C .7K 115
Phoenix Pk. PE19: Eat S .7H 27
SG19: Hat .7G 61
PICCOTTS END .3B 162
Pickering Cl. SG19: Sandy .2J 61
Pickford Rd. AL3: Mark .7E 154
Picton Hall LU1: Lut .6G 159
Piggotts La. LU4: Lut .5F 141
Pikes Cl. LU1: Lut .5H 159
Pilcroft Ho. MK42: Bed .6C 158
Pilcroft St. MK42: Bed .6D 158 (3E 56)
Pilgrim Cen. MK41: Bed .6F 45
Pilgrims Cl. LU5: Harl .7B 120
MK42: Bed .6E 56
MK45: Flitw .3A 108
Pilgrims Way MK42: Bed .6E 56
Pillinge Rd. MK43: Stew .3J 83
Pinchmill Cl. MK44: Sharn .4C 20
Pinchmill Way MK44: Sharn .4C 20
Pine Cl. LU7: Lei Buz .6J 125
NN10: Rush .1A 10
SG18: Bigg .4C 76
Pine Crest M. LU7: Lei Buz .3G 135
Pinemead SG17: Shef .3E 100
Pines, The MK42: Kemp .7B 56
MK45: Amp .5A 96
Pine Vw. Pk. MK45: Maul .6K 97
Pinewood Cl. LU3: Lut .7E 130
Pinford Dell LU2: Lut .1H 151
Pinkle Hill Rd. LU7: Heat R .3J 125
Pinsent Av. MK43: Brom .1E 54
Pioneer Pk. MK42: Bed .5D 56
Pipers Cft. LU6: Duns .3F 147
Pipers Highway MK43: Carlt .6F 29
Pipers La. AL3: Mark .3G 155
LU1: Aley G .3G 155
Pipit Cl. MK45: Flitw .4A 108
Pipit Gro. SG19: Sandy .7H 49
Pipit Ri. MK41: Bed .5E 44
PIRTON .1C 163
Pirton Rd. LU4: Lut .4E 140
SG5: Hol .7G 113
Pitsdean Rd. PE19: Abbot .5J 39
PITSTONE .3A 162
Pix Brook Ct. SG6: Let C .7H 115
Pix Ct. SG15: Arl .5C 102
Pixmore Av. SG6: Let C .7K 115
Pixmore Cen. SG6: Let C .7J 115
Pixmore Ind. Est. SG6: Let C .7J 115
Pix Rd. SG5: Stot .1G 115
Place, The
Bedford .1F 57
Plaiters Cl. MK43: Pave .5B 30
Plaiters Way LU5: Bid .4G 139
Planes, The MK42: Kemp .7A 56
Plane Tree Cl. SG19: Gam .3K 51

Redhoods Way E.—Sadleir's Grn.

Redhoods Way E. SG6: Let C 7G 115
Redhoods Way W. SG6: Let C 7G 115
Red Ho. Ct. LU5: Hou R 5J 139
Red Lion Cl. MK43: Cran 3F 81
Red Lion Ct. LU7: Heat R 3J 125
Redman Gdns. SG18: Bigg 4C 76
Redmire Cl. LU4: Lut 3D 140
Red Oak Cl. MK43: Brom 5C 42
Red Rails LU1: Lut 5A 150
Red Rails Ct. LU1: Lut 5A 150
Redwald Cl. MK42: Kemp 6A 56
Redwood Cl. LU7: Wing 7A 134
Redwood Dr. LU3: Lut 1E 140
Redwood Glade
LU7: Lei Buz 5H 125
Redwood Gro.
MK42: Bed 7E 158 (4E 56)
Redwood Rd. LU7: Wing 7A 134
REED END 1D 163
Reeds Dale LU2: Lut 7K 143
Reeve Cl. LU7: Lei Buz 4A 136
Reeves Av. LU3: Lut 5K 141
Regency Ct. LU6: Duns 3J 147
Regency Ct. Pk. Homes
SG16: Lwr Sto 4E 112
Regent Cl. MK41: Bed 3E 44
PE19: Eat S 3H 27
Regent Ct. MK40: Bed 1B 56
SG5: Stot 6H 103
Regent Gdns. SG5: Stot 7G 103
Regent Link LU1: Lut 6H 159
Regents M. MK40: Bidd 2J 55
Regent St. LU1: Lut 5G 159 (3B 150)
LU6: Duns 1H 147
LU7: Lei Buz 2K 135
SG5: Stot 7G 103
Reginald St. LU2: Lut 1G 159 (1B 150)
Regis Rd. LU4: Lut 5A 140
Rendlesham Wlk. MK41: Bed 6A 46
RENHOLD 3B 46 (2B 160)
Renhold Rd. MK44: Wild 1C 46
Renshaw Cl. LU2: Lut 7J 143
Repton Cl. LU3: Lut 3G 141
MK41: Bed 5H 45
Repton Rd. SG17: Chic 1J 99
Reston Path LU2: Lut 7J 143
Restormel Cl. MK41: Bed 4H 45
Retreat, The LU5: Duns 1B 148
Reynes Cl. MK43: Mars M 5D 82
Reynes Dr. MK43: Oak 1F 43
Reynolds SG6: Let C 5H 115
Reynolds Cl. MK41: Bed 7C 44
MK43: Whar E 1C 80
SG18: Bigg 4C 76
Reynolds Ct. PE19: Eat F 1K 27
Rhineland Way MK41: Bed 3F 45
Ribble Way MK41: Bed 3E 44
Ribocon Way LU4: Lut 2D 140
Ribston Cl. MK41: Bed 2E 44
Richard Daniel's Ho.
SG17: Shef 2C 100
(off High St.)
Richards Cl. LU1: Lut 4K 149
Richards Ct. LU1: Lut 4K 149
Richard's Cres. SG18: Old W 7A 74
Richard St. LU5: Duns 2J 147
Richbell Ct. MK40: Bed . . .1B 158 (1D 56)
Richmond Cl. PE19: Eynes 1K 39
Richmond Ct. LU2: Lut 1D 150
LU6: Eat B 4J 145
Richmond Dr. LU5: Hou R 4A 140
Richmond Hill LU2: Lut 7D 142
Richmond Hill Path LU2: Lut 7D 142
Richmond Rd. LU7: Lei Buz 3A 136
MK40: Bed 1F 57
MK45: West 1A 120
Rickyard, The MK43: Mars M 2D 82
SG6: Nort 5K 115
Rickyard Cl. LU2: Lut 6F 143
Riddy La. LU3: Lut 4K 141
Riddy Local Nature Reserve, The
. . . . .4H 61
Ride, The LU6: Tott 4B 146
LU7: Lei Buz 2B 136
Ridge, The SG6: Let C 7J 115
Ridge Av. AL5: Harp 7J 157
SG6: Let C 7J 115
Ridge Ct. LU2: Lut 1E 150
Ridgely Dr. LU7: Lei Buz 4A 136
Ridge Rd. MK42: Kemp 1G 69
MK43: Kemp 1G 69
SG6: Let C 7J 115
Ridge Vw. MK45: Hou C 4D 84
Ridgeway AL5: Harp 7J 157
LU6: Kens 3A 154
LU7: Wing 6A 134
Ridgeway, The MK41: Bed 5J 45
MK44: Mogg 3E 60
MK45: Flitw 3A 108
SG19: Pott 3H 63
Ridgeway Av. LU5: Duns 7K 139
Ridgeway Bus. Pk., The
MK44: Mogg 2E 60
Ridgeway Ct. LU7: Lei Buz 4J 135
Ridgeway Dr. LU5: Duns 1A 148
Ridgewood Dr. AL5: Harp 7J 157
Ridgewood Gdns. AL5: Harp 7J 157
RIDGMONT 1K 105 (1A 162)
Ridgmont Rd.
MK43: Hus C, Ridg 2G 105
Ridgmont Station (Rail) 6G 93
Ridgmount St.
MK42: Bed 7C 158 (4D 56)
Ridgway Rd. LU2: Lut . . .1K 159 (1D 150)
MK43: Brog 4G 93
Ridings, The AL3: Mark 5G 155
LU3: Lut 1A 150
Riglen Cl. MK43: Lidl 2C 94
Ringmere Ct. *LU2: Lut 6G 143*
(off Telscombe Way)
RINGSHALL 3A 162
Ringshall Rd. HP4: Dag, Ring 7B 152
Ringwood Cl. MK42: Kemp 6B 56
Ringwood Rd. LU2: Lut 2B 142
Ripley Rd. LU4: Lut 1E 148
Ripon Cl. MK42: Kemp 4A 56
Ripon Ct. SG18: Bigg 7C 76
Risborough Ct. MK41: Bed 1H 57
Risborough Rd. MK41: Bed 1H 57
RISELEY 4B 14 (1B 160)
Riseley Rd. MK44: Keysoe 5G 15
Risings, The MK41: Bed 6J 45
Riverfield Dr. MK41: Bed 2J 57
Rivergate Ho. LU1: Lut 4J 159
River Hill AL3: Flam 7A 156
River La. MK44: Mil E 4H 31
Rivermead Gdns. SG19: Sandy 3H 61
River Rd. PE19: Eat F 3J 27
River Row MK43: Pave 5B 30
Riverside LU7: Lei Buz 1J 135
SG17: Shef 2C 100
Riverside Cl.
MK42: Bed 7A 158 (4C 56)
Riverside Ct. SG18: Bigg 4B 76
Riverside Gdns. SG18: Lang 7A 90
Riverside Holiday Pk.
MK43: Pave 4F 31
Riverside Rd. LU3: Lut 4J 141
Riverside Tennis Club 1G 57
Riverside Towers MK42: Bed 4D 158
Riverside Vw. MK44: Mil E 3G 31
River St. MK40: Bed 4B 158 (2D 56)
River Ter. PE19: Eynes 3K 27
PE19: St N 2K 27
River Vw. SG17: Shef 3C 100
Riverview MK43: Pave 4E 30
Riverview Way MK42: Kemp 6J 55
River Way LU3: Lut 4G 141
Robert Allen Ct. LU1: Lut 6J 159
Robert Hunt Gdns. SG19: Sandy 3H 61
Robert Lucas Dr. SG17: Shef 3E 100
Roberts Cl. PE19: Eat S 5H 27
Roberts Dr. MK43: Mars M 2E 82
Robin Cl. MK45: Flitw 4A 108
SG19: Sandy 1H 61
Robin Hill MK41: Bed 5E 44
(not continuous)
Robins Folly MK44: Thur 2F 33
Robinson Cres. LU5: Harl 4B 120
Robinson Ho. MK40: Bed 1C 158
Robinson Pool & Images Fitness . . .7D 44
Robins Reach Archery 6F 17
Robinswood LU2: Lut 4C 142
Robinswood Cl. LU7: Lei Buz 6H 125
Rochdale Ct. LU1: Lut 6J 159
Rochester Av. LU2: Lut 5G 143
Rochester M. *LU7: Lei Buz 3G 135*
(off Church Rd.)
Rochester Way MK42: Short 7K 57
Rochford Dr. LU2: Lut 7J 143
Rockbeck Cl. MK42: Kemp 6A 56
Rock Cl. LU7: Lei Buz 3F 135
Rockingham Ct. NN10: Rush 1A 10
Rockingham Wlk. MK41: Bed 6K 45
Rock La. LU7: Lei Buz 3D 134
(Derwent Rd.)
LU7: Lei Buz 2F 135
(Springfield Rd.)
Rockleigh Ct. LU7: Lei Buz 2G 135
Rockley Rd. LU1: Lut 4J 149
Rodeheath LU4: Lut 6F 141
Rodney Cl. LU4: Lut 6B 140
Roebuck Cl. LU1: Lut 4J 149
Roe Cl. SG5: Stot 1G 115
Roedean Cl. LU2: Lut 6H 143
ROE END 7D 154
Roe End La. AL3: Mark 7A 154
ROE GREEN 1D 163
Roe Grn. PE19: Eat S 2H 27
Roff Av. MK41: Bed 1B 158 (1D 56)
Rogate Rd. LU2: Lut 4G 143
Roise Ct. MK40: Bed 2B 158
Roise St. MK40: Bed 2B 158 (1D 56)
Roman Ct. LU5: Hou R 5H 139
Roman Gdns. LU5: Hou R 5H 139
Roman Paddock MK43: Harr 1E 28
Roman Rd. LU3: Lut 6G 141
LU4: Lut 6G 141
MK45: Bar C 4B 122
Roman Vw. SG19: Sandy 4K 61
Roman Way AL3: Mark 5G 155
MK45: Flitw 2B 108
Romany Cl. SG6: Let C 7E 114
Romney Ct. PE19: Eat F 2J 27
Romney Wlk. MK41: Bed 6D 44
Romsey Way MK42: Els 7E 56
Ronald Cl. MK42: Kemp 1A 70
Rondini Av. LU3: Lut 6K 141
Rookery, The SG19: Sandy 7J 49
Rookery Dr. LU2: Lut 3B 142
Rookery La. PE28: Kimb 1K 9
Rookery Rd. MK44: Wybo 1F 37
Rookery Wlk. SG17: Clif 3H 101
Rooksmead MK41: Bed 5E 44
Rook Tree Cl. SG5: Stot 7J 103
Rook Tree Farm Ind. Est.
MK17: Hulc 2D 92
Rook Tree La. SG5: Stot 6H 103
Rooktree Way MK45: Hay 3E 86
Roosevelt Av. LU7: Lei Buz 1K 135
SG17: Shef 4C 100
ROOTHAM'S GREEN 1E 34 (2C 161)
Ropa Ct. *LU7: Lei Buz 2H 135*
(off Friday St.)
Rope Wlk. MK42: Bed 6E 158 (3E 56)
Ropkins Cl. MK45: West 1B 120
Rosamond Rd. MK40: Bed 1G 57
Rosata La. SG17: Chic 2J 99
Rosebay Cl. MK45: Flitw 3K 107
Rosebery Av. LU7: Lei Buz 2G 135
Rosebery Ct. LU7: Lei Buz 2H 135
Roseby Way MK41: Bed 2J 57
Rose Cotts. SG15: Arl 7C 102
Rose Ct. LU6: Eat B 4H 145
Rose Cres. MK43: Pave 4E 30
Rosedale LU5: Hou R 4A 140
Rosedale Cl. LU3: Lut 2E 140
Rosedale Way MK42: Kemp 6A 56
Rosefield Cl. LU2: Lut 1E 150
Rose La. SG18: Bigg 5C 76
Rosemary Cl. SG18: Bigg 6E 76
Rosemary Dr. MK43: Brom 7E 42
Rosemary La. SG16: Lwr Sto 3G 113
Rose Wlk. LU5: Hou R 3A 140
LU5: Todd 3F 129
MK43: Brom 1E 54
MK45: Amp 4A 96
Rose Wood Cl. LU2: Lut 7D 142
Roslyn Way LU5: Hou R 4G 139
Ross Cl. LU1: Lut 4K 149
Rossendale Wlk. *MK41: Bed 5K 45*
(off Atholl Wlk.)
Rossfold Rd. LU3: Lut 1F 141
Rosslyn Cres. LU3: Lut 4A 142
Rossway LU1: Slip E 2K 155
Rossway St. LU1: Slip E 2A 156
Rothbury Cl. SG19: Sandy 7J 49
Rothbury Ct. MK41: Bed 5K 45
Rotheram Av. LU1: Lut 5K 149
Rother Cl. MK41: Bed 4F 45
Rotherfield LU2: Lut 6H 143
Rotherwood Cl. LU6: Duns 1E 146
Rothesay Rd. LU1: Lut . . .5F 159 (3B 150)
Rothsay Gdns. MK40: Bed 1F 57
Rothsay Pl. MK40: Bed 3E 158 (2F 57)
Rothsay Rd. MK40: Bed 2F 57
Rothschild Rd. LU7: Lei Buz 1G 135
LU7: Wing 7A 134
Rotten Row MK44: Rise 4B 14
Roundel Dr. LU7: Lei Buz 4B 136
ROUND GREEN 7E 142
Roundmead MK41: Bed 6J 45
Roundwood AL5: Harp 7J 157
Roundwood Cl. AL5: Harp 7J 157
Roundwood La. AL5: Harp 7H 157
Roundwood Pk. AL5: Harp 7J 157
Rousbury Rd. MK43: Stew 3J 83
Row, The MK46: Cold B 3A 40
PE28: Up D 1J 7
Rowallan Dr. MK41: Bed 4F 45
Rowan Cl. LU1: Lut 3K 149
Rowan Ct. SG19: Sandy 2H 61
Rowan Cres. SG6: Let C 7G 115
SG18: Bigg 4D 76
Rowans, The MK42: Kemp 7B 56
MK45: Flitw 4B 108
MK45: Sils 2A 110
Rowan Way MK43: Cran 4E 80
Rowelfield LU2: Lut 1G 151
Rowington Cl. LU2: Lut 7J 143
Rowlands, The SG18: Bigg 7E 76
Rowlandson Way MK41: Bed 6C 44
Rowletts Vw. SG18: Bigg 3D 76
Rowley Furrows LU7: Lei Buz 1F 135
ROWSHAM 3A 162
Roxhill Rd. MK43: Mars M 1K 81
ROXTON 6E 36 (2C 161)
Roxton Rd. MK44: Chaw 2E 36
MK44: Gt Bar 4K 47
Royal Ct. PE19: Eat S 3H 27
Royale Wlk. LU6: Duns 3J 147
Royal Ho's. MK45: Bar C 3A 122
Royal London Mall
LU1: Lut 4H 159 (3C 150)
Royal Oak Cl. SG18: Bigg 4B 76
Royce Cl. LU6: Duns 3F 147
Royce Ct. PE19: Eat F 2K 27
Royce Rd. MK43: Whar E 1B 80
Roydon Cl. LU4: Lut 5C 140
Royle Gdns. MK42: Bed 5H 57
ROYSTON 3D 161
Royston Ct. *SG19: Pott 3J 63*
(off Royston St.)
Royston St. SG19: Pott 3J 63
Rudyard Cl. LU4: Lut 6F 141
Rueley Dell Rd. LU2: Lill 6H 133
Ruffs Furze MK43: Oak 2F 43
Rufus Centre, The 2J 107
Runfold Av. LU3: Lut 4J 141
Runham Cl. LU4: Lut 5D 140
Runley Rd. LU1: Lut 2G 149
Runnalow SG6: Let C 7F 115
Runnymede Ct. LU3: Lut 3H 141
Rushall Grn. LU2: Lut 7H 143
Rushbrook Cl. MK45: Amp 4B 96
Rushby Mead SG6: Let C 7J 115
Rush Ct. MK40: Bed 2E 158 (1E 56)
RUSHDEN
Baldock 1D 163
Rushden 1B 10 (1A 160)
Rushden Rd. MK44: Mil E 3H 31
MK44: Sharn, Sould 4B 12
NN10: Wym 2A 10
RUSH GREEN 2D 163
RUSHMERE 5G 125
Rushmore Cl. LU1: Cad 5G 149
Rusper Grn. LU2: Lut 6H 143
Russell Av. MK40: Bed 2G 57
Russell Cen. MK45: Flitw 4A 108
Russell Cl. LU6: Kens 3A 154
Russell Ct. MK40: Bed 1F 57
Russell Cres. MK45: Maul 5F 97
Russell Dr. MK44: Will 1G 59
MK45: Amp 6B 96
Russell Gro. MK45: Millb 3H 95
Russell Pk. 2F 57
Russell Ri. LU1: Lut 7F 159 (4B 150)
Russell Rd. LU5: Todd 3F 129
Russell St. LU1: Lut 6F 159 (4B 150)
MK17: Wob S 2A 104
Russell Wlk. SG5: Stot 3F 115
Russell Way LU7: Lei Buz 2A 136
MK43: Woo 5F 69
Russet Cl. MK41: Bed 2E 44
MK43: Stew 3H 83
Russett Cl. MK45: Amp 4A 96
Russett Way LU5: Duns 1K 147
Ruthin Cl. LU1: Lut 7G 159 (5B 150)
Rutland Ct. LU2: Lut 3E 150
Rutland Cres. LU2: Lut 3E 150
Rutland Gdns. SG19: Sandy 3K 61
Rutland Hall *LU2: Lut 3E 150*
(off Crawley Grn. Rd.)
Rutland Path LU2: Lut 3E 150
Rutland Rd. MK40: Bed . . .3A 158 (2C 56)
Rutters Cotts. MK44: Thur 2C 32
Ryans Ct. LU2: Lut 1D 150
Rydal Cres. SG18: Bigg 7C 76
Rydal Way LU3: Lut 4H 141
Ryder Cl. MK40: Bidd 3J 55
Rye, The LU6: Eat B 2G 145
LU7: Bill 1D 144
Rye Cl. LU7: Lei Buz 2B 136
PE19: Eynes 1K 39
Rye Cres. MK44: Cople 4E 58
Ryecroft Way LU2: Lut 6E 142
Ryefield LU3: Lut 7J 131
Rye Hill LU2: Lut 1G 159
Rylands Heath LU2: Lut 7K 143
Rylands M. LU7: Lei Buz 3J 135
Ryley Cl. SG16: Hen 2H 113
Ryswick Rd. MK42: Kemp 5C 56
Ryton Cl. LU1: Lut 3K 149
MK41: Bed 3E 44

S

Sabel Cl. SG18: Bigg 1E 90
SACOMBE 3D 163
Sacombe Grn. LU3: Lut 7K 131
Saddle Cl. MK41: Clap 2J 43
Saddlers M. AL3: Mark 6G 155
Sadleir's Grn. MK17: Wob S 1A 104

Saffron Cl.—Shelley Rd.

Saffron Cl. LU2: Lut 3B 142
MK40: Bed 3B 158 (2D 56)
SG15: Arl 6C 102
Saffron Ct. SG18: Bigg 6C 76
Saffron Hill SG6: Let C 7G 115
Saffron Ri. LU6: Eat B 4J 145
Saffron Rd. SG18: Bigg 6B 76
Sage Cl. SG18: Bigg 6E 76
St Alban Rd. MK40: Bed 6F 45
ST ALBANS 3C 163
St Albans Cl. MK45: Flitw 2A 108
St Aldates Ct. LU3: Lut 6K 141
St Andrews Cl. LU1: Slip E 2K 155
LU7: Lei Buz 1J 135
MK45: Amp 4B 96
MK45: Flitw 2A 108
SG18: Bigg 5B 76
St Andrews Ct. PE28: Kimb 1J 9
SG18: Bigg 5B 76
(off Church St.)
St Andrews Gro. LU3: Lut 6A 142
St Andrews La. LU5: Hou R 4J 139
(not continuous)
PE28: Kimb 1J 9
St Andrews M. LU3: Lut 5J 141
St Andrews Rd. MK40: Bed 7E 44
St Andrews St. LU7: Lei Buz 2J 135
SG18: Bigg 6B 76
St Andrews Wlk. LU1: Slip E 2A 156
St Andrews Way SG18: Lang 4B 90
St Ann's La. LU1: Lut 5J 159 (3C 150)
St Ann's Rd. LU1: Lut 5K 159 (3D 150)
St Anselm Pl. PE19: St N 1K 27
St Augustine Av. LU3: Lut 6K 141
St Augustine's Rd. MK40: Bed 6F 45
St Bernard's Cl. LU3: Lut 6A 142
St Catherines Av. LU3: Lut 5K 141
St Christopher's Cl. LU5: Duns 1B 148
St Christopher's Pl. LU3: Lut 6J 141
St Cuthberts Ct.
MK40: Bed 3E 158 (2E 56)
St Cuthbert's St.
MK40: Bed 2E 158 (1E 56)
St David's Way *LU5: Hou R 3K 139*
(off Kent Rd.)
St Dominics Sq. *LU4: Lut 5B 140*
(off Tomlinson Av.)
St Edmond Rd. MK40: Bed 6F 45
St Ethelbert Av. LU3: Lut 5K 141
St Francis Ct. *SG17: Shef 2C 100*
(off St Francis Way)
St Francis Way SG17: Shef 3C 100
St Georges Cl. LU5: Todd 2F 129
LU7: Lei Buz 1K 135
St Georges Ct. LU7: Lei Buz 1K 135
St George's Rd. MK40: Bed 7E 44
St George's Sq. LU1: Lut 4H 159
St Giles Cl. LU6: Tott 4B 146
St Helena Rd. MK42: Bed 5F 57
St Helenas Gdn. MK42: Els 6D 56
ST IPPOLYTS 2C 163
ST IVES 1D 161
St Ives Cl. LU3: Lut 6K 141
St James Cl. LU5: Hou R 5A 140
MK45: Pull 6G 109
St James Rd. LU3: Lut 6K 141
St John Cl. LU1: Lut 5K 149
St John's Av. MK42: Kemp 7K 55
St Johns Cen.
MK42: Bed 6E 158 (3F 57)
St John's Cl. LU7: Stanb 4G 137
St Johns Ct. LU1: Lut 5A 150
SG18: Bigg 4C 76
(off St Johns St.)
St John's Homes MK42: Kemp 6K 55
St John's Rd. MK44: Mogg 5B 60
SG15: Arl 2C 114
St John's St. MK42: Bed 5D 158 (3E 56)
MK42: Kemp 7K 55
SG18: Bigg 4B 76
St John's Wlk. MK42: Kemp 7K 55
St Joseph's Cl. LU3: Lut 5J 141
St Kilda Rd. LU4: Lut 5B 140
St Lawrence Av. LU3: Lut 5A 142
St Lawrence Wlk. *NN10: Wym 1F 11*
(off Church La.)
ST LEONARDS 3A 162
St Leonard's Av.
MK42: Bed 6D 158 (3E 56)
St Leonard's Cl. LU7: Lei Buz 5K 125
St Leonards Ct. *MK42: Bed 4D 56*
(off Ampthill Rd.)
St Leonard's St.
MK42: Bed 7D 158 (4E 56)
St Loyes Rd.
MK40: Bed 2C 158 (1D 56)
St Loyes St.
MK40: Bed 3C 158 (2D 56)
St Lukes Cl. LU4: Lut 7G 141
ST MARGARET'S 3B 162
St Margarets Av. LU3: Lut 5K 141
St Margarets Cl. LU3: Stre 2H 131
MK43: Lidl 2C 94
St Margarets Gdns. SG18: Bigg 7D 76
(not continuous)
St Marks Cl. MK45: Flitw 2B 108
St Martin's Av. LU2: Lut 7D 142
St Martins Bus. Cen. MK42: Bed 5K 57
St Martins Way MK42: Bed 5J 57
St Mary's Av. SG5: Stot 7H 103
St Mary's Chu. Path LU1: Lut 5J 159
St Marys Cl. LU7: Teb 6C 128
MK42: Els 6D 56
MK43: Felm 7C 20
MK43: Mars M 5D 82
MK44: Blet 6J 21
St Mary's Ct. LU6: Duns 2H 147
LU6: Kens 1A 154
St Mary's Ga. LU6: Duns 2H 147
St Mary's Glebe LU6: Edles 7J 145
St Marys Pl. SG17: Mep 2B 112
St Marys Rd. LU1: Lut 4K 159 (3D 150)
MK43: Woo 4E 68
St Mary's St. LU6: Duns 2H 147
MK42: Bed 4D 158 (2E 56)
St Mary's Wlk. SG19: Eve 6E 50
St Mary's Way LU7: Lei Buz 2G 135
St Matthews Cl.
LU2: Lut 2J 159 (2C 150)
MK42: Kemp 7K 55
St Mellion Dr. MK40: Bidd 3H 55
St Michaels Av. LU5: Hou R 5G 139
St Michael's Cres. LU3: Lut 6A 142
St Michael's Rd. MK40: Bed 7F 45
St Mildreds Av. LU3: Lut 6A 142
St Minver Rd. MK40: Bed 7F 45
St Monicas Av. LU3: Lut 6K 141
ST NEOTS 2K 27 (1C 161)
St Neots & District Indoor Bowls Club 3K 27
St Neots Camping & Caravan Club Site
PE19: Eynes 4K 27
St Neots Community College Sports Hall 4K 27
St Neots Golf Course 1K 27
St Neots Rd. MK41: Ren 6C 46
(not continuous)
MK44: Boln, Colm 3B 24
PE19: Abbot, Eynes H 1G 39
PE19: Eat F 3J 27
SG19: Sandy 1H 61
St Nicholas Cl. MK17: Ting 2F 119
MK45: Flitw 2B 108
St Nicholas Ct. AL5: Harp 7K 157
St Ninian's Ct. LU2: Lut 2G 159
St Olam's Cl. LU3: Lut 3K 141
St Olives SG5: Stot 7G 103
St Pauls Cl. MK45: Flitw 3B 108
St Paul's Gdns. LU1: Lut 5C 150
St Paul's Rd. LU1: Lut 5C 150
MK40: Bed 3B 56
St Paul's Sq.
MK40: Bed 4C 158 (2D 56)
ST PAUL'S WALDEN 2C 163
St Peter's Av. SG15: Arl 6C 102
St Peters Cl. MK44: Sharn 3C 20
MK45: Flitw 2B 108
St Peters Ct. *SG19: Pott 2J 63*
(off Astwood Cl.)
St Peters Grn. SG5: Hol 7H 113
St Peters Rd. LU1: Lut 3K 149
LU5: Duns 2J 147
St Peter's St.
MK40: Bed 2D 158 (1E 56)
St Saviour's Cres.
LU1: Lut 6F 159 (4B 150)
St Swithun's Way SG19: Sandy 3J 61
St Thomas's Cl. LU2: Lut 5E 142
St Thomas's Rd. LU2: Lut 5D 142
St Vincent Gdns. LU4: Lut 6F 141
St Vincent's MK17: Wob S 2A 104
St Winifreds Av. LU3: Lut 5A 142
Salcombe Cl. MK40: Bed 1G 57
SG18: Bigg 3E 76
SALFORD 2A 92 (1A 162)
Salford Rd. MK17: Asp G 5A 92
MK17: Hulc 5E 92
MK43: Brog 5F 93
Salisbury Cl. SG5: Stot 4F 115
Salisbury Ho. *MK40: Bed 2A 158*
(off Union St.)
Salisbury Rd. LU1: Lut 6F 159 (4B 150)
MK45: Flitw 2A 108
Salisbury St.
MK41: Bed 1C 158 (7D 44)
Sallowsprings LU6: Whip 1F 153
Sallowsprings Nature Reserve 1F 153
SALPH END 3K 45 (2B 160)
Saltash Cl. MK40: Bed 7G 45
Saltcote Way MK41: Bed 2F 45
Saltdean Cl. LU2: Lut 5H 143
Salters Way LU6: Duns 6F 139
Saltfield Cres. LU4: Lut 5E 140
Sambar Cl. PE19: Eat S 2H 27
Sampshill Rd. MK45: West 2A 120
Sandalwood Cl. LU3: Lut 2K 141
Sandell Cl. LU2: Lut 7D 142
Sanderling Cl. SG6: Let C 6G 115
Sanders Cl. MK42: Kemp 4K 55
Sanderson Cl. MK45: West 1A 120
Sanderson Rd. MK45: West 1A 120
Sanders Way MK43: Woo 3F 69
Sandford Ri. SG19: Sandy 3G 61
Sandgate Rd. LU4: Lut 7F 141
Sandhill Cl. MK45: Millb 3G 95
Sandhills LU7: Lei Buz 7K 125
Sandhouse Cotts. LU7: Heat R 7B 116
Sandhouse La. LU7: Heat R 7A 116
Sandhouse Lane Nature Reserve 7B 116
Sandhurst Pl. MK42: Bed 4D 56
Sandhurst Rd. MK42: Bed 4D 56
Sandland Cl. LU6: Duns 1G 147
Sand La. MK45: Sils 7J 109
SG18: Bigg 5C 76
SG18: North 2E 74
SG19: Sandy 3K 61
Sandleford Dr. MK42: Els 7G 57
SANDON 1D 163
Sandon Cl. SG19: Sandy 2J 61
Sandpiper Cl. SG18: Bigg 6B 76
Sandpiper Ct. PE19: Eat S 7H 27
Sandpiper Way LU7: Lei Buz 4A 136
SANDRIDGE 3C 163
Sandringham Dr. LU5: Hou R 5K 139
Sandringham Rd. MK45: Flitw 5K 107
Sand Rd. MK45: Flitt 3F 109
Sands, The *MK45: Amp 4A 96*
(off Woburn St.)
SANDY 3J 61 (3C 161)
Sandyacres MK45: Maul 4D 96
Sandy Bus. Pk. SG19: Sandy 7J 49
Sandye La. MK44: Swin 5A 8
PE28: Lwr D 7G 5
Sandy La. LU7: Lei Buz 5H 125
MK17: Asp H 7A 104
MK17: Wob, Ridg 2G 105
MK43: Hus C 2G 105
PE28: Tilb 1D 8
SG17: Chic 7J 87
Sandy Rd. MK41: Bed 1J 57
MK44: Will 2H 59
SG19: Eve 1D 62
SG19: Pott 4F 63
Sandy Rdbt. SG19: Sandy 3G 61
Sandy Sports Cen. 1J 61
Sandy Station (Rail) 4K 61
Sandy Vw. SG18: Bigg 3D 76
Sanfoin Rd. LU4: Lut 5C 140
San Remo Rd. MK17: Asp G 2D 104
Santa Pod Raceway 1F 19
Santingfield Nth. LU1: Lut 4K 149
Santingfield Sth. LU1: Lut 4K 149
SAPLEY 1D 161
Sarum Rd. LU3: Lut 5G 141
Saturn Cl. LU7: Lei Buz 1B 136
Saturn Way SG18: Bigg 5F 77
Saunders Cl. SG6: Let C 7K 115
Saunders Gdns. MK40: Bed 3A 56
Saunders Piece MK45: Amp 5B 96
Saunton Cl. MK40: Bidd 3K 55
Savannah Cl. MK42: Kemp 5B 56
Savernake Wlk. MK41: Bed 6K 45
Savile's Cl. PE19: Eat F 1K 27
Saville Cl. MK44: Gt Bar 4A 48
Sawfords Mdw. SG19: Temp 3G 49
Sawtry Cl. LU3: Lut 3J 141
Sax Ho. SG6: Let C 5G 115
Saxon Av. SG5: Stot 5H 103
Saxon Cen. MK42: Kemp 6A 56
Saxon Cen., The SG18: Bigg 6E 76
Saxon Cl. LU6: Duns 2E 146
MK44: Rox 7E 36
MK45: Flitw 2B 108
SG6: Let C 5H 115
SG16: Hen 3K 101
Saxon Cres. MK45: Bar C 3A 122
Saxon Dr. SG18: Bigg 6E 76
Saxon Ho. End MK43: Harr 1E 28
Saxon Pool & Leisure Cen. 6E 76
Saxon Rd. LU3: Lut 7A 142
Saxons Cl. LU7: Lei Buz 2A 136
Saxon Way MK40: Bidd 4H 55
Saxted Cl. LU2: Lut 1H 151
Saywell Rd. LU2: Lut 7E 142
Scawsby Cl. LU6: Duns 1E 146
School App. MK44: Sharn 4B 20
School Ho. M. MK45: Sils 2A 110
School La. LU4: Lut 5F 141
LU6: Eat B 4J 145
MK42: Wils 5F 71
MK43: Carlt 6E 28
MK43: Hus C 1F 105
School La. MK43: Stew 3H 83
MK43: Woo 4F 69
MK44: Boln 3J 23
MK44: Colm 5E 24
MK44: Gt Bar 4A 48
MK44: Rox 6E 36
MK44: Wild 5C 34
MK45: G'fld 4E 108
NN29: Pod 4C 10
PE19: Eat S 5J 27
PE19: Eynes 3K 27
SG17: Shef 3B 100
SG18: S'hill 3D 88
School Wlk. LU1: Lut 7J 159 (4C 150)
LU5: Hou R 2K 139
Scotchbrook Rd. MK43: Mars M 5D 82
Scotfield Ct. LU2: Lut 6H 143
Scott Av. MK42: Short 1J 71
Scott Ct. LU5: Duns 1J 147
Scott Rd. LU3: Lut 2E 140
Scotts Cl. MK17: Sto H 1A 124
Scyttels Ct. SG5: Shill 5K 111
Seabrook LU4: Lut 6D 140
Seaford Cl. LU2: Lut 6G 143
Seal Cl. LU4: Lut 6F 141
Seamarks Ct. LU4: Lut 1J 149
Seamons Cl. LU6: Duns 4K 147
Sears, The LU6: N'all 5F 145
Sears Cl. SG17: Clif 2H 101
Seaton Dr. MK40: Bed 1G 57
Seaton Rd. LU4: Lut 6H 141
Sebright Rd. AL3: Mark 6G 155
Sedbury Cl. LU3: Lut 3J 141
SEDDINGTON 6K 61
Sedgwick Rd. LU4: Lut 2D 140
Seed Pl. AL5: Harp 7K 157
Segenhoe Cl. MK43: Ridg 1K 105
Selbourne Rd. LU4: Lut 6H 141
Selina Cl. LU3: Lut 2E 140
Selsey Dr. LU2: Lut 4G 143
Selsey Way MK41: Bed 7G 45
Sergeants Way MK41: Bed 7A 46
Setchel PE19: Eat F 1J 27
Severalls, The LU2: Lut 6F 143
Severn Cl. MK45: Flitw 4K 107
Severn Wlk. LU7: Lei Buz 5K 125
Severn Way MK41: Bed 4E 44
SEWELL 7C 138 (2A 162)
Sewell Cutting Nature Reserve 7D 138
Sewell La. LU6: Sew 7C 138
Sexton Av. MK42: Bed 6C 56
Seymour Av. LU1: Lut 7K 159 (5D 150)
Seymour Rd. LU1: Lut 7K 159 (5D 150)
Shackleton Cl. MK42: Short 1H 71
Shaftesbury Av. MK40: Bed 2G 57
Shaftesbury Dr. SG5: Stot 3E 114
Shaftesbury Ind. Cen.
SG6: Let C 7J 115
Shaftesbury Rd. LU4: Lut 2K 149
Shakespeare Dr. SG18: Up C 3H 75
Shakespeare Rd. LU4: Lut 6D 140
MK40: Bed 7B 44
PE19: Eat S 4J 27
Shaldon Ct. MK40: Bed 7G 45
Shanklin Cl. LU3: Lut 2J 141
Shannon Cl. SG16: Lwr Sto 4E 112
SG19: Sandy 1H 61
Shannon Pl. SG19: Pott 3H 63
SHARNBROOK 3C 20 (2A 160)
Sharnbrook Ct. MK44: Sharn 4D 20
Sharnbrook Mill Theatre 4G 21
Sharnbrook Rd. MK44: Sould 6B 12
Sharnbrook Summit Nature Reserve 4H 11
Sharose Ct. AL3: Mark 6G 155
Sharp Cl. MK45: Maul 6K 97
SHARPENHOE 5G 121 (1B 162)
Sharpenhoe Rd. LU3: Stre 6G 121
MK45: Bar C 5J 121
MK45: Shar 6G 121
Sharples Grn. LU3: Lut 1K 141
Shay La. PE28: Up D 1J 7
Shearley Cl. MK40: Bed 3B 56
Sheepcote Cres. LU7: Heat R 3J 125
Sheepfold Hill MK45: Flitw 3B 108
Sheeplands MK41: Bed 6K 45
SHEEPLANE 6A 116
Sheep La. MK17: Wob 5A 116
Sheep Tick End MK43: Lidl 2A 94
Sheep Wlk. SG18: Holme 2B 90
Sheepwalk Cl. SG19: Pott 4K 63
Sheffield Cl. SG19: Pott 3J 63
SHEFFORD 2C 100 (1C 163)
Shefford Ind. Pk. SG17: Shef 3C 100
Shefford Rd. MK45: Clop 4C 98
SG17: Bead 3E 98
SG17: Clif 2E 100
SG17: Mep, Shef 7C 100
Shelford La. MK44: Colm 4E 24
Shelley Pl. PE19: Eat F 1K 27
Shelley Rd. LU4: Lut 7D 140

Stirling Cl.—Thurlestone Cl.

Stirling Cl. SG19: Sandy 1H 61
Stirling Rd. MK42: Short 1H 71
Stivers Way LU5: Harl 4B 120
Stockbridge Rd. SG16: Hen 2H 101
SG17: Clif, Hen 2H 101
Stockdale LU5: Todd 3F 129
Stocker Way PE19: Eynes 1J 39
Stockgrove Country Pk. 1H 125
Stockgrove Country Pk. Vis. Cen. 1H 125
STOCKGROVE PARK 1G 125
Stockgrove Pk. Ho. LU7: Heat R . . . 1H 125
Stockholm Way LU3: Lut 1G 141
Stockingstone Rd. LU2: Lut 6B 142
Stockton End SG19: Sandy 2K 61
Stockwood Country Pk. 6A 150
Stockwood Ct. LU1: Lut 7G 159
Stockwood Cres.
LU1: Lut 7G 159 (4B 150)
Stockwood Discovery Cen. 6B 150
Stockwood Pk. Athletics Cen. 7A 150
Stockwood Pk. Golf Course 6B 150
Stoke Albany M. MK40: Bed 1B 56
STOKE HAMMOND 1A 124 (2A 162)
Stoke Mill MK44: Sharn 4G 21
Stoke Rd. LU7: Lei Buz 7F 125
Stokers Cl. LU5: Duns 2K 147
Stokesay Cl. MK41: Bed 5J 45
Stondon Rd. SG5: Shill 4C 112
SG17: Mep 1B 112
Stondon Transport Mus. 3F 113
Stone Cl. MK40: Bidd 4H 55
Stonecroft SG19: Sandy 3K 61
Stonedale Rd. MK42: Kemp 6C 56
Stonehenge Works Station
Leighton Buzzard Narrow Gauge Railway 5C 126
Stoneland Av. SG18: Bigg 4C 76
Stoneleigh Cl. LU3: Lut 2K 141
Stoneley SG6: Let C 5H 115
STONELY 2K 9 (1C 161)
Stone Pine Rd. MK43: Brom 6D 42
Stonesdale LU4: Lut 5E 140
Stoneways Cl. LU4: Lut 3F 141
Stoneygate Rd. LU4: Lut 7F 141
Stonnells Cl. SG6: Let C 6H 115
Stony La. LU2: Tea G, Wan E 1K 151
STOPSLEY 5E 142 (2C 163)
STOPSLEY COMMON 3C 142
Stopsley Mobile Home Pk.
LU2: Lut 5D 142
Stopsley Way LU2: Lut 6E 142
STOTFOLD 7G 103 (1D 163)
STOTFOLD GREEN 5H 103
Stotfold Rd. SG6: Let C 7E 114
SG7: Cald 5K 103
SG15: Arl 5C 102
Stotfold Watermill 7J 103
Stour Way MK41: Bed 4E 44
STOW LONGA 1C 161
Strafford Cl. LU5: Harl 6B 120
Strand, The MK45: Clop 4A 98
Strangers Way LU4: Lut 5E 140
Stratford Cl. LU5: Todd 2F 129
Stratford Pl. PE19: Eat S 4J 27
Stratford Rd. LU4: Lut 1K 149
SG19: Sandy 4K 61
Stratford Way MK43: Mars M 2D 82
Strathconon Rd. MK41: Bed 5A 46
Strathmore Av.
LU1: Lut 7K 159 (5C 150)
Strathmore Wlk.
LU1: Lut 7K 159 (4D 150)
Stratton Bus. Pk. SG18: Bigg 1F 91
Stratton Ct. *SG18: Bigg* *5C 76*
(off High St.)
Stratton Gdns. LU2: Lut 5B 142
Stratton M. LU7: Lei Buz 2K 135
Stratton Pk. SG18: Bigg 6F 77
(not continuous)
Stratton Pk. Dr. SG18: Bigg 7F 77
Stratton Way MK41: Bed 6B 46
SG18: Bigg 4D 76
Strawberry Fld. LU3: Lut 2G 141
Strawberry Flds. MK44: Gt Bar 4K 47
Straw Plait Way SG15: Arl 2B 114
STREATLEY 2J 131 (2B 162)
Streatley Rd. LU3: Up Sun 4D 130
Street Cl. MK43: Carlt 5E 28
Stringfellow Cl. MK43: Whar E 2C 80
STRIXTON 1A 160
Stronnell Cl. LU2: Lut 6E 142
Stuart Ct. SG19: Temp 1H 49
Stuart Pl. LU1: Lut 5G 159 (3B 150)
Stuart Rd. MK42: Kemp 6A 56
MK45: Bar C 3A 122
Stuart St. LU1: Lut 5G 159 (3B 150)
LU6: Duns 1G 147
Stuart St. Pas.
LU1: Lut 5G 159 (3B 150)
Stubbs Cl. LU5: Hou R 4K 139
STUDHAM 7J 153 (3B 162)
Studham La. HP4: Dag 6D 152
LU6: Whip 3G 153
Studley Rd. LU3: Lut 1F 159 (1B 150)
MK43: Woo 4E 68
Sturmer Rd. MK41: Bed 2F 45
Styles Cl. LU2: Lut 7G 143
Such Cl. SG6: Let C 7K 115
Sudbury Rd. LU4: Lut 3D 140
Sudeley Wlk. MK41: Bed 5J 45
Suffolk Cl. LU4: Lut 6C 140
Suffolk Rd. LU5: Duns 4B 148
Sugden Ct. LU6: Duns 2G 147
Sullivan Cl. SG17: Shef 2D 100
Summerfield Ct. *SG5: Stot* *7G 103*
(off Regent St.)
Summerfield Dr. MK43: Woo 5F 69
Summerfield Rd. LU1: Lut 2H 149
Summerfields Miniature Railway 1D 86
Summerhouse Hill
MK44: Card 3A 58
Summerleys LU6: Eat B 6J 145
Summers Cl. MK41: Clap 2J 43
Summers Rd. LU2: Lut 1G 151
Summer St. LU1: Slip E 1A 156
LU7: Lei Buz 2K 135
Summer Vw. Ct. *LU1: Lut* *3G 159*
(off Mill St.)
Summer Wlk. AL3: Mark 6G 155
Sunbeam Rd. MK42: Kemp 1K 69
Sunbower Av. LU6: Duns 6E 138
Suncote Av. LU6: Duns 6E 138
Suncote Cl. LU6: Duns 7E 138
Sunderland Cl. *MK44: Rav* *7H 33*
(off Butler St.)
Sunderland Hill MK44: Rav 6H 33
Sunderland Pl. MK42: Short 2J 71
Sunderland Rd.
SG19: Sandy 7H 49
Sundew Cl. MK42: Bed 6H 57
PE19: Eat F 1H 27
SUNDON HILLS 2D 130
Sundon Hills Country Pk. 2D 130
Sundon La. LU5: Hou R 4J 139
SUNDON PARK 2E 140 (2B 162)
Sundon Pk. Pde. LU3: Lut 2E 140
Sundon Pk. Rd. LU3: Lut 7D 130
Sundon Rd. LU3: Lwr Sun 7B 130
LU3: Stre 3H 131
LU4: Chalt, Lwr Sun 7B 130
LU5: Harl 6B 120
LU5: Hou R 4J 139
Sundown Av. LU5: Duns 3K 147
Sunningdale LU2: Lut 6D 142
Sunningdale Ct. LU2: Lut 6D 142
Sunningdale Wlk. MK41: Bed 4G 45
Sunridge Av. LU2: Lut 7C 142
Sunrise Ind. Est. LU2: Lut 7E 142
Sunset Dr. LU2: Lut 6D 142
Sun St. SG18: Bigg 4B 76
SG19: Pott 3J 63
Super Karts Indoor Karting Cen. *7K 115*
(off Pixmore Av.)
Surrey St. LU1: Lut 7J 159 (4C 150)
Sursham Ct. AL3: Mark 6G 155
Sussex Cl. LU4: Lut 5B 140
Sussex Pl. LU2: Lut 7H 143
Sutherland Pl.
LU1: Lut 7F 159 (5B 150)
SUTTON 6H 63 (3D 161)
Sutton Av. SG18: Bigg 5D 76
Sutton Cross Roads SG19: Sutt 6G 63
Sutton Gdns. LU1: Cad 7G 149
LU3: Lut 3F 141
Sutton Mill Rd. SG19: Pott 4H 63
Sutton Rd. SG18: Dunt 7K 63
SG19: Eye 3D 78
SG19: Pott 3A 64
Swaden SG19: Sandy 4A 62
Swaffield Cl. MK45: Amp 4A 96
Swale Path *MK41: Bed* *3E 44*
(off The Wharfe)
Swales Dr. LU7: Lei Buz 4B 136
Swallow Cl. LU4: Lut 5C 140
MK45: Flitw 5K 107
SG17: Shef 3C 100
Swallow Crest SG19: Sandy 7H 49
Swallowfield MK44: Wybo 2F 37
SG18: Up C 2K 75
Swanbourne Cl. SG18: Bigg 6D 76
Swan Ct. LU6: Duns 2H 147
Swan Gdns. LU5: Duns 2J 147
Swan La. SG8: Guil M 7K 79
SG19: Sandy 3H 61
Swan Mead LU4: Lut 5C 140
Swannells Wood LU6: Stud 7H 153
Swann's Cl. SG8: Tad 7K 65
Swan Rd. MK42: Wils 5E 70
Swansholme MK43: Felm 7D 20
Swansholme Gdn. Ct.
SG19: Sandy *3J 61*
(off Swansholme Gdns.)
Swansholme Gdns. SG19: Sandy 4H 61
Swansons LU6: Edles 7K 145
Swanston Grange LU4: Lut 7D 140
Swasedale Rd. LU3: Lut 3H 141
Swasedale Wlk. LU3: Lut 3H 141
Swift Cl. MK41: Bed 5D 44
MK45: Flitw 4K 107
SG6: Let C 6G 115
SG19: Sandy 7J 49
Swifts Grn. Cl. LU2: Lut 4F 143
Swifts Grn. Rd. LU2: Lut 4F 143
Swift Way MK42: Wils 6E 70
Swindale MK41: Bed 3F 45
SWINESHEAD 5A 8 (1B 160)
Swineshead Rd. MK44: Per 5F 9
MK44: Rise 2D 14
Swiss Garden, The 5D 74
Sworder Cl. LU3: Lut 7H 131
Sybil's Way MK45: Hou C 4C 84
Sycamore Cl. LU3: Lut 7E 130
MK45: Flitw 4B 108
SG18: Bigg 3C 76
SG19: Pott 3H 63
Sycamore Rd. LU5: Hou R 3J 139
Sycamores, The MK42: Kemp 7B 56
MK45: Sils 1K 109
Sylam Cl. LU3: Lut 2G 141
Sylmond Gdns. NN10: Rush 1A 10
Sylvester St. LU7: Heat R 3J 125
Symonds Cl. MK43: Brom 1F 55
Syon Path MK45: Flitw 5K 107

T

Tabbs Cl. SG6: Let C 7K 115
Tabor Cl. LU5: Harl 5B 120
Tabor Ct. SG6: Let C 7F 115
Taddy Cl. SG18: Up C 3H 75
TADLOW 7K 65 (3D 161)
Tadlow Ga. SG8: Tad 6J 65
Tadlow Rd. SG8: Tad 1G 79
SG19: Wrest 1G 79
Taft Pl. SG17: Chic 3J 99
Talbot Ct. LU7: Lei Buz 1J 135
Talbot Rd. LU2: Lut 1D 150
MK40: Bed 1G 57
Talbot Way SG6: Let C 5K 115
Talisman Cl. SG19: Sandy 1H 61
Tall Pines LU7: Lei Buz 6H 125
Tamar Rd. MK41: Bed 4F 45
Tamar Wlk. LU7: Lei Buz 5K 125
Tameton Cl. LU2: Lut 7K 143
Tamworth Rd. MK41: Bed 4J 45
Tancred Rd. LU2: Lut 5E 142
Tandys Cl. *MK43: Pave* *4C 30*
(off Brookfields)
MK43: Turv 4C 40
Tanfield Grn. LU2: Lut 1J 151
Tanners Ct. LU5: Todd 1G 129
Tannery La. MK43: Odell 6H 19
Tanqueray Av. MK45: Clop 5A 98
Tansey End SG18: Bigg 6E 76
Tansy Av. SG5: Stot 1H 115
Tansy Cl. MK42: Bed 6H 57
PE19: Eat F 2H 27
Tan Yd. PE19: St N 2K 27
Tarnside Cl. LU6: Duns 4H 147
TARTLETT END 4F 81
Taskers Row LU6: Edles 6K 145
Taskers Row Bungs. LU6: Edles 6K 145
Tattlers Knoll LU5: Todd 2F 129
Taunton Av. LU2: Lut 1F 151
Taunton Cl. MK41: Bed 4J 45
Tavistock Av. MK45: Amp 6K 95
Tavistock Ct. MK40: Bed 1B 158
Tavistock Cres.
LU1: Lut 7H 159 (5C 150)
Tavistock Pl. MK40: Bed . . . 1B 158 (1D 56)
Tavistock St. LU1: Lut . . . 7H 159 (4C 150)
LU6: Duns 7G 139
MK40: Bed 1B 158 (1D 56)
Taylors Cl. SG17: Mep 1B 112
Taylor's Ride LU7: Lei Buz 6H 125
Taylor's Rd. SG5: Astw, Stot 5H 103
Taylor St. LU2: Lut 2J 159 (2D 150)
Teal Rd. SG18: Bigg 6B 76
Teasel Cl. PE19: Eat F 2J 27
Teasel La. SG5: Stot 1H 115
TEBWORTH 6C 128 (2A 162)
Tebworth Rd. LU7: Hock 7A 128
LU7: Teb 6C 128
LU7: Wingf 7D 128
Tedder Av. SG16: Hen 1H 113
Teesdale LU4: Lut 4E 140
Telegraph Hill Nature Reserve 2H 133
Telford Way LU1: Lut 3F 159 (2B 150)
MK42: Bed 5K 57
Telmere Ind. Est.
LU1: Lut 7J 159 (4C 150)
Telscombe Way LU2: Lut 6G 143
Tempest Cres. MK42: Short 7K 57
Templars Way MK44: Sharn 3E 20
Temple Cl. LU2: Lut 4C 142
Temple Gdns. SG6: Let C 6K 115
Templer Way SG17: Chic 2K 99
Temple Way MK45: Flitw 5K 107
TEMPSFORD 1H 49 (2C 161)
Tempsford Rd. MK44: Blun 5E 48
SG19: Eve 3K 49
SG19: Sandy 6G 49
SG19: Temp 5E 48
Tempsford St. MK42: Kemp 6A 56
Tenby Dr. LU4: Lut 6H 141
Tenby M. LU4: Lut 6G 141
Tenby Way PE19: Eynes 1K 39
Tennyson Av. LU5: Hou R 5K 139
SG18: Bigg 6C 76
Tennyson Ho. *LU1: Lut* *5C 150*
(off London Rd.)
Tennyson Pl. PE19: Eat F 1K 27
Tennyson Rd. LU1: Lut . . . 7J 159 (6C 150)
MK40: Bed 2G 57
MK45: Flitw 3K 107
Tenth Av. LU3: Lut 2E 140
Tenzing Gro. LU1: Lut 4A 150
Test Cl. MK41: Bed 2F 45
TETWORTH 2H 51
Tetworth Hill SG19: Tet 1J 51
Teversham Way PE19: Eat F 1J 27
TEWIN 3D 163
Tewkesbury Rd. MK42: Els 7F 57
Thames Cl. MK45: Flitw 5K 107
Thames Ct. LU3: Lut 6K 141
Thames Ind. Est. LU6: Duns 2H 147
Thatch Cl. LU4: Lut 5B 140
Thaxted Cl. LU2: Lut 7K 143
The . . . . . .
Names prefixed with 'The' for example 'The Abbeygate Bus. Cen.' are indexed under the main name such as 'Abbeygate Bus. Cen., The'
Thelby Cl. LU3: Lut 3H 141
THERFIELD 1D 163
Therfield Wlk. LU5: Hou R 3A 140
Thetford Cl. MK42: Kemp 6B 56
Thetford Gdns. LU2: Lut 3B 142
Thickthorn La. MK45: Hou C 1B 84
Thinnings, The MK45: Flitw 2A 108
Third Av. LU3: Lut 2E 140
Thirlmere Cl. SG18: Bigg 7D 76
Thirlmere Gdns. MK45: Flitw 4A 108
Thirlmere Rd. MK42: Kemp 7K 55
Thirlstone Rd. LU4: Lut 1F 149
Thistle Rd. LU1: Lut 3D 150
Thistley La. MK43: Brom 1E 54
Thomas St. LU7: Heat R 3J 125
Thompson's Mdw. SG8: Guil M 7K 79
Thomson Av. MK42: Short 1J 71
Thor Dr. MK41: Bed 6B 46
THORN 3E 138
Thornage Cl. LU2: Lut 2B 142
Thornbury LU5: Duns 7B 140
Thornbury Ct. LU5: Hou R 2J 139
THORNCOTE GREEN 6E 60 (3C 161)
Thorncote Rd. SG18: North 7D 60
SG19: Hat 7D 60
Thorneycroft Cl. LU3: Lut 5H 141
Thornhill Cl. LU5: Hou R 2K 139
Thornhill Rd. LU4: Lut 1H 149
Thorn Rd. LU5: Thor 4D 138
Thorntondale LU4: Lut 4E 140
Thornton St. MK42: Kemp 5B 56
Thorn Vw. Rd. LU5: Hou R 4H 139
Thorpe Cl. MK40: Bidd 1H 55
Thorpe Way MK43: Woo 3F 69
Thrales Cl. LU3: Lut 2G 141
(not continuous)
Thrales End La. AL5: Harp 6H 157
Thrapston Rd. PE28: Kimb 1J 9
Threave Cl. MK41: Bed 4H 45
THREE LOCKS 3C 124
Three Locks Golf Course 2C 124
Three Star Pk. SG16: Lwr Sto 3G 113
Thresher Cl. LU4: Lut 5B 140
Threshers Ct. LU7: Lei Buz 2B 136
Thricknells Cl. LU3: Lut 2G 141
Thrift Rd. LU7: Heat R 3J 125
Thrift Vw. MK43: Cran 2G 81
THROCKING 1D 163
Thrupp End MK43: Lidl 2B 94
THURLEIGH 5E 22 (2B 160)
Thurleigh Airfield Bus. Pk.
MK44: Thur 4B 22
Thurleigh Farm Cen. 5H 23
Thurleigh Rd. MK44: Boln 5K 23
MK44: Mil E, Thur 3J 31
MK44: Rav 6G 33
Thurlestone Cl. MK40: Bed 1H 57

188 A-Z Bedfordshire Atlas

Thurlow Cl.—Waltham Cl.

Thurlow Cl. LU4: Lut .5B 140
Thurlow St. MK40: Bed . . .3B 158 (2D 56)
Thurne Way MK41: Bed .2F 45
Thyme Cl. LU2: Lut .2C 142
Tibbett Cl. LU6: Duns .4K 147
Tiberius Rd. LU3: Lut .3H 141
Tiddenfoot Leisure Cen. & Harpers Fitness .4G 135
Tiddenfoot Waterside Pk. .5G 135
TILBROOK .1B 160
Tilbrook Rd. PE28: Kimb .1H 9
Tilgate LU2: Lut .6H 143
Tiller Ct. LU7: Lei Buz .2B 136
TILSWORTH .4K 137 (2A 162)
Tilsworth Golf Course .3B 138
Tilsworth Rd. LU7: Stanb .4G 137
Timberlands Caravan Site
LU1: Pep .3A 156
Timber La. MK17: Wob .1C 116
Timworth Cl. LU2: Lut .1H 151
Tindall Av. LU7: Lei Buz .7K 125
TINGRITH .2F 119 (1B 162)
Tingrith Coarse Fishery .7E 106
Tingrith Rd. MK17: Ever, Ting .7D 106
Tinsley Cl. LU1: Lut .5K 149
MK41: Clap .2J 43
Tintagel Cl. LU3: Lut .5K 141
Tintagel Wlk. MK41: Bed .4K 45
Tintern Abbey MK41: Bed .2J 57
Tintern Cl. AL5: Harp .7G 157
Tipcat Cl. MK42: Els .6D 56
Tippett Dr. SG17: Shef .2D 100
Tipple Hill Rd.
LU1: Aley G, Wood .1H 155
Titan Ct. LU4: Lut .1H 149
Titchfield Dr. MK42: Els .7E 56
Tithe, The MK43: Felm .7C 20
Tithe Barn MK43: Felm .7C 20
Tithe Barn Rd. MK43: Woo .4F 69
TITHE FARM .3K 139
Tithe Farm Cl. SG18: Lang .5A 90
Tithe Farm Rd. LU5: Hou R .3H 139
Tithe Rd. MK43: Kemp .6D 54
Tiverton Rd. MK40: Bed .7F 45
TODDINGTON .2F 129 (2B 162)
Toddington Rd. LU4: Lut .3D 140
LU5: Harl, West .4K 119
(not continuous)
LU7: Teb .6C 128
MK45: West .4K 119
TODDINGTON SERVICE AREA 2A 130
Toland Cl. LU4: Lut .1E 148
Tolgate Ct. LU6: Duns .3K 147
Tolkien Cl. MK41: Bed .6C 46
Tollfield PE28: Kimb .1J 9
Tollgate Cl. MK43: Brom .1E 54
Tomlinson Av. LU4: Lut .5A 140
Tompions End SG18: Ickw .3E 74
TONWELL .3D 163
Top End MK41: Ren .3C 46
Top Row MK44: Blet .6J 21
Tornay Ct. LU7: Slapt .4B 144
Torquay Dr. LU4: Lut .5F 141
Torre Abbey MK41: Bed .2K 57
Torridge Ri. MK41: Bed .4E 44
Torrington Cl. SG19: Pott .2H 63
TOSELAND .1D 161
Totnes Cl. MK40: Bed .1G 57
TOTTERNHOE .3B 146 (2A 162)
Totternhoe Knolls Nature Reserve .1K 145
Totternhoe Quarry Nature Reserve .2B 146
Totternhoe Rd. LU6: Duns .3E 146
LU6: Eat B .4H 145
Tourist Info. Cen.
Bedford .4C 158 (2D 56)
Dunstable .2J 147
Letchworth Garden City .7H 115
Luton, Bridge St. . . .4H 159 (3C 150)
Sandy .3J 61
Tower Ct. LU2: Lut .1E 150
Tower Rd. LU2: Lut .2E 150
Towers Ho. MK40: Bed .7D 44
Tower Way LU2: Lut .2E 150
Town, The PE19: Gt S .1G 17
Town Bri. Mill LU7: Lei Buz .2H 135
Town Cl. MK45: Wils .7G 71
Town Farm Cl. SG8: Guil M .7K 79
Town Farm Ct. MK43: Oak .1F 43
SG16: Hen .4K 101
Townfield Rd. MK45: Flitw .5B 108
Town Lot La. MK43: Felm .7B 20
Town Mdw. Dr. SG17: Shef .2C 100
TOWNSEND .3C 163
Townsend Cen., The
LU5: Hou R .6H 139
Townsend Cl. MK43: Cran .4E 80
Townsend Farm Rd. LU5: Hou R . . .6H 139
Townsend Ind. Est. LU5: Hou R . . .6H 139
Towns End Rd. MK44: Sharn .3C 20
Townsend Ter. *LU5: Hou R .5G 139*
(off Houghton Rd.)
Townshott MK45: Clop .4C 98
Townside LU6: Edles .7K 145
Townsley Cl. LU1: Lut . . .7H 159 (4C 150)
Tracey Ct. LU1: Lut 7J 159 (4C 150)
Trafalgar Dr. MK45: Flitw .2A 108
Trafalgar Rd. PE19: Eat F .2J 27
Trailly Cl. MK44: Yeld .2B 6
Trap Rd. SG8: Guil M .6K 79
Treetop Cl. LU2: Lut .1D 150
Trefoil Cl. LU4: Lut .5B 140
Trenchard Av. SG17: Chic .1H 99
Trent Av. MK45: Flitw .4K 107
Trent Rd. LU3: Lut .6J 141
MK41: Bed .4F 45
Trent Way LU7: Lei Buz .4B 136
Trescott Cl. LU2: Lut .7J 143
Trevor Dr. MK43: Brom .7E 42
Trevor St.
MK40: Bed .2A 158 (1C 56)
Trident Dr. LU5: Hou R .3K 139
Triggs Way LU2: C'hoe .6J 143
Trilley Flds. MK45: Maul .5K 97
Trimley Cl. LU4: Lut .4D 140
TRING .3A 162
Tring Rd. LU6: Edles .3A 152
Trinity Cl. MK43: Felm .7C 20
MK44: Rox .6E 36
SG18: Bigg .5B 76
Trinity Gdns. MK40: Bed . . .2B 158 (1D 56)
Trinity Rd. LU3: Lut .4J 141
MK40: Bed .3B 56
SG5: Stot .6H 103
Triumph Ct. LU1: Lut 6H 159 (4C 150)
Triumph Way MK42: Kemp .1A 70
Trojan Ct. LU4: Lut .1H 149
Troon Cl. MK41: Bed .4G 45
Troon Gdns. LU2: Lut .3C 142
Trowbridge Gdns. LU2: Lut .7C 142
Trow Cl. MK45: C End .4A 72
TROWLEY BOTTOM .3B 162
Truman Pl. SG17: Chic .3J 99
Truncalls LU1: Lut .7F 159
Trunk Furlong MK17: Asp G .7B 92
Trunk Furlong Est. MK17: Asp G 7B 92
Truro Gdns. LU3: Lut .4K 141
MK45: Flitw .2A 108
Tudor Cl. MK40: Bed .1C 56
MK43: Brom .6F 43
MK45: Bar C .3A 122
Tudor Ct. *LU6: Duns .7G 139*
(off Park St.)
LU7: Lei Buz .2H 135
(not continuous)
Tudor Dr. LU5: Hou R .5A 140
Tudor Rd. LU3: Lut .7K 141
Tudors, The MK44: Colm .5F 25
Tuffnells Way AL5: Harp .7H 157
Tulip Cl. LU3: Lut .2E 140
SG18: Bigg .6E 76
Tulip Dr. NN10: Rush .1B 10
Tulip Tree Cl. MK43: Brom .6C 42
Tunstall Wlk. MK41: Bed .6A 46
Turnberry Wlk. MK41: Bed .4G 45
Turner Cl. LU5: Hou R .4K 139
Turner Rd. PE19: Eat F .1J 27
Turners Rd. Nth. LU2: Lut .7E 142
Turners Rd. Sth. LU2: Lut .7E 142
Turner Way MK41: Bed .6C 44
Turnham Dr. LU7: Lei Buz .4A 136
Turnpike Cl. LU6: Duns .4J 147
Turnpike Dr. LU3: Lut .7A 132
Turnpike Rd. MK43: Hus C .4E 104
Turnpike Way MK41: Bed .6K 45
TURVEY .3C 40 (2A 160)
Turvey Rd. MK16: Ast .3D 52
MK43: Carlt .6C 28
MK43: Stag .6K 41
Tweedsmuir Rd. MK41: Bed .5H 45
Twigden Ct. LU3: Lut .4G 141
TWINWOOD .6B 32
Twinwood Airfield .6A 32
Twinwood Rd. MK41: Clap .7J 31
Twinwoods Bus. Pk. MK41: Clap 2A 32
Twitchel, The SG5: Shill .6J 111
Twyford Dr. LU2: Lut .7H 143
Tyburn La. MK45: Pull .6F 109
MK45: West .1A 120
Tydeman Cl. MK41: Bed .2E 44
Tylecote Cl. MK43: Mars M .5C 82
Tylers Mead LU2: Lut .4C 142
Tyne Cl. MK45: Flitw .4K 107
Tyne Cres. MK41: Bed .3E 44
Tyne Rd. SG19: Sandy .7J 49
Tyrells End MK17: Ever .1A 118
Tyrells Gdns. MK17: Sto H .1A 124
Tyrells Rd. *MK17: Sto H .1A 124*
(off Fenny Rd.)
TYRINGHAM .3A 160
Tythe Barn Cl. MK45: West .1A 120
Tythe Cl. MK44: Sharn .4E 20
MK45: Flitw .4C 108
Tythe M. LU6: Edles .7J 145
Tythe Rd. LU4: Lut .3E 140

U

Ullswater Cl. MK42: Kemp .7A 56
MK45: Flitw .4K 107
SG18: Bigg .7D 76
Ullswater Dr. LU7: Lei Buz .2E 134
Ullswater Rd. LU6: Duns .4H 147
Ulverston Rd. LU6: Duns .4G 147
Underwood Cl. LU3: Lut .7H 131
Union Chapel Ho. LU1: Lut .6H 159
Union St. LU1: Lut 6H 159 (4C 150)
LU6: Duns .2G 147
MK40: Bed .2A 158 (1C 56)
University Hall LU1: Lut .6K 159
University of Bedfordshire
Luton Campus 5K 159 (3C 150)
Polhill Campus .7H 45
University Way
MK43: Cran, Whar E .4B 80
Uplands LU3: Lut .1F 141
MK41: Bed .5H 45
Uplands Ct. LU1: Lut .5C 150
UPPER CALDECOTE 3H 75 (3C 161)
Upper Coombe LU7: Lei Buz .1G 135
UPPER DEAN .1J 7 (1B 160)
UPPER DUNSLEY .3A 162
Up. George St.
LU1: Lut .4G 159 (3B 150)
UPPER GRAVENHURST .2G 111 (1C 163)
UPPER SHELTON .1B 82 (3A 160)
Up. Shelton Rd. MK43: Mars M 1B 82
UPPER STAPLOE .3C 26 (2C 161)
UPPER STONDON 3D 112 (1C 163)
Upperstone Cl. SG5: Stot .7H 103
UPPER SUNDON .4D 130 (2B 162)
Upton Cl. LU2: Lut .3B 142
Upton Ct. MK41: Bed .4E 44
UPTON END .4K 111 (1C 163)
Upton End Farm Bus. Pk.
SG5: Shill .4A 112
Upton End Rd. SG5: Shill .3J 111
Upwell Rd. LU2: Lut .7F 143
Urban Way SG18: Bigg .4C 76
Ursula Taylor Wlk. MK41: Clap 4A 44
Usher Cl. MK42: Bed 6B 158 (3D 56)
Ushers Ct. PE19: Eat S .6H 27

V

Vadis Cl. LU3: Lut .2G 141
Vale Cl. AL5: Harp .7H 157
Vale Ct. MK43: Cran .2H 81
Vale Crematorium, The & Cemetery
LU2: Lut .3F 143
Valence End LU6: Duns .4K 147
Valerian Cl. PE19: Eat F .1J 27
Valerian Way SG5: Stot .2F 115
Valiant Cl. LU5: Harl .6B 120
Valley Cl. LU6: Stud .7H 153
LU6: Whip .4E 152
Valley Rd. LU6: Stud .7H 153
SG6: Let C .7F 115
Vanbrugh Dr. LU5: Hou R .4K 139
Vandyke Rd. LU7: Lei Buz .2K 135
Vanguard Cl. MK42: Kemp .4K 55
Varna Cl. LU3: Lut .5J 141
Vaughan Rd. SG5: Stot .7G 103
Vauxhall Recreation Club .5E 150
Vauxhall Rd. LU1: Lut .5F 151
LU2: Lut .5F 151
Vauxhall Way LU2: Lut .6E 142
LU6: Duns .7F 139
Venetia Rd. LU2: Lut .5E 142
Venetia Rd. Footpath *LU2: Lut .5E 142*
(off Venetia Rd.)
Ventnor Gdns. LU3: Lut .2H 141
Verey Rd. LU5: Duns .7J 139
Ver House AL3: Mark .6H 155
Verne Dr. MK45: Amp .5B 96
Vernon Pl. LU5: Duns .1H 147
Vernon Rd. LU1: Lut .2A 150
Verulam Gdns. LU3: Lut .3H 141
Vespers Cl. LU4: Lut .7C 140
Vestry Cl. LU1: Lut .4F 159
Viaduct Cotts. LU1: E Hyde .3J 157
Vicarage Cl. MK44: Rav .7K 33
SG5: Shill .6J 111
SG15: Arl .5C 102
SG18: Lang .4B 90
Vicarage Gdns. LU7: Lei Buz .3G 135
PE19: Eat S .4H 27
Vicarage Grn. MK44: Thur .6E 22
Vicarage Hill MK45: Flitw .5A 108
Vicarage La. LU7: Wing .7A 134
MK45: Wils .1G 85
NN29: Pod .4C 10
Vicarage Rd. LU5: Hou R .4H 139
LU7: Lei Buz .3G 135
MK45: Sils .2A 110
Vicarage St. LU1: Lut 5K 159 (3D 150)
MK17: Wob S .2A 104
Vicars Cl. MK40: Bidd .2J 55
Vicars Wlk. MK41: Bed .7K 45
Viceroy Cl. PE19: Eat S .4G 27
Viceroy Ct. LU6: Duns .2J 147
Victor Cl. MK42: Short .1J 71
Victoria Cl. SG18: Lang .7A 90
SG19: Wrest .6F 65
Victoria Ct. *SG18: Bigg .5C 76*
(off Back St.)
Victoria Dr. MK45: Hou C .4D 84
SG5: Stot .1J 115
Victoria Pl. LU6: Duns .2G 147
SG18: Bigg .5C 76
Victoria Rd. LU7: Lei Buz .3G 135
MK42: Bed .7A 158 (4C 56)
SG17: Shef .3D 100
Victoria St. LU1: Lut 6H 159 (4C 150)
LU6: Duns .1G 147
Victoria Ter. LU7: Lei Buz .2B 136
Viking Gro. MK42: Kemp .4K 55
Viking Ind. Est. MK41: Bed .5A 46
Villa Ct. LU2: Lut .2G 159 (2B 150)
Village, The LU2: Lut .2F 143
SG18: Old W .7B 74
Village Ct. LU7: Lei Buz .3F 135
Village Rd. MK43: Brom .7F 43
SG19: C Hat .3F 65
Villa Pk. MK43: Cran .5E 80
Villa Rd. LU2: Lut .2G 159 (2B 150)
Villiers Cl. LU4: Lut .6F 141
Vimy Ct. LU7: Lei Buz .2H 135
Vimy Rd. LU7: Lei Buz .2H 135
Vincent Rd. LU4: Lut .4F 141
Vinegar Hill SG19: Hat .7G 61
Vine Row MK43: Turv .3C 40
Vines, The SG5: Stot .7G 103
Vineyard Way MK42: Kemp .5A 56
Violet Cl. MK42: Bed .6H 57
SG18: Bigg .7E 76
Virginia Cl. LU2: Lut .6D 142
Viscount Cl. LU3: Lut .4J 141
Viscount Ct. LU2: Lut .1G 159
PE19: Eat S .4H 27
Vista Ho. LU1: Lut .3G 159
Voyce Way MK42: Bed .4F 57
Vulcan St. MK42: Bed 7E 158 (4E 56)
Vulcan Way PE19: Eat S .6H 27
Vyne Cl. MK42: Kemp .5K 55
Vynes, The LU7: Lei Buz .4A 136

W

Waddesdon Cl. LU2: Lut .7H 143
Wadhurst Av. LU3: Lut .5A 142
Wadsworth Ct. MK42: Els .6E 56
Wagstaffe Cl. MK41: Bed .3G 45
Wagstaff Way MK45: Amp .7K 95
Wakes End Farm MK17: Ever .4C 106
Walcot Av. LU2: Lut .7E 142
Walcourt Rd. MK42: Kemp .5B 56
Waldeck Rd. LU1: Lut .2A 150
LU3: Lut .2A 150
Waldocks Cl. MK44: Rise .3D 14
Waleys Cl. LU3: Lut .1G 141
Walgrave Rd. LU5: Duns .7B 140
WALKERN .2D 163
Walkers Cl. SG17: Shef .2C 100
Walk Ho. Cl. MK43: Cran .3F 81
Walkley Rd. LU5: Hou R .5H 139
Wallace Dr. LU6: Eat B .4J 145
Wallace M. LU6: Eat B .4J 145
Waller Av. LU3: Lut .7H 141
LU4: Lut .7H 141
Waller St. Mall LU1: Lut .4H 159
WALLINGTON .1D 163
Wallis Way MK42: Bed .6J 57
Walnut Acre *LU5: Todd .2F 129*
(off Marlborough Pl.)
Walnut Cl. LU2: Lut .5F 143
MK43: Brom .1D 54
MK43: Pave .5B 30
MK44: Blun .6D 48
SG5: Stot .7H 103
SG18: Bigg .3B 76
Walnut Gro. MK43: Lidl .2B 94
Walnuts, The LU7: Lei Buz .6J 125
Walnut Tree Cl. SG19: Wrest .6F 65
Walnut Wlk. MK42: Kemp .7B 56
Walsingham Cl. LU2: Lut .2B 142
MK42: Bed .7C 158
WALSWORTH .1C 163
Waltham Cl. MK41: Bed .4H 45

A-Z Bedfordshire Atlas 189

Y

HOSPITALS, WALK-IN CENTRES and HOSPICES
covered by this atlas.

N.B. Where it is not possible to name these facilities on the map,
the reference given is for the road in which they are situated.

BEDFORD DAYCARE HOSPICE 1C **56**
    3 Linden Road
    BEDFORD
    MK40 2DD
    Tel: 01234 352015

BEDFORD HOSPITAL 7B **158** (4D **56**)
    Kempston Road
    BEDFORD
    MK42 9DJ
    Tel: 01234 355122

BEDFORD HOSPITAL (NORTH WING) 1E **158** (1F **57**)
    Kimbolton Road
    BEDFORD
    MK40 2NU
    Tel: 01234 355122

BIGGLESWADE HOSPITAL 3E **76**
    Potton Road
    Biggleswade
    BIGGLESWADE
    SG18 0EL
    Tel: 01767 224913

HARPENDEN SPIRE HOSPITAL 7K **157**
    Ambrose Lane
    HARPENDEN
    AL5 4BP
    Tel: 01582 763191

KEECH HOSPICECARE 6J **131**
    Great Bramingham Lane
    LUTON
    LU3 3NT
    Tel: 01582 492339

LUTON & DUNSTABLE HOSPITAL 7E **140**
    Lewsey Road
    LUTON
    LU4 0DZ
    Tel: 0845 1270127

MANOR BMI HOSPITAL 2H **55**
    Church End
    Biddenham
    BEDFORD
    MK40 4AW
    Tel: 01234 364252

NHS WALK-IN CENTRE (LUTON) 5H **159** (3C **150**)
    14-16 Chapel Street
    LUTON
    LU1 2SE
    Tel: 01582 556400

FSC
www.fsc.org

MIX
Paper from
responsible sources
FSC® C005461

SAFETY CAMERA INFORMATION

Safety camera locations are publicised by the Safer Roads Partnership which operates them in order to encourage drivers to comply
with speed limits at these sites. It is the driver's absolute responsibility to be aware of and to adhere to speed limits at all times.

By showing this safety camera information it is the intention of Geographers' A-Z Map Company Ltd., to encourage
safe driving and greater awareness of speed limits and vehicle speed. Data accurate at time of printing.